# Biocapital

# Biocapital
## *The Constitution of Postgenomic Life*

Kaushik Sunder Rajan

DUKE UNIVERSITY PRESS

DURHAM AND LONDON

2006

© 2006 Duke University Press

All rights reserved

Printed in the United States of America on acid-free paper ∞

Designed by Heather Hensley
Typeset in Galliard by Keystone Typesetting, Inc.

Library of Congress Cataloging-in-Publication Data and
republication acknowledgments appear on the last printed
pages of this book.

*For Appa and Amma*

# CONTENTS

# ACKNOWLEDGMENTS

This book has been made possible by a number of teachers, in the university and in the field. Each one has had something special to contribute toward my learning. I wish to thank Michael Fischer for sharing his deep and profound scholarship; Joe Dumit for teaching me how to read; Sheila Jasanoff for passing on to me her deep ethical commitments about writing and intervention in multiple communities of practice (and, related to that, her important lectures to me on lucidity, not always heeded!); and Donna Haraway for her contagious energy and for pushing me to always think beyond boundaries. Learning from them individually and collectively has been a privilege.

No ethnographic work is possible without the informants who make it so. There are many who let me into their lifeworlds, in spite of the huge intrusion my work represented to their time. Many of these people live in worlds where information is guarded with almost paranoid zeal, which makes me even more thankful for the access they gave me. While there are many people who taught me about the worlds of the life sciences and capital, a few deserve special thanks. Mark Boguski made this project possible in the first place, both with his encouragement and by enabling me to attend the Cold Spring Harbor Genome Sequencing and Analysis meetings in 1999, giving me my first initiation into the worlds of genome scientists. At GeneEd, I was made to feel welcome not only as an observer but also as a friend. I wish to thank everyone there, especially Sunil Maulik, Salil Patel, Paul Eisele, and Mai Grant. At the Centre for Biochemical Technology, Samir Brahmachari and Manjari Mahajan were extremely generous with their time and insights. Thanks also to D. Balasubramanian, Kent Bottles, Deepanwita Chattopadhyaya, Debashis Das, Arthur Holden, David Housman, Satish Kumar, Ramesh Mashelkar, Mitali Mukerji, Svati Pande, Ali Pervez, Raji Pillai, Premnath, R. Rajagopalan, M. Samuel, S. Sivaram, Hari Tamanna, Patrick Terry, Uday Turaga, Patrick Vaughan, Akella Venkateswarulu, M. Vidyasagar, Spencer Wells, and Darshana Zaveri for giving me invaluable insights into biocapitalist lifeworlds at various stages of this work.

I have benefited greatly from three intellectual communities that I have been privileged to be a part of—the Science, Technology, and Society Program at the Massachusetts Institute of Technology (especially the graduate student community that was a source of such collegiality during my dissertation years); the Science, Technology, and Society Program at Harvard's John F. Kennedy School of Government; and the Department of Anthropology at the University of California, Irvine. Thanks also to the History of Consciousness Program at UC Santa Cruz for giving me affiliation while I did my fieldwork in the Bay Area. Fieldwork support came from MIT's STS Department, MIT's Kelly-Douglas Fund, and the MIT Graduate Student Council. The constant help and cheerful presence of Chris Bates, Shirin Fozi, Debbie Meinbresse, and Judy Spitzer at STS headquarters at MIT, of Seth Kirshenbaum at the Kennedy School, of Sandy Cushman at UCI, and of Sheila Peuse at Santa Cruz, as well as Jerry Burke's supply of used laptops to take on fieldwork trips, were all vital enabling ingredients.

Many of my friends, who have also been collaborators in various ways, deserve special thanks. The transformation of a completely unwieldy Ph.D. dissertation into a hopefully slightly less unwieldy book owes hugely to detailed comments I received at various stages of its revision from Sheila Jasanoff, Nick King, Bill Maurer, and Rajeswari Sunder Rajan. It also owes greatly to conversations I have had with Etienne Balibar about Marx's labor theory of value; with Lawrence Cohen about questions of theorizing biopolitics; with Joe Dumit, who has generously shared his recent work on surplus health and has included me in his extremely generative experiments reading Marx; with Kris Peterson, for conversations about global capital and therapeutic economies in Africa that highlighted for me just how partial a perspective into biocapital as a global regime is provided by the United States and India; with

Venkat Rao, whose introduction to the history of Andhra Pradesh and strong theoretical sensibilities have been invaluable in writing the sections of this book having to do with the establishment of a technoscientific culture and infrastructure in Hyderabad; and with Elta Smith, for careful and caring readings of my work, and invaluable conversations comparing aspects of this work to parallel emergences in agricultural genomics and biotechnology. For reading and commenting on parts of this work at various stages of research and writing, I also thank Stefan Beck, Joao Biehl, Marianne de Laet, Kim and Mike Fortun, Cori Hayden, Jonathan Kahn, Chris Kelty, Michi Knecht, Andy Lakoff, Hannah Landecker, George Marcus, Torin Monahan, Adriana Petryna, Rachel Prentice, Arvind Rajagopal, Anupama Rao, Jenny Reardon, Chloe Silverman, Karen-Sue Taussig, and Charlie Weiner. Two anonymous reviewers for Duke University Press (who subsequently revealed themselves to be Lawrence Cohen and Kim Fortun) have incalculably improved this manuscript with their detailed, meticulous, and thoughtful comments, for which many thanks, again. Thanks also to my editor, Ken Wissoker, for the support he has given this project, and to Christine Dahlin, Courtney Berger, and Pam Morrison at the press for their editorial assistance. I am grateful to J. Naomi Linzer for compiling the index. The material act of writing this manuscript was enabled at various times by the caffeine and friendliness available at Darwin's Café in Cambridge, Diedrich's Coffee in Irvine, and Bruegger's Bagels in Durham.

A special word of thanks to Naira Ahmad for all her love and support and for making the years spent researching and writing this book so worthwhile. This book is dedicated to my parents, who supported me through my transition out of laboratory-based biology and into the social sciences, and who have constantly been there for me in every possible way. My mother has virtually been a fifth dissertation committee member, teaching, editing, proofreading, and expanding my theoretical horizons. But there is so much more to thank them for than just the materiality of research sustenance. I thank them for genetics and environment, *bios* and capital, support and love.

# Introduction
*Capitalisms and Biotechnologies*

In January 1999, I spent a month in a lab at the National Institutes of Health (NIH), because my Ph.D. dissertation advisor Michael Fischer felt I should experience how it feels to be part of a lab as an observer. It felt pretty uncomfortable, and not just because the only place I had to sit on was an icebox in a corridor outside the lab. At such an early stage in my Ph.D, I really had no story as to why I was there, what my questions were, or what I wanted to find out or study — all of which, of course, were things that the scientists in the lab were curious about.

The lab I was "studying" itself studied signal transduction pathways within cells, and the one thing that struck me was how each researcher's bench had a computer that was constantly downloading DNA sequence information in real time, as soon as the information was released into GenBank, the public-domain DNA sequence repository. I remarked on this to the head of the lab, who said that I must go and meet Mark Boguski, a scientist at the National Center for Biotechnology Information, which runs GenBank. And so I did.

As I said, what was most uncomfortable for me about my encounters with various scientists was that I did not have a story to tell them about my presence. And yet the first words that Boguski said when he met me were: "I've read Paul Rabinow, so I know exactly what you want to do. I think someone needs to write a contemporary history of genomics, and I think you should do it."[1] Boguski was organizing the Cold Spring Harbor genome meetings that year, which was the major annual meeting of the publicly funded Human Genome Project. He waived my registration fees and got me to attend. That is how I started studying genome scientists.

In 1999 I could quite comfortably say that the subject of my research was genomics, at a historical moment when genomics meant the sequencing of the human genome and the generation of software tools to make sense of that sequence. That year was also a conjuncture marked by the "race" to sequence the human genome between the public Human Genome Project and Craig Venter's private genome company Celera Genomics. Over the next few years, genomics remained an important part of this study for reasons that I will try to explain throughout the book, but the objects of my study became inseparable from the larger epistemological and political economic terrains, themselves emergent, within which they were situated. The larger context of what I am studying is what I have called biocapital, but before I explain what I mean by that, it is worth at least setting the stage by mentioning, in the most perfunctory fashion, what was happening in genomics in 1999.

In 1998, Craig Venter was brought in to run a new company, Celera Genomics, that challenged the public Human Genome Project, which had until that point planned to sequence the genome from one end to the other, with a stringent error frequency of not more than one in every ten thousand base pairs.[2] This was ultimately resolved as a fight between "public" and "private" genomics, the key node around which contestation took place being the patentability of gene sequences. Private companies like Celera were keen to patent the sequences they generated and to realize commercial value off them, while public researchers felt that generating sequences was not particularly inventive and that granting them patents would stifle genomic research by making those sequences unavailable in the public domain.

Many things happened over the next year or so, not least the continuous running of sequencing machines in public and private laboratories around the world, so that in June 2000, when the working draft sequence of the human genome was announced both by the Human Genome Project and by Celera, everyone smiled with Bill Clinton for the cameras, and we were told that the "Book of Life" had been read, the "Code of Codes" decoded, and the "Holy Grail" attained.[3]

Such momentous happenings were not necessarily evident to everyone living in the small town of Syosset in upstate New York, the home of the famous Cold Spring Harbor Laboratories, in 1999, as exemplified by the following story. While going to the laboratories for the 1999 meetings (held at the height of the sequencing "race"), I shared a taxi with two people, one a genome sequencer going to the meetings, the other a woman who lived in the town, going elsewhere. The two had the following conversation:

RESIDENT: Are you here doing research?

SEQUENCER: Yes, we've come for the conference.

RESIDENT: What conference is that?

SEQUENCER: Genome mapping and sequencing.

RESIDENT: Of what?

SEQUENCER: Oh, the genome.

RESIDENT: Of what?

SEQUENCER: Human.

RESIDENT: Yes, but of what? What are you mapping?

SEQUENCER: [*increasingly perplexed*] The whole thing.

RESIDENT: But that's already been done, hasn't it?

## Biocapital

We live in a world of rapid changes, many of which force us to ask afresh what we mean by words that are an integral part of our lexicon, words like "life," "capital," "fact," "exchange," and "value." Genomics is one such change, but it is a change, I argue, that reflects more general changes in two broad domains. The first is in the life sciences, which, consequent to the rapid advances in genomics, are increasingly becoming *information* sciences. The second is in capitalism, which is triumphantly acknowledged today as having "defeated" alternative economic formations such as socialism or communism and is therefore considered to be the "natural" political economic formation, not just of our time but of all times.[4] The title of this book, therefore, signals its thesis that the life sciences represent a new face, and a new phase, of capitalism and, consequently, that biotechnology is a form of enterprise inextricable from contemporary capitalism. I will try to explain here what I mean by this, and specifically try to explain how I conceive of the relationship of "biocapital" as a concept to contemporary systems of capitalism and to emergent scientific and technological horizons in the life sciences. I will then provide a brief overview of the drug development marketplace and of genomics in order to lay out the terrain on which I have conducted this study, before outlining the structure of the book.

The object of bioscience, the practice of bioscience, and the locations of bioscience have all been changing rapidly over the past thirty years, and one of the major directions this change has taken has been toward more corporate forms and contexts of research. But this drift toward corporatization has hardly been natural, inevitable, or without contestation. As demonstrated in 1999 by the angry response of public genome researchers toward the possibility that DNA sequences might be patented, the corporatization of the life sciences has simultaneously been rapid and hegemonic on the one hand, and contingent and contested on the other, setting up what I call a *frictioned* terrain on which these emergences take shape. Further, biotechnologies cannot simply be analyzed by studying them "within" laboratories. Rather, all science needs, as Emily Martin (1998) has argued, to situate changes within scientific and technological worlds in larger social and cultural contexts. This has been the practice, over the last decade and a half or so, of the also rapidly emergent field of the anthropology of science. And this contextualization of science cannot, as a number of scholars within science and technology studies (STS) have argued, simply be a unidirectional attribution of causality. In other words, it is too simple to state either that social change is a consequence of scientific and technological development or that science and technology are completely conditioned by "the social," as if "the social" were something unitary and easy to identify and thus purify. STS scholars refer to the mutual constitution of "the scientific" and "the social" as *coproduction*, and it is this coproduction of the life sciences with political economic regimes that I investigate in this book.[5]

An example of such coproduction is evident even in the extremely truncated story of genomics in 1999 that I recounted earlier. As mentioned, there was considerable anxiety among public genome researchers that private companies might patent the DNA sequences they were generating at the time. The legal status of the patentability of the sequences was (and in fact still is) quite ambiguous and rests, among other things, on whether the generation of these sequences could be regarded as an "inventive" activity.[6] In other words, the question of whether DNA sequences should be patented could not at the same time take recourse to externally established criteria of patentability without asking the question of what those criteria meant in the context of new technological possibilities for innovation, in this case the development of automated sequencing machines that could generate DNA sequences at speeds and resolutions inconceivable before. At the same time, further use of these sequences depended in considerable measure on their legal status, either as part of the public domain or as legitimate private property. The legal status of DNA sequences depended on the technological mechanisms that produced them, while the continued production and use of these sequences absolutely depended on their legal status. Neither could a priori be settled without bringing the other into question.

The beginning of the biotechnology industry in the late 1970s and early 1980s was itself marked by a coproduction of new types of science and technology and changes in the legal, regulatory, and market structures that organized the conduct of that technoscience.[7] The "new" technoscience was recombinant DNA technology (RDT), which is a set of techniques that allows the cutting up and joining together of DNA molecules in labs. The biotechnology industry came about largely as a consequence of this technoscientific development in 1973 by Herbert Boyer and Stanley Cohen. This sort of cutting and splicing allows scientists to study the functionality of different genes and DNA sequences by expressing these sequences in organisms (usually bacterial or viral) called vectors. These vectors can be research tools that "house" the DNA to be studied, or can function as production factories for more DNA (if it gets amplified by the polymerase chain reaction, or PCR), or for the protein that might be coded by that DNA. In other words, RDT allows the life sciences to become "technological," where the product that is produced is cellular or molecular matter such as DNA or protein. Some of these proteins could, in principle, have therapeutic effects (especially for diseases that are caused by, or have as a central symptom, an abnormal amount of that protein) and be produced industrially. This, in a nutshell, represented the possibility and the rationale for the biotechnology industry.

While RDT could be said to have "led" to the development of the biotech industry, the emergence of a new technology could hardly in itself be considered sufficient cause for the development of an entire industry. The shift of the technoscience of RDT to industrial locales was evidenced by the emergence of a slew of biotechnology companies in the early 1980s, a development that in turn led to further research and innovation in the life sciences and biotechnology. One can only understand this coproduction in terms of a conjuncture of several events and factors.

One was the willingness of venture capitalists to invest in a technology that had little credibility at the time as a successful business model. A second was the enormous amount of money spent by the U.S. federal government on basic biomedical research through funding of the National Institutes of Health (NIH) consequent to the declaration of a war on cancer in the early 1970s.[8] A third was the 1980 Bayh-Dole Act, which was legislation that facilitated the transfer of technology between academe and industry and thereby enabled rapid commercialization of basic research problems. A fourth was a supportive legal climate that allowed the protection of biotech intellectual property, marked, for instance, by the landmark 1980 U.S. Supreme Court ruling in *Diamond v. Chakrabarty*, which allowed patent rights on a genetically engineered microorganism that could break down crude-oil spills.

While I argue that the life sciences and capitalism are coproduced, I do, however, further argue that the life sciences are *overdetermined* by the capitalist political economic structures within which they emerge. "Overdetermination" is a term used by Louis Althusser to suggest a *contextual* relationship, but not a *causal* one (Althusser 1969 [1965]). In other words, even if a particular set of political economic formations do not in any direct and simplistic way lead to particular epistemic emergences, they could still disproportionately set the stage within which the latter take shape in particular ways. And so, even if capitalism represents particular types of political economic formations, in this current moment in world history, as Slavoj Žižek argues, it "overdetermines all alternative formations, as well as non-economic strata of social life" (Žižek 2004). Therefore, even while emphasizing the historicity and the far from natural emergence of capitalism as a set of political economic forms and structures, it is important to acknowledge the importance of capital as being what Žižek calls the "'concrete universal' of our historical epoch" (ibid.).

This book, then, is simultaneously an analysis and a theorization of the life sciences, especially as they pertain to biomedicine, with an analysis and theorization of capitalist frameworks within which such technoscience increasingly operates. This is the rationale for the term "biocapital." A fundamental assumption of this book is that capitalism, even as it overdetermines the emergence of new technoscience, is a political economic system whose own contours are not unitary or rigid. In other words, capitalism cannot be *assumed* in studies of biomedicine, because capitalism is in itself dynamic, changing, and at stake.

I do not make the argument here that biocapital is a distinct temporal or figural form of, or from, "capitalism" as some unitary entity. Rather, I wish to make the argument, made most powerfully by scholars such as Žižek and Susan Buck-Morss, that what is at stake is the very conception of capitalism as something unitary, eternal, and without history (see, for example, Žižek 1994; Buck-Morss 2002). Rather, capitalism is mutable and multiple; it is always *capitalisms*.[9] Biocapital is one vantage point from which to view the complexities of capitalism(s), and like all situated perspectives, it contains within it both its specificities as well as its diagnoses of more general structural features of capitalism.[10] Therefore, rather than define what I mean by "biocapital" at the outset, I wish to explain next, with a digression through the political economic analysis of Karl Marx as a basis, how I see this relationship of biocapital to systems of contemporary global capitalism writ large.

A major theoretical argument that I make in this book is for a return, not to Marx*ism* in any dogmatic sense, but to reading Marx as a methodologist from whom one can learn to analyze rapidly emergent political economic *and* epistemic structures. Indeed, I believe that Marx himself is often read too simply as heralding inevitable communist revolution. While this was certainly the polemical tone of *The Communist Manifesto* (Marx and Engels 1986 [1848]), one can see that by the time Marx wrote *The Eighteenth Brumaire of Louis Napoleon* in 1852 (Marx 1977 [1852]), he was offering a much more nuanced understanding of capitalist processes that emphasized their *tendential* nature.

*The Eighteenth Brumaire* is a historical treatise concerning the events between 1848 and 1851 in France, during the presidency of Napoleon's nephew Louis Bonaparte. This was a period during which France's National Assembly was dominated by the reactionary Party of Order. The period saw constant tension between the Assembly and Bonaparte, leading finally to a coup by Bonaparte in 1851. Bonaparte ended up being hailed as a revolutionary, as a single individual who took on and overthrew the reactionary forces of Order. Marx disputes this by closely following the political happenings in these years to show how Bonaparte was, in fact, resolutely counterrevolutionary. Further, Marx points out that Bonaparte was not just hailed as a great revolutionary by the bourgeoisie but was very much the undisputed leader of the small peasantry, which was among the most economically depressed sectors of the French populace at the time. Marx's concern in *The Eighteenth Brumaire* is to show how even those sectors of society whose structural relations of production within society would have suggested that they embrace revolutionary communism might put their faith in a counterrevolutionary personage. Moreover, the desire for political stability that was expressed in the faith in a counterrevolutionary dictatorship like Bonaparte's was completely conditioned by the need for *economic* stability in a capitalist society, an economic stability that the peasants and the bourgeoisie alike saw to be in their interests. In other words, *The Eighteenth Brumaire* itself traces a co-constitution of a political regime with an economic one, in which each conditions the other, but in ways whose outcomes are not dictated as they logically ought to have been as a consequence of the structural relations of production prevailing at the time.

Marx, however, also realized that the economic structure of capitalism was multiple. Therefore, in outlining the labor theory of value over successive volumes of *Capital*, Marx begins by outlining a hypothetical system of the production and circulation of capital but proceeds to situate that hypothetical system in the context of "real" systems of capitalism that were emergent (and hardly stable) at the time. By *Capital, Volume 3* (Marx 1974 [1894]), Marx is already analyzing two distinct forms of capital, what he calls industrial capital (which was the primary subject of analysis in the first two volumes) and trading or merchant's capital. This latter form of capitalism is its emergent *commercial* (as distinct from *commodity*) form, distinct only in that its "process of circulation is . . . set apart as a special function of a special capital, . . . established by virtue of the division of labor to a special group of capitalists" (267). In other words, the function of trading capital is not just the production and exchange of commodities as a means to an end (that end being the generation of surplus value) but is commercial activity as an end in itself. This "special type" of capitalist to whom Marx refers is the speculative capitalist, a precursor to the types of capitalists, such as, for instance, venture capitalists or investment bankers, who are central to sustaining the dynamics of contemporary capitalism. In other words, the merchant is to commercial capital what the producer is to commodity capital. And the key function of the merchant is the *advancement* of money in order to set commercial capital in motion. Commercial capital, according to Marx, does not create surplus value in and of itself but does so indirectly by constantly perpetuating the circulation of capital, and by providing it with its own self-perpetuating, self-sustaining logic that does not need to *originate* from the moment of production of commodity.

One can see a similar disjuncture in the forms of production and circulation that biotech or pharmaceutical companies are involved in today, where, on the one hand, there exists the manufacture and sale of therapeutic molecules, but, on the other, there exists an elaborate system of valuation that is essential for the existence of these companies that only indirectly depends on this actual manufacture and sale. The everyday existence of a biotech or a pharmaceutical company, then, involves the coexistence of at least these two simultaneous, distinct, yet mutually constitutive forms of capital, one directly dependent on the production of commodity, the other speculative and only indirectly so. Depending on the institutional and legal structure within which these companies operate, one or the other of these forms can predominate in the creation of value; yet neither of these forms flows seamlessly from the other. And therefore, in India, for instance, there has tended to be a more direct correlation between therapeutic molecule production, sales, profit margins, and the value of a pharmaceutical company. In the United States, where biotech companies are almost always enabled by venture capital funding, and where biotech and pharmaceutical companies almost always become publicly traded companies when the opportunity presents itself (and therefore answerable to investors on Wall Street), valuation is more directly dependent on speculative capital.[11]

Marx further outlines the relationship between merchant's and industrial capital as follows:

> Since merchant's capital is nothing but an individualized form of a portion of industrial capital engaged in the process of circulation, all questions referring to it must be solved by representing the problem primarily in a form, in which the phenomena peculiar to merchant's capital do not yet appear independently, but still in direct connection with industrial capital, as a branch of it.[12]

In other words, Marx first argues for at least two distinct forms of capital, industrial and merchant's. He then proceeds to posit the latter as, simultaneously, a continuation of, an evolution of, a subset of, and a form distinct from, the former. Both these forms of capital exist in close relationship with each other, but one cannot be reduced to the other. Further, the relationship between the two cannot be understood except at multiple registers simultaneously.

I wish to clarify the relationship of biocapital to capital (and to capitalisms) in precisely these terms. Biocapital does not signify a distinct epochal phase of capitalism that leaves behind or radically ruptures capitalism as we have known it. At the same time, there are significant particularities to biocapital that have to do both with the institutional structure within which drug development takes place, and with the technoscientific changes in the life sciences and biotechnologies over the last thirty years, that make it too simplistic simply to say that biocapital is a "case study" of capitalism having to do with the life sciences. Rather, the relationship between "capitalism" (itself not a unitary category) and what I call biocapital is one where the latter is, simultaneously, a continuation of, an evolution of, a subset of, and a form distinct from, the former. Further, biocapital itself takes shape in incongruent fashion across the multiple sites of its global emergence.

Indeed, the relationship of emergent and constantly mutating forms of capitalism to "capitalism" as a theoretical concept describing a political economic system has continued to vex social theorists since Marx, and the agent often implicated in this mutation of capitalism is technological change. An outline of the relationship of a form of a system under analysis to the concept underlying that systemic understanding that I take inspiration from is Jean-François Lyotard's. In *The Postmodern Condition* (Lyotard 1984), a "report on knowledge" written for the Canadian government in the late 1970s, Lyotard is also confronted with theorizing a moment in capitalist modernity that is marked by rapid technological change, much of which had to do with what might be called the information revolution. These technological changes, on the one hand, saw the persistence and reproduction of some "fundamental" aspects of capitalism as diagnosed by Marxism (such as, for instance, structural inequities in relations of production, especially when extended and considered globally) and yet occurred in the context of a different set of political con-junctures, most notably the dissipation, to the extent that it existed, of a strong notion of proletarian class consciousness that was central to Marx's analyses of industrial capitalism. Lyotard's definition of the "postmodern," then, is not a system that marks a radical rupture with modernity but rather one that is a subsumed, incongruent, evolving component of it. In other words, for Lyotard, postmodernism is a *symptom* of modernity, just as I attempt to show biocapital as, among other things, being *symptomatic* of capitalism (with "symptom," of course, itself being a biomedical term), rather than a new phenomenon that is radically distinct from, and rupturing with, the old.[13]

While my relationship of biocapital to capital is similar in form to Lyotard's relationship of the postmodern to modernity, it is also not dissimilar in con-tent. Fredric Jameson, for instance, posits Lyotard's analysis of the postmod-ern squarely in the frame of contemporary capitalism when he says that "post-modernism is not the cultural dominant of a wholly new social order . . . but only the reflex and the concomitant of yet another systemic modification of capitalism itself" (Jameson 2003 [1991], xii).

And yet what is crucial here is not just an understanding of capitalisms (however multiple) as *structures* that form the grounds for the emergence of a certain sort of technoscientific enterprise but also an understanding of political economy as an *epistemology*. I read Marx as himself only able to achieve a critique of capital by means of critiquing political economy as the emergent foundational epistemology of the time that had consequences for structuring social formations.[14]

Many of the life sciences involve production and circulations of many sorts, not all of them geared toward the generation of surplus value. Indeed, Robert Merton (1942) propounded communism as one of the four fundamental norms of science. By this, he meant not a particular system of scientific gover-nance or regulation but a self-imposed scientific ethos that valued the sharing of scientific information and materials. Such an ethos is very much a part of the everyday functioning of much academic life science today: it is, for instance, extremely common for one lab to send another information, or materials such as a DNA clone or a cell line they may have created, without any charge and even if no formal collaboration exists between the labs. At the same time, of course, there is the increased protection of these same forms of information and material as private property, not just among corporate biologists, but even among academic scientists. This protectionism could arise because these academic scientists are themselves, actually or potentially, also corporate entrepreneurs on the side (an increasingly common phenomenon in the United States thanks to the incentive structures of the Bayh-Dole Act that reward the transfer of technology from academe to industry); because the university that employs these scientists seeks to aggressively protect its intellectual property much as a corporation would; or defensively, to protect information or material *from* private protection by industry. Further, the biological "stuff" that circulates, whether information or material, could circulate as objects that have different connotations attached to them. For instance, information could be "raw data" (useful but not worked into anything "theoretical" or "factual"); it could be in the form of an algorithm or some form of software code that might itself be a potential or actual commodity protected by intellectual property rights; or it could be "scientific facts." Therefore, understanding the systems of production, circulation, and consumption of various "biologicals,"[15] including the ways in which these circulations insert into more "general" processes of capitalist circulation, is one side of the analytic challenge of studying biocapital as a system of exchange.

But the other side to its study springs from Marx's analysis of political economy as epistemology, and that is the study of the *epistemic* reconfigurations of the life sciences. In this case, as I have mentioned, these epistemic reconfigurations are co-constituted by *technical* reconfigurations as well. "Biocapital" is a study of the systems of exchange and circulation involved in the contemporary workings of the life sciences, but is also a study of those life sciences as they become increasingly foundational epistemologies for our time. In the former register, it is indeed a subset or "case study" of contemporary capitalism; in the latter, it points to the specifically *biopolitical* dimensions of contemporary capitalism.

Biopolitics is a notion put forward by Michel Foucault to show how modernity put *life* at the explicit center of political calculation (see, for instance, Foucault 1990 [1978]). Through his work, Foucault traced the constitution of modernity, which he felt was marked by a qualitatively different operation of power, leading to the construction of a different type of subject, from the power that operated between a regal sovereign and his subjects in medieval times. Therefore, tracing the processes by which power operates, and looking consequently at ways in which different types of selfhood (such as, for instance, that of the madman, the leper, or the criminal) emerge, was in a sense the purpose of Foucault's analyses.[16] Once again, however, I am interested in the methodologies that Foucault employs to attain such an end.

What Foucault focuses on specifically is the fact that power (which, consequent to having life firmly in its calculus, is a form of what he calls *biopower*) operates through *institutional*, *epistemic*, and *discursive* mechanisms. In other words, Foucault puts together what he calls his archaeology of modernity by looking at the institutions and the disciplines that constitute it. And therefore his corpus of work traces the emergence of institutions such as the prison, the clinic, the school, and the asylum, or disciplines such as demography and psychology.

Of particular interest in terms of the methodological influences on this book is Foucault's "archaeology of the human sciences," *The Order of Things* (Foucault 1973), where he argues, first, that a constellation of disciplines collectively concerning the knowledge of humanity becomes fundamental to the operation of modern rationality, and, second, that three such disciplines of particular importance are biology, political economy, and philology, corresponding respectively to understandings of life, labor, and language.

In a very different register, then, from Marx, and with a very different set of analytic operations, one sees an articulation of "the life sciences" and "political economy" as a central operation of an emergent modernity—an operation that I argue is still very much in process and whose understanding is still very much at stake. What Foucault does explicitly is what I have argued Marx does implicitly, which is consider political economy as consequential not (just) because it is a political and economic *system* of exchange but because it is a foundational *epistemology* that allows us the very possibility of thinking about such a system *as* a system of valuation. The biopolitical, then, does not just refer to the ways in which politics impact everyday life, or in which debates over life (such as, to take an evident example, over new reproductive technologies) impact politics, but rather points to the ways in which our very ability to comprehend "life" and "economy" in their modernist guises is shaped by particular epistemologies that are simultaneously enabled by, and in turn enable, particular forms of institutional structures.

The third peg of Foucault's triad, however, is equally important, and that points to the way in which the *grammar* of life is itself at stake. Layered within my arguments about the articulations between the life sciences and capitalisms in this book are central arguments about the discursive forms that both take, at a moment in the life sciences that might be called "postgenomic," and at a moment when our global political economic systems might unequivocally be called "capitalist."[17] Therefore I argue (most directly in chapter 4) that the sorts of knowledge genomics provides allows us to *grammatically* conceive of life in certain ways, *not* in terms of an Aristotelian poesis, but rather as that whose futures we can calculate in terms of probabilities of certain disease events happening — and this shifting grammar of life, toward a future tense, is consequential not just to our understanding of what "life" now means, but contains within it a deep ethical valence, what Nikolas Rose and Carlos Novas (2005) refer to as a "political economy of hope." Similarly, the current moment in American capitalism, which was grotesquely magnified during the dot.com heyday of 1999–2001, sees speculative capitalism as apparently disproportionately setting the terrain of valuation — a triumph of Marx's "commercial" capitalism over his "commodity" capitalism. Speculative capitalism, as I show most directly in chapter 3, contains its own future-oriented grammar, which is also consequential for value in both senses of the word and pertains to what might, in parallel to Rose and Novas, be called a political economy of hype. In other words, the articulations of life, labor, and language are themselves in formation (and information) that constitute biocapital and postgenomic life, and it is an analysis of these articulations that is a central attempt of this book.

Therefore this book is an explicit attempt to bring together Foucault's theorizations of the biopolitical with a Marxian attention to political economy, labor, value, commodity forms, and processes of exchange as they get constituted alongside the epistemic and technical emergences of the life sciences and biotechnologies.[18] It is, further, an attempt to do so with an explicit attention to the *globalizing* dimensions of capital and, increasingly, of technoscience. To that end, this book is a comparative investigation of postgenomic drug development marketplaces in the United States and India. I elaborate on my reasons for choosing these two sites at a later stage of this introduction, after further explaining the theoretical groundings of this work.

## Materiality and Abstraction

So far, I have outlined the relationship as I see it between biocapital and the life sciences and contemporary capitalism. Central to my analytic method throughout the book is to show how both the life sciences and capital are constituted by relationships at multiple levels between different forms and registers of materiality and abstraction. In this section, I attempt to explain what I mean by this. I show how five distinct domains of analysis in this book — exchange, commodities, valuation, science, and globalization — are all animated by this dialectic. For that, it is important to again digress into Marx's methodology and explain historical and dialectic materialism.

Marx borrows the dialectic from Hegel. The logic is that the dialectic whole inherently consists of two antithetical parts and is an inherently contradictory structure. However, both parts are essential for the constitution of the whole. By showing both objects and systems to be thus contradictorily constituted, Marx both shows the object or system under analysis in its entirety and points to its instability.

Marx, however, inverts the Hegelian dialectic by basing it not in the mind or the idea or consciousness but in materiality. Human activity for him is a consequence of the historical material conditions of human existence. Marx designates consciousness as being "from the very beginning a social product, [remaining] so long as men exist at all."[19] The attempt, according to Marx, should be not to see how consciousness creates social existence but to see how the conditions of existence shape consciousness. Therefore, a simple inter-pretation would suggest that Marx shows material relations of production as underlying the evolution of the social phenomenon that capitalism was.

This straightforward reading of the Marxian method is expectedly too sim-plistic to withstand rigorous analysis, if only because it reduces all politics to the politics of class. But there is something to be grasped from a materialist analysis as it might be applied to biocapital that I shall do before attempting to read Marx's own formulation of materialism in more complex terms.

For instance, as mentioned earlier, one of the things said to be unique about genomics is the way in which it allows us to conceive of life in informational terms. And yet the idea that life is information has been very much a part of the central dogma of molecular biology, which signifies the mechanics of life as being a series of coding operations, where DNA gets *transcribed* into RNA, which gets *translated* into protein — an algorithmic conception of life that has been prominent within molecular biology since at least the 1950s.[20] The difference now is that genomics allows the *metaphor* of life-as-information to become *material* reality that can be commodified. In other words, one does not just have to *conceive* of life as information: one can now *represent* life in informational terms that can be packaged, turned into a commodity, and sold as a database; and this change itself is enabled not so much by conceptual advances as by the development of the technological hardware that enables the generation and processing of information at speeds and resolutions inconceivable before. And indeed, the evidence of genomics as an assemblage of technologies that generates material information that can be commodified was made explicit by the fact of the "race" to sequence the human genome. What was at stake in regulating the commodity status of DNA sequence information was not just Merton's norm of communism but also the fact that whoever owned this *object* that DNA sequence information had now, consequent to genomic technologies, become was consequential to the modes of conduct of subsequent research.

And yet Marx's materialist analysis is rife with moments that defy materialist explanations. Marx's own schema to account for this was outlined in terms of his conception of *base* and *superstructure*. According to Marx, the material relations of production constitute the basic driving force of social activity, and forms of consciousness are "superstructures" that need to be understood in terms of this base. Therefore, for instance, in *The German Ideology* (Marx and Engels 1963 [1845]), he is able to dismiss religion as "false consciousness," as not something grounded in the material relations of production.

By the time Marx outlines the labor theory of value, however, this simple relationship of base as material and superstructure as abstract is considerably muddied.[21] This is evident in Marx's analysis of surplus value, which in many ways grounds his structural analysis of capitalist exploitation. To understand how surplus value leads to exploitation, Marx poses the question of the fundamental contradiction of capitalist political economy that he is trying to resolve, which is how an exchange of equivalents can lead to the generation of surplus.

To answer this question, Marx locates the generation of surplus value not in the labor that the worker exchanges for wages from the capitalist but in the *potential* of the worker to perform work *in excess* of that wage. It is this potential that Marx terms "labor power." As creative potential, labor power is not predetermined value. Therefore the apparent act of equivalent exchange (worker's labor for capitalist's wages) has hidden within it an element of nonequivalence, because wages are fixed remuneration, but the labor, which is actually labor power, is the potential for creation of value *over and above* the money expended in wages.

The key here is that labor power is an entirely abstract concept, and yet it is in this abstract concept that the fundamental dynamics of the labor theory of value, as an explanation of political economy distinct from the bourgeois understanding of it, rest. Historical materialism depends entirely, then, on this fundamental abstraction, but it is an abstraction, in turn, that stems entirely from the structural, material relations of production, because it is an abstraction that can only be enabled by the fact that the capitalist controls the material means of production. Therefore, at the very heart of Marx's analysis of capital is the dialectic relationship between forms of materiality and forms of abstraction.

This sort of relationship between materiality and abstraction runs throughout Marx's work and is a central methodological lesson from Marx that I incorporate into this analysis. For instance, the very act of exchange is animated by this dialectic. This could be the case whether the act of exchange in question is between capitalist and worker, or whether the exchange in question involves the circulation of money and commodities, the contours of which Marx describes at the start of *Grundrisse* and *Capital*. Biocapital, like any other form of circulation of capital, involves the circulation and exchange of money and commodities, whose analysis needs to remain central and at the forefront of analysis. But in addition, the circulations of new and particular forms of currency, such as biological material and information, emerge. One of the things that genomics fundamentally enables is a particular type of materialization of information, and its decoupling from its material biological source (such as tissue or cell line).

And yet, as Marx teaches us, one cannot be satisfied by simply tracing the circuits traveled by various forms of commodity, currency, or capital. Because again, at the heart of Marx's analysis of the circulation of money and commodities is the *mystical* and *magical* nature of the commodity, the fact that it is, in his words, "full of metaphysical subtleties and theological niceties" (Marx 1976 [1867], 163). In other words, at the heart of the interaction between either worker and capitalist or money and commodity is an uncanny kernel of abstraction that eludes capture in purely materialist terms.[22] It is this uncanny kernel that enables the commodity, which as an object is a rather banal thing, to become the mediator of social bonds. Indeed, that Marx alludes to it doing so in a "theological" manner is particularly striking. If, twenty-two years previously (in *The German Ideology*), he dismissed religion as ideological and therefore superstructure, a form of false consciousness, then by the time he writes *Capital*, the "theological" character of the commodity becomes a central symptom of its fetish.[23] It is not surprising, then, that a moment of exchange is also referred to as a moment of conversion, conversion being a process whereby one type of object (money, for instance) gets converted for its holder into another (such as commodity), but *also* being, explicitly, a theological category.[24]

Just as the act of exchange is animated by the dialectic of materiality to abstraction, so too is the act of valuation. Indeed, valuation is an integral part of the exchange process, but with the differentiation of capitalism into its industrial and speculative forms, valuation too starts operating at multiple levels or registers. Therefore, on the one hand, we have registers of valuation that depend on tangible material production — the amount of product manufactured, distributed, or sold by a company, for instance, or its profit margins and revenue flows. On the other hand, and certainly in many ways more central in the dot.com heyday of 1999–2001 that much of this book traces, we have forms of valuation having not to do with tangible material indicators of successful productivity, but with intangible abstractions, such as the felt possibility of *future* productivity or profit. Vision, hype, and promise, as I show in detail in chapter 3, are fundamental drivers of this kind of valuation and are central animating factors in drug development, whether it involves the valuation of start-ups by private investors such as venture capitalists, or the valuation of public companies on the stock markets of Wall Street. As the stock market scandals over the last couple of years indicate, this different level of abstraction is not merely discursive but has led to different, tangible material practices such as creatively articulated accounting mechanisms. Layered on these different registers of valuation is the fact that "value" itself, like conversion, is a double-jointed word that not only implies material valuation by the market but also suggests a concern with meanings and practices of ethics. This is particularly salient for industries such as biotech and pharmaceuticals, which generate significant symbolic capital from being, as they are never averse to pointing out, in the business of saving lives. Just as commodity objects and exchange processes are animated by a certain theological mystique, so too are systems of valuation.

So too, indeed, is science, which operates with its own authority by virtue of its ability to generate scientific "fact." This fact production is itself, as mentioned earlier, never driven by conceptual advances alone but often requires enabling technological advances. Indeed, genomics would have been a nonstarter had it not been for what are called tool companies, the companies that manufacture kits, reagents, and technological machinery that in many ways fundamentally enable genomic research to happen. The development of subjects (as in technoscientific disciplines such as genomics) is, however, always already entwined with the configuration of subjects (as in disciplined agents). In the case of genomics, these latter subjects could, for instance, be patients, or consumers, or experimental subjects, as I trace in chapter 2 and, especially, in chapter 4. This is particularly so when the disciplines in question are those that concern the very meanings of life, as the biological sciences in general and genomics in particular claim to do. In many ways, the particularities of *bio*capital stem from a combination of the specific market terrains of drug development (elaborated hereafter) and the specific epistemologies and subject formations of new life sciences.

So far in this introduction, I have talked about biocapital in delocalized (and implicitly in American) terms. This book, however, is a comparison of biocapital in the interlinked contexts of the United States and India and is specifically attentive to capitalisms as *global* regimes and practices. And indeed, globalization too is animated by a dialectical relationship between materiality and abstraction.

One of the methodological challenges of a project such as this is that symmetrical comparison between American and Indian techno-capitalism is in fact impossible, because there is an evident and wide asymmetry in the resources available to the two countries to do science or to influence the global marketplace. Therefore there are significant, material differences in structural relations of production that are absolutely vital. At the same time, I argue that the actions of Indian actors in this account cannot be explained simply by recourse to structural inequalities, because they are animated by a range of individual and collective *desires*, specifically the desire to be a global free market player. However, this desire, for these actors, always already implies acting *as if American*: there is a marked imitation of an American free market imaginary. In spite of these imitative desires, however, actual emergences of techno-capitalist systems on the ground in India tend often to diverge in incongruent ways from their American models. And these divergences are themselves conditioned both by different structural histories (such as India's colonial past, and five decades of postcolonial state socialism) and by the fact that Indian free market imaginaries are themselves not seamlessly articulated but rather frictioned and in tension with various forms of nationalist indignation at the unequal relations between India and the West. Similarly, the normative attribution of a particularly American mode of globalizing free market imaginary as somehow being the unmarked form of free market capitalism is itself, I show, animated by underlying abstractions such as nationalism, which get articulated differently in the United States than they do in India.[25]

In other words, an account of a system of global capitalism, if one learns from Marx's methodology, cannot simply be a network analysis that traces the various types of technoscientific or capital flows that occur in order to produce and sustain this system.[26] Such an account also needs to understand how these flows are constantly animated by multiple, layered, and complex interactions between material objects and structural relations of production, on the one hand, and abstractions, whether they are forms of discourse, ideology, fetishism, ethics, or salvationary or nationalist belief systems and desires, on the other. These abstractions may be hard to pin down and map in the same diagrammatic fashion as networks and flows, but it is essential to acknowledge them if we are to make sense of what Donna Haraway might describe as the biocapitalist "onion."[27]

## The Upstream-Downstream Terrain of Drug Development

I have argued so far that the complex relationships between materiality and abstraction constitute the nature of the tendential emergences of biocapital, as sets of systems and practices that are simultaneously globalizing and particular in their manifestations. However, these relationships are themselves constituted on certain terrains that have evolved historically. At their simplest, these terrains are overdetermined by logics of capital in our present historical conjuncture. But capitalist terrains are themselves multiple, and different market segments have different market terrains. One of the particularities of biocapital is the particular terrain of drug development that is constituted both by the nature of the drug development enterprise and by the histories of market evolution of the biotech and pharmaceutical industries, which, as I show hereafter, are two distinct arms of the drug development enterprise. In this section, I describe this particular American terrain, referred to as "upstream-downstream," and provide a brief overview of the drug development process, before briefly situating the Indian pharmaceutical industry in relation to this terrain.

The stages of drug development start with the identification of potential lead compounds (what is known as *drug discovery*), through a process of clinical trials (which is the subset of the entire process actually referred to as drug development), to finally the manufacture of a therapeutic molecule that gets marketed. The earlier stages of this process are referred to as *upstream* stages, the later ones as *downstream*.

Biotech and pharmaceutical companies represent two quite distinct arms of the drug development enterprise. They have evolved at different historical moments, have engaged for the most part in quite distinct science, and tend to occupy different locations in the drug development market terrain. The development of therapeutic molecules by the pharmaceutical industry has largely occurred by organic chemical synthesis, where derivatives of often serendipitously found biological substances were created in order to obtain therapeutics with better safety and efficacy profiles than the natural substance from which it was derived. The major driver of new molecule development over the last seventy-five years has indeed been synthetic chemistry. These traditional methods still form the bedrock of the pharmaceutical industry, in spite of considerable investment to make the initial identification of lead compounds less serendipitous and more rational and predictive.

The beginnings of the biotech industry, on the other hand, depend on recombinant DNA technology (RDT), as mentioned earlier.[28] If the logic of pharmaceutical organic chemical synthesis is the production of small chemical molecules that interact with and modify cellular and molecular components, then that of biopharmaceutical development is to engineer molecules that are normally components of the cellular and molecular machinery.

The story of the pharmaceutical industry has arguably been one of the most dramatic stories of industrial growth in the twentieth century. The pharmaceutical industry was actually incubated in, and grew out of, the dye industry, just as the biotechnology industry in the 1970s was initially supported by, and grew out of, the petrochemical industry. The "boom" in the pharmaceutical industry occurred in the 1930s with the discovery of the sulfa drugs, followed by the industrial-scale manufacture of penicillin as part of the World War II effort, which highlighted the importance of the links between defense and security needs during war and pharmaceutical innovation.[29] At the end of the nineteenth century, the two companies that could be called pharmaceutical companies were Bayer and Hoechst. They were joined in the 1930s and 1940s by would-be pharmaceutical giants such as Ciba Geigy, Eli Lilly, Wellcome, Glaxo, and Roche. The burst in natural-product chemistry occurred in the 1940s and 1950s, starting with the successful development of streptomycin for the treatment of tuberculosis. Not surprisingly, the development of biopharmaceuticals has a more modest history, both because the history of the biotech industry is much shorter and because in many ways the synthesis of biopharmaceuticals, which are chemically much more complex than small organic molecules, is often a much trickier process than traditional pharmaceutical development.[30]

If biotech has an origin story, then it is probably to be located in that of Genentech, even though Cetus Corporation, formed five years before Genentech in 1971, is considered the first biotech company. It was Genentech's initial public offering (IPO) on October 14, 1980, however, that really announced to the world the reality of biotech companies on Wall Street and further pointed to the market possibilities of companies that could by definition operate only on promise for years, until tangible therapeutic products could emerge from their R & D efforts.[31]

The innovative capabilities of biotech companies — which tend to be much smaller than pharmaceutical companies — are not simply the consequence of their doing "newer" science but are also a manifestation of a smaller, more adaptable, and managerially supple organizational structure. Nonetheless, there is no questioning the starkly differential positions of power and bargaining that biotech and pharmaceutical companies occupy when they actually do business with one another, and a fundamental aspect of the upstream-downstream terrain of drug development is that, with a few exceptions, biotech companies tend to focus on upstream drug discovery, but do not always have the capital to take molecules through downstream clinical trials processes. Instead they often license a promising therapeutic molecule out to a pharmaceutical company that does have the resources to do so.

To summarize, then, the market terrain of drug development in the United States today is constituted by small biotech companies that tend for the most part to work on upstream drug discovery projects before licensing potential therapeutic molecules out to pharmaceutical companies, and by big pharmaceutical companies that, in spite of some moves toward biopharmaceutical development, still tend to rely for the most part on the development of small therapeutic molecules through organic chemical synthesis. In addition, much of their strategic functioning involves in-licensing molecules from biotech companies or occasionally acquiring biotech companies with promising molecules in their pipeline. This terrain fundamentally structures the dynamics of drug development and provides it with some of its particularity.

Genomics very much occupies an upstream market niche in the drug development process, though the dream of most genome companies, like that of any biotech company, would be to increase capital reserves and revenue flows so as to be in a position to increasingly move their therapeutic lead molecules further and further downstream. From the point of view of the empirical content of this book, which is about postgenomic drug development market-places, pharmaceutical companies are a fundamental animating specter rather than a site of analysis themselves. Different pharmaceutical companies are interested to different degrees in genomics as sources of potential value to them, and some do invest resources in genomic-related research and development. But for the most part, pharmaceutical companies act as the eight-hundred-pound gorilla in the drug development process, the one institutional entity with the capital reserves and the proven history of being able to take molecules to market. As mentioned earlier, the way they often do that with biopharmaceuticals is by in-licensing molecules from biotech companies and then taking them through downstream stages of drug development. In many ways, pharmaceutical companies, in addition to making molecules, could be said to be the regulators of capital and commodity flow in the drug development value chain, often deciding which upstream technologies and molecules are worth investing in, either through a licensing agreement or by buying the upstream company. In this manner, pharmaceutical companies almost act like the investment banks of the drug development enterprise.

The other crucial aspect worth noting here is that there are two economies at stake that are themselves not seamless with respect to each other and that correspond to Marx's "industrial" versus "commercial" capitalisms that I discussed while talking about the relationship of biocapital to systems of capitalism writ large. On the one hand, there is the R & D, manufacturing, and marketing of drugs, the component of the drug development economy that has to do with the production, distribution, and sale of commodities (similar to Marx's "industrial capitalism"). On the other, there is the speculative market, which for pharmaceutical companies (almost all of which in the United States are publicly traded) translates into market valuation on Wall Street (similar to Marx's "commercial capitalism").

Ironically, the larger and more powerful a company is, the harder it is, in some ways, to satisfy Wall Street. This is because while one metric for measuring the value of an investment is its stability and reliability (on which score pharmaceutical companies are extremely sound investments), another, whose importance was particularly magnified during the dot.com boom of 1999–2001, is the ability of a stock to appreciate in value. This is known as earnings per share (EPS), which is the annual percentage increase for an investor in the value of the shares he or she holds in a company. Investors like to see between 12 and 15 percent EPS in any stock they hold; typically, pharmaceutical company EPS has been in the range of 8 to 10 percent. This has largely to do with the time, capital intensiveness, and high risk of drug development. It also has to do with the fact that large, successful, and extremely profitable industries have to do correspondingly more in absolute terms to register an equivalent increase in relative value of a share than a much smaller company. Thus a small biotech company with one therapeutic molecule in its pipeline will generate huge stock market excitement when a second therapeutic molecule enters clinical trials, whereas for a large pharmaceutical company that has, say, twenty patented molecules on the market, seven of them blockbusters, and eight others in various stages of clinical trials, the addition of a ninth into the pipeline, which requires the same amount of development resources and research efforts as it would for the small biotech company, would likely not generate the same amount of investor excitement, because it would not be as defining an event for the larger company relative to its own market history. This is why one can simultaneously have an activist discourse that points to the huge profitability of the pharmaceutical industry as an argument against high drug prices, and an industry discourse that points to the need for high drug prices in order for the industry to survive, as apparently completely antithetical discourses that both make market sense: the former discourse points to the commodity marketplace and the generation of revenues, the latter to the speculative marketplace and the need to satisfy investors.

I have so far talked about the upstream-downstream terrain as descriptive of drug development in the United States.[32] But pharmaceutical companies exist, and have existed for decades, as robust industries in many countries other than the United States. The Indian pharmaceutical industry, for instance, is one of the most interesting national pharmaceutical industries in the world today, in large measure because its character has been so significantly shaped by patent regimes. The 1970 Indian Patent Act granted process as opposed to product patents on drug manufacture. This meant that Indian pharmaceutical companies, unlike their American counterparts, could manufacture drugs that already existed on patent in the market, as long as they came up with their own method for doing so.[33] This helped shape the industry into one that was capable of cheap reverse-engineered bulk drug manufacture, which has in turn enabled Indian drug prices to be among the lowest in the world. In 1995, however, India became a signatory to World Trade Organization–imposed patent regimes, which required the industry there to be completely WTO compliant by 2005. The change in patent regimes toward a WTO-imposed one has therefore necessitated a paradigm shift in the Indian industry, as after 2005 Indian pharmaceutical companies will not be able to take a molecule already on the market, remake it through an indigenous process, and then sell it. Indian companies will now have to focus on novel drug discovery and development in a manner much more closely reflective of the American drug development marketplace.

The major question facing the Indian pharmaceutical industry today is what effect becoming WTO compliant will have on it, a question of what exactly the consequences will be of a paradigm shift toward a property regime that will not allow reverse-engineered bulk drug manufacture. The Indian pharmaceutical industry was not a sick or dying industry in need of market rejuvenation but was, throughout the 1980s, a quite profitable industry. Therefore, changing over to a WTO regime, for this industry, does not just mean adopting new and unfamiliar methods of drug discovery, which necessitates the setting up of R & D facilities; it also means abandoning a revenue-based business model in favor of the potentially lucrative but far riskier growth-based model, in which Indian companies would be evaluated not just by the amount of product that they are able to sell but also by the potential value that investors speculate they can provide, while pitted in direct competition against more powerful Western companies.

There are, however, an increasing number of Indian companies that have been in the process of retooling themselves to become companies that can discover new chemical entities. The stakes are not just profits but global expansion. The niche that Indian companies starting to invest in R & D occupy becomes similar to the one a Western biotech company occupies with respect to a big pharmaceutical company. Dr. Reddy's Foundation (DRF), for instance, is the R & D division of Dr. Reddy's Laboratories, which is one of the Indian pharmaceutical companies best positioned to retool itself away from reverse engineering of generics and toward novel drug discovery and development. But it employs just 250 people (the size of a very small U.S. biotech company); its R & D efforts involve drug discovery rather than development; and its new business model has involved out-licensing the molecules it discovers to big pharmaceutical companies that can take a molecule through clinical trials. From the revenue garnered from such licensing, companies like

Reddy's hope to move further up the value chain by holding on to the molecule longer before out-licensing it. While it is nearly impossible to actually get breakdowns of milestone payments at different stages of drug development when the drug has been licensed from a discovery company to a development company, it is well understood that a molecule's value increases exponentially the further up the clinical trials process it gets before being out-licensed. In other words, the story of drug development in India, from the perspective of its pharmaceutical companies, is one that sees a shift from the reverse engineering of generic molecules for primarily domestic markets, a profitable business model in terms of revenues, to one that much more closely approximates the role and market position of a U.S. biotech company, involved in early-stage novel drug discovery (though still primarily using traditional organic chemistry), that it hopes will allow it to eventually take its molecules further downstream.[34]

While the Indian pharmaceutical industry is well established, India does not have much of a biotech industry. As indicated earlier, this is partly because of the absence of a traditional scientific strength in the life sciences to match that in the chemical sciences, coupled to the risk aversion of pharmaceutical companies that do not want to abandon research in areas of their core strength. However, as I note at many instances throughout the book, Indian state actors are particularly keen to change this situation, and view genomics as the answer to India's developing an emergent biotech industry. As with the Western pharmaceutical industry, the Indian pharmaceutical industry too is not an explicit site of analysis for much of the rest of the book. Rather, I focus on India's biotech and genome ventures, many of which are enabled in considerable measure by the state and strategically constrained and influenced by the global influence and strength of Western pharmaceutical companies. I continue to set the stage for this further analysis by briefly explaining the changing meanings of genomics, both as science and, in the United States, as business model, over the past few years.

## Genomics

One set of background contexts necessary to understanding the assemblages of actors, practices, stories, and events that I narrate in this book concerns the terrain of drug development.[35] However, I also argue that genomics represents an epistemic and technological shift of some significance to biocapital in its particularity. In this section, I provide a quick tutorial on genomics. "Genomics" itself, I wish to show, is not a stable referent, and its own meaning has evolved over the last few years, from the days of the initial conception to map and sequence the human genome at the start of the Human Genome Project (HGP) in the late 1980s to today's postgenomics era subsequent to the completion of the working draft sequence of the human genome. Further, this evolution in what genomics means has not just been consequent to technological innovation or epistemic advances but has also been conditioned, in significant measure, by what is deemed a potentially successful business model at the time.

Genomics itself, then, is multiple things, but it is first and foremost an articulation of experimental with informational science. To this extent, it involves an articulation of different scientific perspectives on biological systems, of mathematics and computational biology on the one hand with molecular genetics and cell biology on the other.

Genomics has to a significant extent been technologically enabled, and analysis has also tended to be driven by automated technology rather than by hypotheses. It represents the rapid, high-volume analysis of information, what is known as *high-throughput* science. The initial attempts of genome scientists focused on mapping and sequencing human (and other) genomes, which has been followed now by more complicated genomic analysis. Therefore the first "phase" of genomics was very much about the generation of databases, and this was very much the prime activity of many of the public labs and private companies from 1999 to 2001, the period that I trace most directly in this book.

An important informational tool in genomic analysis is knowledge of genetic *variability* between individuals and populations, and the potential correlation of that variability to phenotypic variability (i.e., variability in visible traits). Major informational artifacts that enable such analysis are called single nucleotide polymorphisms, or SNPs (pronounced "snips"). SNPs are single base variations in the genetic code that occur about once every one thousand bases along the three-billion-base human genome. Knowing the locations of these closely spaced DNA landmarks both eases the sequencing of the human genome and aids in the discovery of genes variably linked to different traits. A map of all the SNPs in the human species would provide the basic database to perform association studies, which compare the prevalence of particular genetic markers among individuals who possess a certain trait (which may be a disease trait or a predisposition to a disease or to side effects to certain drugs) and those who do not. Association studies can provide insights in unearthing obscure disease-related genes or in helping preventive diagnosis. SNPs, therefore, have a potential value as tools leading to therapy, in a more pinpointed and versatile way than a random DNA sequence. Indeed, the "human" genome sequences generated by the public HGP and by Celera represent a rather small sampling of human DNA sources.[36]

As mentioned toward the beginning of this introduction, the HGP started as a public initiative to sequence the genome. This was officially undertaken by a five-nation consortium, though not surprisingly much of the policy impetus came from the United States. Therefore, at the outset, genomics was hardly overdetermined as corporate. In fact, the initial interest in the project came from the U.S. Department of Energy. Many biologists were skeptical because what was being proposed was not hypothesis-driven science. Indeed, in its guise as a state-sponsored project of big, industrialized science, whose planning proceeded throughout by means of the generation of five-year plans, the HGP could almost be said to have resembled Soviet science in its conception rather than American.[37]

The approach of the genome project was to start by developing genetic and physical maps, and then to sequence regions of interest. All of this could be done only through the concomitant development of technological hardware, and by the parallel sequencing of model organisms.[38] This was followed by the development of database tools to annotate the sequence and the beginnings of the development of functional genomics capability, with a special focus on DNA sequence variations.[39]

All these plans were accelerated by the formation of Celera Genomics, and by Craig Venter's challenge to the HGP mentioned at the start of this introduction. This also marked the upstaging of big state science by entrepreneurial corporate science and was enabled in large part by new automated sequencing machines developed by Applied Biosystems (ABI), whose parent company, Perkin-Elmer, was the company that also seeded Celera. Therefore, while biotechnology's corporate contours had already taken shape in the early 1980s with events such as the Bayh-Dole Act, *Diamond v. Chakrabarty*, and the Genentech IPO, genomics itself only started looking increasingly corporate because of the enabling role played by Perkin-Elmer, a company that until that time had been a completely unglamorous instrumentation company, a nuts-and-bolts company far removed from the sort of cutting-edge research and development associated with biotech.

I have, so far, myself tried to provide some nuts-and-bolts background at the start of this introduction, by outlining what I see as some of the central theoretical terrain that I am trying to cover through an attempt to explain the notion of biocapital, and by explaining all too briefly the market terrain of drug development and a brief overview of genomics. Both these latter contexts are essential to understanding the arguments of especially the first four chapters of this book. I now move on to outline the structure of this book and to describe some of the sites of my analysis.


This is a book that studies a global political economic system and uses ethnographic methods to do so. This is already an incongruent attempt, which effectively sets out resources well equipped to study *locality* and *particularity* in order to map a set of *global* systems, structures, and terrains. In many ways, it is this incongruence that captures the spirit of what George Marcus and Michael Fischer diagnosed for social and cultural anthropology in the 1980s, the constitutive element of what they called an "experimental moment in the human sciences" (Marcus and Fischer 1986), and that indeed typifies the fundamental contradiction of ethnographic practice.[40]

This necessitates reconfigurations of the spatial boundaries of ethnographic practice to map onto the spatial reconfigurations of the relationships between "local" and "global" brought about by global capitalism. Traditional, "single-sited" ethnography, as Marcus and Fischer point out, tends not to be sufficient to capture the complexities and multiple causalities that constitute contemporary social systems and structures. They therefore proposed multisited ethnography as a methodological solution to the problems confronting "experimental" social and cultural anthropology. By multisited ethnography, they do not simply mean a multiplication of the number of field sites that an anthropologist travels to, a quantitative "adding on" to single-sited ethnography. Rather, they have argued that multisited ethnography is a *conceptual topology*, a different way of thinking about field sites in relation to analytic and theoretical questions about the world we live in. This might require different methodological strategies (for instance, involving new types of collaborations, formal and informal, between anthropologist colleagues, or between anthropologists and their informants), access to a different range of sources (for instance, Web sites and other sources of mediated information in addition to participant observation and formal interviews), and different narrative strategies (more dialogic and polyphonic).[41]

The ambition of this book, in a similar vein, is to make social theoretical interventions in science studies and political economy by using empirical ethnographic material. Therefore, on the one hand, this book is about "biocapital"; on the other hand, it is also a multisited ethnography of postgenomic drug development marketplaces in the United States and India. Such a limited demarcation of sites necessarily leads to partial and fragmentary insights into a political economic system. I argue that it is nevertheless in the particularities that constitute global systems that the functioning of those systems can truly be elucidated and understood. Further, as I have argued earlier, if capitalisms are always already multiple and mutable, then the challenge is less one of creating a grand unified theory of capitalism than one of contributing to a proliferation of thick, multiple, locally grounded analyses of technoscientific market regimes and practices. India and the United States are central and in many ways unique sites that contribute to such an analysis, but they by no means capture "biocapital" in any sort of entirety. Rather, they provide windows into global capitalisms, together generating a systemic perspective.[42]

The other challenge of this book is to confront the fluidity of the systems that I am writing about. If capitalism is multiple and mutable, any analysis of capitalism needs to relentlessly emphasize it as *process*. Similarly, biotechnology is a constantly emerging and changing field: to repeat, even genomics fails to be a constant referent over the last five years that could be said to constitute the period of ethnographic investigation for this book.[43] The changes in genomics as an epistemology have paralleled changes in genomic business models, as business plans that in 1999 or 2000 were deemed to be the future of the life sciences (such as, for instance, those based in the creation of bioinformatic databases) now often seem to have been naively optimistic. Indeed, many genome companies that generated their initial investment on the basis of bioinformatic business models are in the process of reinventing themselves as drug discovery biotechnology companies. Perhaps the most notable example of such a company is Celera Genomics, which played such a major role in generating the working draft sequence of the human genome. Meanwhile, changes in Indian technoscience and capitalism have been particularly rapid over the past decade and a half, as the recent dramatic investment in high technology has been matched by drastic changes in an economic and legal environment that has been retooled, both intentionally and as a consequence of global structural constraints, toward an aggressive embrace of the free market.

Therefore, complementary to a multisited ethnographic methodology that emphasizes the spatial scale and incongruence of global systems is a necessary emphasis on *temporality* as a consequence of the fact that these systems are not rigid or eternally resolved structures but processes constantly in formation.

On the one hand, then, this book tells stories of people, places, technologies, epistemologies, business models, and market logics in two countries that are distinct yet interrelated in asymmetric fashion. On the other hand, however, many of these stories are structured by flows of various sorts — of materials, people, money, and information. While I trace the cultures *of* particular sites throughout the book, I am also interested in tracing the multiple exchange relations *between* these sites. I do not, therefore, study and describe the sites in this book as reified, static, or solitary entities, but as nodes in multiple sorts of exchange.

In my fieldwork, I have adopted a combination of different approaches: intensive, medium-length participant observation (one to six months per site); short targeted "probes" (one- to two-day site visits); ongoing monitoring of written products of the drug development marketplace; semistructured, multiple life history and career development interviewing; use of scientific conferences and trade shows as ritual spaces for seeing many of the promotional, competitive, and status constituents enacted and renegotiated; and seminars that I gave at one of my sites (GeneEd, an e-learning start-up based in San Francisco), which emerged as an ethnographer's variant of a focus group technology. In the process, I have physically covered a number of sites in the United States (mainly around Boston and the Bay Area) and in India (mainly in New Delhi, Hyderabad, and Bombay) over a five-year period from early 1999 through mid-2004.

This book is written in two simultaneous narrative registers that implicitly ground its structure. The core theoretical argument of the book is that understanding biocapital involves analyzing the relationship between materiality and modes of abstraction that underlie the coemergences of new forms of life science with market regimes for the conduct of such science. In other words, one can understand emergent biotechnologies such as genomics only by simultaneously analyzing the market frameworks within which they emerge. In doing so, for instance, marketing discourse, the hype and hope surrounding emergent technologies, the fetish of genetic determinism, and the belief in science, nation, and religion all constitute the assemblages of postgenomic life that this book maps at the same time as it maps the technological and epistemic shifts that are both cause and consequence of genomics, biotechnology, and drug development.

The book also maps three sets of terrains: one, the upstream-downstream terrain of drug development that I have already briefly described; the second, terrains within which start-ups deal with investors and customers; and the third, the global market terrains that structure technology and capital flows between centers of innovation such as the United States and aspiring "Third World" peripheries such as India.

In chapter 1, "Exchange and Value: Contradictions in Market Logic in American and Indian Genome Enterprises," I argue that much of the genomics "revolution" is based on technological advances rather than on fundamental conceptual advances. New technological hardware and methodology allow experiments and measurements to be performed at resolutions and speeds inconceivable before. The chapter shows how market logic is as much at stake as technological change, as such innovations always emerge in the context of fluid and contested ownership and intellectual property regimes.

Further, these are exchange regimes in which the apparent binaries of "public" and "private" are in fact hard to maintain as American corporations take strategic recourse to gift regimes at the same time that the Indian state attempts to negotiate global playing fields as a market agent.

In chapter 2, "Life and Debt: Global and Local Political Ecologies of Biocapital," I explore, through fieldwork conducted in the outskirts of Hyderabad and in the center of Bombay, the local political ecologies of indebtedness that are constituted by, and constitutive of, globalization. Biocapital is referred to here in two distinct yet simultaneous analytic frames, more explicitly than at any other point in the book: on the one hand, as the circuits of land, labor, and value (in a classic Marxian sense) that are inhabited by biotechnological innovation and drug development; on the other hand, as the increasingly constitutive fact of biopolitics in processes of global capitalism. In other words, the chapter explores both what forms of alienation, expropriation, and divestiture are necessary for a "culture of biotechnology innovation" to take root, and how individual and collective subjectivities and citizenships are shaped and conscripted by these technologies that concern "life itself." I thereby argue that the playing out of First World–Third World asymmetries in globalization, as opposed to those of industrial colonial expansion, occurs through the reconfiguration of the relationship of imperial power to colony into one of vendor to client.

In chapter 3, "Vision and Hype: The Conjuration of Promissory Biocapitalist Futures," I argue that genomics, and indeed all biotechnology, is a game that is constantly played in the future in order to generate the present that enables that future. I therefore trace the conjuration of corporate promissory futures as a constitutive feature of biocapital, which changes the very grammar through which "life," which now gets transformed into a calculable market unit, is understood, and which structures the strategic terrain on which biotech and drug development companies operate.

In chapter 4, "Promise and Fetish: Genomic Facts and Personalized Medicine, or Life Is a Business Plan," I follow the modes of abstraction that genomic knowledge itself provides and is based on, leading to what I term "genomic fetishism."[44] I reflect the tensions between abstraction and materiality when considering the operation of scientific facts, which themselves are produced on terrains overdetermined by questions of ownership and the public domain on the one hand and vision and hype on the other. I argue that genomic facts centrally imbricate multiple types of risk discourse. These discourses, on the one hand, concern the probability of future disease that genomic technologies can foretell, and on the other hand, they concern the high-risk, capital-intensive process of drug development that biotechnology and pharmaceutical companies are involved in.

In chapter 5, "Salvation and Nation: Underlying Belief Structures of Biocapital," I show how the promises of biocapital are undergirded by salvationary and nationalist rhetorics and discourses. I talk about the structural manifestation of biotechnologies in the United States as promissory salvationary science; show how such salvationary stories are embedded in specific biographies of individuals; and argue that they are embodied in the ethos of specific corporate cultures, and in cultures of the biotechnology and drug development industries writ large. I contrast this to the nationalist manifestations of biocapital in India, in terms of everyday work practices, institutional structures, regulations and mechanisms, biographies of Indian scientists, and the missionary zeal of Silicon Valley–based nonresident Indian (NRI) entrepreneurs and the role they see for themselves as agents in India's development. I thereby conclude that understanding technoscientific emergence in India is not simply a case study of Third World science and technology, but rather that global market terrains are structured by tensions between dominant hegemonic imaginaries (invariably American) and countervailing nationalist imaginaries. These latter simultaneously submit to and resist American market hegemony in ways that lead to manifestations of market logic, state action, and scientific development that diverge in incongruous ways from what gets conceived in ideologies of innovation and technology transfer.

In chapter 6, "Entrepreneurs and Start-Ups: The Story of an E-learning Company," I describe fieldwork at GeneEd, a San Francisco–based start-up that sells e-learning courses in drug discovery and development to biotech and pharmaceutical companies. GeneEd is neither a biotech nor a pharmaceutical company, but it is situated in all three sets of terrains that I concern myself with throughout the book, and therefore is the one site to which I devote an entire chapter of traditional, single-sited ethnographic attention. By virtue of being a start-up, GeneEd negotiates the investment terrain that entrepre-neurial ventures have to contend with, something that much of the biotech industry has had, and continues to have, to do in a market segment where dealing with venture capitalism and venture capitalists is a central constitutive element. Both of GeneEd's founders are Indians in Silicon Valley and, al-though not (yet) directly involved in technology transfer to India, are to varying degrees networked into the Silicon Valley nonresident Indian entre-preneurial community, which forms one of my central links in this book be-tween Indian and U.S. market biotech worlds. And finally, GeneEd sells its products to upstream biotech and downstream big pharmaceutical companies and therefore has a particularly invested, and well-situated, perspective on the upstream-downstream terrain of drug development (a terrain that has itself significantly shaped the emergence of GeneEd's own history as a company). This chapter therefore shows how innovation is structured in start-ups, how start-ups relate to their investors and customers, and how labor and manage-ment practices and core values are impacted within the start-up itself in the course of its evolution.

In my concluding reflections, I return to Marx to redefine what I have meant by biocapital at various points in this analysis. In the process, I try to tease out some of the continuities and some of the novel specificities that the implosion of emergent life sciences with emergent market terrains and logics present to us.

# Part I

*Circulations*

# 1. Exchange and Value
*Contradictions in Market Logic in American
and Indian Genome Enterprises*

In March 1999, undergraduates of Harvard University and the Massachusetts Institute of Technology (MIT) belonging to the Harvard-MIT Hippocratic Society organized a conference titled "Genetic Technology and Society." This brought together leading biotech scientists and entrepreneurs with politicians, antibiotech activists, religious leaders, and bioethicists to debate some of the social issues arising from biotechnology. It was clearly an uncomfortable venue for a number of the attending scientists, academic and corporate, who were evidently not used to presenting their achievements on the same panel as nonscientists who shared less sanguine views of the scientists' efforts than they themselves did.

One of the attending scientist-entrepreneurs was Kari Stefansson, founder and chief executive officer of the Iceland-based genome company DeCode Genetics. The pitch for this company was that Iceland, by virtue of its purported genetic homogeneity, provided an ideal site for population genomics experiments. What in fact made it an especially good site for such experiments was the existence in the country of excellent national medical records dating back to the early twentieth century, coupled with a wealth of genealogical information thanks to a population who took the tracing of their ancestry seriously.

Just as private genome companies in the United States such as Celera Genomics were creating controversy in 1998 (in their case because of their stated desire to patent the DNA sequences that they generated), so too was 1998 a controversial year for genomics in Iceland. This is because the Icelandic parliament had given DeCode exclusive rights to create a genomic database of the Icelandic population by collecting DNA samples and elucidating their genetic sequence, and further by coupling that genotype information to the health records of the population maintained by the state. This venture, called the Health Sector Database, presumed the consent of the Icelandic population. Instead of obtaining the informed consent of each potential participant in the database, DeCode allowed individuals to opt out of it. Unless an Icelander actively opted out of the database, his or her medical information was presumed to be a part of it. Not surprisingly, DeCode's efforts were becoming hugely controversial, not just in Iceland but in debates among American bioethicists, many of whom felt that it was inappropriate for a single company to own exclusive rights to a nation's genetic information.[1]

As a graduate student with nothing to lose, I had e-mailed Stefansson before his arrival in Cambridge in the hope that I might be able to meet with him during the conference, and as expected had not received a reply. At a reception at the end of the first day of the conference, I met him in person, tall and elegant in a light gray Armani suit that matched his silvery beard. I told him that he had not responded to my e-mail, for which he apologized profusely, stating that he received in excess of two hundred e-mail messages a day, but that "we must talk." He suggested that we have lunch together on the following day, just after his own session.

The next day, Stefansson gave a wonderfully sculpted presentation on De-Code, in which he talked about its scientific and business potential, and also about the great care taken by the company to behave in an ethical fashion. He was particularly eloquent regarding the measures taken to protect the privacy of all individuals who were included in the Health Sector Database. One of his copanelists was a soft-spoken bioethicist from the Cambridge-based Council for Responsible Genetics named Martin Teitel, who raised many of the standard objections that opponents of DeCode's efforts had been raising in the previous few months. Stefansson exploded in the middle of Teitel's talk, saying that Teitel was not qualified to speak about the scientific aspects of DeCode's work, as he was not a scientist, and did not have the right to pass judgment on an Icelandic matter, as he was American. Teitel responded gently that if he could not, as a nonscientist, talk about science, and could not, as an American, talk about Iceland, then by that logic, Stefansson did not have the authority to talk about ethics, since Teitel was trained as an ethicist, and Stefansson was not. Stefansson realized that he had made an error, dramatically buried his face in his hands, shook his head, put his arm around Teitel, and apologized to him in public.

After the panel, I hovered expectantly around Stefansson for the promised lunch, but he swept past me, grabbed an associate by the hand, and stomped off with him, saying firmly as he went, "We *must* get ourselves a bioethicist!"

### Grounds, Arguments, and Sites

The circulation of capital is intimately tied to questions of value. Value is one of those nice double-jointed words that always already imply two different things. On the one hand, "value" implies the market value that gets realized through processes of exchange. On the other, it implies the nonmarket values that might be called, in shorthand that has led to the term's own black-boxing as it has been used by members of the life science community, *ethics*. One of the things I show in this chapter is how market valuation depends on notions of value that are deemed somehow "external" to the market, while the "ethical" gets increasingly encroached on, co-opted by, and made answerable to, systems of market valuation.

One of the key transformations in the life sciences that genomics marks, as I explained in the introduction, is that biology increasingly becomes an information science. Therefore an analysis of biocapital involves asking at the outset where value resides as biology becomes an information science, and what work and whose agencies are required to create these values. Answering these questions involves understanding the circulation of information and the changing forms of corporate activity. I theorize the dynamics of information flow and corporate action around the fact that information is something that can be and is now *owned*. This chapter, therefore, offers an analysis of the dynamics of information ownership in the life sciences. Specifically, it focuses on the relationship between genomic information flows and the "speed bumps" created by its private ownership, in order to trace its implications for understanding the operation of the market logic of biocapital. In the process, I wish to show that "market logic" itself is hard to pin down and is very much at stake.

Corporate biotech is a form of high-tech capitalism. Three defining features consequently mark it: the importance of innovation; the role of fact production; and the centrality of information. One of the things happening is that information itself becomes a form of currency, susceptible to commodification and decommodification. Also, information is something that can travel globally, in circuits of exchange tied to, yet independent of, the (in the case of biocapital) living material (often DNA, protein, cell, or tissue) that the information comes from or relates to.

Let me tease out further the different social lives of biological material and biological information. Even though these are different "things," a continuous relationship exists between them. Biological information helps to rationalize experimental laboratory biology. For instance, one can use bioinformatics to determine the probable function of a protein encoded by a particular DNA sequence, by looking for homology between the sequence of interest and other sequences (usually in other organisms) whose function is already known. By thus narrowing the probable functional significance of different sequences, it is easier to experimentally determine the functionality of genes and proteins.

Therefore there is biological information, and the biological material (cell or tissue) from which the information is derived, material that subsequently becomes the substrate of experiments that validate the leads suggested by the information. In the process, information is detached from its biological material originator to the extent that it does have a separate social life, but the "knowledge" provided by the information is constantly relating back to the material biological sample. The database plays a key intermediary role in the transition of "information" to "knowledge": in this case specifically knowledge that is relevant to therapy. It is knowledge that is always relating back to the biological material that is the source of the information; but it is also knowledge that can only be obtained, in the first place, through extracting information from the biological material. The abstraction of information away from the biological material has a specific function in making therapeutically relevant knowledge. This is also why it is so easy to intuitively conceptualize the generation of information as "inventive," and therefore as something that can legitimately be owned.

What is at stake, then, in analyzing biocapital is an analysis of multiple forms of currency, such as money, information, and biological material, all simultaneously dependent on one another, yet not necessarily traveling the same circuits at the same time. These circuits, however, are not simply preordained networks but are often strategically constructed or constrained by various institutional actors, whose actions may be at cross-purposes. The creation of value, then, is a consequence both of circuits of exchange and of strategic articulations of concerned individual and institutional actors.[2]

One of the features of sequence information flow in genomics is the remarkable speed at which DNA sequences are being generated, a consequence of considerable automation and investment in technological hardware in the form of new DNA sequencing machines. Therefore what is relevant is not just that genomic information traverses circuits of exchange but that genomics enables this circulation to occur at resolutions and speeds inconceivable before. The pervasive rhetoric surrounding such rapid information generation is, not surprisingly, almost one of breathlessness, conveying a sense of being overwhelmed with a huge amount of (presumably) valuable data that is virtually impossible to keep up with. As I will show, this is not merely rhetoric (though it is all rhetorical), because it is true that there is a huge amount of data being generated, and while nobody quite knows the biological significance of even a fraction of it, any piece of information in this haystack could turn out to be extremely valuable, therapeutically and commercially.

Speed is also of direct material value, since a delay in the production and marketing of what turns out to be a blockbuster drug could, in the calculation of the pharmaceutical industry, cost a drug company in excess of a million dollars per *day*. Speed manifests itself in two distinct ways: both as qualitatively massively compressed research and production time,[3] and as a number of emerging segments that contribute to, or feed off, speediness. In other words, "speed" in genomics is important not just because change is fast but because "speed" is a material-rhetorical fulcrum used to lever first the government, and then the public and other companies, into responding to "hype" and thus further entangling themselves in biotech.

To stake a claim to the potential value of genomic information, there is a desire, certainly among private genome scientists, to own it. Ownership, however, puts fetters on the seamless flow of information, which is the desired condition for enabling information to be transformed into that valuable "something else," which is often a pharmaceutical product. I will unpack this dynamic in greater detail as the chapter proceeds, but this is the central theoretical problematic that I am trying to contend with: the breathlessness manifested through a speed surrounding information flow, tempered by the speed bumps installed as a necessary consequence of an institutional regime that allows information to be owned. This leads to a frictioned process. I use the notion of friction rather than that of noise (which has commonly been used in information theory to denote obstructions to information that, if overcome, can lead to a seamless flow of information),[4] because such obstructions are not externalities waiting to be subsumed in a seamless flow but are internal to the dynamics of the flow itself. Friction is both the product of things rubbing against each other and suggestive of conflict; it is not just obstructive, but productive. Speed, speed bumps, and friction, therefore, are all inherent to the circulation of genomic information in contemporary capitalism. Further, the forms of "gifting" that I describe later in the chapter, which are articulated as alternatives to regimes of ownership and commodification, are themselves, by virtue of in fact being commensurable with commodification, also obstructive yet productive.

My theoretical arguments in each chapter are made through the use of different sets of ethnographic and empirical material. These, in different cases, include institutional sites, material objects, and individual biographies. In this chapter, I use three sets of institutional and strategic sites and arrangements to analyze notions of exchange and value in biocapital. These include the SNP Consortium; a U.S.-based biotech company that I call Rep-X; and the Indian state. The choice of these three sites and sets of stories reflects my concern to show the stratified dynamics of biocapitalist exchange through mapping its multiple terrains.

As I described in my introduction while explaining the upstream-downstream terrain of drug development, a broad distinction can be made between a genomics company and a pharmaceutical company. A genomics company tends to occupy upstream niches of the drug development process, tended between 1999 and 2001 to focus largely on selling genetic information,[5] and tends to be smaller and newer. A pharmaceutical company tends to focus on downstream aspects of drug development, sells drugs, and is usually much larger and older. A common mode of operation for genomics companies is to license their information to pharmaceutical companies, an arrangement that is often more convenient for the pharmaceutical company than setting up an extensive genomics facility of its own.

Thus genomics companies try to patent DNA sequence information so that they can sell or license it. Pharmaceutical companies usually have to pay upstream licensing fees and subsequent royalties on any therapy they may discover to these database companies. The pharmaceutical companies would, therefore, much prefer information to be accessible in the public domain. Therefore, even public/private debates are overcoded by corporate fights. In other words, and this is crucial: *What distinguishes the drug development marketplace from, say, the software industry is its peculiar upstream-downstream terrain. Drug development is such a capital-intensive process that very few companies have the muscle to actually take a drug to market.*[6]

The analogy of the upstream-downstream terrain of drug development with the software market merits further exploration. I have suggested that drug development is so capital intensive that it makes it very unlikely that small biotech companies will ever really compete with or displace big pharmaceutical companies. Such a capital-intensive environment as a competitive advantage for large companies does not really exist in industries like the software industry. In other words, I have suggested that the very *nature* of drug development makes it that much harder to alter the fundamental power relations between small and big companies. Having said this, the fact remains that in the software industry, few organizations have seriously tried to go up against Microsoft's core business. Many have tried to compete with one or two products or services that Microsoft has offered, but the only significant challenges have come from companies that have fundamentally tried to change the rules of the game (such as Netscape or AOL, or more recently from the open-source movement). The costs of bringing any big product to market, regardless of the industry, are likely to keep the number of competitors low. Nonetheless, the time when the biotech industry was just beginning (the late 1970s) was the time when a little start-up called Microsoft was challenging the established computing giants such as IBM and Wang. Even if Microsoft has an impenetrable hold on the software market today, there has historically (as seen in Microsoft's own case) been the room for the emergence of a small company into a giant corporation that has never happened in biotech.[7]

The SNP Consortium is an attempt by public genome researchers and big pharmaceutical companies to place information regarding genetic sequence variability into the public domain so that genome companies cannot patent such information.[8] In the portion of this chapter dealing with the consortium, I show how such acts of apparent gifting of information to the public domain are strategic and overdetermined by the interests of big pharmaceutical companies. I argue that certain forms of strategic decommodification are part and parcel of "market logic," which in itself is hardly seamless or unitary but rather constitutes a terrain for hegemonic contestation.

Rep-X is a biotech company that aims to collect DNA samples from around the world. It aims, in the process, to become the world's largest corporate DNA repository and hopes to leverage the information it obtains from these genetic samples for commercial value.

My account of Rep-X forms a bridge between the SNP Consortium stories and the stories of the Indian state in this chapter, because it is embedded in both sets of terrains that I am trying to elucidate: the upstream-downstream terrain of drug development in the United States, and the global terrain of First World–Third World relationships around circuits of exchange relating to biological material and information. In the former case, Rep-X represents a new biotechnology company struggling to create a niche to generate market value in the face of the hegemonic clout of the pharmaceutical industry. In the latter case, it represents the powerful First World quasi-colonial entity seen as expropriating genetic material from the "Third World" to create value in the "First."

The Indian state, however, does not just exist as a "colonized" state actor, a constrained victim of biopiracy. The incongruence in my stories of the Indian state arises from the ways in which it paradoxically frames itself as a global market actor in order, simultaneously, to resist acts of biopiracy while leveraging itself as a "global player" in biotech. In the process, I argue that the Indian state itself acts almost analogously to a biotech company, an aspiring "start-up" in a global technoscientific terrain that is always already overdetermined as American *and* corporate.

Biocapital is creating a series of cultural transformations in the materiality and exchangeability of what we call "life." These transformations are created through shifting and variable use of market commodification versus public commons or public goods formation, both of which are disciplined by new forms of capitalist logic, conforming neither to those of industrial capitalism nor to those of so-called postmodern information capitalism. This is the rationale for the term "biocapital," which asks the question of how "life" gets redefined through the contradictory processes of commodification. In other words, in this chapter, I attempt to get at the relationship between the material objects of public goods and commons and the abstract objects of market commodification, in an overall economic structure that might be called material-speculative.

## The SNP Consortium

There is a tendency to conflate genomics with its best-known institutional manifestation, the Human Genome Project (HGP). The HGP, however, is very much just a fragment, albeit a central one, of genomics. First, a primarily state-sponsored venture, the HGP occupies a particular political space vis-à-vis genomics writ large, as an endeavor that has used and continues to use public money to generate gene sequence information. Second, the sequencing of the human genome, a project that just a few years ago seemed so dauntingly far away as to be an end in itself, is today very much conceived of as just the end of the beginning, at a moment when a working draft sequence of the human genome is already complete.

I start by mapping some of the major actors involved in the efforts to sequence the human genome. To start with, there is the National Institutes of Health (NIH), an umbrella term for a state institution that comprises various generally academic research institutes; there are upstream companies, which may be genome companies that sell information (either by simply sequencing, or after annotating, the information), or tool companies; and there are downstream companies, of which pharmaceuticals (and invariably big multinational pharmaceuticals) are the most downstream. Tied into the differentiation of upstream and downstream companies is the upstream-downstream relationship of information itself to its "ultimate" product, the therapeutic molecule (which of course need never actually be realized, but, as I argue in chapter 3, whose existence as a future goal is vital to the operation of the dynamics of the present).

As briefly described in the introduction, Craig Venter threw the genomics community into turmoil in May 1998 by announcing that his private-sector company, Celera Genomics, would sequence the human genome long before the deadline of 2005 set by the publicly funded HGP. By 1999, the HGP was clearly haunted by the specter of Venter. Much as the HGP researchers insisted that the media overplayed the Venter story, he was often talked about in thinly veiled taunts ("combative entrepreneur" and "worm genome detractor" being among the more colorful ones).[9]

"Craig Venter," says *Time* magazine in an issue devoted to "the future of medicine" (January 11, 1999), "is a man in a hurry, and now all the genome mappers are operating on Venter time. . . . Driven, impatient, demanding, irritating, Craig Venter has a knack for making the rest of the world run at Venter speed." This description encapsulates the multiple embodiments of hastened temporality in the contemporary world of biotech, where fast technologies are mirrored by fast CEOs.[10]

Venter's history is controversial. He was at the NIH in the early years of the HGP and was involved in an NIH attempt to patent DNA fragments from brain tissue in 1991 (Cook-Deegan 1994, 311–25). This generated considerable controversy within and outside the NIH. Not surprising, then, that much of the ire of the HGP scientists toward Venter was (at least on the face of it) not just born of a fear of being upstaged but came from the knowledge that Venter would patent the DNA sequences that he generated. If the genomics enterprise has been a race, then it has been one not just for credit but for ownership as well.

It must be emphasized that it was not just Venter but the NIH itself that quite staunchly defended Venter's 1992 patent applications, which were backed strongly by NIH director Bernadine Healy.[11] Major opposition to Venter's patent application came from James Watson, who was heading the HGP at the time and was therefore director of the National Human Genome Research

Institute (NHGRI).[12] Thus this particular polarization into "public" and "private" was a particular contingent outcome of a set of situated politics, perspectives, and priorities, and by no means a "natural" falling out of public versus private roles.

The genomics race between public and private actors continues to be constantly redefined. Now that the working draft sequence of the human genome has been completed, the competition between the NIH and the private sector has shifted to other types of information, such as annotated sequence information or information about genetic variability. This competition, after all, has not just been about finishing first and getting the credit for it — who generates information first has always had huge implications for whether that information goes automatically into the public domain or becomes the property of particular companies. As I try to show later in the chapter, however, this opposition between public and private sectors is more complicated than it might seem simply from looking at the race to generate the working draft sequence.

A consensus among especially younger public scientists in 1999 (at the height of the race) seemed to be that the winner, regardless of who sequenced the genome first, was always going to be Venter.[13] It was felt that he was in a win-win situation simply because he always had the NIH project's sequences to draw on as soon as they were done (since they were immediately released into the public domain), while he did not need to divulge his sequence to the HGP. So effectively the millions of dollars of taxpayers' money going into the HGP have all gone into Venter's project as well, without his having to lift a finger; and there is nothing anyone could have done to stop it.[14]

A story about the interactions between "public" and "private" genome worlds complicates the stark opposition that I have just set up between the two. *Signals* magazine, an online magazine that analyzes biotechnology for executives, has this to say:

> Coming soon: A global genomic map of single-nucleotide polymorphisms (SNPs), the tiny differences between two people's DNA that largely determine everything from who's the natural athlete to who's the klutz to who's likely to get lung cancer from smoking and who's not. In the not-so-distant future, scientists will also be able to tell who's at risk for cardiovascular disease, whatever their lifestyle, as well

as who will respond, or not, to this drug or that. But the techniques now used for discovering or mapping SNPs are costly, tedious and Ph.D.-intensive. The real mark of a SNP-detection assay scale-up will be its downward mobility: For characterizing huge numbers of SNPs among large populations, cheap, fast and easy is the way to go.[15]

The working draft sequence of the human genome does not itself yield any information about genetic *variability* between individuals and populations, which has become an area of increased interest for scientists and the biotechnology industry. The ultimate aim of studying human genetic variation is claimed to be the generation of personalized medicine, which is therapy tailored to individual genetic profiles. Determining human genetic variation is a much more daunting task than sequencing the human genome, both because the sample of humans required to be sequenced is much larger and because a meaningful correlation of genetic sequence and individual or population disease trait would involve identifying the person from whom the sample came, which raises ethical concerns. As the HGP has progressed, however, scientists have paid an increasing amount of attention to informational and technological tools that may help study human genetic variation, and conflicts and alliances have begun to arise around these tools.

The major informational artifacts of this emergent battlefield are called single nucleotide polymorphisms, or SNPs (pronounced "snips"). As described in my introduction, SNPs are single base variations in the genetic code that aid in the discovery of genes variably linked to different traits. SNPs are potentially very valuable markers for diagnostic and therapeutic development, and therefore of great interest to pharmaceutical companies.

In autumn of 1998, the NIH allocated $30 million to the National Human Genome Research Institute to identify SNPs. This was a more than slightly breathless undertaking (or as Francis Collins, head of the NHGRI, put it, an undertaking of "some urgency"). The basic strategy that was decided in December 1997 involved the collection of at least 100,000 SNPs from DNA donated by 100 to 500 people in four major population categories: African, Asian, European, and Native American (Marshall 1997a). Collins first started promoting the project in September 1997, in response to the danger that SNP information would get patented and "locked up" by genomics companies

(Marshall 1997b). In November 1997, Collins coauthored a Policy Forum piece in *Science* with Mark Guyer and Aravinda Chakravarti that argued that SNP data would get locked away in "private collections" if it did not get public support (Collins et al. 1997). Chakravarti has also argued for publicly supported coordinated data gathering, not just for reasons of unfettered access, but for reasons of *ordered* access, saying that "we will lose information if we don't combine it all in one place" (Marshall 1997a). In other words, researchers like Collins have been well aware since before the Venter challenge that the private ownership of DNA sequence information slows down information flow. What is interesting in the SNP story is the strategy that the public researchers devised to get around this, and the speed with which the strategy was employed. This is a strategy that potentially sacrificed some of the scientific quality of the data in the interest of enabling quicker access, an accusation that had ironically been leveled by the publicly funded scientists themselves against Craig Venter's sequencing modus operandi.

In April 1999, the NIH strategy grew into a $45 million consortium funded by the British nonprofit Wellcome Trust and ten major multinational pharmaceutical companies. The objective of the consortium was to generate a full-length SNP map within two years and to place the results into a free public database. The members of the consortium read like a who's who of the pharmaceutical industry combined with the major players of the HGP.[16] The objective was to fill the public databases with enough SNP data to get around anybody's patent. According to SNP Consortium chairman Arthur Holden, "Everybody will be able to do this sort of work without being held hostage to commercial databases."[17]

While the SNP Consortium database was not set up as a commercial database (in that it was not established as a commodity in itself), its setting up was without a doubt a commercial enterprise. In the rhetoric of contemporary capitalism, this is framed not as altruism but as "win-win." Indeed, the setting up of the consortium, which was largely encouraged by the pharmaceutical giant Merck, itself had its genesis in corporate battles. Merck hoped this move would challenge the hold that its rival SmithKline Beecham had on expressed sequence tag (EST) information as a consequence of its exclusive agreement with Human Genome Sciences (see Davies 2001, 100).[18] The move for a SNP

Consortium ensured that, by immediate release of information into the public domain, the major pharmaceutical companies would not have to go through tedious or expensive licensing procedures with smaller genomics companies. It also gave an aura of legitimacy to the big pharmaceutical firms, since it could profitably be projected that consortium members had forgone patent rights on SNP information to facilitate cheap, fast, and easy public access to it. This is a wonderful example of, to use Edward Grefe and Martin Linsky's term, new corporate activism (Grefe and Linsky 1995).

In *The New Corporate Activism*, Grefe and Linsky provide a blueprint and strategies for political action on the part of corporations actively influencing the outcome of issues affecting their organizations. At one level, this is just a corporate public relations manual. However, Grefe and Linsky's call for combining democratic values, human psychology, grassroots organizing, and modern technology into a winning corporate strategy draws explicitly on Saul Alinsky's (1989 [1971]) templates for grassroots activism in the late 1960s and early 1970s and translates easily into a call for hegemonic corporate praxis. Even the key metaphors used—"setting a strategic approach," "framing the message," "mobilizing the troops," "dealing with crisis," and "targeting communications for maximum impact"—are clearly metaphors of the battlefield and come straight from Alinsky.

The dynamics of exchange of the various objects and forms of currency in any capitalist system are not just a consequence of their traversing certain networks. Throughout this book, I argue for the situated ways in which networks of exchange and circulation resolve. These resolutions are not just consequent to the particular locations of actors and institutions within predesignated systems or networks but are also a consequence of the strategic actions of the involved actors.

What is important from the strategic perspective of a "new corporate activism," however, is that such strategic actions not seem *merely* strategic, or mere cynical manipulations. To act strategically, as Grefe and Linsky suggest, involves making the fact, and the act, of strategic action *in*explicit.[19] My account of the SNP Consortium is, then, the tracing of a strategic political act by pharmaceutical companies that provides these companies with both material and symbolic capital *while always already appearing to be disingenuous commitments to the public domain and to the progress of science.*

But even such a strategic masking of strategic action cannot simply be read as an act of cynicism. There is a contradiction inherent in a "new corporate activism" gifting, which is the importance of the *sincere* gift. Dale Carnegie, in his influential manual for businesspeople *How to Win Friends and Influence People* (Carnegie 1998 [1936]), argues that the interest that must be shown in others in order to succeed in business has to be a "genuine" interest (like financial interest, genuine interest creates future value). This leads to the paradox of magnanimity being necessarily interested, as in goal directed, the means toward the garnering of symbolic capital, on the one hand, while on the other hand, it cannot be reduced to a cynical appearance of magnanimity simply to garner symbolic capital. That is why reading arrangements like the SNP Consortium, which are strategic calculations through and through, as merely cynical does not appreciate the genuine sincerity that needs to underlie such arrangements in order for them to function in a way that can in fact garner the desired symbolic capital. The instrumentalism of gifting in market regimes, which itself is a specific form and situation of gifting, cannot be collapsed to utilitarianism.

The SNP Consortium was not the only corporate collaboration formed to hunt SNPs, and it was by no means the first. In 1997, Abbott Laboratories seeded the French genomics company Genset to the tune of $42.5 million in order to construct a SNP map.[20] This is considered to be the first "strategic alliance" (as Genset called it) of its sort in genomics.[21] Like many other alliances between biotech and pharmaceutical companies, and unlike the SNP Consortium, this was an *exclusive* alliance. The division of labor in this alliance was also quite typical of such alliances. While Genset's job was to develop a proprietary map of the human genome with relevant markers and genes associated with responses to particular pharmaceutical compounds, Abbott's was to "develop, produce and market diagnostic systems derived from these genes and markers to clinically test patient response to specific drugs."[22] The SNP Consortium replaces the direct contractual agreement of the Genset-Abbott type with something more "communal" in nature, and at first sight counterintuitive to "market logic." What is evident, however, is that the SNP Consortium is less an attempt to negate market logic than it is to redefine the terrain in such a way that "market logic" is dictated by the strategic interests of the consortium members.

A major figure in the SNP Consortium was Alan Williamson, former vice president of research strategy at Merck, who called the initial meeting in April 1999 to propose the consortium. According to him, "Some companies have a very positive attitude towards the idea of supporting a public database."[23] Statements like this *imply*, in the rhetoric of new corporate activism, that some companies are inherently open to sharing information, while others are spoilers who want to own it all themselves. What they hide is the locations of specific corporations within a larger strategic market terrain where billions of dollars are at stake. And this is where the upstream-downstream distinction comes to the fore again. Even major genomics companies that might fancy themselves as one day becoming pharmaceutical companies do not have the history of pharmaceutical research and development and regulatory infrastructure that the big multinational pharmaceuticals have, and drugs are neither their primary nor an assured product. For SNP Consortium members, however, any possible profit they might make on a SNP patent is small compared to the profit they can make on a drug, and it is in their interests to remove the necessity of sharing that profit with a genomics licensee. As Williamson says, "I don't think a SNP patent per se is going to be worth much. It's the clinical significance that really counts. Each SNP has to be evaluated epidemiologically or pharmacologically."[24]

Therefore, while the SNP Consortium purportedly opposes the ownership of DNA sequence information, it supports owning biologicals per se. Arrangements like this increase the monopoly of the big pharmaceutical partners in the consortium on any therapy that might accrue, at a lower cost to the companies involved. It is not ownership itself but the *modes* and *categories* of ownership that constitute the terrain for hegemonic struggle in genomics. In other words, what is at stake is the rendering of the "raw material" of production "public" — that is, not "owned" — in order to give later ownership advantage to those who control the modes of production.

These disputes highlight issues of corporate agency. While unobstructed access and speedy progress of research remain the stated goals of all parties concerned, clearly for each party research progresses "speedily" only when *they* have unobstructed access, combined with the right, whenever they feel appropriate, to slow down and charge everyone else. The inherent logic of *ownership*, after all, is that the owner can decide what to do with the object (that has, by virtue of its objectification, become alienable) owned. This could include using it as an obligatory point of passage toward what are strategically deemed to be more valuable ends (such as, in this case, by pharmaceutical companies, therapeutic molecules).[25]

The NIH did not want information to be owned because it has a commitment, as an institution of the state generating information with public money, to release the information into the public domain. In other words, for the state as represented by the NIH, information has the status not of commodity but of public good. Of course, in this case "the state" is represented by the NIH and, in the case of DNA sequence patents, defends genomic information as part of a commons for the public good. But it also is the state, in other guises, that constructs the boundaries between public and private goods in ways that, especially in the United States, favor the appropriation of the commons by private companies through intellectual property protection.

The downstream companies do not want information to be owned because their locus of surplus value generation is in selling the drug, and the less they have to dish out to upstream companies on the way, the better for them. However, by framing this self-interest in terms of a "relinquishing" of patent rights on DNA sequences in order to enter into a "partnership" with the HGP to allow "free and rapid" flow of information, pharmaceutical company rhetoric suggests that information is part of a *gift*, rather than a *commodity*, regime.

The idea that information is a gift on the part of big pharmaceutical companies is well in keeping with the tenets of new corporate activism. As Marcel Mauss (1990 [1954]) has shown, the gift has attached to it cultural obligations both to receive and to reciprocate.[26] The field of gifting, reception, and reciprocation is much less clearly delineated in genomics than in the "archaic societies" of Mauss and encompasses that extremely diffuse, undefined, and constantly recruited arena of the "public domain." As Jacques Godbout and Alain Caille have argued, there is a modality of gifting that is internal to capital, with the market absolutely dependent on the existence of a form of gift exchange (Godbout and Caille 1998).[27] To quote: "The mercantile relationship must first be authorized by a gift relationship. In areas where the market has not yet established its 'automatic' rules or where relationships count, we still offer presents. . . . The gift acts to authorize what follows it: a founding act, it establishes the level of confidence required for the mercantile exchange that ensues" (150). This is a gifting that still relies on a calculus of ratios, and on comparability, rather than analogies and substitutability.[28]

There is thus a tension between a linear race toward commodification and the changing status of information from commodity to gift. In other words, the linear race toward commodification has speed bumps inherent to it, speed bumps that push actors to take recourse to mechanisms outside the sphere of commodification, mechanisms that in turn facilitate the "linear" (now purposefully in quotes) race toward commodification. This instability is a consequence of the particular structures of biocapitalist knowledge production, especially its upstream-downstream terrain, which is particularly well demarcated in the U.S. context. Here academic research is at least discursively (and sometimes in actual fact) designated as contributing to the "public domain."[29] But also, public research is naturalized as being the *enabler* of private research, albeit a silent one. In other words, the mantra that innovation comes from the private sector hides one of the fundamental conditions of possibility that makes private innovation possible, which is the role that public institutions play to enable private research.[30]

Information potentially has, in addition to Marxian use value and exchange value, a third form of value, a "moral" value that operates in the realm of symbolic capital. This comes from two sources. For one, as a primary good or gift that the state distributes or as a could-have-been commodity that the (downstream) company relinquishes as gift, information acquires a decommodified status through a mechanism of rhetorical abdication that suggests that its *natural* state is as commodity, and the *decommodification* is an act of virtue — whether by the state or by the (downstream) company, which is portrayed as a willing partner to the state in maintaining the unfettered flow of information, and therefore of science.[31] There is, however, another, more direct manner in which genomic information becomes virtuous, and that is its extensive linkage, rhetorical and real, to *therapy* — a linkage that is made real by the rhetoric. This too is a part of the background culture in which notions of "public" and "private" are being formed. There was a wonderful moment, for instance, at the end of a 1999 industrial genome conference, when Randy

Scott, chairman and chief scientific officer of Incyte Genomics, raised a toast to "the genomic community. Because they aren't in genomics for themselves, they are in it for Life." Mirroring, indeed, Incyte's own corporate slogan, "Genomics for Life."

It is evident that the production of biocapitalist value is to a large extent a discursive act, whether it is through advertising, the selling of futures, the rhetorical creation of a corporate scientific community committed to Health, or many competing companies relinquishing property rights for the common good. Indeed, the creation of this single community has as its internal logic the existence of multiple competing actors, all of whom try to propagate their particular informational value at the expense of their competitors.

It is evident, also, that information has to perform active work, variously material and discursive, in the process of which the corporate drug development community is created as an *ethical* entity, an entity represented (and encompassed) by Incyte's "Genomics for Life." It is not just the subject within the genomics profession who gets informed at this moment; equally in-formed are the subject (as in discipline, endeavor, or venture) *of* genomics and the corporate subject such as Incyte, as ethical subjects that are in the business of saving lives.

This section, then, is about flows, of information and of capital, the former flowing "downstream" from raw DNA sequence information through annotated and more "meaningful" forms of information into the therapeutic molecule that might eventually be produced based on such information. The flows are constrained and enabled by legal regimes and technological advances, but, intuitively at least, by that most nebulous and overarching of entities, "market logic." Market logic plays a friction-producing role in the analysis of capitalism similar to the role that scientific method plays in the analysis of science. These are terms that are at once the ultimate signifiers of the boundaries of actions that the market and science respectively can allow in order to be the market and science, and yet precisely because of that, they assume an almost transcendental position, impervious to analysis themselves. I have not analyzed market logic as a single entity but have tried, through an actor-centered analysis of information and scientific-corporate actors, to tease out elements of what gets called "market logic" as it is played out. In the process, I have tried to argue that the speed with which genomic information is generated, while indeed consequent to technological development, is equally an intuitive outcome of market logic, whereby the speedy progress of science is commercially beneficial. That it is therapeutically beneficial lends speed further legitimacy.

The crucial point is that both the perpetuation of ownership and its obstruction can be argued as being "sound market logic": in the former case, ownership is the reward that functions as incentive to innovation, whereas in the latter the regulation of ownership (or its strategic elimination, as in the case of the SNP Consortium) allows maximally efficient and rapid circulation (which itself can be an incentive). Clearly, therefore, the contestation here is over the very definition of what constitutes market logic, the outcome of which has considerable implications for the overall terrain of cooperation, conflict, and value generation.

Furthermore, market logic goes much beyond a quantitative generation of maximal surplus value — it needs to generate other forms of symbolic capital, which in the case of biotechnology already exists in the rhetorical and real construction of the industry as being in the business of Food, Health, and Hope (to borrow this time from Monsanto's company slogan). Meanwhile there is the NIH, an organ of the state, that has its own interests and constraints as a consequence of being an institution funded by the public, and therefore needs to have a commitment to the public domain — a commitment that again gets justified through "market logic" at a contemporary historical moment when market logic is perceived to greatly exceed the bounds of the market. Such a formulation of market logic as exceeding its boundaries, however, implies that it simply takes over the new terrain it encroaches on (such as that of the state or the university) while itself remaining immutable. Market logic, however, often (indeed necessarily) draws on strategies external to the process of commodity exchange, the gift regime being a major one. The SNP Consortium, for instance, manages simultaneously to espouse "sound market logic" (by allowing "cheap, fast, and easy" circulation of information, leading ostensibly to cheaper, faster, and easier drug production) and to gain symbolic capital by giving up property rights on information, an act that can be projected as a self-sacrificial *abdication* of market logic in the public cause. In the process, by the simultaneous holding up and negation of "market logic," market logic as a terrain of hegemonic contestation is redefined. While the strategies of the various actors redefine the terrain of contestation, they simultaneously redefine their own value as actors, as well as the value of the information they produce.

As Slavoj Žižek says: "The 'normal' state of capitalism is the permanent revolutionizing of its own conditions of existence: from the very beginning capitalism 'putrefies,' it is branded by a crippling contradiction, discord, by an immanent want of balance: this is exactly why it changes, develops incessantly—incessant development is the only way for it to resolve again and again, come to terms with, its own fundamental, constitutive imbalance, 'contradiction'" (Žižek 1994, 330).

I take Žižek's call seriously here. I map contradiction not to show the impending dissolution of capitalism but to map a terrain that highlights, in fact, its flexibility and adaptability, and also to show the amount of work required in sustaining it. My analysis tries to provide an insight into capitalism's adaptive mechanisms, adaptations, however, that question the fundamental mechanisms of capitalism themselves while at the same time upholding them. Capitalism's incessant development is brought about not because of the superiority of its indices (efficient production, competition, market logic, or surplus value generation) but because of its willingness to constantly abandon, redefine, or mutate many of them in contested, unpredictable ways.

In this section of the chapter, I have shown how contradictions inherent to the frictioned circulation of genomic material and information lead to fluid and constantly contested boundaries between what constitutes the public domain and what private property. This is a fluidity essential for the sustenance (albeit a constantly frictioned sustenance) of the exchange regimes and processes in question.[32]

The SNP Consortium perhaps asks us whether we need a new language of public and private to describe such arrangements that seem to transcend such binary formulations. Rather than search for a new vocabulary, I would like instead to take seriously the difficulty of in fact ever having a pure "public" or "private" realm, and ask why it is that making apparent the breakdown of such a powerful modern binary constantly occasions surprise.

**Rep-X**

One of the landmark cases concerning the patentability of human biological material is *Moore v. the Regents of the University of California* (1990; henceforth cited as *Moore*). John Moore, a patient afflicted with hairy-celled leukemia, had his spleen cells excised. The researchers belonging to the University of California were able to convert these cells into a unique cell line (which they named *Mo*, after Moore) and were able to patent the cell line. When Moore found out that derivatives of his spleen cells had been made without his knowledge and consent and had been patented, he demanded a share in the property rights. The case was finally decided in the California Supreme Court, which, while upholding Moore's claim that the UC researchers had shown a breach of fiduciary duty and had not obtained proper informed consent, denied him any property rights in the cell line, which the court claimed was the researchers' "invention."[33]

As already mentioned, the working draft sequence of the human genome does not document genetic variability between individuals and populations. For that, one needs DNA from different individual, patient, or population groups. The development of, for instance, personalized medicine, which many people claim is the ultimate aim of genomics, is vitally dependent on getting large collections of DNA samples (usually obtained as blood samples, occasionally as tissue samples, depending on the disease being focused on). Human biological material is obtained for such purposes from different, often clearly identified, patient or population groups that are strategically selected and then genotyped (i.e., their genetic sequence is elucidated). Through such large-scale analysis, especially when situated across multiple populations or patient groups, it is possible to obtain information about the genetic variability that centrally underlies specific traits or diseases of interest.

The human biological material—*not* information—is usually obtained from hospitals with which researchers draw up specific agreements, though other sources are also occasionally tapped. For instance, the Iceland-based genome company DeCode Genetics obtains material from the general population. That material is stored in a tissue repository of some sort. These repositories could be located within the company that is planning to perform subsequent research (as in the case of DeCode), or in a public-domain tissue collection, or, with increasing frequency, in specific companies who base their entire business models on serving as such repositories. The information that is generated from this material is often converted into databases. These databases are (or so it is hoped by the companies developing them) the precursors of therapy. In an ideal world, the company that generates the database would hold the information and use it in the company's own drug discovery program. In reality, taking drugs to market is so heavily capital intensive that most database companies license their information to big pharmaceutical companies (again, in the case of the Icelandic example, DeCode has licensed its database to the multinational pharmaceutical giant Hoffmann–La Roche). In this way they try to ensure that information pays off.

The key point here, which I will get back to later, is that genotyping alone is not enough to generate meaningful information about the genetic basis of disease: *There is an absolute importance of medical history that can be correlated with the genotype. It is only in the correlation of the two types of information that any sort of therapeutically relevant meaning can be extracted.*[34] Having in addition information about family medical history is even more valuable, but is very rare except in cases like Iceland. Now the dream (at least as articulated as part of the rhetorical justification for sustaining its enterprise) for any company in this business is that they can do all three of the foregoing steps: collect the DNA, generate valuable information, and then develop a drug. In reality, different companies end up concentrating their business models on specific points of this value chain.

The controversy around DNA patenting that I described in the previous section while discussing the SNP Consortium has really only involved the part of the value chain that leads downstream from database to therapy. However, the issues surrounding ownership that most closely resemble the *Moore* controversy have more to do with the part of the chain between repository and database. The field on which intellectual property debates in biotechnology take place is framed by these two sets of debates.

In this section, I focus on ownership issues that arise when one deals with the part of the value chain concerning itself with creating databases from corporate DNA repositories. What sorts of ownership barriers underlie the business models of the companies that concentrate on this part of the value chain? I will specifically talk about one company, a commercial DNA repository based in the northeastern United States, that I will refer to as Repository X (Rep-X).[35]

In its corporate description, Rep-X calls itself "a functional genomics company with a comprehensive, clinical approach to discovery, focused on developing high value, proprietary intellectual property for its own account and in collaboration with major biopharmaceutical companies. Rep-X maintains the [Rep-X proprietary repository],[36] an unparalleled, large-scale resource of clinical research material, including human DNA, serum and snap-frozen tissue samples, linked to detailed medical information collected from patients worldwide. To date, Rep-X has recruited more than 100,000 patients in its effort to build the [Rep-X proprietary repository], and collections continue."[37] In other words, what Rep-X wants to become is the world's largest commercial DNA repository, collecting DNA samples from all over the world, including India, genotyping them and then leveraging them for profit.

Obviously a business model such as this can be deemed by many as ethically somewhat fraught. So clearly bioethics is a key area in which Rep-X takes an interest, which is not unusual for a biotech company these days. Indeed, Rep-X has its own in-house bioethicist, a bioethicist being an emergent form of expert mediator in the ethical debates that surround new biotechnologies.[38] In fact, the CEO of Rep-X says of hiring bioethicists: "I'm surprised more companies don't do it. It doesn't cost us anything, and in the end it may save us [money, time or reputation]. I mean, the whole idea of it is so reasonable. We've always said that if we are going to be on the front page of the *New York Times* we'd better make sure we get it right."[39] In other words, bioethics is an integral component of Rep-X's business model.

Rep-X has not yet made it to the front page of the *Times*, but it has made it to the business page of a leading U.S. newspaper. The article is typically celebratory and paints a picture of dynamism, speed, and incessant progress, none of which is unusual in a character sketch of a young biotech company: "When the FedEx driver rings the bell on the loading dock at [Rep-X], it's a call to action. The driver unloads bundles of special envelopes marked with the biohazard symbol: fresh samples of tissue and blood from patients nationwide. Within minutes, technicians scurry to open individual plastic kits. Glass vials of blood, each identified only by a bar code, are quickly scanned into the computer—like a giant grocery checkout in reverse. Processing the samples is a carefully choreographed blend of tedious hard work and blazingly fast robotic automation."[40] And so it goes on: the combination of speed and genius combining to create value from a novel business model, the rhetoric reflecting the seamless operations of an aggressive young company.[41]

Now the big "ethical" issue that Rep-X confronts is not the fact that it can own samples but the fact that it should collect them properly; as their CEO suggested in the earlier quote, "doing it" is not the question as much as "doing it right" is. In other words, like the judges who constituted the majority opinion in *Moore*, Rep-X is most worried about getting proper informed consent. The company knows that in the United States at least, getting exclusive property rights on the samples does not really constitute the bottleneck. This is reflected in Rep-X's fascinating statement of what it calls "Rigorous Ethical Standards," which states:

> [Rep-X] is committed to maintaining the highest ethical standards possible, and to that end, meets quarterly with a distinguished Bioethics Advisory Board that has been invaluable in developing innovative solutions to the range of ethical problems posed by genetic research. In addition, [Rep-X] has created a proprietary system for anonymizing collections while ensuring data quality and protecting patient confidentiality. Informed consent and patient rights are key to [Rep-X]'s operations, and ensure sample quality while maintaining pristine ethical standards. Working with international leaders in the area of informed consent for genetic research, [Rep-X] has developed consent procedures appropriate to the repository context.[42]

Not only does Rep-X in statements like this portray itself as the embodiment of ethical practice; it also sets up the idea that an institutionalized bioethics provides expertise that can transcend national boundaries and contexts, in the same way that the genetic samples Rep-X collects do. Indeed, Rep-X's statement is quite typical of the disclaimers that are central to many of the companies that occupy the part of the value chain between repository and database, and concerns itself with proper informed consent procedures for sample collection, privacy, and confidentiality. Of course, what is notably missing in this statement is anything to do with ownership rights, which, as in the case of *Moore*, are deemed nonnegotiable. This is because it is the company doing the genotyping that is deemed to be doing the "inventive" work; where samples come from merely constitutes source, which, because of present law, gets written out of intellectual property agreements.

Unfortunately for Rep-X and the retinue of "expert" bioethicists who profess transnational and universal problem-solving capabilities, the expertise of institutionalized bioethics, professing as it does primarily American (and sometimes European) codes for ethical governance, does not translate well into other sociopolitical and geographical contexts. The final section of this chapter has to do with the friction that Rep-X's seamless rhetoric encounters in the practical context of collecting genetic samples from India. This is a friction that, of course, is left out of the narrative that institutionalized bioethics, the business press, and Rep-X's own public relations apparatus construct for it.

The question of why bioethics concerns itself so little with questions of ownership is an interesting and important one to address. A major reason is disciplinary and pedagogical: institutionalized bioethics, especially in the United States, draws largely from analytic philosophy, which engages normative questions much more readily than questions that are more explicitly "political." My suspicion, however, is that *Moore* has served as more than just a legal precedent: it has further served as a normative precedent, which suggests somehow that ownership issues are "settled." This is why challenges to intellectual property regimes come much more often from that messy and unpredictable space of the public domain, and through the messy and unpredictable routes of politics, than through institutionalized spaces that, at some level, do exist to channel and regulate this messiness through the "sanity" of expert mediation. In other words, it is not just the *content* of bioethics that I find problematic. It is the bioethicists' mediation in such debates *as experts*, to the exclusion of other participating voices, that makes institutionalized bioethics such an undemocratic institution, even when it manages to be an "ethical" one.

There is a substantive underlying conceptual question at stake here, which is that, first, bioethics therefore ends up representing particular interests and, second, sets itself up as a universal discourse. In other words, I do *not* argue here for a relativist position that somehow reifies an "Indian" bioethical position that should be regarded as distinct from a "Western" one and therefore left untouched or unquestioned. Nor do I argue that the particularities of situations that bioethics is called on to deal with in different contexts necessarily resolve along national lines. (And so my mention of "Indian" versus "Western" bioethics is merely shorthand for the different sorts of ethical-political emergence in the two sets of sites I study in this project.) What I argue is that the posing *as* universal of very particular, situated interests and value systems makes institutionalized bioethics a supremely ideological enterprise, in the sense in which Marx and Engels critiqued ideology as being opposed to materialist understandings of the world in *The German Ideology*.[43] Further, it must be remembered that bioethicists, when deployed in the corporate cause such as in the case of Rep-X, do not act simply as what Donna Haraway calls "value clarifications specialists";[44] they also serve as value *creation* specialists, creating value in all senses of the word. They both lend legitimacy to the corporate and scientific enterprise that they "adjudicate," and structure which questions get asked as ethical.

The question that is left hanging for me, then, is what a genuinely transnational bioethics would look like, since I do believe that biotechnology as a global regime needs transnational, democratically accountable systems of governance and regulation. I think one good way to start would be to reexamine the connotations of the word "ethics." "Ethics," like many of the other terms that I have described or analyzed (such as "genomics" or "capitalism"), is again not a stable referent. The universalizing tendencies of institutionalized bioethics are not just consequent to a *spatial* uncoupling of ethical *adjudication* from the context of the emergence of an ethical dilemma. They are also consequent to the fixing of "the ethical" as somehow an eternally valid adjudication — as, in fact, a statement of a *moral* position.

In this regard, I find Michael Fortun's distinction of the ethical from the moral extremely relevant. Fortun, in writing about the DeCode controversy for Mannvernd, the leading organized Icelandic opposition to the Health Sector Database, says:

> Ethics puzzles me — which is good, since I believe that if you're ever *not* puzzled by ethics, you're in the realm of moralism, and moralism doesn't puzzle me — it disturbs me. Of all the things I could write about ethics here, let me start with just

one: to me, ethics is not about a good or bad answer, or a good or bad action, so much as it is about a certain quality of an encounter. I'm deliberately leaving that rather vague for now. But it suggests some shared space between ethics and ethnography: each involves the careful staging of some sort of encounter.

Or layers of encounters.[45]

Fortun does not seek to abandon the ethical as a notion. But by placing ethics squarely as that which emerges from an encounter, as always already indeterminate rather than simply "right" or "wrong," as that to which one is constantly obligated to *work through*, he moves ethics beyond the realm of simple moral adjudication. He also moves it beyond the binary of universality and relativism. Both transcendental, universal ethical positions and their relativist counterparts that simply celebrate particularity assume that the ethical can be decided purely with reference to some kind of self-contained value system — the only dispute being whether that value system holds across communities or is distinct between different communities. Fortun's understanding of the ethical points instead to the absolute impossibility of ethics in either universal or relative frames of reference unless one recognizes the sorts of incongruent discourses and value systems that come into contact in order to create an "ethical" question demanding resolution in the first place.[46]

Building on this Derridean sensibility, the "transnational" bioethics that I invoke here is not simply an alternative moral framework within which ethical disputes or dilemmas can be resolved. Nor is it a relativist celebration of the multiple possible ethical resolutions of problems arising from new biotechnologies. It is, rather, an acknowledgment of the *impossibility* of an ethical regime that trusts moral adjudication that is based on a situated set of principles and referents (drawn largely from philosophical precepts central to advanced liberal societies) to successfully deal with bioethical dilemmas that take shape "elsewhere." But it is simultaneously also an acknowledgment of the *necessity* of dealing with bioethical dilemmas "elsewhere," in an era of global capitalism where even societies that do not have the same historical development as advanced liberal societies are nonetheless deeply connected to them materially and ideologically. The ethical-political terrain of technoscience is increasingly constituted by its global reach, and elucidating this terrain requires a set of tools that takes the nature of global interactions and encounters into serious account.[47]

My stories in the next section are ones of exchange and value in a situation that sees the interaction of a Western corporate entity (Rep-X) with a non-Western, noncorporate entity (the Indian state). They are stories of ethics, where the ethical is *not* a clash of incommensurable worldviews or value systems but a series of encounters that are structured by, and in turn structure, the global terrain of biocapital. These are stories of population genomics, which is a technoscientific assemblage that requires as its very condition of possibility a multiplicity of genetic samples, and legal regimes that regulate the circulation and ownership of these samples in a manner consistent with certain established principles. These principles include values such as privacy and informed consent that ensure the rights and dignity of the persons who constitute the source of the samples.

But these are also stories where the agent collecting the genetic samples happens to be an American company. The terrain on which the activities of this company play out is not a seamless terrain of articulation, where ethical rules are accepted without friction across national or private-public boundaries. Rather, this terrain is striated — the very grounds on which Rep-X constructs "ethics" are disarticulated in significant ways from the grounds on which the Indian state negotiates "ethics." It is this disarticulation that needs to be taken seriously into account in any attempt to come to terms with "the bioethical."[48]

### The Indian State

India occupies a particularly interesting and ambiguous space in global technoscience writ large, a space that is particularly accentuated in areas relating to biotechnology and drug development. At one level very much a Third World country with some of the lowest human resource indices in the world, India has always privileged science and technology as a springboard into globally competitive playing fields. Presently, India's technoscientific establishment is undergoing a period of profound change, as the institutional socialist model of primarily state-sponsored research and development is giving way to a more market-oriented approach. However, some of the most aggressive market players in Indian biotech are not companies, which are still by and large reticent and risk averse, but Indian public-sector labs.

Genomics is an area that the Indian government has been particularly interested in. India did not get into the Human Genome Project in the early 1990s, a fact that its scientific policy establishment was regretting by the mid-1990s, when it became evident that genomics was where the action — and the fame and money — was at. Therefore the Centre for Biochemical Technology (CBT), which for the previous thirty years had been a dilapidated center that had housed biochemical reagents, was reinvented as India's cutting-edge public genome lab.[49] Typically for these new market-oriented public institutions, CBT is very interested in protecting its intellectual property.

CBT's primary research focus is population genetics, because India's population is one that can be leveraged for genetic information in two ways. First, a number of India's indigenous populations are considered genetically homogeneous and might therefore be suitable groups on which to perform the sorts of studies that DeCode performs in Iceland. Second, even India's "general" population is a strong candidate population for genetic studies, because the prevalence of large families with very little genetic counseling will allow the family genetics of disease to be traced in a way that is difficult to do in the West.[50] CBT is therefore aggressively involved in these studies, with patient samples collected largely from public hospitals with which it enters into collaboration.

Public labs in India such as CBT, therefore, see Rep-X's sample acquisition in a very different light from Rep-X.[51] They maintain that Rep-X's samples are worthless, even if extensively genotyped, without detailed medical records. These medical records are collected along with the samples from Indian hospitals. Therefore, this argument goes, the Indian hospitals should have a share in the intellectual property (IP). (Indeed, some American companies do draw up extensive legal arrangements with the hospitals they obtain samples from.) This argument says that if Rep-X shares IP with Indian hospitals, it can have all the samples it wants. But if it does not, then it is stealing. What complicates this analogy is that many of the best-known research hospitals in India are public institutions, whereas in the United States, most such hospitals are private and function as corporations. Therefore this argument of the Indian state paradoxically frames the state itself as a corporate entity. This is very much in keeping with a post-1990s ideology of economic liberalization that has been prominent in Indian elite and policy circles whose idea of India is as India Inc.[52]

In fact, these demands have been codified in a set of ethical policies relating to the human genome, genetic research, and services put forth by the Department of Biotechnology (DBT) of the Ministry of Science and Technology (DBT 2001).

The DBT guidelines explicitly mention intellectual property rights in an "ethics" document. They also claim that intellectual property rights are in the "national commercial interest" (DBT 2001, 2), a rather odd combination of terms normally associated with clearly demarcated "public" and "private" spheres. The various ways in which benefit sharing is incorporated as ethical guidelines are enunciated in article VIII.5 of the document (DBT 2001, 12, which says: "It will be obligatory for national/international profit making entities to dedicate a percentage [e.g., 1–3 percent] of their annual net profit arising out of the knowledge derived by use of the human genetic material for the benefits of the community"); article IX.1 concerning DNA banking (13: "If any commercial use is made of the samples in the Repository, appropriate written benefit sharing agreements, consistent with the policies stated earlier, must be jointly signed by the donor, sample collector and Repository Director"); and article X.3 concerning international collaborations (15: "In international collaborative research, when genetic material from India forms the primary basis of such research, intellectual property rights should be protected with a majority share of the patent, if any, being held by the collaborating Indian institution/organization. At least 10% of the benefit accruing from such a patent should be used by the individual institutions to develop better services for the population(s) that provided genetic materials. A minimum of 10% of Intellectual Property Rights should be held by Indian institution/organization in any international collaborative research").

With Rep-X unwilling to draw up IP sharing agreements with Indian hospitals, all the samples that they had collected from India since October 1999, under the authority of the Indian Council for Medical Research (ICMR), were prevented from leaving India.

The resistance from the Indian state has been of a particular order that in itself poses vexed questions of the status of "market logic" as employed by an institution that exists to function in the public good. It does not want IP because it thinks that the source of genetic information should be valued. It wants IP because it realizes that generating medical records is part of the inventive procedure. In fact, at first sight, the argument that public *hospitals*, not *patients*, should share in IP might seem rather peculiar. Nor is it the Indian state as represented by the ICMR that wants to share IP, as an institution that can distribute those rights through *all* hospitals, regardless of where samples are obtained, as public good. All that the ICMR stipulated is that the same market principles for licensing and ownership sharing that get applied in arrangements between hospitals and research institutions in the West be reapplied in the Indian context. This is a position that can be deemed problematic both from the point of view of a distributive justice argument and in the way a public institution frames itself as a corporate entity.[53] In the global (South–North) travel of genetic material, the South or Third World gets framed as "source" — and this is of course a framing with a colonial legacy, which even anti-imperialists in countries like India buy into, often legitimately. The Indian argument here is that Rep-X's taking samples from India and patenting them is not colonial expropriation but industrial theft.

There is a larger contradiction, which is embodied in the stance of the Indian state, one that is not merely conceptual but also strategic. As mentioned earlier, on the one hand, the Indian state in this case frames itself as a market entity engaged in "corporate" fights with a Western corporation over intellectual property rights. On the other hand, however, the impetus to do so comes largely from a nationalist indignation about "neocolonial" expropriation, which is not merely the position of activists on what might broadly be called the Left, but very much the motivation for scientists involved in the science policy establishment in India who have some say in charting the state's responses to situations like the one outlined here. This occurs at a moment in Indian history when nationalism as necessarily a secular anti-imperialist gesture has been seriously called into question by Hindu nationalist postures that script a much more aggressive and exclusionary cultural nationalism. The fact that the Bharatiya Janata Party (BJP), the political wing of the Hindu nationalist movement, was the party leading the coalition government in power in India from 1998 to 2004 is not insignificant for science policymakers, since that makes the BJP their political masters. Thus there is always already inherent a tension in the articulation of a nationalist position as an anti-imperialist gesture in a situation such as this.

Perhaps the more acute tension for the purposes of understanding biotechnology as an integral part of the phenomena of globalization, however, is that Indian state actors are only able to take recourse to anti-imperialist postures by coding them as "corporate" fights, and that this posture, while effective to the extent of preventing Rep-X from exporting samples from India, is still partial and fragmentary. While the Indian state, and certain Indian state actors, are keen to negotiate IP sharing agreements with Western companies, there is a reluctance to aggressively push for such models at international forums because it is felt that such a move might jeopardize foreign investment into India, which is eagerly sought after in the current climate of economic liberalization, regardless of the ideological persuasions of the parties in power.[54] In other words, nationalism is completely enmeshed in the phenomenon of globalization, both as a contradictory component and as an outcome as well.[55]

It is, however, the corporate coding of "the nation" that is of particular interest to me here. Brahmachari, for instance, in a presentation to the United Nations Educational, Scientific, and Cultural Organization (UNESCO), claims that natural resources (in this case, the citizens and their biological matter) are the *property* of the nation-state, a framing that both denotes legal and contractual commodification of the resources in question, and the nation-state itself as a quasi-corporate entity (Brahmachari 2001). This situation is further complicated in CBT's case because it is involved, literally, in a market venture of its own.

In addition to reinventing the agenda of a public laboratory, Brahmachari has, along with the Indian pharmaceutical company Nicholas Piramal (NPIL), seeded a genomics start-up called Genomed on its premises.[56] In other words, someone like Brahmachari, when he gets involved in policymaking that regulates the flow of genetic material from India while encouraging the state to frame itself as a global market player, is also a cofounder of a real biotech start-up with its own global strategic interests.

### Conclusion

It is impossible to talk about a concept without it flowing over inescapably. And so there are two things that can happen with the notion of "exchange." On the one hand, it can be hammered, analyzed, dissected, and critiqued —

dare I say "deconstructed"—in ways that can make us think more carefully about words like "commons," "gift," "commodification," "public," "private," "market logic," and "value." But it can also, in a very literal sense, be the subject of deconstruction, because it gets deferred.[57] Getting a handle on exchange means never quite being able to get a handle on it, always having it slip away, but having other things, objects and concepts, present themselves.

This is precisely what has happened with the larger project that this book attempts to describe and capture. What started as a study of American genome companies quickly became one about a system of production and exchange and a market regime—biocapital—that, as capitalist regimes do, refused to be contained within the crucible of the "innovative center" of the United States. Therefore, already, very quickly, I found myself trying to get a handle on capitalism and globalization, in ways that would make them specific, by calling them "biocapitalism."

I have tried in this chapter to emphasize contradictions in market logic within state-corporate formations in particular contexts, such as the United States; but I have also compared these sets of contradictions in different state-corporate formations of North and South, First World and Third World. Therefore I have tried to highlight the radical incongruence of the playing out of globalizing market logic in these two contexts. To reconfigure regimes of exchange and maximize value, one sees, in the United States, corporations taking strategic recourse to a gift economy, and, in India, the state taking strategic recourse to a market economy.

I am also trying to argue that intellectual property debates, whether around the patentability of DNA sequences or in the context of collecting genetic material from so-called Third World peripheries and moving them to the "inventive" centers of the First World, cannot be understood simply in terms of inventiveness. Rather, they have also to be understood in terms of materiality. I am seeking to question the very *notion* of invention as the definitive notion that underlies the playing out of IP agreements on the ground. In this sense, I am reading IP disputes much more in the sense that Rosemary Coombe does as she traces what she calls the "cultural life" of intellectual properties (Coombe 1998).[58]

Coombe sees intellectual property not simply as a set of rights or as (reductive) attributions of inventive genius. Rather, she shows it as a constitutive object in commercial and popular lifeworlds, as a source and sink of social power. Perhaps most in consonance with my own sensibility is her call for what she calls an "ethics of contingency with respect to the use of commodified social texts" (Coombe 1998, 5).

The question then becomes how the fluidity of intellectual property translates into ethical-political complexities, especially in regimes of global information flow, where the information in question has to do with "life itself," and where the information often travels along with tangible material objects such as blood and tissue samples. John Frow, for instance, echoes an argument made by many Third World opponents of global intellectual property regimes such as the General Agreements on Tariffs and Trade (GATT) and the World Trade Organization (WTO) on the grounds that they directly disadvantage these countries (Frow 1996). While I broadly agree with such sentiments, I am also keen to tease out the constantly contradictory ways in which politics on the ground trouble such easy political positions, especially in countries like India that refuse to take their "Third World" status for granted.

Therefore, at one level, genomics in India would to a considerable degree just not be possible without sequence information and other bioinformatics resources that are generated in the West being accessible in the public domain, since private databases are often too expensive to afford for most Indian research centers. However, a number of "disenfranchised" groups, such as patient advocacy groups in the West, and indeed even CBT in India, are involved in leveraging intellectual property arrangements in strategic ways for their own benefit. This might be, in the former case, to ensure that rare genetic disorders that would otherwise never get researched do get research attention;[59] in the latter case, as a mechanism to ensure a certain return in revenue for what gets framed as the "Indian" public good. Indeed, it is hard to take an excessively comfortable position on intellectual property issues in biotech and drug development writ large when major proponents of DNA sequence patents are some genetic disease patient advocacy groups, and major opponents are big multinational pharmaceutical companies.

One of the classic examples invoked to point to the "biopiracy" of Western corporations patenting Third World natural resources is the case of the patenting of neem, traditionally used in India for its medicinal properties for centuries. In 1994 the U.S. Department of Agriculture and the American multinational company W. R. Grace were granted patents for neem-derived products.[60] Paradoxically, it was *not* India's Council for Scientific and Industrial Research (CSIR) that cried foul over this issue of piracy, even though it was CSIR that had to fight the case in global intellectual property courts (a case that CSIR won, thereby enabling the neem patent to be overturned). CSIR, however, points to the attempted piracy of neem not as the case in point of biopiracy and neocolonialism but as the ultimate proof of the fairness of global multilateral trade arrangements such as the WTO that provide mechanisms to overturn attempts at piracy. This is not to argue that I either agree with CSIR's position or disagree with it, but to point out, once again, that "politically correct" positions that are in fact probably better informed by the inequities of global trade systems than CSIR's (which, after all, is operating on politically constrained terrain, much as it is an enthusiast for globalization itself), are almost invariably infinitely more complicated on the ground. The position taken by CSIR in this case is an instance of an organization that might be expected, from its structural positioning, to have a certain "Third World" consciousness resolutely failing to do so. This "failure," further, is not on account of ignorance or coercion, but rather is a conscious strategic decision. Therefore even acknowledging an intellectual property system as being stratified is often not sufficient to enable one to understand its effects, unless one is attentive to its (often unpredictable) political manifestations.

Indeed, CSIR's embrace of globalization as signified by the WTO is not just at odds with its structural position as a governing body of "Third World" public research institutions but is even at odds with pre-1990 political currents in India. I have suggested that the 1990s saw a profound shift in the economic ideology of the Indian state, away from a state socialist agenda and toward aggressive market-oriented policies of liberalization, changes that have very much been central to the direction charted by India's technoscientific establishment as well. Of course, while 1991 did represent a watershed of sorts, being the time when India proclaimed through a series of visible measures its intentions to open its markets, India's global leanings were already in evidence in the 1980s, as both Indira Gandhi and her successor Rajiv Gandhi initiated economic liberalization in more modest but definite ways. And yet Indira Gandhi addressed the World Health Assembly in 1982 with the following words: "The idea of a better-ordered world is one in which medical discoveries will be free of patents and there will be no profiteering from life and death" (cited in Braga 1990, 253). The extent to which CSIR's current views on global trade regimes, which include WTO provisions on biotechnology and drug development, differ from even Indira Gandhi's twenty years ago (let alone Jawaharlal Nehru's fifty years ago), of course, suggests changes in ideological direction. But such differences also suggest various coproductions of law and corporate ethos and prevailing political ideology. These are themselves influenced by structural constraints, such as a huge balance-of-payments crisis in 1991 that provided the immediate impetus for economic liberalization; or the Uruguay Round of GATT and the pressure brought to bear by the West on the Indian government to be a signatory. They are also influenced by the agency of individual actors (such as S. K. Brahmachari or the director general of CSIR, Ramesh Mashelkar, whose role I discuss in chapter 5), who chart seemingly irrevocable courses.

The challenge in understanding biocapital, then, is that it is a global regime that sees exchange between sites, such as the United States and India, that are radically asymmetric in the power they command in the global techno-scientific marketplace. How, then, might it be possible to understand biocapital as it emerges on multiply striated global market terrains, marked by the upstream-downstream terrain of drug development, but also by bilateral and multilateral market and regulatory pressures that impact the United States and India in different ways?

I have shown that the global exchange regimes that both constrain and are constructed by biocapital see an implosion of different sorts of exchange that are normally understood as binary counterparts to one another. For instance, exchange in the public domain conflicts with the exchange of private property, yet in different situations each reinforces the other in unpredictable ways. Similarly, it is hard to sustain binaries between commodity regimes and gift regimes.

One thing that is common both to a market regime that depends on future returns on current investments and valuations and to a gift regime is forms of indebtedness, whether structured as monetary debt or as moral calling. In other words, indebtedness is itself a form of valuation of circulatory systems of exchange, again in both senses of the word "value." It is the biopolitics of indebtedness as constituted by global circuits of biocapital that I explore in the next chapter.

# 2. Life and Debt
*Global and Local Political Ecologies of Biocapital*

The first sign that one is greeted with in 2004 upon disembarking at Hydera-bad airport advertises Genome Valley, which claims to be the "biotech hub of India." It is a six-hundred-square-kilometer area of land in and around Hyderabad city that will, it is hoped, become the hub of academic and corpo-rate innovation in the life sciences. In the last fifteen years, between 1989 and 2004, more than three thousand farmers have allegedly committed suicide in the southern Indian state of Andhra Pradesh, of which Hyderabad is the capital. Three out of four farmers' suicides in the country during this time are estimated to have occurred in this state, which prides itself on being one of the high-tech havens of India. This has included two phases, in 1997–98, and again recently in 2003–4, which have seen a concentrated spate of suicides. The normal reasons attributed to these suicides are drought, crop failure, and mounting debt. However, the most recent spate of suicides has occurred in spite of rising agricultural productivity and normal rainfall in 2003–4, suggest-ing that debt was the overwhelming factor that precipitated the crisis.[1]

The Andhra Pradesh state government during much of this time (1994–2004) was led by N. Chandrababu Naidu. I describe Naidu's vision and gover-nance style and provide greater context about his regime later in the chapter. Suffice it to say at this point that his government stopped paying compensa-tion to families of suicide victims in 1998, on the perverse grounds that com-pensation for suicides would provide an incentive for farmers to kill them-selves. This has made it difficult to ascertain the number of farmers who have in fact killed themselves, since the most reliable way of accounting for such deaths is through an accounting of state compensation.

One of the major policy documents of the Naidu regime is "Vision 2020," which articulates Naidu's modernist vision of the state as embedded in a dream of rapid technological progress and material prosperity attained through globalization and an aggressive embrace of the free market.[2] In the agricultural sector, Vision 2020's focus is on pesticides and agro-chemicals. Mechanization, modernization, genetic modification, and a reduction of the number of people on the land from 70 percent to 40 percent of the population are central tenets of this policy document. A large part of the investment for these modernizing changes is envisaged by Vision 2020 to come from the private sector.

### Grounds, Arguments, and Sites

In this chapter I explore, through the lens of emergent biotechnology initiatives in India, the local political ecologies of indebtedness that are constituted by, and constitutive of, globalization. "Biocapital" in this chapter operates explicitly in two distinct yet simultaneous analytic frames: on the one hand, as the circuits of land, labor, and value (in a classic Marxian sense) that are inhabited by biotechnological innovation and drug development; on the other hand, as the increasingly constitutive fact of biopolitics in processes of global capitalism. In other words, on the one hand, what forms of alienation, expropriation, and divestiture are necessary for a "culture of biotechnology innovation" to take root? On the other hand, how are individual and collective subjectivities and citizenships both shaped and conscripted by these technologies that concern "life itself"?

As I outlined in the introduction, I use "biocapital" as a concept to mean multiple things in relation to "capitalism," itself a shifting concept with multiple meanings. Specifically, I have argued that biocapital simultaneously manifests as a specific *case study* of systems of capitalism — one situated lens through which we can view the emergence of capitalist logics and systems writ large — and as a *particular form* of capitalism made specific because of emergent technologies and epistemologies of the life sciences. My analysis of biocapital swings between these two relationships to capitalism. Thus at least part of the specificity of my stories in chapter 1 had to do with the emergent possibilities of analyzing the "fundaments" of life as information that could be commodified and could operate as currency. In this chapter, on the other hand, I analyze biocapital in terms of how biotech enterprises shed light on emergent (and in some ways continuing) manifestations of capitalism, globalization, and biopolitics.

Biopolitics, to recapitulate, is a notion propounded by Michel Foucault, whereby life becomes the explicit center of political calculation. Foucault's analysis of the biopolitical was largely situated in the empirical context of the historical transition in Europe from absolute monarchy to the modern state, where *accounting for* and *taking care of* the population becomes central to the rationality of government. This emergent rationality, Foucault shows throughout his work, takes place along with the emergence of *institutions* and *techniques* such as the prison, the census, the clinic, and the asylum, and of *disciplines* that produce the knowledge that underlies these calculations, such as biology, demography, psychology, and political economy.

In other words, Foucault argues that emergent governmental rationality is intimately connected to emergent institutions and techniques of governance, and to emergent forms of knowledge production.[3] Also, this is a governmental rationality whose *territorial unit* is the *nation-state*.

It is not surprising, then, that an emergent moment in world history which is marked by globalization should present to us questions of the rationality of global governance. And as we start thinking about governance in more global terms, it is not surprising that biopolitical regulation — the regulation, calculation, accounting for bodies, decisions about who lives and who dies — becomes central to the calculus of this new governmental rationality.

The larger theoretical challenge here becomes one of mapping the articulations of technoscience, capital flows, and global governance, and of asking how these articulations enable us to understand emergent forms of knowledge production and technological innovation, emergent forms of capitalism, and the relationship between various levels — global, regional, national, and subnational — of governance.

Foucault's primary concern with biopolitics had to do with an analysis of the state as an agent of political calculation as very much at stake, and this concern was in consonance with the increased role of the state as a defining authoritative institution of modernity. We are in the midst of a historical shift toward increasingly corporate regimes of governance. This is not a shift that automatically implies a reduced role for the state — indeed, in this chapter, I show very much the opposite — but one that does pose questions about the change in the state's role.

In other words, by the phrase "corporate regimes of governance," I imply two things. On the one hand, corporations themselves are taking on agential responsibility for dispensing services that, in the liberal ideology of the welfare state, were "state" services.[4] On the other hand, the state itself is seen adopting corporate strategies or forms of governance, which are often particularly explicit in the Indian context. I have narrated one instance of this in my stories of the Indian state positioning itself as a quasi-market player in order to leverage value from "Indian" genetic material in chapter 1.

In this chapter, I situate the circulatory processes and strategies described earlier in the context of the ways in which governance — which is always already a melding of "state" and "corporate" forms and rationalities — manifests on the ground in India. I address these questions through ethnographic fieldwork conducted in the rural outskirts of Hyderabad city and in the urban center of Mumbai. In the process, I argue that First World–Third World asymmetries in globalization, as opposed to those of industrial colonial expansion, play out through the reconfiguration of the relationship of imperial power to colony into one of vendor to client. I also persist, thereby, with my structural concern with circulation, and the circulatory structures, processes, and regimes that are called into account in these global-local systems and strategies of biocapitalist governance.

Central to these issues is a concern with indebtedness as a governing value system, in both senses of the phrase, of capitalism today. I showed in the previous chapter the ways in which supposedly pure market forms are completely enmeshed in certain forms of gifting (even if those are forms of gifting that are always already open to being co-opted by the market and therefore not quite the gift in the Maussian sense). Also there is the existence of the state as an institution that "gifts" to the public good and thereby calls into account certain forms of indebtedness to the nation. Therefore, at one level, indebtedness operates as moral currency.

But there is also indebtedness in more direct monetary forms of market valuation, at multiple levels, and most certainly in American society. There is, for instance, the central importance of individual creditworthiness, with the credit card industry as an obligatory node of contemporary American capitalism. Debts are also constitutive at an institutional level, in ways that are difficult to tease out into monetary and moral connotations of the term. Indebtedness is marked, for instance, in interactions between corporations and their investors, whether they be large, public corporations and Wall Street, or entrepreneurs who are forced to relinquish control over their companies by venture capitalists to whom they are indebted, in both senses of the word, for the capital that enables their company in the first place.

Then there is the symbolic capital that is called into account by the biotechnology and pharmaceutical industries in particular, as I emphasized in the previous chapter, by virtue of their being in the business of "food, health, and hope" — suggesting how consumers should be indebted to these companies for undertaking high-risk, decade-long drug development ventures to produce therapies for otherwise untreatable diseases. This is an indebtedness that rationalizes not just symbolic capital for the industry but also some of the most expensive drug prices in the world.

Indebtedness operates at multiple levels or registers, as one structural facet of a contemporary historical moment marked by particular arrangements of capital flows, as a symptom of a free market system that is always already a value system in all its multiple senses, and, more specifically for an analysis of biocapital, the ways in which indebtedness becomes biopolitical and biosocial.[5] It is not incidental, of course, that the American nation-state is itself the largest debtor nation-state in the world.

Such multiple registers of indebtedness are at play in India as well. The immediate impetus for India's embarking on its rapid program of economic liberalization and globalization in 1991 was a huge balance-of-payments crisis. At the time, India's foreign exchange reserves had fallen to $585 million, which was sufficient for financing just one week of exports. As a consequence, imports had to be curtailed, and there was a high rate of inflation, which led to an increase in domestic prices that further made the export environment unfavorable.[6] Additional structural factors were brought into play because of the first Gulf War, which led to an increase in oil prices and a reduction in remittances from Indian expatriates in the Gulf.[7] Ironically, a major reason for India's indebtedness at the time was a more tentative, but nonetheless very real, push toward liberalization initiated in the late 1980s under Rajiv Gandhi, marked by what Partha Chatterjee calls a "mindless spending spree" (Chatterjee 1997 [1989], 201).

In spite of all these structural factors that evidently pointed to crisis, crisis was itself evident only in its own production by "market logic." Jayati Ghosh, in her analysis of the initiation of liberalization programs, shows that at this time both agricultural and industrial output were normal, and inflation not particularly high (Ghosh 1998). What was key, however, was that India's balance-of-payment crisis was not inspiring confidence on the *speculative* marketplace. Once again, one sees the dissonance between "commodity" and "commercial" capitalism.[8] Just as a successful industry in terms of product manufacturing and revenue generation like the Indian pharmaceutical industry was deemed to be a failure from the perspective of a growth-based model and was made under WTO-imposed constraints to retool its business models, so one sees an entire nation's economic strategy similarly retooled because of a perceptible "failure" in the eyes of a speculative market rationality that does not necessarily seem like such a failure when seen in terms of a manufacturing and production rationality.

In response to the 1991 crisis, the immediate solution adopted by the Indian government was to take out a loan from the International Monetary Fund (IMF), putting India into a further state of indebtedness. Once again, both monetary and moral registers of indebtedness were called into account, because the conditions of the IMF loan necessitated embarking on structural adjustment policies in order to be more "fiscally responsible." The explicit juxtaposition by the World Bank/IMF of the fiscal responsibility or irresponsibility of its (Third World) debtor countries with the "rewards" or "punishments" as the case may be (which imply the extent of further creditworthiness) is strikingly direct and paternalistic. Therefore, simultaneous to invoking a system of monetary payback came, immediately, a call for moral reform — a reform that demanded that India shed an "irresponsibility" that was *not* profligacy but prudence, an *absence* of the profligacy, exuberance, and risk of embracing the free market.

I wish here to explore the Third World Other that is India, not in relativist, or even explicitly comparative, terms to the "center" of much of the techno-scientific innovation in my stories, the United States, but rather *as a constituent* of the American imaginaries that India currently inhabits in incongruent ways. The relationship of India to the United States as I am trying to configure it, therefore, is *not* the relationship of an outside to an inside (a binary or rela-tivist framing from which no project of strictly symmetrical comparison can completely escape) but the story of the outside that is always already within the hegemonic inside — but within it in ways that make the inside uncomfort-able, distend it, but never turn it "inside out."

In this chapter, I continue the sensibility introduced in chapter 1, inspired by what Rosemary Coombe calls an "ethics of contingency" (1998, 5). I simultaneously insist on locating India as a constituent of a hegemonic terrain that is *not* of its own making, while refusing to acknowledge for it a Third World status that is known in advance. In the process, many of the tactical and strategic articulations of the Indian state tend not to be "resistance" to global orders of technoscientific capitalism, even while they might rescript hege-monic imaginaries in ways not imagined.

With this context, this chapter narrates ethnographic fieldwork at two sites that I consider exemplary for studying the relationships between global capital flows and local forms of indebtedness, and for showing the ways in which biocapital "touches down" in different contexts in India.[9] The sites that I choose in this chapter are once again institutional assemblages, each of which is located in a distinct political ecology. I do not use the phrase "political ecology" in the sense that environmental studies scholars do,[10] but rather employ it as shorthand for a "local" that is particular not just because of its spatial circumscription but also because of a political economic environment already conditioned by local and global histories and presents.

The first site is the ICICI Knowledge Park, known simply as "the Park," a biotechnology park started by the Indian financial services company ICICI and the government of the state of Andhra Pradesh, with help from nonresident Indian (NRI) entrepreneurs based in Silicon Valley. The Park is located about forty kilometers outside Hyderabad, which, as mentioned earlier, is the capital of Andhra Pradesh and one of the fastest-growing "technoscience cities" in India. The second site is Wellspring Hospital, a hospital started by the Indian pharmaceutical company Nicholas Piramal India Limited (NPIL) in Parel, in the heart of downtown Mumbai. The hospital houses Genomed, a genome start-up seeded jointly by NPIL and the Centre for Biochemical Technology (CBT), India's flagship public-sector genome lab.

These sites are significant to my stories of biocapital at the level of the institutions they represent and the political ecologies within which they are situated. Both the Park and Genomed/Wellspring are start-ups in a country that has very few start-up entities of the kind seen in the United States, most markedly in Silicon Valley. The attempt to imitate a U.S. "start-up culture" in both these experiments is quite explicit. The Park reflects start-ups at multiple levels—it is itself a start-up venture with considerable investment in capital and expertise put in by the investing parties, and its function is to enable the incubation of biotech start-ups on its premises.

Yet both of these start-ups require significant, and explicit, state involvement. The Park is enabled, as I will show, in large measure by the Andhra Pradesh state government, while CBT, a publicly funded lab of India's Council for Scientific and Industrial Research (CSIR), is an equity holder in Genomed.[11] Hence both are examples of hybrid state-corporate assemblages set up *in order that* India (the nation-state) become a "global player" (in the global marketplace) through corporate entities whose very conditions of possibility are provided, in large measure, by the state. In other words, both are institutional reflections of the active, resource-intensive interest taken by the Indian state in fostering biotechnology innovation, which largely does not exist in India at this point and is configured, from its initiation, as a global market venture.

However, the two sites inhabit completely different political ecologies. Needless to say, India's size implies a huge heterogeneity in what constitutes "the nation-state" on the ground. Mumbai and Hyderabad, in many ways, represent two epochs of India as an industrializing country, with Mumbai exemplifying the phase of industrial growth through manufacturing, and Hyderabad (along with Bangalore) exemplifying a "postindustrial," high-tech capitalism.

Saskia Sassen makes the argument that cities are constituent nodes in the capital flows of contemporary globalization, in ways that simultaneously question the centrality of the nation-state while instantiating its importance (see, for instance, Sassen 2000). Cities trouble the centrality of the nation-state to the extent that their nodal positions in global capital flows are not simply a consequence of their being a component of a nation-state, as was the case in the era of industrial colonial expansion. While cities are very much constituents of nation-states, they are also, in direct and emergent ways, constituent nodes and passage points in flows of transnational capital. Equally importantly, Sassen calls for an attentiveness to locality, not as an oppositional category to "the global" but as a constituent of the global. In other words, *place matters*, and Sassen refuses to completely evacuate the role that particularity plays in shaping the ways in which globalization manifests or "touches down." This is very much in line with my argument in making "comparisons" between the United States and India, in my attempts to trace the radically incongruent manifestations in India of processes whose ideologies purport to be a seamless homogenizing force. But it also shows up starkly in my comparison in this chapter of political ecologies within India, which have consequences for understanding the questions of governance with which I opened this section. It becomes clear, especially in my accounts of the role of the Andhra Pradesh government in fostering the Park and a culture of biotech innovation writ large, that "governmentality" is not just complicated in contemporary capitalism by the melding of state and corporate forms of governance, but the "state" in question, while never ridding itself of the specter of the nation, cannot automatically be assumed as the *nation*-state in its strict modernist understandings.[12]

Both the sites that I write about in this chapter, of course, are also related to questions of governmentality not just in the sense of instruments and strategies of governance but as explicitly *biopolitical instruments and strategies*. The incorporation (quite literally) of cultures of innovation as governing ideologies of state-corporate formations invested in enabling and facilitating global capital flows has consequences for the ways in which the lives of subjects of the state are reconfigured. These reconfigurations have everything to do with historical and emergent relations of production, and with fundamental Marxian concerns such as access to land and the encroachment of rural space by urban expansion (in this case, in the explicit cause of technoscientific development), urban proletarianization and deproletarianization, alienation, divestiture and expropriation, and, as a governing framework, indebtedness.

This chapter does not offer a subjective narrative from the perspective of those displaced by, or recruited into, these start-up attempts at biotech innovation. Rather, it is an attempt to map a structural terrain marked by a transition from one era of industrial capitalism (emblematized by agriculture, and by, in Mumbai's case specifically, textile manufacturing) to another, high-tech capitalism.

## The ICICI Knowledge Park

I start my story of life and debt in rural Andhra Pradesh by talking about Chandrababu Naidu, who was chief minister of the state from 1994 to 2004, and the political party that he heads, the Telugu Desam. This is among the younger, and yet more powerful, of what are known as "regional parties," parties that draw their political affiliation from a particular region (usually a single state) in India. On the one hand, these are parties whose ideologies and identities are intensely shaped by a sense of locality, in opposition to the centralizing tendencies of the Indian state that are most acutely upheld by the Congress party, which has ruled India for forty-four of its fifty-seven years of independence. On the other hand, these parties have become increasingly central to national governance as the erosion of the Congress's pan-national hegemony has seen the emergence of coalition governments at the center, likely to persist as the norm rather than the exception in the coming years of India's parliamentary democracy.

What is interesting for me here is how in many ways a regional party such as the Telugu Desam is increasingly enrolling itself as a *transnational* facilitator of capital flows into India, as the upholder of the "Telugu nation" turns out to be the most aggressive and sophisticated political player in the game of globalization. At one level, of course, it is not such a surprise that a political party that depends on an ideology that is opposed to the centralizing tendency of the state should find natural allies in entrepreneurs who are themselves opposed to such centralization. Political decentralization and market decentralization seem to find common cause in movements such as Naidu's Telugu Desam.[13]

Speed, information, and selling were the key modes of governmentality for Naidu: "An Indian chief minister in today's global economy has to be a salesman. If he rests on his pride nothing will be achieved. He also has to be like a chief executive who makes things happen. Speed is of the essence" (Naidu 2000, 9). And further: "The only course at that point was to go out and market the state. That is what I set out to do. By going to every investors' forum, domestic or foreign, making Power Point presentations on what Andhra Pradesh has to offer" (134). Naidu learned much from management pedagogy, as any good chief executive would. He says: "Politicians must be acquainted with the managerial wisdom of Peter Drucker and Jack Welch" (21). His attempt has been to turn governance into an *expert regime* that is founded, further, on imitating the United States.

This is governmentality, however, not of the *nation*-state but of the *state*-state: the entity that Naidu was seeking to manage was, quite explicitly, Andhra Pradesh, which after all *is* the region that the Telugu Desam in its very inception claimed most directly to represent. Further, Naidu constantly emphasizes the competition *between* states for rapid economic growth and attraction of foreign investment, as if each state were a corporate entity.

But even the notion of Andhra Pradesh as a single state is a problematic one. There is an increasingly strong movement for statehood in the region of Telengana, which comprises the mostly interior parts of Andhra Pradesh. This is a movement that has existed since India's independence, with Andhra Pradesh, as a state, being the legislative conglomeration of three regions, coastal Andhra, Rayalaseema, and Telengana. It is a movement that has gained force recently because of the continued deprivation of Telengana, and also because statehood has been given to three other regions in India that have fought for autonomy for many years. Telengana provides most of the minerals and raw materials that go into sustaining Hyderabad, and the relationship between the center and the periphery of this state has very much been one of relatively straightforward expropriation, with little development being channeled back to Telengana. Indeed, Telengana has been the site of many of the farmer suicides over the last decade.

Naidu, as mentioned earlier, effected a number of reversals of the founding Telugu Desam ideology. While it received its *discursive* identity from the notion of a federally strong Telugu statehood opposed to the Congress party's tendency to concentrate power in Delhi, Telugu Desam received its popularity from the populist measures of its founder and former chief minister N. T.

Rama Rao. Central to Rama Rao's policy was providing cheap rice and huge agricultural subsidies, and imposing prohibition, which had been the demand of many women in urban and rural Andhra Pradesh. Naidu brutally reversed all of these at the altar of fiscal management, structural adjustment, and pragmatism. And yet, central to his art of politics was his ability to project these brutal reversals, first as policies that were not imposed by an antipopulist state, and second as policies that represented the continuation of Rama Rao's legacy while they reversed it.

Vision, then, was fundamental to Naidu's mode of governance: it allowed him to project attractive futures to investors and his electorate alike, to set milestones for himself and his government to achieve, and was precisely the mechanism that allowed a silent reversal of Rama Rao's legacy, because it implied, rhetorically, a legacy in itself, which Naidu artfully took credit for, but always as an inheritor of a mantle, in a state where Rama Rao's populism makes his legacy an extremely useful one for electoral purposes.[14] Naidu posits vision in explicit opposition to planning, which has always been undertaken by the Indian state on Soviet lines, in terms of five-year plans. "For a vision," says Naidu, "a reasonable time-span is 20 years" (Naidu 2000, 12). In other words, in the terms of Antonio Gramsci,[15] vision, for Naidu, is strategic, whereas speed is tactical: vision is the distant promissory horizon to set for oneself, whereas speed is the means by which to narrow that distance as energetically as possible.[16]

There are direct links — of ideology, capital, and locality — between Naidu and the nonresident Indian entrepreneurial community in Silicon Valley. One of the more perverse mimetic borrowings has been that of the ideology of venture capital. Naidu saw that venture capital was the engine that has fueled entrepreneurialism in Silicon Valley. He therefore believed that Andhra Pradesh should have lots of venture capitalism. The state, therefore, has itself decided to provide venture capital, by setting up a fund to which the contributors are the Andhra Pradesh Industrial Development Corporation Ltd., the Small Industries Development Bank of India, and the AP Industrial and Infrastructure Corporation Ltd. (see Naidu 2000, 139). In other words, Naidu set up a system of public investment as "venture capital" funds, a completely oxymoronic conception of venture capital, which by its American definition comes out of huge private investment funds that expect an extremely high return on investment. Naidu's "venture capitalism" is, effectively, a euphemism for government subsidy for high-tech industry.[17] The fostering of an "entrepreneurial culture" in this way ultimately involves the removal of subsidies from one sector, agriculture,[18] and the concomitant provision of subsidies to another, high-tech—but primarily high-tech *services* rather than high-tech *innovation*—where the services themselves are often performed for Western corporations and exported.

Naidu's ideology might be called an "intervention of no intervention," premised as it has been on the ideology of *minimal* state intervention, an ideology that, in order to be upheld, requires *massive* state intervention.[19] One of the critical points to be made regarding such governance is that things like information technology, biotechnology (together referred to in India quite commonly as HIPAA-BT), and tourism, which were all central to Naidu's strategy for attracting foreign investment into Andhra Pradesh, have all tended to be emphasized at the expense of rural development.[20] Let me explore this further by talking about one such state initiative to enable biotech innovation in the Hyderabad area.

This is the ICICI Knowledge Park, which consists of a set of infrastructure facilities developed by the state government in collaboration with the private venture capital and financial services company ICICI. It consists of a set of laboratories that can be leased out to companies who want to set up research facilities. The rationale for this, according to Naidu, is that "a lot of multinationals are interested in doing research in India because of the availability of high quality scientific manpower" (Naidu 2000, 147). This is a rationale, again, that is at complete odds with a rationale of doing *innovative* technoscience and *basic* research by local scientists. In other words, the structure of something like the ICICI Knowledge Park is best suited, from the perspective of the state's own investment in it, not necessarily to encourage basic, cutting-edge science locally but to encourage the setting up of facilities to do research at a fraction of the cost that it would take to do similar research in the West. This is, of course, research that will use state-subsidized infrastructure but will quite possibly translate into scientific and commercial advances that get re-exported back to Western markets, even though the stated rationale for such ventures is that some of the value generated will remain in India.[21]

The Park is conceived as an idyllic research environment. All the labs are extremely open, and a lot of the space has been given to terraces that look out over fields, fountains, and ponds, with a number of ducks thrown in for good measure. Indeed, this is an aesthetic that ICICI is consciously trying to cultivate, as was evident from constant and anxious questions asked to me by the CEO of the Park throughout my visit as to whether everything looked scenic enough. It certainly did.

ICICI's job here is to act as an estate manager and provide the enabling conditions for companies to get together and do work in a workspace where a number of labs are in close proximity to one another, thereby presumably encouraging collaboration. While the job of ensuring smooth execution is ICICI's, the land has been made available by the Andhra Pradesh government (this area is part of a tract of land designated by Naidu's government as "Genome Valley"). The Park has its own substation providing the labs with electricity, and it has created its own tank to hold rainwater, thereby taking care of the two big worries that plague any wet-lab researcher in India. Also, the Park is not meant for companies with manufacturing facilities, as manufacturing would lead to pollution. The state government has declared a twenty-five-kilometer zone around the Park as a no-pollution zone.

The built-up area when I visited in summer 2001 had space for ten labs, and there were plans to erect more buildings in the future. One of the central features of the Park is a customs shed. A major problem that Indian researchers face is the absence of a standardized import policy for research materials, which means that quite often valuable and perishable materials languish in customs sheds without ever reaching their intended recipient. ICICI, however, has ensured that any research materials coming to the companies housed in the Park would be delivered straight to the Park, where the customs officials would come the next day and clear the material. (This, of course, is yet another enabling feature that is "provided" by ICICI but actually enabled by the government.)

Parks like these raise a number of questions, and in India the immediate one is whether such ventures are huge steps toward becoming a "developed country" or a "global player," or whether they are simply white elephants. The answer may well depend on who rents the lab space in the Park. While in the three years of its operation, a number of start-up ventures have leased space in the Park, Indian industry has never been geared to take risks, as it has grown up in a largely protectionist environment. The brief high-tech boom and the desire of NRI entrepreneurs based in Silicon Valley (who see in Naidu a great supporter of their own wishes to transport a "culture of innovation" into India) notwithstanding, India is a long way off from having what might be called a start-up culture, certainly in biotech. ICICI believes that providing the enabling infrastructure for starting up companies will change this, but an adequate material environment alone does little for entrepreneurship unless it articulates in creative ways with both long-term capital sources and a certain sort of ideology of risk taking that is necessary for an entrepreneurial culture to take root.[22] Another problem that industry has to tackle is the question of how to leverage academe as an incubator. It is particularly ironic that a "start-up space" is being envisaged forty kilometers outside Hyderabad, when the city itself has some of the top academic life science research institutions in the country, such as the Centre for Cell and Molecular Biology (CCMB).[23]

The biggest question, however, comes back to the role of the state government. The tragedy of water reservoirs being created and used for high-tech "global" research in what is not a water-rich region, and the gifting of land by the government for the Park in a state that has seen a spate of farmers' suicides over the past decade as a consequence of unbearable debt, are structural manifestations of global capitalism that have to be taken especially seriously in Andhra Pradesh, a state with revolutionary peasant movements completely inscribed in its history and present.

The land in itself is easily made available by the state government because 10 percent of the land around Hyderabad belonged to its precolonial ruler, the Nizam, and is known as *sarf-e-khas* (literally implying crown land, or land of the king). The government still has control over these lands to dispose of as it pleases. Real estate has boomed in Hyderabad over the last decade, in large measure because the government has encouraged the growth of high-tech so assiduously. Thus the land in areas like Shamirpet, where the Park is housed, has become extremely valuable, but this area itself was not significantly agricultural land. Therefore the government has not had to appropriate land for ventures like the Park. To this extent, the Park does not represent a dispossession of agricultural land for high-tech development. What it does represent is an index of the priorities of the Naidu government, especially a vision of development that has involved leapfrogging the agrarian sector.[24]

What makes it so easy to conceive of such land as somehow "ideal" for setting up high-tech enterprises is a conception of these areas as simply the extension of Hyderabad city. The Park is itself located close to Turkapalli village, which is officially a part of Rangareddy district. It is, however, roughly halfway between Hyderabad and Medak, the district headquarters of Medak district. A few figures from the 1991 Andhra Pradesh census indicate what a stark difference exists between urban Hyderabad and the surrounding rural districts that are being made into an extension of urban Hyderabad.

Hyderabad has a literacy rate of 71 percent, compared to 49 percent for Rangareddy district and 32 percent for Medak district. In a 217-square-kilometer area, Hyderabad has 177 hospitals and 1,062 high schools. In a nearly 7,500-square-kilometer area, Rangareddy district has only 45 hospitals and 1,032 high schools. In a nearly 10,000-square-kilometer area, Medak district has 49 hospitals and 1,363 high schools.[25] Twenty-one percent of the population of Rangareddy district is involved in cultivation and agricultural labor, as is 35 percent of the population of Medak district (compared to 1.4 percent of the population of Hyderabad). In other words, stark differences exist in the levels of development between the city and the countryside, which are presumably to be bridged by some inchoate notion of wealth trickling down.

It could be argued that the networks between Hyderabad and Silicon Valley are in many ways stronger than those between Hyderabad and Medak. Even the relationship between Hyderabad and Silicon Valley emphasizes various histories and trajectories of indebtedness. The very opening up of the Indian economy to global capital flows that has enabled the easy repatriation of capital and expertise from Silicon Valley back to India stemmed, as I have mentioned, from a situation of state indebtedness. The interest taken by the Silicon Valley entrepreneurs, as I will show in greater detail in chapter 5, comes from a feeling of indebtedness toward India, as many of these entrepreneurs received a highly state-subsidized higher education in India before leaving to settle down in the United States. The solution to India's balance-of-payments crisis led to the implementation of IMF/World Bank structural adjustment policies that exacerbated the indebtedness of local farmers, a situation that is part of Andhra Pradesh's political economy to the extent that it is not in any other part of India. The regional political complexities arising from Naidu's government being subjected to the constraints of representative democracy (an indebtedness to the people of the state for being in power in the first place), and of a state that has a history of both peasant revolutionary movements and movements from autonomous statehood for Telengana, further serve to accentuate the particularities within which biotechnology transfer, a supposedly seamless homogenization of India's market culture with that of Silicon Valley, and a form of "technology transfer" that is completely about global capital flows, actually manifests on the ground.

## Wellspring Hospital

Michael Fischer, adapting an imaginary from Gilles Deleuze, proposes the term "ethical plateaus" as a means of thinking about the intersections and interactions of different technologies and ethical-political emergences in ways that are always already stratified (Fischer 2001). One lens through which the tactical emergence of ethical-political terrains can be viewed is clinical trials, which are techniques within which values, in all senses of the term, get incorporated. I wish here to talk about clinical trials in an Indian context by drawing on some of my fieldwork at the Centre for Biochemical Technology (CBT) and its associated start-up, Genomed.

As mentioned in chapter 1, Genomed is a start-up that has been seeded by CBT in partnership with the Indian pharmaceutical company Nicholas Piramal India Limited (NPIL). There were two physical lab spaces in which Genomed is housed, very different from each other. There is one Genomed on the premises of CBT in Delhi, and another in a private hospital owned by NPIL, Wellspring Hospital, in Mumbai.[26]

The two Genomed sites quite literally represent different worlds and different forms of life and indicate vividly how place matters in understanding technoscientific production in situated and complex ways. On the one hand, there is the evidently different environment in which the two branches of the company are located: one drawing directly on all the academic researchers, facilities, and work happening in CBT, the other not, for instance. But there is also a difference in the types of work being performed at the two. In addition to doing population genomic research on schizophrenia (which parallels similar projects being done on asthma and type 2 diabetes in Delhi), Genomed Mumbai also studies pharmacogenomic drug response in clinical trials.[27]

Wellspring Hospital is primarily an experimental site rather than a therapeutic one. It is, indeed, a "five-star" hospital in appearance: glittering marble floors, comfortable sofas littering the hallways, and hospital beds with bright yellow bedcovers all make Wellspring seem more like a hotel than a hospital, and very different from, say, the All Indian Institute of Medical Sciences, India's premier referral hospital in Delhi, with which CBT Delhi has collaborative projects under way. What makes Wellspring even more unlike anything resembling "normal" Indian hospitals is the striking and almost complete absence of patients.

This absence is because the major interventions that take place at Wellspring are clinical trials. A stated purpose for ventures like the Human Genome Project, or studies of genetic variability such as the SNP analysis that I described in chapter 1, is that they make the process toward developing a therapeutic molecule more rational. However, the path from DNA sequence information to the development of a drug is extremely tortuous, for both scientific and business reasons. Scientifically, this is because the genetic etiology of disease is extremely complex and multifactorial. In terms of business rationalities, it is because an increase in the number of targets for the development of a therapeutic molecule, which is what genomics provides, does not necessarily decrease the high capital risk associated with drug development for biotech and pharmaceutical companies. There is a tendency among the latter, in any case, to make drugs for existing indications (the so-called "me too" drugs) because, in a certain market calculus, that is less risky than searching for drugs for new indications. They also have very little guarantee of success.[28] The risk for drug development companies here operates at two levels — the three phases of clinical trials, especially phase 3 trials that need to be performed on a few hundred to a few thousand volunteers, are extremely capital intensive. Also, even a small percentage of adverse responders could lead to the drug not getting FDA approval for marketing in the United States.[29]

While the genetic etiology of disease is complex, that of drug response is relatively simple and is associated with the Cytochrome P450 group of drug-metabolizing enzymes. Therefore it is expected that the safety profile of a drug correlates strongly with the patient's Cytochrome P450 genetic profile.

Pharmacogenomics is the correlation of genetic profile with response to drugs. Because the genetics of drug response is so much less complex than the genetics of disease, pharmacogenomics is much more easily realizable than developing therapy based on DNA sequence information. Meanwhile, if patients can be stratified based on their likelihood of developing an adverse response to a drug, then it might be possible to market a drug only to that segment of the patient population who are *not* adverse responders. This could save millions of dollars for pharmaceutical companies, who might otherwise see drugs like Pfizer's Trovan fail to come to, or stay on, the market altogether because of an adverse response of a small percentage of people taking the drug. Thus pharmaceutical companies are extremely interested in pharmacogenomics. The key here is how the epistemic reconfigurations promised by genomics — such as allowing correlations between genetic profiles and response to drugs — implode completely with economic considerations. The emergence of particular rationalities of clinical trials is completely a coproduction of economic or market considerations and possibilities with epistemic possibilities, each providing the conditions of possibility for the other.[30]

In addition to the money that could be saved for pharmaceutical companies by incorporating pharmacogenomics into their clinical trials regimes is the money that could be saved by taking the trials to the so-called Third World, where trials are significantly cheaper to perform. While Wellspring/Genomed does research on the genetics of schizophrenia and type 2 diabetes, a third major project, and potentially its most lucrative one, concerns pharmacogenomics.

The pharmacogenomics work is explicitly conceived of as research that can be of interest to Western biotech and pharmaceutical companies that might wish to contract clinical trials out to Wellspring/Genomed. But the resource in question that would make this attractive is not just the emergent pharmacogenomic capabilities in India as a result of state investment in biotechnology, but the *population*. As the director of CBT and board member of Genomed S. K. Brahmachari admits, India's cross section of populations covers the spectrum of the world's populations. "If they want Caucasians, we'll give them Caucasians; if they want Negroids, we'll give them Negroids; if they want Mongoloids, we'll give them Mongoloids."[31] Thus India becomes the melting pot of clinical trials.

The idea that a local pharmaceutical company would invest in building a state-of-the-art hospital almost solely as an experimental site in itself makes Wellspring an interesting institutional component of a genomic assemblage. What makes it even more interesting, and pertinent in terms of my arguments for situating ethical understandings in political economic contexts, is the larger urban ecology within which Wellspring is situated.

Wellspring is located in Parel, in the heart of downtown Mumbai, but also in the heart of the part of Mumbai that houses the textile industry. Mumbai's economy grew largely on the strength of a textile industry that rapidly disintegrated through the 1980s and 1990s, leaving visible from the windows of Wellspring the empty shells of once prosperous mills.[32] Parel, therefore, is teeming with unemployed millworkers, who have gone through periodic cycles of unionization over the last decade, but whose struggles to reoccupy and reopen the failing mills have probably, once and for all, ended in defeat. Hospitals like Wellspring now abut both the poverty of recent deindustrialization (a very different space of poverty from that of, for instance, Daravi, widely regarded as Asia's largest slum) and the new wealth that is displayed through other monstrously glamorous erections, such as a nearby shopping mall that sells a range of foreign brand-name consumables that can be afforded only by the rapidly ascendant middle-class consumer population. Such shopping malls are clearly, at least partly, built in anticipation of the mills finally being torn down and replaced by high-rise apartment blocks, since Parel represents prime real estate in a city with some of the most expensive real estate prices in the world.

In other words, Wellspring's location in Parel is almost certainly not accidental, as there lies available to the researchers a huge unemployed local population that ends up being easily recruited into clinical trials, which do, after all, compensate their volunteers. Even if the correlation between the hospital's locality and the nature of the work performed is not direct or premeditated (something I have been unable to ascertain), there is at the least an incongruent breaking of a pattern that is otherwise prevalent in Mumbai. Normally, private hospitals tend to be located in elite areas, whereas Wellspring is an unusual example of a private hospital located in a mill area.[33]

The ethics of such clinical trials can only be understood and evaluated if situated within the local ecologies of their conduct, ecologies that trouble the very notion of a trial "volunteer" in ways that are not relativist but situated and historically, materially produced. Just as Marx describes the forced proletarianization of the working class during the Industrial Revolution in volume 1 of *Capital* (Marx 1976 [1867], 873–942), so one can see how forced deproletarianization as a consequence of the crippling contradictions of capitalism leading to the virtual death of an entire industry in Mumbai leads in Parel to the creation of a new population of subjects who are created as sites of experimental therapeutic intervention.[34] What is at stake here is not simply a judgment of the dubiousness or other character of clinical trials recruitment strategies on their own terms, but rather the question of how regulatory and ethical regimes of pharmaceutical governance happen on the ground. Specifically, what is at stake is an understanding of the relationship between national-global enterprises of clinical trials and local forms of indebtedness.[35] In this process, biosociality itself gets configured as a relationship between vendors and clients, just as globalization is.

### Conclusion

In this chapter, I have looked at the co-constitution of biopolitics with global capital flows, which are themselves constituted by relations of indebtedness, leading to localized, particular manifestations of global technoscientific capitalism, and raising questions, simultaneously, of exchange (a Marxian concern) and governmentality (a Foucauldian concern).

My comparisons highlight the particularities of place. But once again, the comparisons between Wellspring and the ICICI Knowledge Park are not meant to be symmetrical. Rather, they are situated juxtapositions that highlight forms of incongruent manifestations of the apparently homogenizing process of installing a "start-up" culture. Of course, these particularities have everything to do with local histories, such as that of Mumbai's textile industry or the history of rural development in Andhra Pradesh, which are themselves conditioned by historical, global relations of production.

The history of the Mumbai mill districts is too long and rich to do justice to in this chapter. Briefly, I have hinted at Mumbai's transformation away from being a center of the textile industry toward being almost exclusively a business center—a transformation from commodity to commercial capitalism, leading to massive retrenchment among Mumbai's textile workers, most of whom live in the mill districts of the city, Parel and Byculla. Most of these retrenched millworkers now make their living either as sidewalk hawkers or as security guards in newly built shopping malls.

There is considerable union activity in Parel. Through much of the 1980s and 1990s, the unions focused on reopening mills, but they now focus primarily on documenting retrenched workers and their qualifications and ensuring both tenancy rights and employment for them in new real estate and businesses that come up in the mill districts.

The trope that union leaders use to describe the changes taking place in Mumbai in terms of the lives of the workers there is *sacrifice*. For instance, Datta Isswalkar, the founder of a community organization demanding the right of retrenched workers to work, describes the consequences of Mumbai's rapidly changing landscape (both built and market) in the following terms:

> Har waqt gareeb ka hi bali kyon dete ho? Hum to development ke khilaaf hain hi nahin. Lekin iske jo sufferer hai, uske liye kya suvidha aapne banaaya? Woh kyon har waqt wohin pichda rahen? Mera kehna hai ki poore duniya ke saamne globalization ke jaap karte ho, vikas ki baat karte ho, lekin har time vikas aur globalization mein jo bali jaata hai woh gareeb jaata hai. . . . Investor yehi dekhte hain na, ki security hai ki nahin usko? Lekin mazdoor apni suraksha nahin dekhna? Usko adhikaar nahin chahiye? Yeh kaunsa satya hai? Iska matlab, vittha, capital ko aap zyaada mahatva de rahe hain insaan se? To yeh kaunsa vikas hai bhai? Yeh kaunsi globalization hai?[36]
>
> [Why do you always sacrifice the poor person? We are not against development. But the sufferer of this, what help have you created for him? Why should he always lag behind? What I'm saying is that you go on about globalization to the whole world, you talk about development, but every time the person who gets sacrificed by development or globalization is the poor person. . . . After all, don't investors look to see whether they have security for their investments? So shouldn't the worker also look for his security? Does he not want rights? What sort of truth is this? This means that you are giving capital more importance than people? What sort of development is this, brother? What sort of globalization is this?]

The story of Parel, then, can be situated along two theoretical frames. The first is the Marxian frame of proletarianization and deproletarianization, having to do with shifting modes of production, the collapse of textile manufacturing, and the experimental recruitment of retrenched workers.

The second is a biopolitical frame. Michel Foucault's notion of biopolitics is an account of the ways in which, through techniques of normalization, standardization, visualization, and enumeration, populations get included, and thereby *accounted for*, within "state rationality" in its broadest sense. In an elegant inversion of this logic of *inclusion* of populations into a biopolitical calculus, João Biehl shows how biopolitical techniques of governance, in the case of the management of AIDS by the Brazilian state, create an *excluded* population — an exclusion by systems of enumeration of afflicted, treatable, and treated patients that, as integral to the rationality of such enumeration, *fails* to count those who, as a consequence, are left to die (see Biehl 2001; Biehl et al. 2001).[37]

Both in Biehl's case and in Isswalkar's description of the situation in Mumbai, the excluded population in question is a *sacrificial* population. When this excluded population gets incorporated into logics and circuits of global capitalism (such as into clinical trials regimes), however, this population shifts away from being sacrificed to being *consumed*. The worker's body becomes available to systems of capital, and also to systems of science, as a source of value generation, and as a source of knowledge production.

Scholars such as Biehl and Susan Greenhalgh (2003) in her work on China show how *acts* of state enumeration have as integral to their logic and method *in*actions; "seeing like a state," to use James Scott's phrase (see Scott 1999), leads to certain forms of blindness *as a part of the rationality of a certain mode of seeing and accounting for the population*.

Similar Marxian and biopolitical frames of reference present themselves in the Andhra Pradesh story, though the particularities and historical specificities are different. The stories of the Andhra Pradesh government creating a culture of technoscience in and around Hyderabad by embracing ideologies of innovation and technology transfer necessarily involves configuring state priorities, and state subjects, in certain ways that lead to exclusions, primarily an excluded population of indebted farmers, whose interests do not get accounted for in circuits of global capital flow.[38]

The thick historical and institutional contexts within which such biopolitical emergences take place, of course, are hardly so simple; even exclusion is not seamless. The biggest contradiction that faced Naidu in his attempts to create a culture of innovation in the Hyderabad area has to do with the fact that he himself was subject to the vicissitudes of representative democracy. In other words, it is the excluded population of local peasants who vote politicians like Naidu into or out of power, not the Silicon Valley entrepreneurs or IMF/ World Bank experts. This is a contradiction realized both by Naidu and by Western free market ideologues.

Therefore, on the one hand, part of the art of Naidu's governance is his ability to give audience, and a certain form of voice (albeit not necessarily equal voice) to both sets of interested parties, free market capitalists and indebted electorate. For instance, it was possible for me (no doubt aided by the symbolic capital of being a graduate student at MIT) to get an appointment with Naidu simply by e-mailing him out of the blue. On the other hand, the complaints of NRI capitalists and the Indian middle class regarding India's poor competitive position in global markets with respect to, especially, China represent a thinly disguised dismay at the constraints imposed on an unbridled exercise of the free market by representative democratic mechanisms. This is evident, for instance, in a special issue of the *Economist* published in 2001 that surveyed the first decade of India's economic reforms. The last section of the *Economist* survey calls itself "A Management Guide: How to Run India Inc." It starts by saying that "if India were listed on the stock market, it would be a juicy takeover target. A corporate raider would see an enterprise that has raised its game in the past ten years but remains constrained by caution. Surely India's assets could deliver higher returns under new management" (Unger 2001, 19). It becomes evident that only certain prescriptions can flow from a framing of "India Inc." as a "takeover target" for a "corporate raider," India simply needing "correction" so that it can achieve its "full potential." What needs "correcting," not surprisingly, are things like "wages and salaries," which need, of course, to be corrected with that wonderful attribute of the Wall Street trader, "draconian pragmatism" (ibid.).

In Parel, a different regime of biopolitical inclusion and exclusion is at work. This is the enrollment of a certain population that has become excluded from mainstream economic activity because of the radical collapse of the city's major industry, getting recruited then as subjects in clinical trials, thereby becoming, quite literally, both source for genetic material that enters extremely contested circuits of exchange, and also *experimental subjects*.[39]

Thus the stories about the Park are about the types of policy prioritization and consequent neglect and alienation of certain sectors required for a culture of innovation in biotechnology to take root in India. While the story of Parel is also one of global capitalism, it also concerns the effects of the *epistemic* changes being brought about by genomics and biotechnology.

In chapter 1, I talked about the indignation of Indian public scientists at what they perceived to be the expropriation of Indian genetic material by Western researchers or companies. I pointed to the irony that the mechanisms of preempting such acts by the Indian state were market mechanisms, imply-ing that the state acted as if corporate; but here the irony is doubled as, *at the same time* that the state acts as a quasi-market agent to protect "Indian" in-terests against Western corporate interests, it acts (through the company it seeds) as a full-blown market agent in making Indian populations available to Western corporate interests as experimental subjects. Of course, in such situa-tions, Wellspring/Genomed becomes a contracting agent, so at one level, this is simply a consistent enforcement of the desire on the part of the Indian state that the same market principles that get applied by Western companies con-tracting with other Western corporate entities also get applied when these companies do business with "Indian" genetic material.

The incongruence arises because, in relationship to the state, populations such as the unemployed millworkers of Parel are configured as a particular type of subject, *citizen*.[40] Indeed, it is precisely the *citizenship* — a modernist category of representative democracy — of peasants in Andhra Pradesh that al-lows them, by virtue of their ability to vote, to bring friction into the seamless imaginary of technology transfer that Naidu would otherwise have bought into. The biopolitical incongruence of the Parel population resides in the way in which they become, simultaneously, *experimental subjects* and obligatory nodes in systems of global exchange consequent to their citizenship. It is, after all, a consequence of citizenship that the people from whom Rep-X collects samples get represented by the Indian state, which enters into contractual relationships to act on behalf of, or in the name of, the sample donors. It must be remembered that the populations from which Rep-X collects samples and the population of Parel are not necessarily, or at all, overlapping; however, they do share the subject position of citizenship and thereby get interpellated into particular relationships to the state, market, and state-market formations.

Adriana Petryna proposes the term "biological citizenship" in her analysis of Chernobyl survivors in Ukraine (Petryna 2002). In her formulation, these survivors, who are also citizens of the new nation-state of Ukraine (which is itself built on the debris of both Chernobyl and the former Soviet Union), *configure* and *perform* their citizenship by virtue of their status as victims of radioactive fallout. Reparations for Chernobyl victims are integral to — indeed, are defining of — Ukraine's legitimacy as a nation-state distinct from the Soviet Union. However, these reparations can only be constituted by systems of enumeration such as acceptable radioactive exposure that qualifies for reparation and designates victims as quantified (and therefore qualified) in certain ways for remuneration. These systems of enumeration exist in specific relationship to an emergent idea and institution of a nation-state that has been constituted in the shadow of radioactive catastrophe. In other words, Petryna argues, the very conditions of constitution of citizenship in Ukraine are biological.

In India, an older nation-state than Ukraine, citizenship preexists such (in the case of Ukraine, catastrophic) moments that instantiate the *biological* as underlying a citizenship order.[41] This is evident in the Andhra Pradesh stories, which show citizenship to be quite similar to what liberal political theory tells us it is — a right to exercise electoral franchise. In Parel, however, citizenship gets reconfigured.

More generally, this reconfiguration occurs alongside the *epistemic* changes that genomics, always already overdetermined as market science, makes possible or brings about. What one sees here is the ability of information to describe "life itself," and to accrue value through insertion into transnational circuits of exchange. This reconfigures subjectivity in ways that turn populations into source (in intellectual property considerations), experimental subjects (in clinical trials regimes), and obligatory passage points without which the global exchange networks that get constituted could not thus be constituted. Since it is the Indian *state* that happens to be the most entrepreneurial agent in Indian biotech today, the relationship of this emergent subjectivity to citizenship comes to be at stake. This is especially so when the state enters into market contracts that involve populations that it claims to represent by virtue of its statehood. Even if the citizenship in question does not exactly parallel the biological citizenship Petryna speaks of, there is no question that a component of citizenship at stake in these emergent, global, postgenomic transactions is undeniably "biological," and equally configured by relations of indebtedness at multiple levels.

The first part of the book, then, has been concerned with circulation. This is a circulation, as I have argued, that can be described and discerned in two distinct narrative registers or ethnographic perspectives — that of circulatory systems, with the vital importance of the obligatory passage points of those systems; and that of particular locales, with the vital importance of the fact that these locales are positioned within global circulatory systems.

I do not wish here to preordain the consequences, for whomever and in whatever form, of the circulatory processes I am studying. At the same time, I do not resist this preordination to fetishize, instead, the empirical, local, or agential, in a fashion that *reduces* outcomes of processes that are undeniably constrained by the structural edifices within which they are contained (or fail to be adequately contained) to mere contingency.

The first two chapters have dealt with the conditions of possibility of exchange, and the tendential ways in which these processes of exchange, which always already relate to value in both senses of the word, manifest on the ground in different globalizing locales. The second part of the book concerns the ways in which globalizing regimes of exchange (both techno-scientific and market) articulate. Chapter 3 investigates the promissory grammatical structure of biocapital that structures the operations not just of corporate statements (public relations) but also of scientific statements (facts). Chapter 4 maps the forms of individual and social subjectivities that get configured through such grammars of promissory articulation that concern "facts" about "life itself." Chapter 5 outlines the underlying belief systems, such as nation and religion, that form the grounds or conditions of possibility or the terrains of enablement for such forms and practices of articulation. And chapter 6 provides a case study of some of my arguments throughout the book in an ethnographic account of a San Francisco–based start-up company.

# Part II
*Articulations*

# 3. Vision and Hype
*The Conjuration of Promissory Biocapitalist Futures*

The L. V. Prasad Eye Institute (LVPEI) in Hyderabad is a premier not-for-profit research and treatment center for eye disease. To understand the epidemiology of blindness, the institute undertook a major study called the Andhra Pradesh Eye Disease Study (APEDS). This study threw up some staggering results, which suggested that 80 percent of the state's population (and, by extrapolation, India's population) of blind people had avoidable, treatable, or easily operable forms of blindness, such as cataracts, or simply lacked access to eyeglasses.[1] To rectify this situation, LVPEI has become part of a World Health Organization initiative called Vision 2020: The Right to Sight.

A prominent researcher at LVPEI who is involved in its Vision 2020 initiative is D. Balasubramanian. A former director of Hyderabad's prestigious academic research institute, the Centre for Cellular and Molecular Biology (CCMB), Balasubramanian is also one of the architects of Andhra Pradesh's biotechnology policy, some elements of which (such as the support to knowledge parks) I described in chapter 2. He was, in the process, involved in another Vision 2020 initiative, that of the former chief minister of Andhra Pradesh, Chandrababu Naidu. Vision 2020 was the cornerstone of much of Naidu's public relations apparatus.

Getting an appointment with Chandrababu Naidu was remarkably easy and simply involved e-mailing him out of the blue. His office had an electronic cell, which forwarded my message to his joint secretary, who set up my meeting. Such online (or, for that matter, off-line) responsiveness is generally quite unheard of in Indian politics, but Naidu had a reputation for responding to e-mail requests, especially if they either came from someone based in the United States or had anything to do with science and technology.

Much of the "meeting" was, not surprisingly, waiting, but that too was quite an interesting experience. Naidu met with people every evening, and there were two separate rooms outside his office for people to wait, one for the "common man" and the other for VIPs. I had, no doubt by virtue of my MIT affiliation, been classified in the latter category. The arrangement reminded me of a Mughal emperor's court, with a separate *Diwan-e-am* and *Diwan-e-khas* for public and special audiences respectively. My waiting-room companions included a prosperous-looking nonresident Indian from Washington, D.C., who worked for Sylvan Learning Centers. The second was an even more prosperous-looking nonresident Indian from Denver, who was chaperoning an elderly, clearly "local," gentleman who was rehearsing his presentation to the chief minister from a bright pink folder labeled "Tirumala: Vision 2020." Tirumala is the site of the Tirupati temple, arguably the most sacred pilgrimage spot for South Indian Hindus. Clearly, in Naidu's regime, religions and religious institutions had to be visionary, too. And it helped to have someone with American connections to articulate that vision.

Visions, of course, are articulated all the time in corporate America and perhaps were never more consistently or extravagantly articulated than at the height of the dot.com boom in Silicon Valley, the event and place that served as a source for much of Naidu's own visionary inspirations. Perhaps the most dramatic example of a company that operated solely on the basis of extravagant vision and hype was the bioinformatics company Doubletwist.[2] My own first encounter with this company was at its stall at a 1999 industrial genome conference organized by Craig Venter's Institute for Genomic Research (TIGR). At this time, the company was called Pangea but was on the cusp of reinventing itself as Doubletwist. It was without a doubt the loudest and most visible presence at any of the public relations events at the conference, typifying the dot.com corporate attitude of the time, and clearly spending huge amounts of money to stay garishly visible. Indeed, at one point, there was even a billboard advertisement for the company on Highway 101 as it entered San Francisco, possibly the most expensive spot for roadside advertising in the United States. Pangea's transformation into Doubletwist was the transformation of a bioinformatics company that wrote annotation algorithms into a dot.com company that was, in the words of its vice president of marketing Rob Williamson, "a life science portal for online genetic research geared to go directly to the scientist" — in another words, a Web site that would put other genomic database resources into one place for easier access.[3]

The story of Pangea/Doubletwist is a fundamental part of stories of vision and hype in Silicon Valley high-tech worlds that run in significant measure on the basis of venture capital funding. Indeed, the role of venture capitalists in Doubletwist's saga led a number of its employees to refer to the company as "Double-Crossed."

Pangea was started by two Stanford graduates, Joel Bellenson and Dexter Smith. Bellenson and Smith were crack programmers who wrote the code, as contract workers, for the first version of Incyte's gene expression database, LifeSeq, which became the industry-standard expression database and the major source of Incyte's value in the late 1990s. As contract workers, the two did not get any share in the intellectual properties or royalties Incyte received. This was something that Bellenson and Smith felt very bitter about, though equally something that Incyte felt was hardly to be expected, given that the two had been hired as contractors, not employees. In starting Pangea, Bellenson and Smith were offered $10 million by one of the most famous Silicon Valley venture capital firms of the dot.com boom.[4] In exchange, the venture capitalists wanted 50 percent of the company, which Bellenson and Smith, not knowing any better, gave up. Indeed, on the back of this investment came a number of other extremely prestigious venture capitalists.

Now, this venture capital firm had also seeded a small bioinformatics company in San Diego that was going nowhere in particular. They suggested to Bellenson and Smith that Pangea should buy the small company. Since the venture capitalists had a substantial ownership share in the acquired company, the acquisition served to further dilute Bellenson's and Smith's share in Pangea. In other words, the venture capitalists had managed to get Bellenson and Smith to spend their money in order to further relinquish hold on their company. Eventually the venture capitalists managed to so dilute Bellenson's and Smith's holdings in the company that they finally even got rid of the founders from the company's board.

Meanwhile, Affymetrix, a tool company based in Santa Clara, California, was hoping to go beyond being a tool provider and turn into an informatics and drug discovery company. They were hoping to do this by acquiring a promising young bioinformatics company. Pangea/Doubletwist, perhaps by virtue of its high visibility, was the company that Affymetrix initially sought. In March 2000, Affymetrix offered to buy Doubletwist for $300 million, quite a staggering figure to offer for a company that really had not developed any genuine value-added commercial products. Doubletwist, however, felt they were worth much more than that, and turned Affymetrix down.

This failed acquisition was perhaps the most fortuitous event in Affymetrix's history. Seven months later, they had acquired Doubletwist's competitor Neomorphic instead. Doubletwist, meanwhile, spiraled through its huge reservoirs of venture capital money, attempted and failed thrice to go public, and finally, in a symbolic gesture of supreme insult, was offered to be bought for $10 million by Celera Genomics at the end of 2001. Spurning that last offer as well, Doubletwist finally ran out of money and closed its doors in March 2002. It had managed to burn through $78 million of venture capital money, a remarkable amount for what was purely a software company, with no wet-lab facilities, but with one of the most aggressive public relations and investor relations outfits in Silicon Valley biotech.[5]

If Chandrababu Naidu's vision failed because of the exigencies of representative democracy that saw him voted out of power, then Doubletwist's failed because they spent all their money on articulating their vision. Nonetheless, both Naidu and Doubletwist, failures in one reckoning, managed fundamentally not just to epitomize the capitalist terrain of their time but also, in significant measure, to contribute to a definition of a culture of innovation that was marked in Silicon Valley and markedly imitated in Andhra Pradesh. As I attempt to show through my arguments in this chapter, such a culture of innovation, driven by vision and hype, is not simply a waste or unreal but rather an extremely productive mechanism of value generation in a speculative marketplace.

### Grounds, Arguments, and Sites

In many ways, this is the most theoretical chapter of this book. It investigates the *grammar* of biocapital. As I have mentioned, Michel Foucault (1973) has argued that an understanding of modernity can be grasped by tracing the changes that have occurred in life, labor, and language. This chapter most explicitly concerns itself with language and investigates the discursive apparatus of biocapital.

The grammar of biocapital is a consequence of the type of capitalism that it is. As a type of high-tech capitalism, biocapital is, certainly in the U.S. context, often *speculative*, a reflection of commercial capitalism almost to the exclusion of commodity capitalism.[6] At the same time, because biocapital is a technoscientific enterprise, its component institutions are involved in the production of *scientific fact*, and in technological *innovation*. Biocapital is the articulation of a technoscientific regime, having to do with the life sciences and drug development, with an economic regime, overdetermined by the market. The life sciences are involved in fact production that enables the creation of new technologies and therapeutic products (innovation). The outcomes of innovative experiments are by definition unknowable; the market inputs into these experiments, on the other hand, need to calculate and look forward to a return on their investment. Therefore a speculative marketplace lends itself to innovation, while innovation breeds a speculative marketplace. An evident example of this relationship between speculation and innovation is the high-tech dot.com boom in Silicon Valley between 1999 and 2001.

Speculation and innovation both involve the articulation of *vision*. But it is articulation that takes a certain form, that of *hype*. Vision and hype are both types of discourse that look toward the future. Therefore, tracing the grammar of biocapital involves asking theoretical and conceptual questions about *temporality*.

I have started my analysis in this chapter, then, by providing a set of keywords: grammar, speculation, innovation, scientific fact, vision, hype, and temporality. All of these are keywords that get unpacked, individually or together, as the chapter proceeds. All of these are also keywords that relate to the generation of *value*. To provide further context at this point, I spend a little more time unpacking each of these.

The accounts in this chapter are particularly relevant to the U.S. context. Parenthetically, in the Indian context, vision functions differently for two reasons. First, as mentioned at a number of points in the book, the most entrepreneurial actors in Indian biotech have tended, for the major part, to be state actors. Meanwhile, Indian corporate actors have tended to embrace a different logic and yardstick by which to judge themselves, one that has to do more with Marx's commodity capitalism than with commercial capitalism. In other words, the yardstick by which Indian biotech and pharmaceutical companies have tended to be judged is by their *manufacturing* success, and consequently by revenues and profits. On the contrary, in the United States, most biotech and pharmaceutical companies tend to be deeply answerable to their investors, whether they are private (since most biotech companies are venture capital funded) or public (because of the fundamental importance of Wall Street in the valuation of American companies, thanks to the basic fiduciary duty of an American corporate CEO, under U.S. law, to maximize investors' value).[7] I indicated this difference briefly in the introduction while talking about the United States and Indian pharmaceutical industries, and emphasize it again in this chapter by recounting the story of the initial public offering of Genentech, one of the best-known U.S. biotech companies, and juxtaposing that briefly to the story of Biocon, one of India's most established biotech companies. Biocon, like Genentech, is more than twenty-five years old, but it had its own IPO more than two decades after Genentech had its.

Most of my analysis in this chapter, therefore, is pertinent to a speculative capitalism that is a much more hegemonic form of capitalism in the United States than it is in India. My use of the term "biocapital" in this chapter, then, is shorthand, for the most part, for manifestations of techno-capitalist logic in the hegemonic center of biotech innovation and free market ideology, the United States.

The biotech industry could be said to have come of age in the early 1980s, when a slew of biotech companies went public. This occurred during a period of marked deregulation, the explicit embrace of the irrational exuberance of the free market, and the symbolic valuation of the "entrepreneurial spirit." In many ways, the apparent excesses of the Silicon Valley dot.com boom of the late 1990s were anticipated in the early to mid-1980s. The coproduced relationship between the changing face of high technology and the changing face of capitalism implied, on the one hand, the emergence of a particular upstream-downstream terrain of drug development in the marked, often company-specific, division of labor that we now associate with the enterprise of therapeutic molecule development, and on the other hand, a more general shift in capitalist practices and value systems toward one that more explicitly embraced an ideology of risk taking.

The ideology of the free market as it manifests in, for instance, Silicon Valley, sees a specific *ethos* at play, one quite distinct from the rational accumulation of Max Weber's Protestant ethic (see Weber 2001 [1930]), and more similar to Clifford Geertz's description of deep play (Geertz 1973). This is an ethos marked by an apparent *ir*rationality, excess, gambling. Georges Bataille argues in *Principles of General Economics* that excess is a "fundamental" impulse of capitalism (Bataille 1988 [1967]). What is particularly interesting here is the way in which excess gets *valued* — seen as source of surplus value, and valued as a moral system.

High-tech capitalism is a form of capitalism that Susan Strange (1986) calls casino capitalism, where gambling becomes constitutive to the capitalist ethos (certainly in the United States, the crucible of these changes). It is a form of capitalism that is millennial in its spirit.[8] As I explore in chapter 5, the born-again messianic overtones of this value system are all too evident in the case of biotech and drug development in the United States.

The current strategic promissory horizon of genomics in the United States is a form of therapeutic realization, personalized medicine. But what is also at stake, of course, is commercial realization, for all involved corporate actors, but also increasingly for academic or state actors as they act, more and more, as if corporate. This commercial realization, as in any other capitalist enterprise, involves a successful venture that provides a high return on investment, increased revenue earnings, and corporate growth — value systems whose ideologies are increasingly globalizing and homogenizing, but whose contours, as I have argued in the first two chapters, are still highly specific and tendential.

What brings therapeutic and commercial realization into proximity to each other is the ideology of innovation — a high-risk, free-market frontier ideology that is simultaneously particularly American and globalizing. Innovation is a qualitatively different (albeit related) concept from the Industrial Revolution or Marxian concept of surplus value generation. It implies not just the generation of infinitely greater amounts of things that already exist (capital or commodity), which itself, as Marx shows, is a mystical and magical generative force, the source of capitalism's power. Rather, innovation implies, in Michael Lewis's phrase, the creation of the "new, new thing" (see Lewis 1999). The magic of technoscientific capitalism is not the magic of the endless pot of gold but the magic of being able to pull rabbits out of hats. Therefore one side of the ethos, authority, and magic of technoscientific capitalism has to do not just with capitalism's generative potential but with its *creative* potential.

The life sciences also produce scientific facts. Because these are facts about something as fundamental as life, they are valued in certain ways. And because they are *facts* (as opposed to, for instance, hypotheses, theories, or speculations), they operate with a certain authority. Genomics is a set of epistemic and technological assemblages that allows the creation of certain types of scientific fact, and allows a certain sort of rationalization of the drug development process, toward the much-hyped goal of "personalized medicine."

I investigate personalized medicine as a set of fact- and identity-producing technologies and epistemologies in the next chapter. In this chapter, I concern myself with the implosion of enterprises of scientific fact production with those of capitalist value generation in ways that make considering one without the other require a profound denaturalization of the categories and understandings of the involved actors. Joseph Dumit calls this overdetermination of scientific research by the market "venture science."[9] It is the grammar of venture science — promissory, risk laden, steeped in the ideology of innovation, and in many ways American (even if globalizing) — that I concern myself with in this chapter.

Investor relations and public relations are central to the functioning of all corporations. These are forms of discourse. They are also, invariably, hype. Hype is not about truth or falsity; rather, it is about credibility or incredibility. A successful investor relations pitch for a company is one that sounds credible, even if no one who is being pitched to quite believes what is being said.

I argue that in biocapital the "classical" scientific binaries of truth and falsity are *articulated* with those of credibility and incredibility. These are articulations of noneconomic forms of sociomoral values that trouble the normative structure of science as propounded by Robert Merton.[10] For the contemporary biotechnology corporation to exist and survive, it is (to investors, for instance, who would need to sink huge amounts of money into a biotech venture to enable it in the first place) credibility rather than truth that is essential to start with. At some fundamental level, it does not *matter* whether the promissory visions of a biotech company are true or not, as long as they are credible.[11]

The promissory statement of biocapital relates to corporate PR and is quite similar to the promissory discursive terrain of much high-tech as seen during the Silicon Valley dot.com boom. But the other form of statement that emanates from biotech companies, as mentioned earlier, are scientific facts. Meanwhile, even the promissory statements of corporate PR are made on a terrain constrained by certain regulations that exist to prevent *fraudulent* corporate behavior. In other words, while corporate PR is, in every sense, hype, *biotech* corporate PR is constrained by two regimes of "truth," where in each case truth means something different and operates within a different value system. One form of truth is scientific fact, established by adherence to a rigorous scientific method (albeit a method that has been shown by STS to be much more contingent than the seamless ideology of technoscientific progress makes out), subject to peer review. The second form of truth is that which constitutes ethical business practice, more generally applicable to all companies, which primarily implies a moral order that discourages the sorts of untruth that constitute a defrauding of investors. Therefore, if PR is about credibility, then ethical business practice and scientific facts are both about truth in different forms, and the question becomes one of the nature of the articulation of discursive forms that deal with credibility and with different forms of truth telling in an enterprise that is always already one, simultaneously, of fact production, therapeutic product development, and surplus value generation. The question of such articulation lies at the heart of understanding the epochal shift that venture science represents from the scientific ethos expounded by Merton, and gets at the question of the consequences of the implosion of the political economic with the epistemic, which is the implosion that makes biocapital a specific exhibition of capitalist systems, regimes, and processes writ large.

In terms of the rhetoric or structure of promissory marketing, I make two arguments that relate the generation of commercial value from biotechnology and drug development to necessary temporal lags. First, to generate value in the present to make a certain kind of future possible, a vision of that future has to be sold, even if it is a vision that will never be realized. Excess, expenditure, exuberance, risk, and gambling can be generative because they can create that which is unanticipated, perhaps even unimagined. But this can only be so if the temporal order of production is inverted, away from the present building toward the future and instead toward the future always being called in to account for the present. It is this realization of the operation of temporality, intensely value laden, that needs to be taken very seriously if one is to understand the functioning of promissory futuristic discourse, hype. I argue that hype cannot simply be cynical but is, rather, a discursive mode of calling on the future to account for the present. A central theoretical insistence of this chapter, then, is that hype cannot be opposed to reality, as is too easily done when hype is read cynically. Rather, hype *is* reality, or at least constitutes the discursive grounds on which reality unfolds.

Vision, hype, speculation, and temporality all relate to questions of value. As Friedrich Nietzsche says: "It might even be possible that *what* constitutes the value of those good and honored things resides precisely in their being artfully related, knotted and crocheted to these wicked, apparently antithetical things, perhaps even in their being essentially identical with them" (Nietzsche 1973 [1886], 16).

This chapter is about discourse of a certain sort: promissory. But it is discourse conditioned by specific institutional grounds, by the question of a specific type of implosion — of the *sciences* with *capitalism*. It is this implosion that leads to the shift away from Merton's description of science to venture science. This has consequences for value in both senses of the word. On the one hand, this implosion makes technoscience more driven by market value; on the other, it troubles, displaces, and puts at stake a normative structure of science based on values of universality, disinterestedness, communism, and organized skepticism.[12]

It is as easy to dismiss Merton's norms of universalism, communism, disinterestedness, and organized skepticism as it is to dismiss corporate PR as "simply hype." After all, one has only to look at the grossly unequal distribution of research budgets and facilities, within and between countries; the increasing encroachment on science's stated commitment to the public domain by private interests, especially as enshrined in intellectual property law; the active pursuits of credit and profit by often less-than-honorable means by many scientists; and the fact that peer evaluation of scientific results is as dependent on brand value (from whom and where do these results come?) as it is on objective, unbiased, rigorous peer review to conclude that Merton's norms perhaps exist only in name in the real world, to the extent that they exist at all.

At the same time that legal, political, and ideological mechanisms promote the seamless corporatization of science, however, is the fact that this seamlessness *does* encounter friction. The incongruence of venture science is not that "public" science is getting seamlessly incorporated but that this apparently seamless incorporation is taking place, as if natural, *at the same time* as it causes much disconcertment among involved actors and the larger polity. I have, for instance, already alluded to the aversion that scientists of the publicly funded Human Genome Project have exhibited toward genome companies patenting DNA sequences. A good deal of this aversion, no doubt, comes from a fear of being upstaged. And equally, a good deal of this aversion is voiced by public scientists like Eric Lander, who is also cofounder of Millennium Pharmaceuticals and Infinity Pharmaceuticals and one of the most avid and successful scientist-entrepreneurs to symbolize the emergence of venture science. Nonetheless it is undeniable that at least some of the public scientists' opposition stems from a sensibility that the norm of communism is important to uphold in practice.

In other words, Merton's ethos, even if partial, fragmentary, perhaps even residual, is still a strong organizing principle of the value system of science. Biomedical journals, for instance, still have strong disclosure requirements of their authors so that links to industry are clearly made explicit. But at the same time, research divisions of public universities receive huge amounts of funding from private companies in ways that cannot but change the ethos of science away from disinterestedness.[13] Lander leads vocal opposition to the patenting of gene sequences but at the same time is on the board of one of the most aggressively growing biotech companies in the world. S. K. Brahmachari vehemently opposes the expropriation of genetic material from Indian populations by Western companies at the same time as he seeks to leverage value for his start-up by licensing genetic information from Indian populations to Western companies. Scientific fact produced by biotech companies goes through the same peer-reviewed mechanisms that academic scientists go through, yet it is considered perfectly natural, at the same time, to issue press releases that are indeterminate, sometimes even misleading (if never, legally, fraudulent). This is the knot of venture science — not the seamless replacement of one value system by another, but the implosion of two apparently distinct value systems into one where each feeds off the other — a quasi-symbiotic, quasi-parasitic gob.

If *this* is venture science, then the value of Merton's science — initially configured, by Merton, purely in the realm of the normative — gets realized through another form of value, that of the free market. And it gets realized through the market to such an extent that the *only* way normative value, not just monetary value, can be realized is through the exercise of market mechanisms. It is this form of encroachment by the market on science that allows the naturalization of assertions such as the one often made by pharmaceutical companies that if they are not given free rein to set drug pricing (to the exorbitantly high levels that one sees in the United States in particular), the alternative would be no new research, and no new therapies for unmet medical needs.

Hence the prescience of Nietzsche's quote — that both the material and symbolic value of "good and honored" things (like Merton's norms of science) might in fact reside in their being "artfully knotted and crocheted" to "wicked, apparently antithetical things" (corporate encroachment). The word "artfully" is the key here: venture scientific articulations are hardly natural consequences of technological, legal, political, and ideological constraints. Rather, they are strategically crafted forms of discourse and practice. That does not mean, at the same time, that they can be reduced to cynical manipulation. The "artful knotting" — promissory conjuration as a means of discursive strategic articulation, "hype," or PR — is the subject of analysis of this chapter. The "becoming identical" of Merton's science with corporate science is no doubt a disconcerting emergence, but it is undeniably a powerful and consequential one that gets naturalized and globally disseminated, and forms the grounds on which such strategic articulations take place.

The sites through which I make my arguments in this chapter are not necessarily locales or institutions. My first site is, simultaneously, an individual and a performative space. The individual is Randy Scott, the founder of Incyte Genomics, one of the leading genome companies of the late 1990s. More recently, he has founded Genomic Health, a "consumer genomics" company whose story I tell in chapter 5. Scott is a recurring and central biographical figure in this book. He is so both because of his individual stories and articulations and, especially in this chapter, because of his embodiment of a certain type of public figure in the worlds I am trying to trace, the scientist-entrepreneur-manager. (Unlike many start-up founders, Scott tends to stay on to manage, in some capacity and for a significant period of time, the companies he founds.)

My accounts of Scott are, in fact, accounts of his public persona, rather than accounts consequent to privileged ethnographic access (as my accounts, for instance, of S. K. Brahmachari are). This is partly because I did not have privileged ethnographic access to Scott.[14] But it is also because I am keen to analyze Scott's persona *as* performative, because it is the performative aspect that allows him to do the work of promissory conjuration and creation of symbolic capital that I am writing about.

The performative space in which I have seen Scott is at conferences, either industrial genome conferences that served as trade shows, or conferences aimed primarily at investors.[15] Therefore the audiences that he targets at these sites of speech are investors and consumers, those who provide the conditions of possibility for his corporate entities to exist. I tell stories of Randy Scott's performativity in sites of speech targeted to investors and consumers in order to conjure promissory futures, and the existence of his companies in the present. On Wall Street, these forms of performative conjuration are referred to as "story stocks."

My stories of Scott are an attempt to portray conjuration *as process* — simultaneously as discourse and as drama. My second site moves away from persona to event. This is Genentech's initial public offering, the first ever biotech IPO, which closed in October 1980 after raising $35 million when the company did not even have a product on the market, exceeding all expectations. The Genentech IPO highlights both the necessity of conjuration for biotech companies and its enormous potential. It both heralded the arrival of the biotech industry in the investment marketplace and anticipated the "irrational" enthusiasms of the dot.com boom in the late 1990s. The Genentech IPO stories lead to structural questions about the periodic market cycles of boom and bust in the biotech industry, questions that I argue can be answered by paying attention to the promissory discursive terrain that provides both the conditions of possibility for the industry and the contradictions within which those conditions of possibility are constrained. I contrast Genentech's story to that of an Indian counterpart, Biocon, which was founded as far back as 1978 but did not have its own IPO until 2004. In the tale of these two companies lies the tale of the differential salience of the speculative marketplace (at least at this point in time) in India and the United States.

The third site is a discursive apparatus and legal instrument, the "forward-looking statement." This is a statement allowed by the U.S. Securities and Exchange Commission (SEC) that exempts companies indulging in forms of promissory articulation (such as press releases or similar forms of PR) from being held accountable if actual events differ from those predicted in the statement. And yet care is taken to distinguish the forward-looking statement from intentionally fraudulent statements — from the lie. An analysis of forward-looking statements allows me to explore in greater detail the relationship between truth and credibility in promissory corporate worlds.

Promissory corporate articulation is legally sanctioned and constrained by the forward-looking statement. This legal sanctioning and constraint allow boundaries to be drawn between that which is not true because it cannot possibly be predicted with accuracy (the exact historical and material evolution of the company making the promissory statement), and that which is not true because it is an intentional lie (thereby constituting a defrauding of investors, for instance). Of course, as illustrated by the recent spate of corporate scandals in the United States, many of them involving technology companies and almost all of them blamed on the "irrational exuberance" of the dot.com years, the line between these two forms of nontruth are contested, blurred, and often easy to cross. Throughout these three sections, I elaborate first on the types of performance central to the "story stocks" of biotech; second on the promissory speculative terrain that has allowed the biotech industry to develop in the United States; and third on the consequences of this performativity for theoretical understandings of truth and credibility to biocapital.

## Randy Scott

In this section, I describe the discursive performativity of one of the key entrepreneurs of the genomics revolution, Randy Scott. The stage that I describe is at the Hilton resort in Miami, at an industrial genome conference in 1999 organized by the Institute of Genomic Research, the nonprofit organization headed by J. Craig Venter, at the time the CEO of Celera Genomics. That year was a particularly interesting one for genomics, as the genomics community was on the verge of generating a working draft sequence of the human genome. It was also a year when the genomics community was particularly fractured between the publicly funded Human Genome Project and a number of private-sector genome companies (of which Venter's Celera was simply the most visible). The Miami conference was a site of gathering for the latter.

The company that really stole the show in Miami in 1999 was not Celera but its rival, Incyte Pharmaceuticals (now Incyte Genomics). In the context of the 1999 Miami conference, the keynote address by Incyte's chief scientific officer Randy Scott marked the turning point of the proceedings into an Incyte conference. The visibility had been there, the publicity had been there, but it had been built up for a purpose: Scott knew his business, and he executed it well.

A lot of his talk was about biology, about the various projects under way at Incyte. What was interesting, however, was its *visionary* nature — Scott was selling a vision for the future. This involved outlining a timed series of projections, through 2010, by which time, according to Scott, would be achieved a real understanding of biological pathways — and a systematic, annotated, accessible informatics understanding of it, with Incyte as the major creator of that understanding.

The beauty of a futuristic vision, of course, is that it does not have to be true. Legally, for instance, many futuristic pronouncements are qualified with disclaimers disowning the responsibility of the visionary to actualize the vision.[16]

Let alone legally, visions do not even have to be true to sell. Scott's talk was simultaneously addressing another audience, as much as or more than the strictly scientific audience: the audience of investors, who were clearly going to form their business judgments through events like this talk. For investors, of course, sinking money into such visions is risky. This is particularly so with genomics, which does not yet have many tangible drug products to show for itself. But by selling his vision for the future, Scott could be assured of having money to go into that future, irrespective of what might actually be produced.

The product of a genome company is the creation of (some form of) information that is in turn a condition of possibility for the creation of a drug. The conditions of its *own* possibility (and thereby the actual conditions of possibility of the drug) can only be created by the *performative* creation of the conditions of possibility of the drug, that is, through a vision. This is, however, a vision whose realization is not communal but, in the first instances at least, the responsibility of the company. Further, while not contractual in a legal sense, this is a vision that functions as a direct plea to the investor to make possible its (possible) realization by investing capital in the company. This is why the promissory vision of the future creates the conditions of possibility for the existence of the company in the present. While this does not guarantee the realization of the vision in the future, it is a necessary condition for such a realization.

A guarantee is a vexed idea, as well. While the implicit guarantee of the genome company's promissory vision is toward the investor investing capital in it ("We will realize your investment by enabling the creation of this product"), the performative of the vision is directed to a number of listeners and functions differently for each of them. The primary audience in the conference, whom Randy Scott was addressing, for instance, was of scientists, who were interested in his visions from the perspective of enabling their own research. The pharmaceutical companies, which are downstream from the genomics company, are particularly interested parties, since they actually produce the drugs potentially enabled or facilitated by genomics. For the general public, this is a vision in a much less immediately interested manner; for policymakers this interest manifests differently. The performative of the future thus functions to create very different futures for the different concerned actors, irrespective of the actual future product that may (not) be produced.

There is also a slight but tangible difference that depends on whether the company making the investor pitch is a public or a private company. In the latter case, the investors in question are often venture capitalists or other private investors; in the former case, it is Wall Street, and the public stock market, that are listening. The explicitly speculative nature of recent, especially technoscientific, capitalism is indeed a function of Wall Street's acknowledgment of the nature of the performative operation of the promissory statement: those public companies that are still years away from making a tangible product (usually biotech companies) but are driving their stock prices by virtue of promise alone (something that was particularly marked with genomics companies in 1999–2000) are, as mentioned earlier, referred to on Wall Street as story stocks.

But there was something else going on in Scott's talk, and it had to do with the symbolic capital of genomic information as information that is a precursor to therapy. There was that wonderful moment at the end of the Miami conference (in a party organized by Incyte) when, as recounted in chapter 1, Scott raised a toast to "the genomic community. Because they aren't in genomics for themselves, they are in it for Life" — mirroring, as I pointed out, Incyte's own corporate slogan, "Genomics for Life."

Derrida makes the claim that speculation is always theoretical *and* theological. It is perhaps not insignificant to the story of Randy Scott that he is an evangelical Christian. But I am not indicating this with a wish to attribute motives — I am *not* saying that Scott is a good genome entrepreneur because he is a good Christian. Rather, I am arguing for a natural cohabitation of discourses, the visionary discourses of corporate bioscience being morphologically akin to messianic discourses. Scott's ability to cohabit the two worlds of science and religion clearly allows him to use the discourse particularly well, and I will elaborate on this in chapter 5. Biotechnology, therefore, occupies a messianic space, of technology and of Life linked through capital, which becomes, naturally, the object mediating the fetish.

Indeed, this messianic space is a structural part of the biotech industry and has to do with much more than Scott's Christianity or lack thereof. This is evidenced in Barry Werth's description of Joshua Boger, founder of Vertex Pharmaceuticals and Jewish, in his history of that company, *The Billion Dollar Molecule*. Here is an extract from Werth's account of Boger's pitch to investors, and how that pitch is always already positioned as a religious and salvationary project:

> Boger knew that stories have to be accessible and that what investors want most
> from them is affirmation, so he molded Vertex's slide show not as a disquisition on

science or business strategy, but as a quest. The grail — the object of the quest — was structure-based design and its transcendent prize of safer, smarter, more profitable drugs. The impetus, as always in such stories, was a combination of righteousness and greed. (Werth 1994, 96)

Nonetheless, the salvationary-cum-profitable structure of this performative discourse was undergirded and overdetermined by Boger's own background and attributes, just as Scott's Christianity is not determining, but definitely significant, for the types of stories he tells and the ways in which he conjures up futures as scripted by Incyte. As Werth proceeds:

That was the text. There were also subtexts that Boger didn't mention, the most intriguing being about himself. Boger never referred in his slides to his relationship with Merck [where he had formerly been an employee before starting up Vertex], but he was seldom introduced anywhere without it being mentioned. To listeners with a knowledge of the drug industry, his defection was the most tantalizing part of Vertex's story, introducing, as it did, a whiff of patricidal intent, of vengeance. Here was Boger, a scion of America's Most Admired Corporation, the most productive drug company in history, Wall Street's gold standard, rejecting all that it had to offer because he thought he could do better. It didn't take a rereading of Genesis: Boger's saga of defiant departure was as old as Adam. (96–97)

The thematic constitution of motifs such as quest, messianic articulation, salvation, and defection asks questions of discourses of hope, risk, happiness, and success in American investment talk in particular, and in American culture more generally. Indeed, all these elements exist in the attempt to sequence the human genome, often articulated as a quest for the "Holy Grail" of life itself. It is uncanny, also, that the head of the public HGP at the time that the working draft sequence of the human genome was published was Francis Collins, also a born-again Christian. Collins has said that his passion for tracing disease genes is like "appreciating something that up until then, no human had known, but God knew it. . . . In a way, perhaps, those moments of discovery also become moments of worship" (quoted in Davies 2001, 72).

In his many flashes of brilliant performance, then, Scott establishes that the real goal is saving lives; that genomics is the vehicle through which lives can be saved; and that the genomics community, led by the vanguard scientists at

Incyte, merely exists to fulfill that vision. Genomics, in this performative, is not vocation but calling. Scott's employees are not scientists but missionaries.

Further, the missionary zeal, at least in Scott's case, is not tied to some abstract utopian desire for Health but embedded and embodied by real stories of suffering. So that Scott finished his talk with a perfect, poignant story that speaks to the motto and vision of "Genomics for Life": a story of Scott's friend, recently diagnosed with cancer, who ten years later could have been saved by genomics.

And at this perfectly poignant, perfectly appropriate moment, after a talk that was perfectly orchestrated, Randy Scott, chairman and chief scientific officer of Incyte Pharmaceuticals, broke down and cried.

### The Genentech IPO

I have argued that the promise(s) of biocapital provide the conditions of enablement for a certain type of present.[17] What, however, actually happens in the present, and how does the promise by its very nature create contradictions that make the present untenable simultaneously to making it possible? There is a more directly historical way of posing this question: how does one explain stock prices in the hundreds of dollars for companies less than a decade old with no tangible therapeutic product even on the horizon during the dot.com heyday of 1999–2000, and how does one explain the equally dramatic slump that sees those same stock prices operating sometimes in the single digits today? The simple answer, of course, is to take recourse to that ultimate agency, the market, and attribute the fall in biotech stocks to the general slump in the market. There is, I argue, a more complicated set of answers, relating to the political economy that hype works within and creates.

The biotech industry has in fact been experiencing cycles of boom and bust pretty much since its inception in the mid- to late 1970s, and these cycles have been morphologically highly akin to the dot.com boom and reality check bust of the last five years. Biotech has played to highly inflated stocks in the past with no sign of a tangible product even in the context of a 1980s economy that was much more conservative and that was much less willing to go along with the Silicon Valley mode of (apparent) high-risk investment that has marked the dot.com economy. The apparently irrational response to promise has in fact been the single factor that has enabled the existence and growth of an industry that would otherwise just not have been able to survive the extremely long periods of time and high amounts of investment required to bring drugs to market. The realization that promise rather than pipelines could create enduring value started dawning as early as October 14, 1980, the day Genentech went public.

The Genentech IPO closed with one million shares at thirty-five dollars each, an amount that exceeded all expectations, and an incredible amount for a company whose first product (recombinant insulin) would not appear on the market until 1982. In the next six years after the Genentech IPO, another nineteen biotech companies went public and together raised $542.3 million through their IPOs (Cetus, which was the second biotech company to go public, alone raised $107 million).[18] Clearly, therefore, promissory visions have been much more than just a feature of the biotech industry: they have enabled it to exist.

There is, however, a gap that opened up at the very heart of this promise, and that is the gap between infinite promise and what has to be necessarily measured as inadequate in relation to such promise. So while the promise creates the conditions of possibility for the present, it also, necessarily, creates the conditions for its own failure of realization, and the consequences of that. This gap is the place of the spectral, and of marketing and public relations. In other words, really successful long-term marketing and public relations are not the articulation of vision but the closure of the gap between what is envisioned and what is (inadequately) achieved. The periodic cycles in biotech have to be thus understood. The gap that opens up between promise and its realization is where *events* occur, and where *politics* — speed and tactics — take over. If promissory visions have made the biotech industry possible, then they have also placed the risk that attends all drug development — in this case, the risk of not fulfilling one's promise — at the heart of the calculus of biotech.[19]

I have been arguing at various stages of this book, however, that speculative capitalism in India is far less developed in relation to manufacturing capitalism, which suggests that sales and profits, rather than the conjuration of futures, are likely to be the driving dynamic of the Indian biotech and pharmaceutical industries. This, of course, is a situation that is changing along with India's attempts to "go global." Nonetheless there is a qualitative difference in the grammar of capitalism as it has manifested in Indian drug development. I wish to illustrate this by contrasting the story of Genentech to that of Biocon.

Earlier I indicated that whereas the Indian pharmaceutical industry is an established industry, Indian biotech is a fairly recent phenomenon, and still not very established. While this is true for the most part, Biocon, based in Bangalore, is a notable exception. It was founded in 1978 by Kiran Mazumdar, making it just two years younger than Genentech.[20] For much of its existence, Biocon focused on enzyme synthesis, a not particularly glamorous or innovative business model. But in the months leading up to its IPO, it came to emblematize the global, U.S.-inspired shift of Indian biotech, as reflected in Biocon's new slogan, "The Difference Lies in Our DNA." From an enzyme manufacturer, Biocon is in the process of reinventing itself as a drug discovery and development company.

Nonetheless, even this reinvention is publicly marked by manufacturing scale-up. While the "expansion" of U.S. biotech companies such as Genentech, Amgen, or Millennium typically implies either the licensing of products from other companies or the acquisition of other companies, "expansion" in the case of Biocon just before their IPO involved announcing the construction of new facilities that would allow a manufacturing scale-up. This is not to say that U.S. biotech companies do not scale up their manufacturing as they expand — it is just to say that manufacturing scale-up is not the aspect of their business that gets play as part of corporate PR and investor relations, as the activity fundamentally driving valuation. On the other hand, Charles Cooney, a professor at MIT and member of Biocon's scientific advisory board, talks of Biocon's strategy looking forward in the following terms: "Build technical capability, validate that capability by selling products into the marketplace in competition with global companies, and expand the technical and product portfolio while earning profits along the way."[21] This, a call to build a company through the validation of its manufacturing capability, is virtually the opposite of Genentech's history.

As an article in *Business India* puts it, "Biocon's real growth story is only three years old."[22] For the first two decades of its existence, Biocon called itself a biotech company, but in a tie-up with Unilever, it focused on enzyme synthesis. This was still biotechnology, but not the biotechnology that was driven by hype in the United States, which has become the focus in recent Indian biotech vision epitomized by documents such as Naidu's Vision 2020.[23] Indeed, Biocon has only recently entered the generic pharmaceutical market, looking specifically to reverse-engineer blockbuster generics that go off patent. While their focus has largely been on cholesterol-lowering drugs (the statin family), they were also in 2004 planning to launch recombinant insulin to the market. This is in some ways a coincidence in terms of drawing comparisons to Genentech: as mentioned earlier, Genentech's first marketed therapeutic product in 1982 was recombinant insulin.

The story of Biocon, read against that of Genentech, shows that biotech in India has not necessarily lagged behind biotech in the United States by two decades. However, an enterprise of biotech in India that subscribes to an American technoscientific imaginary of biotech — driven by growth, and focusing on therapeutic molecule development — is a recent development even for Biocon, occurring at a time when Indian science and Indian economic policy attempts to "go global." Clearly, going global implies, at least in part, doing the sorts of science that sells in the West, and attempting to open up both domestic and Western markets in the process. But even then, this attempt to go global, in an American image, manifests in incongruent fashion. Biocon still is not (and does not necessarily need to be) driven by speculation to the extent that American drug development companies are; manufacturing still remains the company's primary source of value. Indeed, when I asked a senior manager at Biocon about the effects of going public, he replied that there was not much difference in terms of the company's day-to-day functioning. The only tangible differences, he said, were that there would be greater transparency in the accounting of the company, and that it would "look good" for a company that claimed it was becoming a global player.[24]

### The Forward-Looking Statement

So far in this chapter, I have talked about the *performance* of visionary discourse (by actors like Randy Scott), and about the value and political economy of hype in biotech. But this pertains mainly to market value. Also at stake, as I have indicated, is symbolic capital and moral value when Merton's norms of science get troubled by venture science, and regimes of scientific fact implode with regimes of PR. I explore the discursive regime of PR in this section through an analysis of the forward-looking statement. Specifically, I explore through its lens questions of truth and credibility in techno-capitalism and argue that visionary practice in such enterprises is an act of fabricating the truth, which does *not* equate to fabricating a lie.

The forward-looking statement is not something specific to biotech companies. This section, therefore, is one of those in this book that is not specific to biocapital but concerns capitalist processes writ large. There are, however, a number of reasons, as follows, why an analysis of discursive forms such as the forward-looking statement is essential to an analysis of biocapital.

As mentioned earlier, the 1980s saw the coevolution of the biotech industry with a larger Reagan-inspired free market ethos. This was a neoliberal ethos that *valued* promissory conjuration in a qualitatively different manner from the value systems of liberal capitalist economy. Both the biotech industry, which was itself emergent at this time, and this discursive promissory terrain helped reconfigure the contours of the drug development marketplace into the upstream-downstream terrain that we now recognize. New biotechnologies, such as genomics, have similarly inserted themselves as subsequent upstream elements in this terrain. Thus the upstream-downstream terrain of drug development is strongly correlated, even if not causally linked in any manner, to the discursive terrain of corporate promissory conjuration.

Drug development companies are situated within the context of the high-tech economy. Promissory conjuration is a constitutive part of the lives of all technology companies, both because many of them are relatively young and formed within an ethos of neoliberal valuation, and because technology companies tend to require a high level of capital investment before they can show product and realize value.

With biotech, this situation is further exacerbated, because not only is drug development a highly capital-intensive venture, but its ultimate realization in a therapeutic molecule, assuming it were ever to be realized, is a decade or more away from the initial research toward it. Considering that most biotech companies in existence today are less than two decades old, a significant proportion of their lives and histories are stories of these companies having to sell visions of their future products as much as or more than selling the products themselves. Therefore, while the forward-looking statement as a discursive instrument (and more generally promissory conjuration as a form of life) is a constitutive feature of contemporary American capitalism writ large, its stakes are significantly exacerbated when biotech companies are involved because of the high-risk, time- and capital-intensive nature of drug development.

Finally, as mentioned earlier, the crucial specificities of biocapitalism stem from the involved implosions of the economic with the *epistemic*, and further with epistemologies concerning "life itself." While all biotech companies claim to be in the business of drug development, the more upstream components of drug development marketplaces tend primarily or mostly to be involved in drug *discovery*. Much of this upstream discovery work is not about the *production* of an object or commodity as much as it is about, on the one hand, the identification of possible lead molecules that might successfully be converted to therapeutic molecules, and on the other hand, the initial testing activities that suggest that such a molecule would not be incredibly toxic the minute it enters a living system.

Therefore, even in traditional pharmaceutical development through organic chemical synthesis (which, twenty years after the start of the "biotech revolution," still remains the most common and most reliable way of making drugs that function optimally in human systems), there is an entire element of scientific fact production and testing, primarily relating to protein kinetics and dynamics, that precedes the work of developing the drug, putting it into human clinical trials, and (if successful) manufacturing enough to market it.

With the emergence of biotech and biopharmaceutical development, this upstream epistemic component becomes even more important. Effectively, what biotech promises is the development of pharmaceuticals that insert into, and set right abnormally functioning, bodily biochemical processes. This puts an understanding of bodily physiological and biochemical processes, often at the cellular or molecular level, front and center in the preliminary processes of therapeutic molecule development.

With genomics, the upstream scientific knowledge as conditioning the entire drug development process gets even further exacerbated. At one level, as briefly mentioned in the previous two chapters, genomics further bases the understanding of bodily biochemistry (and biophysics) into information that can be objectified and commodified. It also (as I discuss in the next chapter) makes it much easier to create molecular diagnostic tests than therapeutic molecules. This is because the patterns of inheritance that genomic information can shed light on can instantly highlight future probabilities of disease in each individual who gets tested, without in any way altering the timeline, level of uncertainty, or capital intensity of therapeutic molecule development. Perhaps even more to the point, the complicated multifactorial nature of almost any disease event makes it extremely difficult to engineer a therapeutic entity that can "set it right" at the genetic level, and the way therapeutic molecules, even those "rationally" derived from genomic information, will actually act in human systems is likely to remain indeterminate, and ultimately only resolvable through perhaps even more complicated clinical trials procedures.

What this means is that the emergent assemblages of personalized medicine are likely, more and more, to focus on regimes of scientific knowledge of future probable health and illness, around *diagnostic* capabilities. In other words — and this is fundamentally the question that this chapter and the next, taken in conjunction, together ask — the specificities of biocapital stem from a question of how the legally enshrined, discursive forward-looking statements of corporate PR articulate with the epistemologies and scientific facts of genomics and personalized medicine.

A forward-looking statement is defined as

(A) a statement containing a projection of revenues, income (including income loss), earnings (including earnings loss) per share, capital expenditures, dividends, capital structure, or other financial items;

(B) a statement of the plans and objectives of management for future operations, including plans or objectives relating to the products or services of the issuer;

(C) a statement of future economic performance, including any such statement contained in a discussion and analysis of financial condition by the management or in the results of operations included pursuant to the rules and regulations of the Commission;

(D) any statement of the assumptions underlying or relating to any statement described in subparagraph (A), (B), or (C);

(E) any report issued by an outside reviewer retained by an issuer, to the extent that the report assesses a forward-looking statement made by the issuer; or

(F) a statement containing a projection or estimate of such other items as may be specified by rule or regulation of the Commission.[25]

The Private Securities Litigation Reform Act of 1995 provided a "safe harbor" for forward-looking statements, which means that the issuers of such statements (usually corporate investor relations departments) are not liable in case of the failure to fulfill any promises or predictions made within the statement. It is immediately evident from the act, however, that a failure to fulfill a promise or prediction does not constitute a lie, to the extent that a lie, indicating intent, might be indicative of fraudulent behavior. Indeed, the safe harbor provision is not available to issuers who have committed certain felonies or misdemeanors such as false reports, bribery, perjury, burglary, forgery, counterfeiting, fraudulent concealment, embezzlement, fraudulent conversion, or misappropriation of funds or securities, all of which might be said to be acts of lying.[26]

What sort of not-truth (as opposed to untruth), then, is a forward-looking statement? For that, I will turn to an example of such a statement that I quoted in an earlier footnote, which was put out by Incyte while announcing a collaboration with the Huntsman Cancer Institute to study the role of genes in the diagnosis, treatment, and prevention of cancer.

> Except for the historical information contained herein, the matters set forth in this press release, are forward-looking statements within the meaning of the 'safe harbor' provisions of the Private Securities Litigation Reform Act of 1995. These forward-looking statements are subject to risks and uncertainties that may cause actual results to differ materially. For a discussion of factors that may cause results to differ, see Incyte's SEC reports, including its Quarterly Report on Form 10-Q for the quarter ended June 30, 1999. Incyte disclaims any intent or obligation to update these forward-looking statements.[27]

The truth ingrained within the forward-looking statement is the implicit statement on the part of the issuer that "I will not have lied, and that is the truth." In other words, regardless of the outcome of Incyte's collaboration with the

Huntsman Cancer Institute, Incyte would not have *defrauded* its readers with its promises — even if some of those readers might have invested in Incyte as a consequence of expectations raised by those very promises. What the forward-looking statement formalizes is the fact that, as Derrida points out, it is impossible to locate an unfulfilled promise *as* a lie even as it is always perceived — even perhaps accepted — as a nontruth. In that sense, a forward-looking statement quite nicely fits in with Derrida's formalization of the popular-cultural conception of the lie. He says, "For structural reasons . . . it will always be impossible to prove, in the strict sense, that someone has lied even if one can prove that he or she did not tell the truth" (Derrida 2001 [1995], 68).

The tension of biocapital, as a form of venture science, then, is the tension between the "lie" of corporate PR and the "truth" of science; where corporate PR "will not have been a lie," and science is *authoritative* as truth when its statement is one of scientific fact. This tension becomes even more acute when such facts are accorded *inherent* truth (inherent as in essential to the statement, but also, when the facts concerned have to do with knowledge about "life itself," inherent as in essential to the self that gets constituted by the "true" fact). This is of particular importance in understanding the constitution of subjectivity by genomics that I explore in the next chapter.

What, then, is the truth of venture science, as opposed to the truth of Merton's conception of science? It is that *the truth lies somewhere*, "lying" here meaning both existing and being the thing that is not the truth. The truth of venture science is always already under erasure; it is ~~truth~~. But this ~~truth~~, which is *not a lie*, is also *not an error*.[28] If a lie could be said to be an intentional falsehood, then an error might be said to be an unintentional mistake, a failure to calculate adequately the uncertain circumstances that might lead a promissory statement to "not pan out." A forward-looking venture scientific statement cannot be a failure to calculate correctly, because the futures it promises are precisely *incalculable* (and therefore it becomes even more important to calculate them).[29]

What constitutes a venture scientific statement is itself a question, since it is not the formalized scientific statement that goes on to constitute "fact." Indeed, it could be argued that scientific facts do remain the same, regardless of where they are produced. I am not arguing that corporations produce different scientific facts from academic labs; I am arguing that the sorts of scientific ventures that get undertaken in the first place change, that the agenda of scientific practice changes as it becomes venture science, and that this changed agenda has everything to do with the sorts of *non*scientific ~~truth~~ claims that constitute corporate public relations and investor relations. Further, this difference is constituted by the different actors that define these market terrains, such as investors and venture capitalists, pharmaceutical company and patient consumers, and Wall Street speculators, which become a central part of the assemblages of biocapital and venture science as distinct from an academic science conducted in the image of Merton's norms. Corporations, like academic labs, can produce erroneous scientific "facts" (those that get falsified subsequently and at that point stop operating as facts), independent of the context of the production of ~~truth~~ claims through which they operate.

There is a question of temporality that resides in the relationship of a lie, or of a truth, to error. In the case of the ~~truth~~, the statement precedes, and indeed often performs or conjures, the event (or fails to do so); in the case of the error, the event (such as, for instance, the result of a genetic test) leads to a statement that then becomes a "fact." As I have been arguing until this point, venture science is constituted by the dialectic between the ~~truth~~ — truth that is always under erasure and pertains primarily to formally nonscientific articulations that create the conditions of possibility for science to occur (such as the existence of the company, and capital, in the first place) — and fact, which *may* be erroneous on occasion, but does not have to be. Regardless of the particular error that may or may not occur, however, fact operates on the fact that it is, authoritatively, true.

In terms, then, of working toward a typology of truthlike statements in drug discovery and development, one could talk about promise, which operates both in the interactions of companies with investors and in the public relations apparatus of companies; about fact, which operates during discovery; and about *evidence*, which is what clinical trials produce, and necessarily has associated with it notions of regulation and expert mediation (in the case of U.S.-based clinical trials, by regulators at the Food and Drug Administration). Each of these constitutes a different type of ~~truth~~-producing enterprise that collectively constitutes biocapitalist corporate envisioning. Further, the enterprises that produce fact, evidence, and PR are completely intertwined. This is why dismissing hype as "simply cynical," a mode of dismissal that is fundamentally what I am writing against in this chapter, is not a fruitful way of understanding the mechanisms of its operation. Attributions of cynicism serve to erect a simple binary between the truth and the lie (hype always being somehow associated, not just typologically but normatively, with the lie), a binary that just does not serve to understand the ways in which the truth and the lie are co-constituted as different types of ~~truth~~.

The key here is that forms of corporate PR are tied to the production of scientific fact, which is supremely authoritative and is moreover in this case scientific fact about "life itself." Therefore, simultaneous to exploring the rhetorical and discursive apparatus of corporations is the need to explore the sorts of scientific facts that genomics provides, especially when its "ultimate" aim, or current strategic promissory horizon, is personalized medicine. Personalized medicine refers not just to new types of therapeutics but to a new ensemble of techniques, practices, and institutional structures of medicine, one that is determined to a significant extent by the market. It is in this larger context of technical and institutional assemblages that the facts of genomics and the promise of personalized medicine need to be situated, and it is this that I undertake in the next chapter.

## Conclusion

I have attempted to do three things in this chapter in relation to the grammar of biocapital: to explore its performative articulation, its institutional effects, and its consequences for corporate credibility and scientific truth-telling. I started this book by tracing global systems and processes of exchange in the life sciences and capitalism. Exchange here involved the circulation of capital and commodities, but more specifically, biological material, therapeutic products, and, particularly consequent to genomics, *information* of various sorts, all of these operating as related but distinct forms of currency, as sources of material and symbolic value, surplus value, and moral or ethical value. In the process, I have argued for the constant overflowing, slippage, and contradictions within these forms and systems of exchange.

I have started examining the discursive grounds on which biocapitalist articulations occur, where "articulation" always already refers, simultaneously, to the capacities of, and possibilities, for utterance and to the process of linking together in striated, hegemonic fields of action.

These discursive terrains are constituted at multiple levels, especially in the context of the hegemony of speculative capitalism in American high-tech. There is the promissory conjuration — hype and PR — that is a fundamental part of the discursive apparatus of contemporary capitalism, though it is perhaps exacerbated in types of high-tech capitalism, drug development in particular, where the tangible product (the therapeutic molecule) is temporally and in terms of capital and resource investment very far away. A discursive terrain of promissory conjuration, where a vision of the future is sold to create the conditions of possibility of the present, is consonant with an ethos of neoliberal capitalism, as well as with an ideology of innovation, and is less evident in a situation such as India's, where manufacturing capitalism still predominates in drug development.

However, some of the key specificities for biocapitalism stem from the epistemic changes taking place within the life sciences, and this is where genomics becomes a conjuncture of profound consequence. I am keen to pursue the argument that biotech, as a form of venture science, does not just see the implosion of Merton's ethos of science with the ethos of the free market, but also sees the reconfiguration of ideas of "life itself" that lead to the implosions of the valuation of life with valuations of the market. In terms of staying attentive to grammar, it could be argued that if the Aristotelian grammar of life conceived of it as poesis, then this new grammar sees life as something that can be invested in. This new grammatical tense that the discourse of biocapital speaks in might be called "future perfect, present tense," an indication of future pronouncements leading to current uncertainty, which relate equally to the discursive terrain of corporate articulation, and to the epistemic terrain of scientific fact production. Such a grammar, I argue, configures life as a business plan.

If this chapter has paid particular attention to corporate discursive articulation, then the next pays particular attention to the epistemic articulation of fact, especially to facts produced by genomics. I analyze the current strategic promissory horizon of genomics, personalized medicine, which itself is an assemblage that is an implosion of the corporate and the scientific. Personalized medicine is both the future that is conjured by genome companies to realize value in the present, and the future that is promised by the sorts of information genomics has already provided or is expected to provide in the future. An analysis of personalized medicine is an analysis of the promise and fetish of the scientific facts of genomics.

# 4. Promise and Fetish
*Genomic Facts and Personalized Medicine,*
*or Life Is a Business Plan*

In outlining the history of the discovery and functional elucidation of transfer RNA (tRNA), Hans-Jörg Rheinberger argues that the material culture in which experimental biology is situated profoundly impacts both the type of "knowledge" produced and the manner in which it is produced (Rheinberger 1997). Similarly, the materiality of a functional genomics lab suggests the sorts of transformations, technological and disciplinary, that genomics marks. An example of this is the Whitehead Institute's Center for Functional Genomics, one of the major basic research labs working on single nucleotide polymorphisms (SNPs).[1]

The Whitehead Institute in Cambridge, Massachusetts, is one of the most prestigious centers for academic biology research in the world. It is a semi-autonomous institute with links to the Massachusetts Institute of Technology (MIT). Much of the Whitehead's recent clout comes from its prominence as one of the major centers in the Human Genome Project (HGP). Indeed, the Whitehead has been responsible for generating about 30 percent of the public genome sequence, making the institute the largest of the public sequencing centers in the United States.[2] There is much more to the Whitehead Institute than its Genome Center, but in terms of space, the Genome Center has somewhat taken over the Whitehead. So in addition to the original Whitehead Institute building on Main Street, Cambridge, there are two other buildings in different parts of the town that house the Genome Center. There is a building in which sequencing takes place, and one that houses the functional genomics unit. It is the latter that is responsible for making sense, in some of the many ways possible, of genome sequence information. Both buildings of the Genome Center are part of the Lander lab, Eric Lander being the head of genomics at the Whitehead in addition to being one of the superstars of the HGP, and a cofounder of Millennium Pharmaceuticals.

The Whitehead functional genomics lab is located at 1 Kendall Square, which is what my informant there called a "vanity address."[3] It is a rather characterless and incongruous block of office buildings rising up in the middle of an otherwise lively array of shops and restaurants located around a red-brick square.

The inside of the center looks more like a corporate office than a lab: plush orange carpeting, a reception hall with a secretary, no smells or lab coats or chemical muck. No signs of any of that even on the bench of the post-doc showing me around, where a computer was the only sign of any work; this could have been a cubicle out of *Dilbert*. Behind her desk were three workbenches.

It was on one of these workbenches that I got my first glimpse of the famed Affymetrix chips. Affymetrix, a biotechnology company based in Santa Clara, California, is the inventor and manufacturer of DNA chips, what they call GeneChip arrays. The DNA chip is a 1 cm x 1 cm silicon wafer substrate that has genes tagged to it, on which hybridizations can be performed to compare two sets, and "states," of genetic samples to see which genes are selectively regulated in response to certain events, or predispositions to events. These events are usually biochemical interactions that trigger certain genes being turned on or off, or trigger cascades of biochemical interactions constituting a biological pathway. In other words, the chip itself maps clusters of genes to provide broad views of gene expression. DNA samples are hybridized onto a silicon chip to create the DNA chip. Both a commodity and an object of knowledge production, the chip has within it the mysticism and authority associated with each.

Essentially a machine, DNA chips are also an experimental site, an entire laboratory on a single silicon wafer,[4] and a bearer of scientific fact, as they are tools that not only provide a profile of gene expression across whole clusters of genes (conceivably across whole genomes) but also are said to enable people to know their predispositions to various traits once those gene expression profiles are adequately correlated with them.

There are three enabling facets to the DNA chip. First, it enables the rationalization of the earliest stages of therapeutic development by helping to look for gene candidates that might be therapeutic targets (though the sorts of information provided by the chip are a very early stage in the possible development of any therapy actually based on such information), and by looking for gene markers that could be used to develop diagnostic tests (a much easier proposition). Second, therefore, DNA chips can be used to develop diagnostic tests, which are central to the assemblage of technologies and health management practices that constitute "preventive medicine." And third, the DNA chip allows *high-throughput* gene expression studies: massively parallel analyses of whole genomes or parts of genomes that can increase the speed of discovery manyfold.

For example, a major early publication that showed the utility of the Affymetrix chip used it to differentiate acute myelogenous leukemia (AML) from acute lymphocytic leukemia (ALL) (Golub et al. 1999). This was a landmark paper because it enabled the classification of these two cancers based on differential gene expression patterns of fifty genes, without any prior biological knowledge. Normally, tumor classification would require clinical, pathological, and cytological analysis. Classifying these cancers is of crucial importance in choosing the right treatment regimen, and the regimens for these two types of leukemia vary considerably. Often cells that follow different clinical courses look similar in biopsies, and traditional diagnosis of one or the other form of leukemia requires a complicated battery of tests. The DNA chip enabled this form of cancer diagnosis to move away from systems based on visual analysis to molecular-based systems and, in this experiment, allowed the comparative measurement of activities of nearly seven thousand genes expressed in bone marrow samples from thirty-eight patients.

Performed in the Lander lab, this study points simultaneously to the scientific, specifically diagnostic, possibilities of the Affymetrix chip and to the terrains of academic-industrial collaboration that enable such possibilities. The Whitehead study was funded by a consortium consisting of Affymetrix, the multinational pharmaceutical company Bristol-Myers Squibb (which is a market leader in oncology therapeutics), and Millennium Pharmaceuticals, a biotechnology company that wants to become a biopharmaceutical drug development company and was cofounded by Lander himself.

In other words, the DNA chip not only allows the identification of patterns of genetic variability across individuals and populations, or in different diseased states, but allows such identifications in a high-throughput manner. *Speed* and *information* are of central importance here. The possibility of such high-throughput analysis has everything to do with the particular material nature of the chip. The hybridizations themselves are made possible by the nature and contours of the silicon wafer,[5] but also because of *miniaturization*. Increasing the density of hybridization makes it possible to speed discovery by obtaining more information from a chip at one go. Thus the material structure of the chip has everything to do with the nature of scientific fact that can be produced, and this is recognized by a series of intellectual property protections that cover the Affymetrix technology.

The chips themselves were encased in a small rectangular sheath, making them look rather like fancy microscope slides. But the process of hybridizing and detecting on them is a complicated one, and completely automated. At the Whitehead lab there was a large room that housed only the machines into which the chips are locked, buttons turned on, and readouts obtained. There were also, on the postdoc's bench, some glass slides that were in the process of being turned into more inexpensive, homemade DNA chips.

In the center of the floor was a bizarre spiral staircase that looked like something out of a spaceship in a 1960s version of *Star Trek*. Downstairs was what is called the "variant" group, which did comparative genomics work. This looked like a more typical "wet" molecular biology lab, though much larger — almost more like a factory than a lab. This floor had an area to pour gels in, shelves stacked with measuring cylinders, and proper lab benches. Much of the upstairs, where the bioinformatics work happened, housed secluded offices. My conversation with the postdoc did indeed revolve around organizational structure, and the office was a peculiarly organized place, with these two groups, that seem hardly to interact at all, constituting the interdisciplinary space of "functional genomics."

The architecture at the Whitehead was situated in the context of larger institutional relationships, with the functional genomics group's lab meetings often being attended by people from Millennium Pharmaceuticals, which is housed a few floors below in the same building. As mentioned earlier, Eric Lander is one of the cofounders of Millennium, a leading genome company. The Whitehead lab meetings are quite literally physical sites of diffusion of academic research into industry, and, in the opinions of many genome scientists that I have talked to, a major source of competitive advantage for Millennium.[6] The interaction between the Whitehead and Millennium, indeed, does not take place only at the level of architecture or informal interaction. The Whitehead functional genomics group, as mentioned, is funded by a consortium that comprises Millennium, Affymetrix (whose DNA chips are extensively used at the Whitehead), and Bristol-Myers Squibb (with whom Millennium has close ties in the area of oncology pharmacogenomics and therapeutics). The Whitehead consortium therefore brings together the major components and actors of the drug development marketplace with a functional genomics company, a tool company (as two distinct types of upstream providers), a big pharmaceutical company downstream, and an academic lab that is funded by all three and feeds basic research into the development programs of its industrial partners. Such arrangements typify the venture science worlds epitomized by genomics.

### Grounds, Arguments, and Sites

So far in this book, I have introduced a number of empirical and theoretical issues that I propose to tackle explicitly in this chapter. The first is that biocapital is the implosion of an emergent economic regime with an emergent epistemic one. The second is that the biotechnology and subsequent genomics "revolutions" are techno-capitalist assemblages that allow analyses, and create types of knowledge, that reconfigure definitions, understandings, even the grammar, of "life itself." The third is that the articulations of biocapital are those of corporate PR and promissory conjuration with those of scientific fact, at a time when Merton's norms of science are simultaneously consequential and at stake in emergent venture scientific assemblages.

All of this means that it becomes particularly important to seriously analyze and understand the technoscience that is genomics, in terms both of its epistemologies and of the ways in which it is likely to reconfigure drug development terrains as well as the practice of medicine. I do this here at a number of levels. First, I explore in greater detail the logic and rationality of pharmacogenomics and personalized medicine, two related yet distinct postgenomic assemblages that I argue constitute the current strategic promissory horizon of genomics. Next, I show how the sorts of knowledge provided by these genomic technologies and epistemologies are likely to shift the drug development enterprise, especially to the extent that it depends on genomics, toward *diagnostics* rather than *therapeutics* as its endpoint, or at least as a subsequent obligatory passage point.[7]

These are the sorts of knowledge that have consequences for the configuration of subjectivity, especially when genomics sees the fetishism of scientific fact implode with the fetishism of the gene as being understood to somehow designate or represent the entire organism, sometimes even whole populations.[8] I describe what I mean by this "genomic fetishism" and contextualize it in relation to Marxian commodity fetishism, essential in a venture scientific terrain that sees the implosion of enterprises of scientific fact production with those of market innovation and surplus value generation.

The key to understanding the implosion of these two value systems, I argue, is to see how they articulate around the question of *risk*. The types of knowledge provided by genomic representational devices, such as the DNA chip that I have described, inherently have to do with foretelling the future risk of disease of individuals who undergo the test. Meanwhile there are multiple levels of risk that the biotech and pharmaceutical industries confront. Especially for biotech, genome, or other upstream companies, of course, there is the very risk of being a start-up entity in a capital-intensive, high-risk marketplace, where such companies' existence is wagered against the vagaries of drug development as well as the muscle of big pharmaceutical companies. But even for big pharmaceutical companies, there is the high risk of drug development, constituted by the high expense and immense uncertainty of clinical trials, in a marketplace deeply indebted to Wall Street and stock valuations. All of these constraints put enormous pressure on biotech and pharmaceutical companies to increase their markets, which for pharmaceutical companies in particular are still very much in the domain of therapeutic rather than diagnostic development.

In other words, genomic information that configures individual subjectivities as those of patients-in-waiting by foretelling future possible illness also very much configures their subjectivities as *consumers*-in-waiting for drug development companies looking to increase their market. This enlargement can be achieved, at least in substantial measure, by constantly enlarging the domain of the "therapeutic," as shown particularly vividly in studies of psycho-pharmaceutical development by authors such as Joseph Dumit (2003, 2004), David Healy (1997, 2002), and Peter Kramer (1997). Of course, this constant enlargement of the domain of the therapeutic in a U.S. market system conditioned by the valuations of Wall Street must also be situated in a global context where millions of people die of diseases such as AIDS at least partly because of exorbitant drug pricing by multinational pharmaceutical companies, because such people do not have the purchasing power to constitute a significant market for these companies.[9]

What is key for my argument in this chapter, regarding the shifts brought about by genomics as an epistemic-technical assemblage and venture science as an emergent institutional and normative assemblage, is that two understandings of risk, one having to do with patient illness profiles, the other having to do with market risk, are constantly at play and in relation to each other. Indeed, in the venture scientific worlds of genomics, these two forms of risk constitute each other, to the extent that individual DNA profiles are market calculations, both for the interpellated individuals and for the market entities whose valuations depend on being able to generate and act on such forms of knowledge. Life, for biocapital, is a business plan.

In this chapter, I refer to the way in which genomic facts function authoritatively as "genomic fetishism." What that means, as I unpack in the chapter, is that while, on the one hand, genomics is not deterministic, on the other hand, genetic determinism does exist in our conceptual understanding of our selves. This implies that a form of abstraction is at play in the interface between science and "culture." As Friedrich Nietzsche says: "One ought not to make 'cause' and 'effect' *into material things*, as natural scientists do . . . one ought to employ 'cause' and 'effect' only as pure *concepts*, that is to say as conventional fictions for purposes of designation, mutual understanding, *not* explanation" (Nietzsche 1973 [1886], 33; italics in original).

In this book, I have not tackled the question of genetic determinism explicitly, but there is no question that its specter haunts the subject and analysis of genomics. It also becomes the straw man in nature/nurture wars. Recently, for instance, the noted cognitive scientist Steven Pinker, a believer in the existence of a biological basis for psychology and cognition, has devoted an entire book to attacking the perceived "environmental determinism" of proponents of "nurture" over "nature," "culture" over "biology" (Pinker 2002). This is a debate I wish to skirt, not least because the reduction of biosociality to such simple binaries is a puerile process of simplification and purification. However, I do argue that a central source of authority for genomics stems from "genomic fetishism"—the fetish, simultaneously, of the authority of scientific fact as something that is definitive and ultimate, and *not* the result of contingent, fragmentary, contested, and constantly revised processes of knowledge production; and of the authority of the gene as somehow standing in for, or representative of, entire organisms, populations, or species.[10]

I embrace, instead, Paul Rabinow's notion of biosociality (see Rabinow 1992), which involves an attentiveness to the coproduced ways in which biological and social structures mutually evolve, and therefore involves having a fundamentally different understanding of *causality* than sociobiology has. To posit causal explanations in some sort of binary opposition to explanations of pure contingency is a mistake. Rather, inspired by Weber (and by Rabinow's use of Weber), I make the argument for staying attentive to the multiple, layered causations that lead to emergences of certain social worlds instead of others. Of course, as Pinker would argue, there is a biological basis for understanding disease or cognition. The maneuver that I reject, whether the question is of the relationship of genes to traits, or of genomics to capitalism, is the purification of a set of complex, multifactorial interactions (which are multifactorial both at the genetic level and in the interactions of "genetic" and "environmental" factors) into a relationship of simple linearity, the making of "cause" and "effect," in Nietzsche's words, into "material things."

That this occurs in molecular genetics and genomics, even (perhaps especially) in academic genome worlds, is undeniable. An example of this was powerfully in evidence at the Institute of Genomic Research genome conference in Miami in 2000. Richard Gibbs, a high-profile public genome researcher who ran the Human Genome Project sequencing center at the Baylor

College of Medicine, gave a general progress report of the HGP, which ran along expected lines, indicating how well everyone had done, how the challenge was only beginning, how the public and private enterprises were cooperating as they ought to, and so on. The talk got interesting at the end, however, when Gibbs said that the real thing to do next was to start correlating genes with disease.

Gibbs then made the remarkable *scientific* claim that five thousand single-gene diseases are likely to exist. Further, Gibbs was justifying his claims with evidence from scientific literature: how an increasing number of articles in journals such as *Nature Genetics*, for instance, were talking about "a gene/ mutant *for*" diseases, thereby suggesting such simple correlations.[11] He was not quite allowed to get away with his assertion, as Craig Venter, CEO of Celera Genomics, argued that claiming single-gene correlation for diseases is like looking under the lamppost for keys dropped elsewhere because it is best lit under the lamppost.

Genetic determinism is scientific fact, to the extent that a matter on which a scientific journal pronounces is scientific fact. But genetic determinism is also, as Venter was hinting, merely artifact that gets reified into fact. In fact, one of the scientists who worked on the initial development of GenBank, the public DNA sequence database, later expressed profound disgust to me about Gibbs's talk, claiming that one cannot, by definition, have such a thing as a single-gene disease, since the very fact that every disease manifests itself at different times in different individuals suggests that there is more than one gene involved in regulating its onset. Further, he mentioned that the notion of a "single-gene disease" was developed as a classification category in GenBank, as shorthand for genes that might be classified as not obviously complex in a database that depended on such shorthand classifications for its creation. He claimed to be dismayed at the way in which a classificatory maneuver had been so completely appropriated by even credible and well-known scientists to represent the "fact" of the existence of five thousand single-gene diseases.[12]

Nietzsche's phrase "as conventional fictions" is particularly resonant here. The persuasive argument against reifying maneuvers such as genetic determinism lies not in arguing against the *content* of "fact" derived from scientific method but in the process of purification that simultaneously holds up the method of investigation as natural, infallible, a transparent representation of "the real world" rather than the process of contingent negotiations, guesswork, and constant revision; and that reifies complex, situated, multifactorial (in this case, biological) processes into a simple phenomenon of cause and effect. It is this work of purification that Bruno Latour argues is symptomatic of modernity (Latour 1993), and it is this combination of reifying maneuvers that is the fetishistic process. Thus my critique of "genomic fetishism" is not a critique of the question of the relationship of genes to traits (which I do believe is consistently more complex than Richard Gibbs, for instance, made out in the talk I described) but a critique of the maneuvers and processes that make a certain, hardly natural articulation of these relationships seem natural, supremely authoritative, and the way things "really" are to the exclusion of other, more hybrid possibilities.

One form of abstraction that is at work in subject constitution by genomics, then, is the shorthand operational at the level of *production* of scientific fact that posits a correlation as a relationship of causality. A second form of abstraction, related to the first, is the way in which subject formation *takes recourse* to the "objective" scientific fact once its production gets black-boxed. Joseph Dumit refers to the latter as "objective self-fashioning" and describes the objective self thus:

> The objective self is an active category of the person that is developed through references to expert knowledge and is invoked through facts. The objective self is also an embodied theory of human nature, both scientific and popular. Objective self-fashioning calls attention to the equivocal site of this production of new objective knowledge of the self. From one perspective, science produces facts that define who our selves are objectively, which we then accept. From another perspective, our selves are fashioned by us out of the facts available to us through the media, and these categories of persons are in turn the cultural basis from which new theories of human nature are constructed.[13]

Dumit's notion of objective self-fashioning calls attention to the equivocal dialectic between the objective and subjective when the subject formation in question is a consequence of an encounter with an "objective" discourse that derives its supreme, fetish-producing authority from that very perception of objectivity — even though it is an objective knowledge that, in cases like personalized medicine or positron emission tomography (PET) scanning (which is the case Dumit analyzes in the passage referred to here), is created precisely to inform the subject who gets interpellated by it. In other words, facts provide the grounds for the creation of subjects at the same time that facts are constituted by information derived from the very subjects they constitute in particular ways. These acts of subject constitution by facts that are simultaneously subject dependent yet objective are made possible because they are *facts*, the supremely authoritative statement that derives its authority by virtue of being derived scientifically.

"The person," the *subject* of objective self-fashioning, is an important category or identity to explore further. Dumit weaves elegantly away from the unmarked "self" to categories of persons that form "the cultural basis from which new theories of human nature" (which often themselves acquire performative force *as facts*) are constructed. In other words, scientific fact can operate in the ways it does because it is universal, *not* culturally specific. And yet the modes of subject interpellation by these facts are specific. While the "subject" of personalized medicine need not be marked or explicit, in that a technology like the DNA chip could potentially tell any individual his or her genetic profile and consequent future probability of illness, the ways in which genomic technologies like the DNA chip operate are in fact quite specific and, not surprisingly, show variation and incongruity between, for instance, the United States and India.

The interpellated subject of genomic fetishism in this chapter, except in cases otherwise mentioned, is the American who gets foretold his or her probability of future health or illness by a technology such as the DNA chip. Such a subject, I argue, becomes a patient-in-waiting. But personalized medicine as a biocapitalist assemblage demands constant attention to the fact that produced epistemologies and technologies, particularly in the U.S. context, are overdetermined as commodities and therefore require a market for their consumption. In other words, I argue for the objectively self-fashioned (American) patient-in-waiting as always already being a *consumer*-in-waiting, an intertwining of subjectivities that fundamentally underlies the rationality of personalized medicine in the U.S. context.

Indian populations could conceivably be consumers of personalized medicine, and no doubt India's desire to be a global player would be fulfilled when it becomes possible to automatically conceive of a reified "Indian subject" of personalized medicine as a patient or consumer-in-waiting. However, as I argued in chapter 2, the tendential axes of global asymmetry on which biocapital plays out imply that the more likely subject position for Indian populations with respect to genomics is not that of *consumer* as much as that of *experimental subject*. Genome profiles of a participant in a pharmacogenomic experiment conducted by the Indian start-up Genomed in Parel, Mumbai, for example, are much more likely to be useful in a pharmacogenomic analysis whose outcome could prove valuable to a Western biotech or pharmaceutical company in a clinical trial. Having already focused on the configuration of the subject of pharmacogenomic experiments in Parel as experimental subject in chapter 2, I focus in this chapter on the configuration of the subjectivity of the (probably, but not necessarily, American) patient-in-waiting as consumer-in-waiting consequent to his or her objective self-fashioning by genomic fact.

This focus allows me here to conceive of subjectivity through an unmarked "subject," who could conceivably be subjected by biocapitalist emergences regardless of his or her geographical subject position, but who is, at least today, most likely in fact to be an American, or at least a Western (neo)liberal, subject.

The disconcertment, then, is this. I believe it is possible to conceive of the ways in which the implosions of epistemic and economic rationalities lead to particular configurations of subjectivity, such as (as I describe in this chapter) biocapital's configuring of the subjects of personalized medicine as simultaneously patients- and consumer-in-waiting. And further, the global reach of, and global desire expressed toward, such technologies imply that there is no reason to believe that personalized medicine should not configure its Indian subject as it would a Western (neo)liberal subject.[14] And yet, as I have been arguing, the tendential alignments of global biocapital at present lead to a situation where Indian subjects of personalized medicine (similar, in all likelihood, to African American or other similarly marked population category subjects of personalized medicine in the United States) are likely to be primarily configured as experimental subjects instead.

It is important to consider why it is so easy conceptually for a chapter such as this, considered theoretically to be about "subjectivity," to analyze this concept in a "placeless" fashion, *at the same time* as the subjectivity of experimental subjects in Parel marks them otherwise (and Other-wise) as "Indian." This is a serious question for ethnography and for theory.

Ethnography has always prided itself on deriving its analytic and empirical power from its ability to localize, and make specific, what might otherwise be left to the vague generalizations of "theory," generalizations that often fail to account for the actual, particular manifestations of the systems, regimes, and processes that are being theorized in the first place. And yet science derives its analytic and empirical power from its universality, from the fact that a *fact-producing* experiment will produce the same fact regardless of the locale of its performance.

In other words, a DNA chip, for instance, will produce the same *fact*, for example about genetic variability between individuals (though the particulars of the information generated will be different), regardless of whether it is used to analyze pharmacogenomic profiles of an unemployed Indian millworker in Parel or of a biotech corporate CEO in Palo Alto. And yet it is likely that the subjectivities configured in the two cases will be different.

In the first two chapters concerning circulation, I have been particularly keen to emphasize how even an absolute imitation of a particular American neoliberal free-market imaginary by Indian actors, *because* of the act of imitation, changes the conditions of emergence for those same market systems, leading to incongruence between the two locales. Similarly, I make the argument here that the replication of an epistemic system, in which the science is resolutely the same whether performed in India or the United States, leads to incongruent manifestations of, for instance, subjectivity in the two contexts, in ways that allow one (Indian) to be conceived and written of as particular, localized, contingent, and "empirical," and the other (American) to be conceived and written of as general, subscribing to epistemic rationality, placeless, and "theoretical."

In other words, if biopolitical (and in this case, biocapitalist) emergence can be theorized in the way that I do in this chapter, with the footnote that such an emergence in, for instance, India would diverge in significant ways from this theorization, then how is it possible to explain that "exception," such as India, while *still* insisting on those "exceptional" emergences as structural, tendential, and *not* reducible simply to contingency? Or—if we are to take biopolitics as a theoretical concept seriously, as we ought to do—then how can we account for "biopolitics elsewhere" in ways that do not reduce the "elsewhere" emergences to explanations of contingency?[15]

## Pharmacogenomics and Personalized Medicine

In this section, I provide an overview of personalized medicine, which, in the hype of promissory life sciences, is at some level the "ultimate" dream of genomics (implicitly replacing, therefore, the genome sequence as its Holy Grail). I use the vision of personalized medicine to talk about genomics *as* scientific fact, and argue for its ability to constitute subjectivity by virtue of the fetishism attendant on this fact. I will then reflect on what insights these facts can provide into understanding relationships of production, consumption, and subjectivity in biocapital.

The question of personalized medicine gets to the heart of what exactly postgenomic drug development is all about. The steps involved in what might be called a "genetic approach" to the diagnosis and treatment of disease could be said to consist of the following: first, the identification of a disease with a genetic component; second, the mapping of the gene(s) involved in the disease to specific chromosomal regions; and third, the identification of the involved gene(s). At this point, one could develop diagnostics to identify the presence or expression of the involved gene(s) in patients to determine predisposition to the disease in question; use the gene itself as a drug (gene therapy); or understand the underlying biology of the disease to "rationally" develop therapeutics to target the molecular mechanisms of disease etiology. The diagnostic tests could further be a precursor either to steps taken to prevent the onset of disease (which could either be interventionist or involve lifestyle changes) or to what is known as pharmacogenomics, which involves tailoring prescriptions and drug regimens to individuals based on their likely, genetically determined, response to these drugs.[16] Of course, some of these advances are likely to be more easily realized than others. The development of diagnostic tests, for instance, is relatively straightforward. Targeted therapeutics based on the underlying biology of disease are much more complicated, since diseases are always complicated multifactorial events that are difficult to understand at the molecular level, and further not necessarily easy to target and set right even if ever properly understood. Gene therapy, too, has been hindered by the lack of finding optimal methods of gene delivery and was further hindered by the death of a volunteer, Jesse Gelsinger, in a trial in 1999.

Most scientists, when they write or speak of "histories of" or "prospects for" genomics, do admit that some of these advances are more immediately realizable than others. Francis Collins and Victor McCusick's way of summarizing this is that "the rate of progress for applying a genetic approach to the diagnosis and treatment of each disease will be different depending on the research investment and the degree of biological complexity underlying the disease. . . . Diagnostic opportunities may then come along rather quickly, but will be of greatest clinical usefulness once prevention measures are developed that have proven benefit to those at high risk. . . . In general, full-blown therapeutic benefits from identification of gene variants will take longer to reach mainstream medicine" (Collins and McCusick 2001, 543). And yet I argue that it is this temporality — the different likely rates of realization of each of these genomic advances — that is the real issue and gets elided as a relatively linear and equivalent set of outcomes in accounts such as this. It is what might be called the therapeutic lag that is actually both the ethnographic window and the political terrain of postgenomic drug development, and it is the ensemble of events in the world that happen during the therapeutic lag that will determine whether, how, and what "full-blown" therapeutic development actually takes place, and when. Making what seem suspiciously like Soviet-style five-year and ten-year predictive plans, as Collins and McCusick do in their article, closes down this ethnographic window at the expense of relatively banal crystal-ball gazing (though, as I have argued in the previous chapter, such modes of prediction themselves have powerful influences in creating ethnographic windows and political terrains).[17]

Both intuitively and from the hype that surrounds personalized medicine, it seems evident that there are many potential benefits. There is the obvious potential benefit to patients if drug treatment can be tailored to each individual: more effective drugs, more precise prescriptions, and better therapeutic outcomes. But there are also benefits at various stages of drug development for companies involved in the process. These include a higher success rate, faster time to market, reduced costs, and greater market share.

In this section, I investigate the hype that proclaims these benefits, especially when set against the contradiction at the heart of the pharmacogenomic promise, which is the fragmentation of pharmaceutical markets, which in an era of personalized medicine would be defined not just by the disease but also by the target population. What I want to emphasize at the outset, however, is that, as mentioned in the previous chapter, an investigation of hype cannot simply be an exposé of hype's hollow promises. Rather, it enables one to track the intertwining of possible therapeutic benefit with market opportunity as the "win-win" of biocapital. I will elaborate on the argument for this intertwining, its effects and affects, in the next part of this chapter while developing the notion of genomic fetishism.

It is important at this point to escape conflating pharmacogenomics and personalized medicine. Personalized medicine is not equivalent to pharmacogenomics but is, rather, a combination of pharmacogenomics and predictive testing. Pharmacogenomics does not aim to provide deep insights into proximal causes of disease: its primary aim is to maximize the efficiency of therapeutic intervention, at the level both of pharmacokinetics (what the body does to the drug) and of pharmacodynamics (what the drug does to the body). Nonetheless, pharmacogenomics is likely to be the most immediately realizable and practical manifestation of personalized medicine for some time to come. The reason for this is that there are important differences between genetic effects on diseases and on drug action. The major difference has to do with the fact that the genetic etiologies of disease are often extremely complex. The combination of this complexity with the extreme rarity with which disease-causing mutations occur makes the therapeutic or predictive value of any single gene relatively limited. Rather, arrays of potential disease markers have to be determined or studied in an integrative fashion.

On the other hand, it has been realized that single-gene effects significantly modulate the action of many common drugs. These include genetic effects on metabolism that alter pharmacokinetics and effects on pathways of drug action that alter pharmacodynamics. Most of the former can be localized to genes that code for drug-metabolizing enzymes (DMEs), mainly belonging to the cytochrome P450 (CYP450) class of oxidative enzymes (though there is a small minority of drugs that do not undergo transformation by CYP450 before elimination). Therefore genetic studies of drug action are likely to provide more therapeutic insights of commercial value than similar genetic studies of the pathogenesis of disease.

The study of molecular genetic variation and its relationship to drug response is not new. There is, however, a historical shift from *pharmacogenetics*, which is a basic study of genetic variance, to *pharmacogenomics*, which is a commercially driven, industrialized, high-throughput science that has emerged consequent to the genomics revolution. Therefore the shift from pharmacogenetics to pharmacogenomics is a shift to an approach that is driven by *process* from one that was driven by *observation*. Once again, I emphasize the importance of the high-throughput nature of this enterprise, marked by speed, its desire and actualization, in industrializing life sciences such as genomics, as changing not just the paradigms of knowledge *production* but also, as I will elaborate later in the chapter, the very *nature* of the knowledge produced.

Pharmacogenetics as a concept was put forth as early as 1957 by Arne Motulsky, the term was coined in 1959 by Friedrich Vogel, and the first book on the subject was written as early as 1962 by Werner Kalow, in which Kalow documented several examples of inherited traits that he confirmed as affecting drug response or toxicity in human populations. Indeed, the long-entrenched notion of taking a family history as part of a conventional medical examination is itself based on an understanding that a patient's genetic makeup, however little known, has a bearing on decisions regarding therapeutic intervention.

The shift to a process-driven pharmacogenomic approach has the advantage of no longer requiring an a priori detection of an altered phenotype. In other words, one does not have to have pathology before studying the underlying genetic causes; one can study genetic variability to predict future pathology (and I will elaborate on this in the next section). The major driving force behind this shift is largely technological, with the availability of high-throughput methods for genetic analysis.

There are three steps to a pharmacogenomic process. The first step is the *discovery and definition of the multiple variations within genes*. A powerful marker that enables such discovery is the single nucleotide polymorphism (SNP), which is described in chapter 1. After discovery, SNPs must be *correlated* with clinically documented variations in drug response. They can then be used to develop *diagnostic tests* to determine whether or not a patient has a genetic profile that is predicted to correlate to a specific drug response.

The process leading from the analysis of genetic variations to the creation of the best drugs as a consequence of that analysis has three steps: *target identification*, *target characterization*, and *target validation* (Jazwinska 2001). Each of these steps correlates to different technologies and business models. Most important for my larger arguments about biocapital, however, is the manifestation of a basic contradiction of speed and information when one tracks these different steps. This is that the bottleneck quickly shifts away from being a problem of inadequate information to being one of too much information.

Target identification is the conventional (one can now almost say "historical") conception of the role of genomics, made famous by what I call "first-generation" genome companies, or target ID companies. However, within a year after the generation of the working draft sequence of the human genome, and five to seven years into the lives of many of these companies, it became clear that target identification had ceased to be the major bottleneck in drug discovery and development through genomics. In fact, target identification has created a host of new problems, in large measure because of its success: the problem now is not generating new targets as much as it is trimming early discovery portfolios to manageable proportions and identifying which targets have the largest probability of success. Further, the identification of molecular defects is useful in early diagnosis of disease and gives clues about the biochemical pathways through which disease onset progresses. However, there is no guarantee that this information is in any way useful in the development of therapy.

Target characterization can be defined as the use of genetic analysis to define the degree of variation within a gene encoding a potential drug target (Jazwinska 2001). Thus target characterization involves first the definition of variants and second the definition of the *impacts* of variants. A recent analysis of variation in seventy-five candidate genes involved in hypertension identified SNPs in seventy-four of them (Halushka et al. 1999). This study suggests that there is a high likelihood of finding genetic variation in any gene selected as a potential drug target.

Target validation can be defined as a process by which knowledge of genetic variation is exploited to show an association between particular targets and disease processes (Jazwinska 2001). This is typically useful in saving costs during clinical trials by predicting before the clinical trials process whether the pharmaceutical intervention might have a desired therapeutic effect by demonstrating the association between target gene variation and clinical process. Target validation steps are twofold: first, the identification of well-characterized clinical populations of specific relevance; and second, the identification of variants within or close to the test gene.

The technical challenge of pharmacogenomics is very different from genomic sequencing. The focus here moves away from new gene *discovery* (which underlies the business models of the target ID companies) and toward the elucidation of correlations and statistical analyses between genetic variations and various types of response. In other words, pharmacogenomics and personalized medicine constitute a different scientific-corporate enterprise from the genomics of 1999–2000.

So far in this section, I have talked about how the *upstream* scientific and corporate issue for genomics, as it comes to be about personalizing medicine, shifts away from the identification of targets to their characterization and validation. Next I want to theoretically ponder some of the subjective consequences of these emergent sorts of genomic knowledge operating as scientific fact. The ability to create diagnostic tests based on information relating to genetic variability is a major part of this shift, and the impetus to move further toward a testing society originates in upstream technoscientific and business genome worlds.

As I have argued, pushing through a bottleneck in genomic drug discovery can, by virtue of the amount of information generated, create a fresh bottleneck. This has been the case with target identification, which has created the need for new methods that can actually characterize the targets identified. A major reason why target identification is only a very preliminary step toward personalized medicine is that identifying a target provides no guarantee that it can be targeted therapeutically. With the explosion of SNP identification technologies, another bottleneck is arising: a huge volume of SNP information, with no guarantee that any particular SNP will be predictive of an actual therapeutic target, or even therapeutic response at a chromosomal level. It is in this context that *haplotyping* assumes increased importance.

A haplotype is a combination of SNPs on a particular chromosome, usually within a particular gene. Common haplotypes exist because in most genes SNPs tend to be coinherited. While SNP genotyping has many benefits in terms of generating information that could be used toward personalized medicine, haplotyping has greater promise for two reasons. First, haplotype analysis greatly reduces the complexity of genetic analysis. Due to linkage disequilibrium, only a small number of haplotypes are generally found in a population, in contrast to the up to ten million SNPs that are said to exist in the genome. For example, thirteen SNPs have been identified in the β2-adrenergic receptor. Theoretically, these could assort into $2^{13}$, or 8,192, haplotypes. However, the β2-adrenergic receptor has been found to have only twelve haplotypes, with only four of these found commonly in the population. More importantly, haplotypes are thought to predict gene *activity* more precisely than genotypes. This is because individual polymorphisms may have different effects on the functioning of a gene. Therefore the predictive therapeutic value of any single SNP within a gene is relatively limited. A haplotype integrates these effects and thereby provides the *sum of the effects of all the polymorphisms*. The move from genotyping to haplotyping is a move away from assaying arrays of potential mutations and toward generating integrative markers of disease (Housman and Ledley 1998).

However, there are issues affecting the practicality of integrating haplotype analysis into a program of therapeutic development. Haplotypes are markers. They are closely linked to disorders, but that does not mean that they contribute to them. Therefore haplotype analysis is most likely to be used as a diagnostic tool, as it has been in the past.

Hence haplotypes could diagnose likely inheritance of a disease but still be poorly predictive of drug response. In other words, there is a logical move toward a diagnostic test as an endpoint of personalized medicine from an upstream perspective as haplotypes emerge as manageable scientific knowledge about genetic variability as it corresponds to chromosomal location and coinheritance.

To sum up: on the one hand, there is the downstream therapeutic molecule, with therapeutic intervention often being viewed as the endpoint of the practice of medicine. On the other hand, there is an upstream ensemble of diagnosis, prognosis, monitoring, and management of disease, what might collectively be called preventive medicine. It is between these upstream and downstream assemblages of objects and practices that historical and ethnographic windows open up to strategic praxis on the parts of the involved players, and analytic intervention on the parts of social theorists.

Meanwhile, both upstream and downstream assemblages have invested in them significant corporate interests with considerable capital and political muscle. While the emergent diagnostics industry is heavily invested in preventive medicine, downstream pharmaceutical companies are heavily invested in therapeutic development.

One can see, however, that there is a pressure on pharmaceutical companies that stems from a downstream logic to move *therapeutic* intervention to earlier and earlier stages of disease manifestation, indeed toward a regime of therapeutic intervention at the *suggestion* rather than explicit manifestation of disease, which has been seen particularly in the increased prescription and use of psychotropic drugs such as Prozac for depression, or Ritalin for the recently constructed "epidemic" of attention-deficit hyperactivity disorder (ADHD) (see, for instance, Kramer 1997; Healy 1997, 2002). This move, I argue on the basis of my analysis of the emergence of the upstream diagnostic ensemble as key corporate actors in the practice of medicine, stems not just from a desire on the part of pharmaceutical companies to enlarge markets but also from a manifestation of the pharmaceutical industry *acting as its own insurance industry*. The only way for big pharmaceutical companies to insure against diagnostic encroachment on the domain of therapeutics is to shift the domain of what counts as disease into earlier and earlier stages of its manifestation—to the point, of course, that new diseases often get created, and old ones get significantly redefined on the basis of shifting the moment that demands therapeutic intervention. This is a rationality of "self"-governance—a larger cultural shift in notions of when it is desirable to care for the self, through diagnostic testing and therapeutic intervention—that in fact originates very much in a governance *of* selves by the complex of strategic actors that constitute the emerging moment of postgenomic medicine.

I have focused here on the productive aspect of personalized medicine, looking at what sort of technoscientific production it is, and what the various stakes are for the producers. In the second part of the chapter, I will explore how genomics quite literally translates to consumers as a set of scientific-corporate practices and consumables, but also, more importantly, as scientific fact. I continue by looking at the *affects* of genomics, as corporate venture and as science, thereby highlighting the importance of understanding and theorizing *risk* as the defining heuristic with which to make sense of the way bio-capital constitutes both business opportunity and subjectivity.

### SNP Chips, Genomic Fetishism, and Polymorphic Subjects

I now explore the question of the relationship of epistemic shifts to the constitution of subjects where scientific knowledge derives its authority from its perceived objectivity, making this a question, similar to the one asked by Joseph Dumit in his analysis of objective self-fashioning, of the relationship between what he calls the objective body and the lived body (Dumit 1998). It is a question that demands an understanding of the functioning of facts as "facts-in-the-world" (86).

My argument is that it is the interstices between epistemic shift and subject constitution that need to be examined to understand the *constructed* and *contingent* relationship between knowledge and subjectivity, in this case between the subject (as in discipline) and the subject (as in constituted person) of genetics. My question is therefore concerned with the *mechanisms of articulation* of the "bio" and the "social" that allow emergent manifestations of bio-sociality. I ask these questions around the node of SNPs.

I will start by making the distinction between the study of mutants and mutagenesis. Mutants have always been important to genetics. But the ability to generate mutants intentionally is quite a different thing and has become more and more directed, more pinpointed, through the course of the past century. In a mutation, a gene gets knocked out. Before recombinant DNA technology, however, there was no way of knowing where in the gene the mutation had occurred, and how — single base change, insertion of DNA, or deletion of DNA. Gene cloning and sequencing therefore empowered mutagenesis by allowing the knocked-out gene to be *localized*. This means that recombinant DNA technology (RDT) allows the isolation and study of *single* genes. Mutagenesis is not new, but the specificity and *site-directedness* that RDT allows bring the gene into play as the mutated subject. While specificity is the key idea here, the level of specificity operates at the level of the individual gene.

In other words, mutants now are not there to just be studied: they can precisely, at the level of genetic engineering, be *created*.

A mutant subject cannot exist without the formulation of the corresponding concept of the wild type. Now "wild type" is an interesting term: a term that in its most simplistic guise is used to denote an organism that is not mutated, but is often understood, by its very construction, to denote an organism as it is found in the wild. A wild-type organism is, however, very much an artificial construct. Nature is extremely unlikely to have wild types (indeed, the very concept of a genotype that is not mutated is an anachronism, since genotypes themselves have arisen as a consequence of both natural selection and mutation), only a range of uncontrolled and uncharacterized mutants, some with a greater selective advantage than others. "Wild-type" strains, therefore, like so many other constructions of the laboratory, are analytical tools rather than replicas of nature, as their name would have us assume. Equally, and more important for the argument here, they are *essential* analytical tools in a world of mutagenesis, where the mutant needs to be in oppositional relationship to a "normal" referral point, of which the mutant is an error. But a mutant, further, is an error of a particular type — a type that has *value* attached to it. Mutants are not just different from wild types; they are *deviants* from the wild-type norm.

A wild type, therefore, is not a "normal" entity, in the sense that it is not an entity that one would normally find in nature. But it is a norm. A norm, according to Georges Canguilhem, "does not exist, it plays its role which is to devalue existence by allowing its correction" (Canguilhem 1989 [1966], 77). A norm is also, as Jacques Derrida points out, an equivocal concept, since "it encompasses both the concept of moral, ethical, political law as well as the concept of factuality. The norm is also sometimes imposed as a fact, in the name of which one normalizes precisely" (Derrida 2002b, 199). A wild type serves as the reference point compared to which mutants are devalued.

Mutants are studied to understand relationships between gene structure and function. A far-fetched, but certainly not untrue, extension of this function in the context of the laboratory-clinic interface is that mutants can thus tell scientists of disease. A state of not being well is identified, studied, and treated as a disease because people get sick and tell doctors about their disease. A way of understanding disease without requiring people to fall ill first is to use model organisms—so scientists *create* mutants (or study appropriately existing ones) so that abnormalities can better be detected and understood when manifested as human disease. The mutant helps advance knowledge about normal organisms. And that is where the distinction between the normal and the norm can be teased out: a mutant needs a wild-type nonmutant in order for it to be a mutant, but the insights into normality that the mutant provides are not necessarily facets of "normality" that any particular wild type actually exhibits—it is an idealized normality that is only itself defined in terms of the "pathological" mutant, a normality that is defined not in terms of natural occurrence but in terms of absence of pathology. In other words, a mutant serves to tell us how a nonmutant would not work, rather than telling us how a wild type works. Lab mutants, therefore, operate on a *terrain* of normality versus pathology and have attached to them the (generally negative) *value* of deviance with respect to a referent norm. The minute one grants that genes, and pathways, interact with one another, one must acknowledge the existence of feedback effects mediated by various components on the activities of others. Mutants, as metaphorical constructions, and genes, as conceptual vantage points, offer vital perspectives on biological systems, but these are at best partial perspectives that pose as complete.

One limitation, then, of a mutant or single-gene view of the world is that phenotypes tend to get equated with the existence of single genes, rather than with their interactions with others. The other limitation is that one needs a phenotype in the first place to get talking. In the language of mutants, if you do not have a phenotype, you do not have a conversation.

The shift from classical to molecular genetics accords a new place for, and understanding of, mutants: from anomalous organisms that help understand evolution to specifically altered genes that help simulate deviance in order to understand normality. But when one goes beyond the study of model organisms to the understanding of diseases in humans, many of the imperfections in the mutant's-eye view of the world could be damning imperfections. Even without entering the nature-nurture debate, the fact that most diseases are polygenic makes it impossible to evolve an understanding of human disease on the basis of human gene information that does not take into account the multiple biological interactions responsible.

There is a discontinuity in molecular biology that allows this necessary discontinuity in perspective, and that is the SNP. At one level, the discontinuity from mutant to SNP is one that has technological causes and consequences: SNPs become possible and feasible markers because of the Human Genome Project, but they are simultaneously landmarks that make human genome sequencing both easier and potentially more lucrative (in terms of helping generate pegs on which the translation from gene sequence to therapy can be made). There is a subtle change in perspective that SNPs bring about from mutants. An equation of one mutation with one phenotype in the former case gets subtly altered to become an equation of a number of variations with the probability of a particular phenotype. SNPs, therefore, bring about discursive and conceptual shifts in the language and understanding of molecular biology. Further, SNPs bring a different perspective to light, a perspective that has to do with *risk* rather than deviance. SNPs talk about susceptibilities and predispositions, rather than abnormalities or aberrations. The key difference between mutations and SNPs is one between *deviation* and *difference*. Obviously SNPs, unlike mutants, do not show a strict correlation between individual phenotype and genetic aberration. A human who is considered in every respect to be healthy could well have variations at the nucleotide level, but these variations do not constitute deviance against a constructed standard of normality — they do, however, constitute the possibility of risk, of future pathology. A SNP is not pathology but *anomaly*: something that, according to Canguilhem, can "shade into disease but does not constitute one" (1989 [1966], 140).

SNPs are not about the simple correlation of a mutation to its phenotype: they are about variations in genomes, rather than differences in genes; and variations within and between whole populations, rather than differences between a "normal" and a "mutant" individual. In terms of level, therefore, SNPs provide a peculiar bifocal perspective. On the one hand, the immediate level of analysis is even smaller than the gene, it is the nucleotide; but on the other hand, it is an analysis that can only be undertaken when the nucleotide is set in the context of whole populations. Few SNPs are likely to be involved in disease, the way a mutation is involved in giving rise to an aberrant phenotype: what SNPs allow is the identification of patterns of inheritance that affect health.

This implies a contradiction at the very heart of the sorts of knowledge that personalized medicine relies on, a contradiction that has to do with the fact that this is a knowledge gained from an increasingly molecular understanding of life itself. The more things get reduced to their molecular components, however, the more one needs to rely on statistical, population-based data to "individualize" therapy. This means that one can individualize therapy *only* on the basis of population classifications. These are classifications that are extremely difficult to construct, as Jenny Reardon's work on the history of the Human Genome Diversity Project shows (see Reardon 2001). In fact, what is at stake from the beginning is the question of what in fact "populations" are, as opposed to "races," or other forms of ethnic categorization, in order to be subjects for genetic analysis.

These dilemmas of classifying populations, and defining what sorts of categorizations need to be assumed as "populations" in the first place before the act of classifying *within* those categories can take place, are particularly evident in India, where something like race, as a "natural" unit within which to classify populations, does not have the same ready-made social-scientific valence as it does in the United States. Classifying populations for genetic studies on the basis of caste is equally fraught, both politically and epistemologically, and is made more complicated by the fact that kinship patterns, which would profoundly affect the purported genetic "homogeneity" of the population in question, vary widely between different parts of India (North Indian communities being traditionally more exogamous than South Indian communities). And yet classifying populations for genetic studies is essential for a genomic endeavor, such as that of the Indian state as driven by CBT, which has identified population genetics as the way to establish India's presence in global genomic knowledge production. Research at CBT has population genetics as its cornerstone, which means that researchers at CBT really need to be able to define what populations are in order even to begin to tackle the scientific agenda that they have set for themselves.

Such definitions, I discovered, are usually made by taking recourse to the anthropological survey of India's voluminous atlas *People of India* (Singh 1992). However, sometimes more random and violent classificatory methods are adopted. Thus I encountered one project that claimed to be an attempt to discover the genetic differences between Aryans and Dravidians, categories that are not merely politically fraught (especially when expressed in those very terms) but also, in the real world, quite difficult to establish, since they exclude a wide range of non-Brahmin, non-Dravidian people who might well trace back to "Aryan" and "Dravidian" (or some combination of both) roots. The DNA samples of "Aryans" and "Dravidians" that this particular researcher was collecting, further, came from students who were identified as belonging to one or the other category in nearby Delhi University: a particularly cosmopolitan site for sample collection, in all probability teeming with donors containing all manner of genetically hybrid DNA. Six months into the project, this researcher, himself a Brahmin (and thereby, I suppose, of the population category "Aryan") abandoned it because he could not find genetic differences of statistical significance between the two groups. Instead of acknowledging this as a possible consequence of the genetic *similarity* between different population groups, as Richard Lewontin (1993), for instance, argues, this researcher indicated his frustration that the samples probably came from "genetically impure" people, descendants of such — to the researcher — unthinking ancestors who intermarried across these wonderfully convenient (and probably for the researcher, sacrosanct) population binaries. It was hard to discern whether this researcher felt greater contempt because his experiments could not provide elegant answers to the fundamental genetic differences between Aryans and Dravidians, or at the thought that the Aryan forebears of his experimental subjects might have been "contaminated" by Dravidian blood.[18]

While much of this chapter focuses on genetic determinism as *individualized* (an idea that plays out especially in regimes of personalized medicine), the purpose of this story is to show that myths of genetic homogeneity among populations are an equally powerful constituent of this determinist knowledge-producing enterprise. Indeed, this tension between the genetic myths that underlie population genomic projects that seek ultimately to be vehicles of personalized medicine, and the individualized risk of genetic determinism as a consequence of regimes of personalized medicine that imply personalized DNA diagnostic profiles, is seen equally powerfully in the controversial case of the Icelandic Health Sector Database of DeCode Genetics. DeCode was a company that was pitched as unique because its DNA samples came from the "genetically homogeneous" Icelandic population. On the one hand, the myth of the *value* of genetic homogeneity for population genetics experiments has been questioned by entities such as the Irish company Hibergen, which claims that it can still generate population genetic information as valuable as DeCode's even though the Irish population is less genetically homogeneous than the Icelandic is supposed to be.[19] The idea has further been questioned by population genetics enterprises such as CBT, which bases its business model on the assumption, in contradiction to DeCode, that the genetic *heterogeneity* of the Indian population, coupled with large Indian family sizes and as yet very little genetic counseling, allows CBT to do the sorts of extensive linkage analyses across families that are just not possible to the same extent in places like Iceland, Ireland, or the United States. On the other hand, the myth of genetic homogeneity itself seems to be getting eroded by the sorts of knowledge DeCode has started producing, which suggests, rather as the experiments of the CBT researcher I mentioned do, that more contaminating mischief was probably happening in the Icelandic ports with sailors of non-Icelandic stock than the Icelandic myths of genetic homogeneity are willing to admit.

Of course, the purpose of this argument is not simply to show how classificatory categories may take recourse to mythical and ideological conceptions of pure population histories that are debunked by the very impure stories that the DNA tells. It is also to show the epistemic violence that would be enacted when these classificatory artifacts might start operating as scientific fact (see Bowker and Star 2000)—a violence that might very well have both been enacted, and been more than simply epistemic, had the CBT researcher in fact claimed to find genetic differences between Aryans and Dravidians.

But a little bit more about discontinuity—how do discontinuities, and shifts in concepts, metaphors, and perspectives, occur? One way I have alluded to is the technological. But another way of looking at discursive shifts within science is by locating them in the context of discursive shifts outside science, as

Ludwig Fleck's studies on the course of syphilis research do (Fleck 1979 [1935]). A similar relationship between macrocultural anxieties and the rhetorical practices of science might be posed for the risk discourse surrounding SNPs by situating them in the contemporary societal context of what Ulrich Beck calls the "risk society."

In his book *Risk Society*, Beck (1986) describes how contemporary society can be visualized not in terms of the class-based logic of wealth distribution but in terms of a new inverse logic of risk distribution. Two ideas here are significant in the context of this chapter: first, the importance in contemporary (at least Western) society of having a *knowledge* of the risk one is at; and second, the importance of the breakdown of traditional class alliances and a concomitant *individuation* of society. Although the risks of disease that SNPs foretell are not specifically risks of modernization, the importance of SNPs highlights the pervasive influence of risk discourse in late modernity. Indeed, comparing the risk discourse around SNPs with the risk discourse that Beck traces shows how the discourse that arose in the 1960s and 1970s around environmental issues has been displaced by one intensely associated with lifestyle and genetics.

A number of facets of Beck's vision of risk society play interestingly with a SNP perspective on the world. For Beck, risk society is a society that always has potential catastrophe within its calculus — the "exceptional condition," according to him, "becomes the norm" (Beck 1986, 24), as indeed is the case with SNPs, where variability, rather than a constructed "normality," is the norm. Second, according to Beck, "science's monopoly on rationality is broken" (29). And so with SNPs: SNPs do not tell us the *truth* about a human condition as much as they express probabilities of how that human condition might evolve in the future — SNPs ultimately operate within a framework of probability statements. For Beck, risk society has "no perfect system, no perfect human being" (30); and indeed, SNPs do not have room for wild types.

The other important perspective is the individuation of contemporary risk society, in which there are no "natural" class-based alliances. The risks associated with possible disease are intensely individual risks, and theoretically each individual has his or her own profile for risk or probability of illness that could be calculated from a SNP profile.

The therapeutic intervention that is envisaged by SNPs is personalized medicine. As the contemporary discursive terrain of knowledge production is also inevitably the capitalist terrain of value generation, each probabilistically interpellated polymorphic subject becomes not just a target of possible intervention but also a consumer-in-waiting. Moreover, the *possibility* of personalized medicine is *insurance* (for the patient, against future illness), just as the always already existent patient-as-consumer is insurance for the pharmaceutical company. As Francois Ewald (1991) has argued, the concept of risk is deeply tied into the concept of insurance, to the extent that risk itself is capital. In other words, SNPs are implicated in two distinct types of risk discourse: the patient's risk of future disease (the individuation that Beck speaks of) is inseparable from the pharmaceutical company's risk of high investment in therapeutic development that must be realized in an eventual commodity.

My argument so far has been that a particular discursive-epistemic shift allows a reconfiguration of subject categories away from normality and pathology toward variability and risk, thereby placing *every* individual within a probability calculus as a potential target for therapeutic intervention. There is, however, an abstraction at play here, one that depends on the fetish of scientific fact, as follows.

The fetishism of scientific knowledge operates by mechanisms similar to Marxian commodity fetishism.[20] Indeed, the moment of mystification through fetishism is less through the "illusory" appearance of scientific knowledge as *true* than through the appearance as *natural* of something that is contingent and socially constructed. I call this mystification of scientific knowledge as a natural thing-in-itself that merely awaits ready-made discovery rather than the material-semiotic-conceptual outcome of real historical processes of knowledge production *epistemic fetishism*.[21]

The ideological power of epistemic fetishism comes from the fact that the mystification that elevates a statement established by rigorous scientific method into that natural thing-in-itself, the Scientific Fact, is invisible. Genetic determinism acquires the status of scientific "fact" at the same time that scientists hasten to tell us that SNPs are merely a set of probability statements. The irony — and power — of epistemic fetishism is that probability statements start operating with determinate legitimacy. Probability statements therefore acquire performative force. When confronted with the question of what one *does* when confronted with a probability statement, the absence of an obvious response allows the probability statement to harden into a reified statement of prophecy. Therefore it is a fetishism that is at once an operation of *naturalization* (the denial of the history of construction of a statement) and an operation that, while naturalizing the statement, shifts it from being a statement of *association* to one of *causality*.

Yet statements alone are often necessary yet insufficient to in-form subjects, which require material allies. It is the articulation of the deterministic statement to or as a representational device, the DNA chip, that ties the statement not just to the constitution of facts but to the constitution of subjects.

"Preventive medicine" is an assemblage of technologies, business models, and health management practices that has diagnostics as central to its calculus. One of the many things genomics promises us, as I have been arguing, is the possibility of diagnostic development without the concomitant development of therapeutics. In itself, the DNA chip *is* a decoding device, one that will allow association between gene expression and disease predisposition and will therefore be used to develop diagnostic tests, and some of its most promising, and potentially profitable, uses stem from this fact.

My analysis of epistemic fetishism so far owes much to Donna Haraway's concept of gene fetishism (see Haraway 1997). Gene fetishism, operating as it does in a capitalist framework that naturalizes gene-as-property, is a capitalist fetish and yet is distinct from commodity fetishism. For Haraway, the moment of the fetish is not just the naturalization but the *becoming corporeal* of the gene as not just a thing-in-itself but a thing-in-itself that stands in for and completely represents what is essentially a relationally constituted subject (whether gene or organism). I would like to take Haraway's notion a little further, to argue that gene fetishism is a form of *subjective* fetishism, in which the fetishism of the object (which is simultaneously, in the case of SNPs, the chip, the information on the chip, and the fact represented by the information on the chip) operates *not by alienation* — the assumption of a transcendental thing-in-itself status — *but by interpellation.*[22]

It is through the constitution of a polymorphic subject that the ideological-scientific "fact" of genetic determinism gets constituted. However, this subject constitution occurs in an epistemic and ideological space in which the determinants — information, representational device, and subject — are always already overdetermined as "naturally" potential commodities. In other words, the oppositional tension between commodity fetishism as alienating from subjective association, and noncapitalist ("precapitalist") fetishism as intensely subject associated, implodes through scientific-capitalist technologies of representation such as SNPs, SNP databases, and DNA chips. Subjects get constituted through genetically determined probability statements simultaneous to their constitution as future probable targets of individual therapeutic intervention. In the latter case, they are constituted as *capital subjects* — as (future) buyers of (future) therapies. Thereby the ideology of the inevitability, beneficence, and naturalness of the pharmaceutical market as the means to therapy is constituted simultaneously with the constitution of subjects and of scientific facts. Genomic fetishes are market(able)s.

To explore the notion of fetishism further, I analyze an extended quote from William Pietz:

> If the notion of fetishism is to have any useful specificity, it must refer to objective phenomena that are valued with an exceptional intensity by individuals or by a society in general. The history of the discourse about fetishism suggests that fetishes may be conceived as excessively valued material objects upon which the very existence and identity of an individual, cultural group, or society, is experienced as depending. This would in turn suggest that a critique of fetishism should begin with a materialist phenomenology of historically particular fetish objects. The embodiment relations and institutional structures articulated by such inquiry into socially valued objects should then follow two paths: first, a Marxian analysis of such objects should locate their excessive valuation in the conflicts and contradictions between the structures of social power reified in the multiplicity of institutions that compose a given social formation; second, the intensely personal investment of individual identities in such objects should be studied by relating them to those arguments and those dramatized scenarios of the libidinal imagination wherein people express their own understanding of the ground of their own self-worth (or lack of it). That is, the critique of fetishism should begin with value objects and then trace these forms of value to objective structures of social power and to subjective conceptions of personal worth. (Pietz 1993, 558–59)

There are two imploding articulations of fetishism that are completely resonant with the imploding articulations of value in a political economic and
epistemic structure such as biocapital. These concern the Marxian notion of
commodity fetishism and the Freudian notion of fetishism.

An analysis of fetishism must begin by acknowledging two important ideas.
The first is that while the fetish is a mode of abstraction, it has to be understood and traced in historical, materialist terms. Indeed, fetishes are abstractions *of* the material, referring to the ways in which mundane material objects
are imbued with mystical, magical power. And thus the second is that fetishes
are *lively*, especially when the objects of fetishism — in this case, of capital,
commodities, and scientific facts — are themselves as emergent and at stake as
they are.

The "objective phenomena" that are valued in genomic fetishism are those
that provide capitalism (as a system and as a set of material objects of currency)
and science (as episteme and as a set of facts, in this case about "life itself") with
their supreme authority. These are phenomena that are valued with equal
intensity, albeit in different ways, in the United States and India. In the United
States, the fetishism of both the free market and scientific fact occurs by their
naturalization, the free market as the only successful political economic formation of our times, and scientific fact as always already "true" rather than contingent and provisional. In India, the fetishism of both manifests in the ways in
which they become objects of explicit desire. The "excessively valued" objects,
in both cases, are simultaneously material and abstract — commodities *and* a
free market system or imaginary; tangible information, biological material,
therapeutic objects, research facilities *and* "culture of innovation."

What Pietz argues for in a critique of fetishism is a "materialist phenomenol-
ogy of historically particular fetish objects." In other words, a useful handle on
which to base a critique of fetishism is to locate the fetish in an emblematic
object that might itself be the object of fetishism or somehow represent the
fetishes whose critiques are at stake. In this chapter, one such object that I have
used is the DNA chip.

What is so useful about the DNA chip as an object through which to study
genomic fetishism is that, as an instance of what Donna Haraway (1997)
would call a constitutive "material-semiotic" object of biocapital, the DNA chip

provides multiple grounds and directions for analysis. Material-semiotic objects, as Haraway shows, cannot simply be described as objects-in-the-world by referring to their objective properties, but nor can they be analyzed without serious attention to those very properties. The DNA chip, for instance, would not be what it is if it were not miniaturized, not a silicon wafer substrate, or not a template for hybridization because of DNA molecules stuck to its surface by a proprietary photolithographic process, not least because this material nature of the chip allows it to be patented and made a *commodity* of knowledge production. Equally, the DNA chip points simultaneously in two directions that a critique of fetishism needs to consider—"embodiment relationships" and "institutional structures."

Pietz mentions a number of terms essential to a critique of fetishism that, when applied to genes, genomes, DNA chips, venture science, genomics, or drug development, point nicely to the implosion of capitalism with "life itself" that I am tracing in my analysis. These terms include "valuation," "institutions," "personal investment," "individual identities," and "libidinal imagination."

Value refers simultaneously to capitalist surplus value generation and to the ethical and moral values that operate in the realm of the normative. However, epistemologies, especially when they are explicitly about knowledge of "life" or "humanness," also have considerable implications for configuring individuals as subjects of particular sorts. When the outcome of an emergent epistemic configuration is something like personalized medicine, the stakes for individual identity formation and subjectivity are evidently acute.

Therefore, as Pietz concludes in the quoted passage, the implosion of these different regimes of value—of the free market and of the life sciences, in this case—relates simultaneously to "structures of social power" and "subjective conceptions of personal worth."

On the one hand, the chip reveals distinctive markers of genetic traits or predispositions for diseases; at the same time, it is acknowledged that there is no direct or simple cause-and-effect relationship between the markers and their statistically corresponding genetic traits or disease predispositions. As Marx already identified, the reification occurs not just because of the use value of the chip but because of its potential for exchange, in this case, specifically, its nature as a promissory instrument involved in the risk-laden raising of venture capital without which the current biotechnology research cannot proceed. Indeed, it is impossible to disentangle the nature of the scientific "fact" provided by the chip—of predispositions to future illness—without looking at such "fact" as itself an authoritative form of information about DNA sequence variability between individuals and populations, where the logic of diagnosing such future illness is completely intertwined with the logic of the diagnostic and preventive medicine industries *as* business models. If genomic fetishes have everything to do with both the scientific and the market frameworks within which they are generated, then life, in the techno-corporate worlds of biocapital, is always already a business plan.

### Consumer Power and Capital Subjects

I wish now to emphasize the importance of generating a more elaborate theory of consumption without reducing capitalist dynamics today to the dynamics of consumption. Specifically, I argue for the need to understand new modes of consumption of surplus, see whether and how surplus consumption is a defining dynamic of biocapital, and further position risk distribution as itself a perverse form of surplus consumption.

I begin my analysis by recounting Marx's analysis of surplus *production*. The key source of exploitation that Marx identifies in the capitalist system is its generation of surplus value. To understand how surplus value leads to exploitation, one must first understand that the fundamental economic contradiction that Marx is trying to resolve is the question of how an exchange of equivalents can lead to a generation of surplus, and then to understand Marx's concept of labor power.

That it is labor power rather than labor that the worker exchanges with the capitalist is crucial because labor power, as creative *potential*, is *not* predetermined value—it has the potential for generating surplus ingrained within it. Therefore the apparent act of equivalent exchange—worker's labor for capitalist's wages—has hidden within it an element of nonequivalence, because wages are fixed remuneration, but the labor, which is actually labor power, is the potential for the creation of value that is *over and above* the money expended in wages.[23] Surplus value, "in general, is value in excess of the equivalent" (Marx 1973 [1858], 324; hereafter cited in the text as *Grundrisse*). Wages therefore constitute for the capitalist *productive consumption*:

> Living labor belongs just as much among capital's conditions of existence as do raw material and instrument. Thus it reproduces itself doubly, in its own form, [and] in the worker's consumption, but only to the extent that it reproduces him as living labor capacity. . . . The payment of wages is an act of circulation which proceeds simultaneously with and alongside the act of production. Or, as Sismondi says from this perspective — the worker consumes his wages unreproductively; but the capitalist consumes them productively, since he gets labor in the exchange, which reproduces the wages and more than the wages. (*Grundrisse*, 676)

And further:

> If the worker needs only half a working day in order to live a whole day, then, in order to keep alive as a worker, he needs to work only half a day. The second half of the labor day is forced labor; surplus-labor. (*Grundrisse*, 324)

Especially when there is a reserve labor force, wages can tend toward the theoretical minimum amount of that which the worker needs to sustain him. As long as the worker is further not given enough to be able to not work, labor power is constantly renewable. This is how, therefore, the exchange of equivalents leads to the creation of surplus.

> By virtue of having acquired labor capacity in exchange as an equivalent, capital has acquired labor time — to the extent that it exceeds the labor time contained in labor capacity — in exchange *without equivalent*; it has appropriated alien labor time *without exchange* by means of the *form* of exchange. . . . The use-value of labor capacity, as value, is itself the value-creating force; the substance of value, and the value-increasing substance. In this exchange, then, the worker receives the equivalent of the labor time objectified in him, and gives his value-creating, value-increasing living labor time. (*Grundrisse*, 674; italics in original)

Marx therefore distinguishes between necessary and surplus labor-time, the former being the labor-time required for the worker to reproduce his means of existence, that is, the labor-time that goes into the production of use values. Everything over and above that is surplus labor-time and leads to surplus value for the capitalist. In order to generate maximal surplus value, the worker is (theoretically) only remunerated with enough wages to maintain his subsistence; the attempt of the capitalist is always to maximize surplus labor-time.[24] It is here that the exploitation of the worker takes place, in the creation of surplus value.

If the first step in developing an understanding of "consumption" relevant to biocapital (and I purposely hold consumption, for the time being, in quotes) is an understanding of surplus value from the productive process as being the node of exploitation of the worker, then the second step is to understand what is meant by subject, which, after all, does not at all necessarily mean worker. It is this gap between political economic, mainly Marxian, analyses of *labor* (as somehow having to do with class, proletariat, relations of production, and so on), and Foucauldian analyses of *subjectivity*, that needs to be bridged if one is to attempt, as I have been doing, a theorizing that is equally attentive to a Foucauldian politics of "life, labor, and language" as it is to a Marxian politics that emphasizes relations of production. In other words, one could say that the relationship between consumption and production is that consumption provides a subject for the object of production. Thus there is a coming together of questions of labor and subjectivity in the dialectical relationship of production to consumption.

In this context, I move back to talk about risk, the defining heuristic around which the consumer subjectivity of personalized medicine takes shape. It becomes important to explore how, as we move toward a diagnostic regime with the patient-in-waiting as always already a consumer-in-waiting, the question is not what "new subjectivity" is created in the process (as if that "subjectivity" can be defined entirely with reference to itself) but rather what changes occur in the entire system of normative structures that combine to create a subject *as* consumer, subjected to corporate evaluations and (their own and others') risk calculus. For this, it is important to talk about risk in terms of some of the questions I posed in the previous chapter regarding vision and hype.

Fundamentally, risk is implicated in a dialectical relationship between prophecy and contingency. Prophecy here means two things. First, it is a way of *calculating* contingency, through risk-benefit analyses, calculations of insurance premiums, investment decisions based on "due diligence," and so on, when the patient-consumer subject's risk of future illness can *only* be situated *as* risk when it is acknowledged that it is a risk that is calculated in the midst of a whole range of calculations of risk that see risk *as* capital. Second, it is a means of *taming* contingency, at least partly by conjuring a tendential future *through* the prophecy, very much as I described the operation of hype in the previous chapter. Therefore the calculation of risk as a mode of prophecy, which is always already a process of prophesizing as a mode of coming to terms with risk, could be about getting investors to invest in companies through investor pitches and story stocks but could also, *in the same way*, be about getting patients-in-waiting to undertake preemptive or prophylactic actions on the basis of diagnostic tests.

There are all sorts of risks to a company developing drugs that need to be adequately calculated and tamed. These include the possibility that a person might never develop a particular symptom and become a patient, and thereby never become part of the market that consumes a particular drug; that a drug in the pipeline might fail to get developed in the first place for the diagnosis because of a failed clinical trial; or that a particular drug that gets developed does not become the prescription of choice for a particular patient (market competition).

In other words, a diagnostic test, which is a marker of an individual's risk of future illness, is *also* a counter to offset the drug development company's risk of limited market size (not enough patients with a disease), limited market share (too many other drugs for that indication), and failures in drug development or adverse events after marketing. By changing the equation from a "healthy" patient to a "patient-in-waiting," by suggesting that *every* person, no matter how healthy, is possibly someone who might fall ill, the potential market for a drug is enlarged from "diseased" people to, conceivably, everyone with purchasing power, just as the domain of the therapeutic is enlarged progressively further back toward prophylactic uses consequent to the moment of diagnosis.

I make the argument here that this enlargement of the domain of the therapeutic, and of potential consumer markets, is enabled by the sorts of knowledge that genomics provides, and by the ways in which genomics inserts into a distinct regime of medicine called preventive medicine. However, the impetus to move toward a testing society and enlarge the market is evident in marketing strategies of biotech and pharmaceutical companies even without explicit recourse to genomic epistemologies or technologies. This is seen, for instance, in the marketing strategies of the so-called lifestyle drugs, the most profitable of which are cholesterol-lowering drugs such as Lipitor. Joseph Dumit analyzes such marketing strategies as part of what he calls a "pharmaceutical grammar" (Dumit 2003).

Therefore an enlargement of the therapeutic moment toward the diagnostic, and of therapeutic markets to include "patients-in-waiting" rather than just "diseased" patients, is not at all restricted to genomic-derived therapeutics. My argument here is that genomics, whose own grammar is articulated by representational devices such as the DNA chip, allows, by virtue of operating in probability statements and configuring all subjects as patients-in-waiting, a subject configuration that completely reinforces the drug development companies' need to show consumers-in-waiting and thereby to both create for themselves and prove to their investors the existence of future markets for their therapies. In other words, what genomics allows is an *epistemic rationality for a market discourse*.[25]

The key to the calculus of personalized medicine is that risk minimization and prevention are *not* dictated by the discriminatory practices of employers or health management organizations, or by the expert (and thereby, it is implied, forcible) interventions of physicians, but by patients themselves, who necessarily have to be configured as rational actors in the way that advertising conceives of them thus, and have to be given the appearance of "free choice" among a highly constrained set of options that are available, in any case, only to those who occupy the class position from which to exercise such "free" choice. Diagnostic tests and preventive or therapeutic options, in the business models of personalized and preventive medicine, become consumables in exactly the same way that soap or perfumes are. The DNA chip is precisely such a technology that creates "free" (in the utilitarian sense of having rational choices of self-governance) subjects of uncertainty, who are subjected to a rationality of perpetual possible consumption, and a rationality that simultaneously demands "rational" self-governance — a governance itself that is effected through further consumption.

In this situation, then, one confronts questions of what Foucault calls governmental rationality, or governmentality (Burchell et al. 1991). After all, "rational" consumer choice, as assumed by corporations selling to those consumers, cannot afford to be quite as banal or simplistic in its assumptions of consumer rationality as rational choice sociology or political science can, since the very future of the company is at stake if consumers act "irrationally." Indeed, there are clearly many ways in which people can respond to the results of genetic tests, as responses to Myriad's breast cancer tests for the *brca* genes has shown. Throughout this book I mention actors — including venture capitalists, entrepreneurs, pharmaceutical companies, biosocial agents, policymakers, and patients as/and consumers — who need constantly to calculate their futures precisely *because* of the difficulty of calculating them. The important question is how such governances articulate at and through different institutional sites, national contexts, and historical and strategic conjunctures. The consumer subject of biocapital is a form of neoliberal subject, no doubt, but it is important to remember that it is the *epistemology* of biocapital — what I have, in shorthand, referred to in the previous section as genomic fetishism — that is involved in this subject constitution.

Personalized medicine or genomics or drug development is not the teleological outcome of technoscientific progress, as scientists like Francis Collins and Victor McCusick portray it, but is ultimately an assemblage of technologies and epistemologies that are coproduced in tendential fashion along with the political economic grounds for their articulation, grounds that are overdetermined by global relations of capital and by the hegemony of the free market.[26] I try in this book to stay attentive both to the structural constraints that form these grounds and to the strategic and contingent articulations that give them shape.

## Conclusion

I have been arguing that biocapital implies an implosion of an emergent political economic regime with an emergent epistemic one, and in this chapter I have placed the question of the epistemic and technological implications of genomics at the forefront of analysis. This also continues my concern with language and the discursive, where I suggest that scientific fact, just like corporate promissory articulation, is a particular type of performative discourse that carries with it its own authenticity and authority by virtue of its factuality. That this factuality ties simultaneously into information about "life itself" and into an enterprise of drug development that is overdetermined as corporate implies reconfigurations in subjectivity, even a different grammar of "life," as credible futures we can all invest in.

This brings to the fore an analytics of risk, more broadly a need for calculation that is always already dually inflected—calculations by patients/consumers-in-waiting entwined with calculations by corporations. It is the relationship between these two forms of calculation that this and the previous chapter together attempt to put into relief. As Niklas Luhmann points out, "Modernity has influenced probability calculations just in time to maintain a fictionally created, dual reality. The present can calculate a future that can always turn out otherwise" (1998, 70). In the case of personalized medicine, this calculation is much more explicit, and also much more vexed, as the ethical dilemmas around genetic counseling make evident.[27]

In the case of personalized medicine, the phrase "a future that can always turn out otherwise" implies two simultaneous yet distinct figurations. The first is that, since the statement of genomic fact such as that foretold by the DNA chip is simply one of *probability*, the actual outcome is, in any given instance, ultimately contingent. For instance (as is already well documented), while the test for *brca* genes (markers for the risk of breast cancer) is the most popular, and most hyped, of genomic diagnostic tests, it is possible for people who have these genes to not develop breast cancer (though it is impossible to evaluate that "not" against the probabilistic statement of the diagnostic test beyond a "not yet"—the possibility of developing the disease always remains inscribed within the probability calculus of a person who has tested positive for these genes), just as it is possible for people who test negative on a *brca* test to develop breast cancer. Therefore it is quite possible for a future to always turn out "otherwise" from the probability indicated by a diagnostic test, *even without the test having been somehow erroneous.*

If the first reading of Luhmann's phrase points to the constant element of contingency in a statement of probability, the contingency that ultimately makes the probability statement *not* be a statement of prophecy, then the second points to the *calculability* of life that I have been arguing for. Personalized medicine can always make the future turn out otherwise, because *it indicates the possibility or necessity of action* that could make the future turn out otherwise. This action could be prophylactic therapeutic intervention (thereby enlarging the domain of the therapeutic, and increasing the market for companies developing drugs), already seen with cholesterol-lowering drugs, for instance, or through lifestyle changes. In other words, personalized medicine can make the "future turn out otherwise" by functioning as a *eugenic technology*.

This ability to explicitly calculate a future, to give it a quantifiable rationality, is the temporal inverse of the phenomenon of corporate promissory conjuration I described in chapter 3, which involves conjuring a future to create the present, instead of calculating in the present to create a particular future. Of course, there is an explicit risk calculus in conjuration, as well, especially when corporations or investors sink huge amounts of capital into ventures based on the belief that the promises of the future will in fact be realized. And of course, those futures could turn out otherwise as well, and the forward-looking statement is one form of insurance to protect against the consequences of that.

Luhmann argues that probability provides a "provisional foresight." I have argued that the moment of fetishism is when this provision is substituted for an understanding of determinacy, when probability *reifies* into prophecy, as it did in Richard Gibbs's speech on single-gene diseases that I recounted earlier in the chapter. Meanwhile, Derrida (2002b) reminds us that being situated in provisional worlds brings with it an obligation.

Derrida's deconstructive method is easily misread as a *failure* to respond, a *failure* to make decisions or effect closure. Rather, what deconstruction demands, as Gayatri Spivak (1976, 1985, 1988) points out, is the importance of acknowledging, and making explicit, the difficulty of closure, the slippery character of texts, analytic structures, or ethical dilemmas, in ways that make it imperative to act *in full knowledge of the provisional nature of one's actions*.[28] The aim of this chapter is to show how the provisional, risk-laden, probabilistic, indeed always deferred, nature of the operation of both scientific and corporate discourse in biocapital, and of the fetishistic maneuvers that attempt to stabilize these into firm, risk-minimizing statements of prophecy, as *not* deferred but eternal and without history, operate. This analysis is a provisional intervention to denaturalize these maneuvers of purification. Because it is within the space provided by provisional facts and probable futures that our lives are being configured.

This book is configured throughout by a simultaneous consideration of both the "economic" and the "epistemic," where the epistemic in particular is almost always articulated in writing, as discourse, as inscription. In other words, while the economic always already pertains to regimes of value, the epistemic always already pertains to the book. Meanwhile, value is always already configured as both capital and moral.

It is therefore impossible to analyze and study the economic, especially when the system in question is capitalist, without locating it squarely in the context of at least two other major historical and ideological formations. The first is religion, especially Christianity; the second is nation.

Capitalism, religion/Christianity, and the nation are, of course, three of the prime institutional and ideological edifices of modernity, and one of the reasons they have become such edifices is because they are, simultaneously, institutional *and* ideological. The relationship between capitalism and Christianity and their coproduction has been famously analyzed by social theorists such as Max Weber and Walter Benjamin (Weber 2001 [1930]; Benjamin 1996 [1922]), and indeed their mutual implication is suggested in the double sensibility of the word "value." However, like capitalism, Christianity is hardly immutable, and if Weber's Protestant ethic, as I argued in the previous chapter, is being replaced by a neoliberal capitalist ethic of the irrational exuberance of innovation, then Christianity itself might be said to have transformed, certainly in the United States, to an aggressive, salvationary, "born-again" form.[29]

Meanwhile, the relationship of the imagination of nation to the rise of capitalism, particularly print capitalism, has been famously documented by Benedict Anderson (1991 [1983]). At the same time, and in a fashion that, as Arvind Rajagopal (2001) argues is itself completely mediated, nationalism and religious consciousness reaffirm and reinforce each other in a fashion that is, across religions, evangelical in form.

The purpose of this book is not just to analyze the coproduction of epistemic and economic regimes with respect to one another but to situate these emergences in the context of understanding larger social structures and ideologies that are themselves emergent and at stake. This continues my emphasis on articulations, which, in chapter 3, focused on the discursive articulations of corporate public relations, and in this chapter focused on the ways in which these articulations in turn articulate with science as a discursive enterprise of *fact* production. In the next chapter, I explore the ways in which biocapital is embedded in salvationary and nationalist tropes and imaginaries, by making the argument that in the United States, one can explicitly see biocapital in terms of a "born-again" messianism, while in India, what becomes explicit is the relationship of these emergent assemblages in terms of concerns and debates around nationalism. This is not an attempt to set up a relativist binary of "salvation" versus "nation" between the United States and India but rather one, influenced by Weber's analysis of the multiple causalities that underlie emergent social forms, that shows how the grounds that condition the imaginaries of global techno-capitalist regimes are themselves shifting and at stake.

# 5. Salvation and Nation
*Underlying Belief Structures of Biocapital*

I begin this chapter with two illustrative tales of national pride, one Indian and one American. In addition to the high-tech software and biotech professionals who are the most powerful and visible part of the Indian diaspora in Silicon Valley are a large number of Sikh taxi drivers. Their often fierce sense of nationalism was reflected in a conversation I had with one of them as he drove me to a friend's house near Berkeley. As I spoke to him initially in Hindi, his heart immediately warmed to me. I learned that he had moved from Amritsar just three years previously and was pining for home. He asked me whether I planned to settle down in the United States, and I replied that while I would probably end up doing so, my heart was still in India. At this, he turned around, smiled broadly, and said, "Han bhai. Is behanchod desh mein reh rehke khoon bhi safed ho jaata hai" (Yes, brother. Staying in this sisterf——ing country too long turns even one's blood white). He refused to charge me for my ride, even though ferrying another Indian around must hardly have been a novelty for him in an area that has a huge concentration of Indian expatriates. And yet, as he said, "Apne mulk ke aadmi se kaise paise le sakte hain?" (How can I take money from someone who is from my country?).

For my second story, I shift setting to reflect on the recent spate of scandals in corporate America, through an account of a forum at the Kennedy School of Government, Harvard University, entitled "Corporate Fraud and Rattled Investors."[1] The speakers at this forum included Jon Corzine, Democratic senator from New Jersey and former CEO of Goldman Sachs; Richard Breeden, chairman of the Securities and Exchange Commission under the presidency of George Bush (Sr.); and Catherine Kinney, copresident of the New York Stock Exchange.

Unanimous among all the participants was the view that the corporate scandals by no means reflected a systemic failure. On the one hand, they pointed to the exceptional nature of the crisis; on the other hand, they insisted that no amount of legislation would make the problem of corporate fraud go away — this latter because corporate fraud, they claimed, is a *moral* problem, not a systemic one. The contradiction in saying that something is simultaneously exceptional and inherent was never reflected on.

Clearly, then, there was something reassuring for all the participants, who represented a spectrum of ideological and political positions, in emphasizing that corporate scandals were a consequence of a moral rather than a systemic breakdown. This tendency can be attributed to two reasons: one, the discursive structures of morality, salvation, and redemption that could be called into account by such a diagnosis; and two, the larger implications of admitting systemic failure could thereby be sidestepped. Diagnoses of moral failure allow the identification of crises in, and the *reduction* of crises to, the specific personae and actions of individuals (or corporations). They also point to the always existing possibility of redemption, thereby implying that white-collar criminals are always on the verge of repentance and reform.

More pertinent to a diagnosis of nationalism, however, are the implications that stem from acknowledging systemic failure in the case of scandal, from reading them as structural lapses rather than as aberrations. Admitting to systemic failure is not just admitting to a failure of free market capitalism but acknowledging, as SEC chairman Breeden constantly emphasized, a failure of free market capitalism that is uniquely laden with *American* values, and a free market capitalism that is uniquely positioned toward garnering America's global power. In other words, structural diagnoses that undermine a culturally particular, ritualized manifestation of free market excess are viewed as undermining not just a system of political economy but a national value system. In contrast to the kind of "naturalized" nationalism that this episode reflects, nationalism in India at this historical juncture is a sentiment both more openly expressed and more regularly interrogated.

## Grounds, Arguments, and Sites

In this chapter, I look at the belief systems within which biocapitalist vision and hype are embedded, specifically in religion and in nation. Inspired by Max Weber, I attempt first to generate a typology of salvationary undercurrents and manifestations of biocapitalism—first, by looking at the multiple (and mutual) coproductions of religion, science, and capitalism that occur; second, by situating these productions in performative sites of speech and ritual; and third, by theoretically analyzing the discursive and rhetorical structures of salvation and nation that underlie life science and capitalism.

This chapter, then, attempts to generate typologies of salvationary manifestations of biocapital in the United States and of its nationalist manifestations in India. There are multiple levels or registers at which salvationary as well as nationalist imagination and discourse operate. For instance, capitalism is not just a formation that is conditioned by religion (as Weber argues in *The Protestant Ethic*), but also a religious phenomenon. Indeed, one could approach this through the dual meanings of the word "conversion," which, on the one hand, has a religious definition, indicating wholesale transformations in religious belief, and, on the other, refers to the hardly momentous transformations of use value to exchange value. Salvationary discourses, which are often embedded in, and disseminated through, ritual, are paternalistic, cultic, and libidinal.[2] Therefore salvationary discourse and practice are also explicitly *gendered* in multiple ways.

Nationalism, as Benedict Anderson (1991 [1983]) famously argued, is the imagination of a community, and it inflects differently when the nation in question is a postcolonial entity such as India, whose very existence as a nation in the world was born of a modernist imaginary that was formed in ways simultaneously inspired by, and opposed to, the colonial power.

For much of the first forty years of India's independence, the conception of "nationalism" was still largely formulated in terms of secular anti-imperialism. But in the last fifteen years, this comfortably hegemonic understanding of nationalism as something natural, common in sentiment to all Indians (who in this conception are marked, after all, by their consciousness as postcolonial subjects), and generally secular-progressive, has come under increasing attack. Political developments that have helped constitute this increasingly ambivalent, contested position for Indian nationalism can, in many ways, be traced to the breakdown of the effortless pan-Indian hegemony of the Congress Party, the dominant party of India's freedom struggle.[3] For instance, there has been increased political movement for greater federal autonomy for states within the Indian union, and consequently "regional" parties, mainly representing particular states/or regions of India, have grown to be major political players.[4] Identity politics, often built around caste, have been playing an increasingly prominent role in the Indian polity as well. And a cultural Hindu nationalism, which was a constituent element of Indian politics throughout the freedom struggle (albeit a suppressed one relative to the Congress's secular nationalism), has grown more prominent, as indicated by the rise to power in 1998 of a coalition government led by the Hindu nationalist Bharatiya Janata Party (BJP, or Indian People's Party).[5] In the midst of these changes (and certainly in many ways coproductive of them) has been India's aggressive new program of economic liberalization, marked by an ambivalent attitude of attraction and repulsion toward the West, represented now by the United States rather than Great Britain.

In other words, it is possible to speak of biocapital as salvationary in the United States but nationalist in India, but not because of some essential "cultural difference" between the two locales. There are historical and material reasons for this difference. For one, discursive, ritual, cultic expression is a constitutive element of American technoscience and corporate culture; for another, nationalism's meaning in the present conjuncture of cultural resurgence and globalization is up for grabs in the Indian polity today. That it is even possible to make the statement "the United States : salvation :: India : nation" is not a little incongruent. After all, it is a *religious* nationalism whose resurgence is reshaping the grounds of Indian politics today. At the same time, it is evident that an explicit, aggressive nationalism is increasingly becoming a defining feature of American culture and policy.

Of course, as with all the other concepts I have used to define rubrics for the chapters in this book, the terms "salvation" and "nation" are not meant to function as binaries at all, but rather as dialectic counterparts to each other. The consolidation of the Hindu Right is a movement not just about religious identity but about Indian *national* identity. Its attempt is less to create some sort of "global" Hindu consciousness (except insofar as such consciousness can translate into questions of what it means for India to be a secular state) than it is an interrogation of, and a challenge to, a particular conception of a nation-state as it has historically evolved. At the same time, American nationalism, especially in the guise of the Bush administration, is explicitly messianic in its overtones. Religion is about national identity (in India), *at the same time* as national consciousness becomes messianic (in the United States).

I begin by showing how the conception of drug development as a *miraculous* enterprise pervades its stories, and how stories about the miracles of pharmaceutical development constantly crop up at each "revolutionary" moment in the industry's history. These stories are not abstract and disembodied structural figures but have to do with real lives that new miracle cures have saved (in the linear progressive historical renderings of science, these miracles are, of course, always subsequently deemed as having been inadequate). Consider, then, the following three stories, the first two recounted by Barry Werth (1994) in *The Billion Dollar Molecule*, and the third by Cynthia Robbins-Roth (2000) in *From Alchemy to IPO*.

The miraculous story of the use of penicillin during World War II had as its key moment the drug's administration in 1942 to a woman who was dying of streptococcal fever and not responding to sulpha drugs. But, says Werth: "At 3.30 Saturday afternoon, when she received her first shot of Merck's penicillin, her fever was 105 and she had 'well over' fifty bacteria per cubic centimeter of blood. By 4 the following morning, her temperature was normal. By Monday, her blood was sterile. She was still alive in 1990 and living in Connecticut" (Werth 1994, 123–24).

Later in that decade, it was cortisone that became the miracle drug. Says Werth: "In September 1948, Merck shipped six of its ten grams of cortisone to the Mayo Clinic for the treatment of a twenty-nine-year-old woman so crippled with rheumatoid arthritis that she couldn't roll over in bed. The woman had already received massive doses of penicillin, streptomycin, gold salts, and sera with no improvement. Three days after her first injection, she was able to raise her hands above her head. Four days later, she went shopping, declaring, 'I have never felt better in my life'" (Werth 1994, 129).

Robbins-Roth starts *From Alchemy to IPO* with the story of Betsy Patterson, diagnosed with non-Hodgkin's lymphoma (NHL), who was suffering as much, if not more, from her chemotherapy regimen as from the disease itself. Consequences of the chemotherapy, which did succeed in pushing her cancer into remission, included a premature menopause, diabetes, severe folic acid deficiency leading to anemia, and peripheral nerve damage. Eighteen months later, another spot showed up on a chest scan, threatening yet another battle with chemotherapy. It was at this point that she decided she wanted to try Rituxan, a new monoclonal antibody treatment for NHL that had been developed by IDEC Pharmaceuticals. As a consequence of the Rituxan treatment, according to Robbins-Roth (2000, 6–7):

> The nodes in her neck were completely gone, and those in her back and groin were disappearing and were no longer painful. CT scans in June prior to her second dose continued to show a substantial reduction in her tumors.
>
> This great response was not accompanied by toxicity. And there were few side effects. . . .
>
> Biotechnology has completely changed to way we discover and develop new drugs and has allowed us to help patients with previously untreatable diseases. Stories like Betsy's are one reason so many people have invested their time, money and careers in biotech.

The purpose of these renderings is neither to pour scorn on, nor to express cynicism toward, these stories, but rather to point to their constant structure of miracle, a structure, further, that is founded on the inadequacy of previous therapies (even though they too were once miracles). It is a structure of linear progress that is embedded and embodied in specific salvationary stories, heroic rescues of individual, extremely sick patients (that all the "rescued" patients in these stories are women is a further feature worth noting).[6] It is a structure of the type "If you relent and submit to penicillin or cortisone or Rituxan (each at the time of these stories relatively experimental therapies), then you will be saved." It is *not* the trope of public health, in which therapy intervenes to prevent the spread of plagues or epidemics. In other words, the symbolic capital for the drug development industry *does not* come from the story of ridding Africa of AIDS. Further, these stories describe not just cures but resurrections; what is at stake in these stories is not just survival, or getting better, but living life to the full, again.[7]

If drugs as instruments of salvation echo one structure of biocapital as reflected in these three origin stories, then markets as instruments of moral purpose have been equally articulated as part of the missionary enterprise since the nineteenth century. Around the time that Marx was writing about the theological nature of the commodity, for instance, David Livingstone was undertaking his expeditions in Africa with the firm belief that commerce and Christianity went hand in hand. The mid-nineteenth century, indeed, marked the coproduction of a metropolitan imaginary of Africa as a site for both evangelization and raw materials to feed the productive demands of the Industrial Revolution, and indeed endures today (as seen, for instance, in the efforts of the Christian Coalition's media magnate Pat Robertson in evangelizing and mining in western Africa [see Roth 2002]).

Thus the trope of drug development in the United States is *not* the trope of public health. Here again is potential for incongruence with respect to India, which, as a relatively poverty-stricken country that has followed socialist welfare state policies for much of the first forty years since its independence, has tended, at a formal and popular level, to conceive of drug development (even if not always explicitly) as a way of meeting public health goals. Once again, this incongruence is a consequence of distinct national, historical, and institutional contexts. And incongruence here manifests not so much between a U.S. "salvationary" trope and an Indian "public health" trope as it does between the Indian imitation of an American culture of innovation and the actual divergent manifestations of these imitative attempts on the ground. Even these attempts at imitation are in many ways out of joint with patent regimes in India, which, before the nation became a signatory to the World Trade Organization, were structured in ways that configured Indians less as sovereign consumers of drugs and more as a "public." Even if drug development in India, as in the United States, has always tended to be a private enterprise, Indian patent laws have allowed the reverse engineering of generic drugs (by allowing only process, not product, patents on drugs), thereby allowing free market competition and keeping Indian drug prices among the lowest in the world.

The attempt to bring about a culture of innovation in India, both by concerned state and market players within India and by nonresident Indian entrepreneurs in the United States, contains within it the germ of a contradiction, when such a culture, always already neoliberal at its core, comes into conflict with a value system that privileges therapeutic *access* as a public good of sorts (albeit one provided by the market). Indeed, India's patent regime is very much at stake as India has become a signatory to the WTO, a patent regime that much more closely resembles American rather than Indian intellectual property structures.[8] India's decision to join the WTO is not something that I explore in great detail in this book, but I mention it here as a stellar example of the contradictory desire and ambivalence of the Indian nation-state, business community, and polity toward globalization. On the one hand, a regime that is likely to be detrimental to the Indian pharmaceutical industry and likely to raise drug prices is seen by many as an example of American neocolonialism calling forth an anti-imperialist, nationalist indignation; on the other hand, at the same time, there is India's desire to be a global player, also a nationalist desire, leading to an embrace of a culture of innovation and its associated transnational regimes like the WTO.

In other words, a value-laden ideology such as innovation manages to be globalizing and apparently homogenizing in its application but in fact calls into account different registers of salvationary and nationalist discourse and consciousness depending on the sites of its manifestation. Further, because this "homogenizing" globalization is in fact occurring between locales that are situated far apart on a global axis of asymmetry, innovation is not likely to be realized in uniform or expected ways. Therefore I show in this chapter how, while attaining a culture of *innovation* is the rationale offered by many Indian actors who embrace global techno-capitalism, the route to its potential realization is *contract work* for Western companies, work that is *not* innovative and for which intellectual property resides with the contracting agent.

The overarching tension between, on the one hand, a consciousness of colonialism that sensitizes state policy regarding unequal exchange relations, and on the other hand the post-1990s determination to become a major player in the global market system, plays itself out at the level of everyday work practices; state policy statements, initiatives, incentives, and regulations (such as the Department of Biotechnology guidelines regarding the travel of genetic material from India discussed in chapter 1); and the struggle between self-reliance and the use of science and technology to solve local problems (the Gandhian, Nehruvian, and Indian Marxist development ideologies) versus its use to leverage the global playing field. To juxtapose the salvationary articulations of biocapital in the United States to its overtly nationalist ones in India is an invitation to take seriously the ways in which different historical terrains — in the Indian case, marked particularly by colonialism and a subsequent four decades of state socialism — lead to differential manifestations of apparently homogenizing "global" regimes and practices. In India, such contradictions are symptomatic of its postcolonial condition of, in Lawrence Cohen's phrase, "as if modernity" (Cohen 2003).

Crucial actors that link American and Indian techno-capitalist worlds, that indeed attempt to configure Indian high-tech worlds "as if American," are nonresident Indian (NRI) entrepreneurs based in Silicon Valley. The category NRI was officially coined by the Indian government in 1973 through the Foreign Exchange Regulations Act, thereby recognizing Indians abroad, through formal systems of state classification, as a distinct group with a clear incentive structure set up for them to reinvest capital back in India. Indeed, I argue that citizenship for NRIs is defined almost solely in terms of their ability to repatriate capital. This is partly because the Indian government, until 2002, did not allow dual citizenship. The 1973 act, however, also recognizes a category called "person of Indian origin," which is anyone who has at any time held an Indian passport or is the female spouse of such a person (male spouses of women of Indian origin are not considered to be of Indian origin), and provides similar investment incentives for these people as it does for NRIs who are Indian passport holders (Ramachandran 1992; see also Rajagopal 2001, 241–42). Further, the formal citizenship for even NRIs who possess Indian passports is somewhat nominal, as they are, rather perversely, unable to vote in Indian elections unless they are physically present in India at the time of elections or are government officials stationed in a foreign embassy. Therefore citizenship for NRIs is defined solely in terms of their ability to repatriate capital, and the Indian state has a quite conscious agency in shaping such a definition. Conversely, the repatriation of capital, for NRIs, becomes the defining act of citizenship (whether they are formally still NRIs or have abdicated Indian citizenship to become merely "persons of Indian origin"). Capital, quite literally, becomes the social bond that links Indians abroad to their homeland, but it works as such a bond only because there are other, less structural, ties already in place.

There are four sites, broadly conceived, that I situate together in this chapter. The first is a patient advocacy group for a rare genetic pigmentation disorder, pseudoxanthoma elasticum (PXE). The advocacy group is called PXE International and is based in the United States but networked throughout the United States and Europe. What makes this group particularly interesting is the way in which it is always already predisposed to framing itself as if corporate, and how this corporate framing is a consequence of a firm belief in the free market on the part of one of its founders, Patrick Terry, a belief that goes hand in hand with the fact that he is an evangelical Christian. This has led not just to PXE International's being an organization that adopts market strategies and tactics in its negotiations with corporate actors, but also to Terry's co-founding of a genome company, Genomic Health, with Randy Scott, who founded Incyte Genomics and has already figured in this book.

In form, this account is uncannily similar to accounts of India's flagship public-sector genome lab, the Centre for Biochemical Technology (CBT), narrated in chapters 1 and 2. There too is a not-for-profit entity framing itself as a market player to leverage global market terrains, and in the process also spinning off an associated start-up, Genomed. The difference is that while in CBT's case, its relationship to its strategies is marked by an ambivalent nationalist desire to resist American global hegemony while embracing it, in PXE International's and Terry's case, it is marked by an unbridled faith in the free market and in Christianity, both of which are value systems shared by Scott. In both cases, the associated start-up reflects the configuration of subjectivities in each context — in Genomed's case, Indian subjects as experimental subjects who get recruited into clinical trials; in Genomic Health's case, U.S. subjects as sovereign consumers. This is indicated by Genomic Health's business model, which claims that it is a "consumer genomics" company.

My second set of sites consists of sites of speech and ritual. Conferences are key sites at which unfolding dynamics and emergent networks of techno-capitalism can be traced. Ritual elements of industrial genome conferences are parties, which also mark a certain Silicon Valley start-up corporate culture. These parties are explicitly libidinal sites of extravagant expenditure and excess consumption and often signify the gambling and deep play of casino capitalism. I narrate stories about these parties to point to the ritualistic, cultic expressions of capitalism, which lead to the performative creation of brand value and vest power in the bodies of particular corporations. This is not just important in interesting investors and consumers but essential in fostering loyalty among the employees of these companies, not just to the "business of saving lives" they are engaged in, but to the causes of the specific corporations by which they are employed.

While talking about the India/nation side of the equation, I return to talk about the Centre for Biochemical Technology (CBT) in terms of a larger institutional context. This is the context of India's Council for Scientific and Industrial Research (CSIR), an umbrella organization of forty national research laboratories and institutions that is at the forefront of engineering India's scientific priorities toward more global, market-driven agendas. I look at the global context within which these labs do their research, one that is very much stratified and unequal in favor of the West, a situation that engenders much nationalist indignation among Indian scientists working in these labs. At the same time, the orientation of research agendas in these labs is very much toward the global, with a clear articulation of the desire to be like the global Other signified by the United States.

A driver of these changes is the current director general of CSIR, Ramesh Mashelkar. The institution that he came from, the National Chemical Laboratories (NCL) in Pune, was an early mover in the Indian technoscientific establishment's desire to go global. I narrate stories of NCL here, paying attention to the multiple contradictions inherent to its desire to become a global player in a situation of radical global asymmetry. I contrast that with a story from another CSIR lab, the Centre for Cellular and Molecular Biology (CCMB) in Hyderabad, which suggests a very different articulation of nationalism and national interest, one that is oriented much more directly toward a state socialist idea of meeting the needs of the Indian population through a technoscientific agenda that focuses on local and national needs while embracing global technologies. Crucially, these alternatives are not between science and antiscience, or an embrace of nationalism versus its repudiation. Rather, both points of view place a modernist faith in the progressive potential of science, one that has been consistently hegemonic since India's independence, and both are explicitly concerned with national interest. Susan Buck-Morss (2002) argues that the apparent oppositions of capitalism and communism as they emerged throughout the twentieth century in fact represented different articulations of the same modernist impulse in ways that made them uncanny (if incongruent) mirror images of each other. One can make a similar argument with respect to the global free market versus state socialist impulses in Indian science, whose negotiation remains an explicit tension in CSIR labs today.

My fourth site is Silicon Valley, and specifically Silicon Valley nonresident Indian entrepreneurs, almost all of whom were educated in state-subsidized Indian universities and research institutions and are key actors in repatriating a culture of innovation back to India. I describe these entrepreneurs, and the entrepreneurial organization they have set up (most notably the Indus Entrepreneurs, or TiE), in juxtaposition to other NRI groups that are involved in the repatriation of capital from the United States to India, the most active of which are Hindu nationalist organizations such as the Vishwa Hindu Parishad (World Hindu Forum, or VHP). A major figure I discuss in the context of TiE is Kanwal Rekhi, one of TiE's founders and arguably the best-known Indian entrepreneur in the United States. While I have corresponded with Rekhi in a number of contexts,[9] he functions less as a traditional ethnographic informant and more as a public figure in these narratives, much in the manner Randy Scott does.[10]

### PXE International and Genomic Health

I begin this section by referring back to Randy Scott's speech that I described in chapter 3 in the context of the stories of miraculous therapeutic intervention I have recounted in this chapter. Like these stories, Scott's pitch for Incyte, couched as a pitch for genomics (where genomics meshes into Genomics for Life), is an origin story, revolutionary and paternalistic; all attributes that go hand in hand with a performative of futurity.

The paternalism that inhabits these miraculous tales is not simply a part of their rhetorical structure. Sometimes that rhetorical structure can be embodied in specific corporate ventures that are explicitly, sometimes painfully, salvationary. The story of Patrick and Sharon Terry, PXE International and Genomic Health, in which one of the costars is Randy Scott, is indicative of this. The story of PXE International is a story of many things: of biosocial communities, of intellectual property, and of the effect of the Internet. Here I tell it as a story of the salvationary promise of biocapital.

Patrick Terry used to be in the construction business, and got involved in biomedicine when he and his wife discovered that their two children had pseudoxanthoma elasticum (PXE), a rare genetic pigmentation disorder that usually leads to blindness by the mid-twenties. Terry therefore got into science not through the normal routes of formal training but as a layman who was forced to take an interest in it. He calls his a "perspective informed by experience."[11] He and his wife found out as much as they could about PXE, networked with other parents of PXE-afflicted children in both the United States and Europe, and started a patient advocacy group, PXE International.

In addition, Pat Terry is one of the cofounders, along with Randy Scott, of a biotech company called Genomic Health, whose vision, according to Scott, is

> to build a new arm to the healthcare system. New genomic technologies will enable the world to characterize every patient's disease and health status as a complete genomic package. Every disease has a molecular basis and some level of genetic-encoded response. Individuals respond to therapy based on the molecular alterations of their disease and their own genetic code. Genomic Health's mission is to one day provide physicians and patients with an individualized molecular analysis that enables the treatment team to utilize relevant treatment guides for all diseases. Our ultimate goal is to make personalized medicine a reality and to dramatically improve patient care.[12]

One of the things the Terrys have done is negotiate agreements with companies like Genomic Health, to which PXE International members donate DNA samples for research, whereby the patient advocacy group shares in the intellectual property that the company generates.

Patrick Terry starts his talks by laying out all the things that he is — parent, PXE International administrator and Genomic Health cofounder, researcher (it is interesting to note that he does not emphasize his Christianity in the formal structure of his talks but often does so immediately in personal conversation, or even in discussions after the formal component of his talks).[13] It is a style that completely mirrors Scott's, who often starts his own presentations with a similar outline of his multifaceted set of involvements, responsibilities, and motivations. As a part of his work, Terry is both a typical and a unique example of a venture scientist. He is involved heavily in policy activities, through an alliance of genetic disease patient advocacy groups called the Genetic Alliance. Through PXE International, he is involved in a worldwide effort to initiate, conduct, and fund PXE research. Much of that is through the establishment of research collaborations, such as those just mentioned, which involves the need to negotiate intricate contracts, alliances, and understandings.

All of this, however, stems from Terry the parent. PXE International is a paternalistic venture, not in any abstract discursive sense but in terms of the actual structure of its genesis. In addition, Terry claims that his alliance with Scott had everything to do with their shared beliefs, in terms of their libertarian bend toward the free market and their conversant religious beliefs (Scott, as mentioned earlier, is an evangelical Christian, like Terry). Scott is, according to Terry, "a regular guy, a super guy, a nice guy, a family guy."[14] It forms the basis of a trust that Terry does not necessarily feel toward other businesspeople, and there are those who he feels have betrayed PXE's cause after indicating interest.

Terry and Scott merge their belief in Christianity with their belief in the market. Terry strongly believes in the market not just as the route to therapeutic *production* but as the route to therapeutic *knowledge* and *dispensation*. What Genomic Health is about, as much as or more than a wet-lab research-based company, is empowering consumers by providing them with "actionable therapeutic information."[15] The goal is nothing less than to foster what Terry calls a "consumer genomic revolution." Terry thinks in terms of "consumers" and "targeted therapeutic interventions" rather than "patients" and "cures": he does not like the normative overtones of the latter terms. What he also does not like is the role of the physician as expert gatekeeper, which he feels hinders the patient-consumers' ideally individualized quest for self-knowledge. He thinks, therefore, of medicine in salvationary terms, but he also thinks that the market has to intervene for medicine to change in ways that can enable it to attain its promise of salvation. While articulating his belief in the market, Terry also *performs* this belief.

Further, PXE International does not just operate as an institutional structure that acts as a formal negotiating party: it acts quite literally as a networked biosocial community, with all the peer pressures attendant on small, intimate communities. Terry, for instance, says that the community uses peer pressure to "push good habits" such as getting members to stop smoking. Terry's biography is an exploration of the relationship between the market and subjectivity, as the grieving father becomes an entrepreneur, who is also a political figure and a religious figure, forcing us, therefore, also to ask what concepts of family are embedded in these entrepreneurial-religious-political-capitalist lifeworlds.

The case of Genomic Health, the company that Terry and Scott have co-founded, is suggestive of some of the arguments that I am trying to make, in terms of salvation, promise, performance, and the market. To analyze Genomic Health, it is important to revisit Scott's modes of prophecy. When Scott was pitching Incyte, for example, at the Institute of Genomic Research (TIGR) industrial conference in Miami in 1999, it was an investor pitch where his potential consumers were pharmaceutical companies. With Genomic Health, his potential consumers are laypeople, the patients and consumers-in-waiting that I have talked about in this and the previous chapter. This leads to an entirely different understanding, different timelines, analogies with the computer industry, and a coincidence with Terry's line about patients and consumers.[16]

In his pitches for Genomic Health, Scott divides the history of genomics into decades — the 1980s, when the first companies brought products into the market based on classical DNA efforts; the 1990s, an era of industrialization and high-throughput technologies; and the first decade of the new century, which he calls the era of consumer genomics, where merging biological information with Internet capabilities will be key. In other words, the driving assemblages of emergent "postgenomic" medicine, in Scott's opinion, are biological information (such as diagnostics), communications technologies that mediate such information as it travels to lay patients (the Internet), and the consequent networking of biosocial communities such as patient advocacy groups. It is a vision that has as its kernel the sort of consumption power that is evidenced by groups such as PXE International.

Scott thus has a vision of "consumer genomics" that is completely entwined with his vision of Genomic Health as a company, a vision that sees patients directly buying access to information and technologies, thereby seriously minimizing the role of physicians. Pharmaceutical companies, in this vision, are still involved in therapeutic development, but Scott realizes that the lag between the development of diagnostic and therapeutic capabilities creates an ethnographic window, one that is absolutely critical to the existence of Genomic Health as a company.

Scott outlines his notion of consumer genomics as follows:

> Genomics is inherently personal. This is not about big industrial units that are bringing out products for other companies.[17] Every one of us sits here with a genome, and a genome is our own particular story. My family has its story . . . they were a perfectly normal family, they thought they had no genetic disease, no genetic defects. . . . [But] no matter how healthy we may think we are, ultimately we will all face the reality of our genetic faults, and the diseases that are coming at us in the future. So we are all in this together.[18]

In this one quote, Scott points at many of the arguments I have worked through in the course of this and the previous chapter. He encapsulates his own visionary biography, superimposed on the history, as he sees it, of genomics — moving away from and beyond the vision of Incyte (which he leaves at a moment when its own business model threatens it with obsolescence), a movement that is portrayed as naturally following the course of the history of a science that is always already a corporate endeavor. But it is also a personal voyage, an individuation whose limitations are immediately evident, because it is an individuation that cannot be made sense of without being placed in larger population contexts. Scott adroitly avoids the fundamental difficulties of classifying populations that I have pointed to in the previous chapter — difficulties that are an acute scientific and business reality for those who invest in population genomics as their vision of, and route to, future monetary and therapeutic salvation. He automatically uses the family as the basis of his relevant population unit — a unit, of course, that is comfortably Christian, moral, and value laden, for one who himself is driven considerably by his Christian faith. Ultimately everyone is enrolled in a Christian odyssey toward his or her respective genetic days of reckoning, but in the process, as Scott managed to do for his employees at Incyte (as I show later in the chapter), he conjures up the image of a community, the community of patients-in-waiting, who are always already consumers-in-waiting. Lest we forget this voyage is overdetermined by the market, Scott immediately proceeds: "So the issue is how we bring these products to the market, how we bring them to the consumer."[19]

Stories such as those of Terry and Scott highlight the rhetoric and language of salvation as it manifests as underlying belief structure, as market enterprise and business model, and as therapy/medicine/health. They show the co-constitution of highly individualized stories of personal motivation, calling, and human interest with the structural messianism inherent to the market, science, or nation. Saving lives melds into saving a company's corporate interests or, in the case of India, making a "Third World" country a "global player." Meanwhile the sacralization associated with the business of life and death melds into the sacralization mediated through the fetish of the commodity that simultaneously, as Marx shows, alienates it from human association while making it the mediator of social bonds.

While the social power of the enterprise of the life sciences emanates from the implosion of these two sources of the sacred, it still does not explain the social power of individual corporate entities, that lead, among employees of life science corporations, not just to loyalty to the *cause* of eradicating disease through the market development of therapeutic products, but to loyalty to *specific* companies. It is this latter question, of how life sciences and life science corporations *both* acquire performative salvationary force, that I explore next.

### Parties

Jean-Joseph Goux, in an analysis of the value system of neoliberal capitalism, says that "whereas the profane is the domain of utilitarian consumption, the sacred is the domain of experience opened by the unproductive consumption of the surplus" (Goux 1990, 207–8).

The salvationary potential of biocapital resides in the very nature of the enterprise of drug development, being as it is in the business of making sick people better. And yet this alone is insufficient to make drug development a salvationary enterprise of the sort that it is in the United States. For that, the therapeutic potential of drug development has to be articulated with other belief systems, especially the neoliberal faith in free market innovation. In other words, the salvationary potential of biocapital has to do not just with the value accruing from "bio" but also from the value accruing from "capital." This relationship of capital to the theological was recognized by Marx to exist even in the days of the Industrial Revolution, but it acquires different performative force when the magic, as in the case of high-tech innovation, involves pulling rabbits out of hats rather than just generating infinite surplus.

While capitalism, as Marx famously suggests in his analysis of commodity fetishism (Marx 1976 [1867]), has always been theological,[20] the explicit treatment of the relationship between capitalism and Protestant Christianity, of course, has been provided by Weber (2001 [1930]). If the "spirit" of capitalism could persuasively be said to have been animated by a Protestant ethic, then the spirit of biocapitalism, certainly in the United States, could be said to be animated by a "born-again" ethic. I take inspiration here from Weber's demonstration in *The Protestant Ethic* that the connection between the Protestant ethic and the spirit of capitalism occurred historically, and at a place in the social structure that tends to hive off other forms.

Weber does, however, set up a particular, contextually situated dichotomy between asceticism and mysticism in *Economy and Society* (Weber 1978 [1968], 541–56). It is the *collapse* of this dichotomy that is so important to trace — if mysticism is, in Weber's terms, "world-fleeing" (might we say thus in the case of science in the guise of Merton's norms — abstract, knowledge, truth?), and asceticism is "world-serving" (the symbolic capital of drug development, as being in the business of saving lives), then the mystical and ascetic aspects of Merton's science and Weber's capitalism respectively collapse most evidently in venture science.[21]

I argue here for the impossibility of purifying accumulation and surplus value generation in (bio)capitalist worlds, especially in the United States, without serious attentiveness to the apparently irrational expenditure of the neoliberal free market, similar to the potlatch of "archaic" societies described by Marcel Mauss (1990 [1954]), but different from it in the millenarian and ultimately goal-directed (in ways overdetermined by market ideologies) form of this excess.

Essentially, it is this recalibration of Weber in the light of contemporary capitalism, while remaining faithful to the methodological form of his analysis, that I attempt in this section. Goux, whom I quoted earlier, is an inspiration to me here, as on the one hand he reads the neoliberal ideologue George

Gilder's enthusiasm for free market innovation, and on the other draws on analyses of capitalism by Georges Bataille (1988 [1967]), who argues for a "general theory" of economics that postulates that capitalism's "fundamental impulse" is expenditure.

On the one hand, Bataille's totalizing reduction of capitalism to a fundamental, singular logic is precisely the maneuver I resist throughout this book, and my juxtaposition of the United States to India is one means to resolutely resist the idea that capitalism has a singular logic (though it undeniably has hegemonic and subordinate logics at different stages of its history). On the other hand, I do find it very useful to pay attention to the importance of "irrationality," exuberance, expenditure, and excess, *not* as aberrations but as constitutive to the forms of capitalism that I trace, certainly in the United States. More importantly, these are the forms of excess that make capitalism, and specific corporate entities, the cults that demand to be bought into. The cultic power of specific corporate entities is a form of social power that undeniably works through a performative of futurity—hype and public relations—but that again cannot just be understood by attributions of cynicism. There is the necessity of mystification that occurs through ritualized modes of performance.

For actors like Randy Scott and Patrick Terry, biotech has an element of calling that Weber points out was introduced by the Reformation (Weber 2001 [1930]). But this is a calling coupled not to asceticism but to *expenditure*, to worldly pleasure. Even if such excess is not practiced by born-again figures like Scott and Terry themselves, it is a part of a certain ritual structure of corporate biotech. And yet it is a ritual structure of excess that is hardly irreligious, if one is to understand religion in the sense that Clifford Geertz (1973) articulates it, as a source of power that derives its authority from the enactment of ritual.

I recount two examples of this now. These are especially marked in the American situation and reflect an allegiance similar to that of allegiance to sports teams. It is, however, an allegiance that involves not just a certain degree of time and emotional or monetary expenditure but a devotion of labor to the corporate cause. Further, there are certain companies that are able to build what might be called "cultlike" images around themselves, a consequence both of their visionary status and of the way in which that visionary status is articulated in hegemonic ways to foster loyalty.

My first story is from an industrial genome conference organized by the Institute of Genomic Research (TIGR) in Miami in 1999. If any one company stole the show at this conference, it was Incyte. They had sent out letters and pamphlets to attendees beforehand; Incyte TV was a closed-circuit TV channel that the company had arranged in all the attendees' hotel rooms, giving Incyte added visibility.

A central event at which this conference crystallized as an "Incyte" conference was at the concluding party. I was with Puneet,[22] an Indian graduating with a master's degree in computer science, who had spent much of the conference looking for jobs in a bioinformatics, genomics, or pharmaceutical company. At the party, he was in his final frenzy of collecting and collating job offers. Earlier in the day, he had been offered a job by Pangea Systems, a Bay Area bioinformatics company,[23] and that evening Pangea's main rival, Neomorphic, had come up with an offer, too. Puneet had actually done an internship with Neomorphic earlier in the year and had many friends and attachments there, which made him ambivalent about going to work for Neomorphic's direct competitors. Nonetheless he was now saying that he would rather join Pangea because they were a bigger company.

But further conversation had to be restricted as an extremely loud brass band started playing and the festivities really began. We met James Kirk, an employee at Incyte, and Puneet endeared both of us to him by telling him with unabashed enthusiasm how Incyte had completely stolen the show at the conference. This was clearly a feeling that the Incyte people shared, and it was evident from the multitude of cheerful light blue T-shirts sponsored by Incyte that they were feeling extremely cocky about the way things had gone. Indeed, the relative performances (in both senses of the word) of Incyte and its major rival, Celera, at the conference were evident just from the size of the contingents of each company present at the party. At this point, there were hardly any Celera dark blues to be seen against the Incyte light blues.

The rest of the evening was dance, music, spectacle — and what a lot of it! This really was a *big* party, and there was clearly a sense of celebration, abandon, confidence, aggression about this group of people. These were powerful and happy people, and they knew it. In the middle of an extremely crowded dance floor, Puneet met the one Incyte person he had been looking for throughout the conference: a friend of his brother's, Sid ("Squid") Collins. And for all his efforts, all his anxieties, all his attempts to woo the Incyte people with his accomplishments and his background, all he really needed to do was meet Squid—the minute Squid realized that Puneet was his friend's brother, he offered him a job at Incyte.

Was Puneet happy. *This* was what he had been waiting for. Neomorphic and Pangea and Curagen were all very well, Roche and Millennium were enticing and worth thinking over, but this moment was all about Incyte, and Squid's offer had made Puneet a part of that moment. And indeed, the party seemed increasingly to be about Incyte — they were the ones present and taking over.

Puneet's story brings me to the issue of brands: how is it that a company's name can be so attractive that it makes people forget individual relationships and principles just to be a part of that name? How is it that people can be so completely a part of a name that they can mold their actions and characters into the actions and characters signified by that name (and here the question of these multiple corporate "cultures," at once individual and yet totalizing, comes up)? And yet shift allegiances so easily that when they get a better offer from a better name, they shift themselves not just physically but in so many other intangible ways as well? How is it that Puneet could change sides so many times, in two days, between companies that were mutual rivals, just at the *prospect* of belonging to one side or the other? So somehow, in some intangible way, value had been added to the Incyte brand. In pure Marxian terms, this is surplus value of a sort, but it is not easy to completely capture in simple Marxian categories of value, either. What is this value that is born of the fetish of intangibles, of excess, of visions, of futures, that is located neither in persons nor in things but in trademarks and company names?[24]

The final set of announcements was a public acknowledgment of the shadowboxing between Celera and Incyte throughout the conference, as a woman representing the absent Craig Venter (then CEO of Celera) took digs at Scott, which Scott, now in complete control, rebutted with ease. Now the finale was clearly Randy Scott's moment of triumph, and the moment when he could show it off. As he walked onto the stage, the air was filled with chants of

"Randy! Randy!" On the other side, the few brave darker blue shirts were mustering a few halfhearted taunts and jibes. Puneet was by now very much a part of the light blues, swept away by the Incyte frenzy, a chanting and completely assimilated fragment of the corporate collectivity that Incyte at this moment, in this place, was.

Scott gave a toast. To the genomics community. Because, as he said, "There is not a single person in this room who's in genomics for themselves. They're in genomics for Life."

As I walked away, I passed Scott as he was being led out onto the dance floor by a young blonde woman. My last glimpse was of Scott's ginger dance steps, hands clasped behind his back, a light blue handkerchief sticking out of his back pocket. A happy, powerful, and triumphant man.

My second story, about Genentech, was told to me by a former employee, whom I will keep anonymous. I do not transcribe the story verbatim but rather will recount the gist of it.

Genentech had just won a patent infringement case, and to celebrate, they called all of their two thousand employees into a makeshift tent constructed on the premises in order to make the announcement. As soon as the announcement was made, according to my informant, the entire tent broke into a standing ovation (which my informant could not understand, since, as she said, most of them had "pretty crummy jobs"), after which the company threw a party, with lots of food, music, drink, and rose petals being strewn from the makeshift stage. After an adequate amount of revelry, the employees were all called out of the tent to witness a fireworks display put on by the company. Since Genentech is in South San Francisco, just north of San Francisco International Airport, it became an urban myth in the company that Genentech was able to stop flights into and out of the airport for fifteen minutes while it put on its own fireworks display. My informant herself would not have been surprised if that had been the case; what she was more impressed by was the ostentatious display of extravagance on the part of the company, and invincibility felt by its employees, who completely bought into the company's extravagance as a matter of course. In the process, a corporate aura and a sense of belonging to a larger cause — which was not simply the cause of eradicating disease but also the activist cause, in itself, of committing oneself to Genentech—were inscribed. The calling, in biocapital, thereby comes both from the symbolic capital accruing from being in the business of "life itself," and from capitalism—being part of a specific, embodied, corporate ethos that itself gets constructed through ritual excess. This leads to a therapeutic salvationary discourse that finds itself completely entwined with faith both in the market writ large and in specific corporate entities.

Indeed, as suggested by the story of Incyte's party, a performance marked by excess is a ritual mode of inscription of a corporate presence in the lives of its workforce, where a larger question of branding is at stake. Indeed, the backdrop to the Incyte party at TIGR 1999 was a party thrown by Celera at the same venue in 1998, which was on Miami beach and signified the 1998 conference as a Celera conference (this occurred in the aftermath of Craig Venter's announcement that he would sequence the human genome before the public researchers). Indeed, it was Celera's first act of public display since its formation earlier in 1998, and it was the TIGR party, as much as Venter's announcement regarding the genome sequence in May 1998, that in some material, embodied sense catapulted Celera into a certain sort of public vision as the company that was racing to sequence the human genome.

That the 1999 party had managed to turn that year's proceedings into an Incyte conference was clearly not lost on TIGR, which, after all, was an organization that had close links to Celera at the time.[25] Sure enough, at the TIGR conference in 2000, Incyte was conspicuous by its absence from the organizational scene of such revelry. This was because, as I learned from an annoyed Incyte employee, TIGR had not allowed them to stage any of the major conference parties and had not allowed them to advertise as easily as they had done the previous year. For much of the 2000 conference, Incyte was reduced to advertising its presence through giant blimps flying overhead.

Celera, meanwhile, needed not just to register its presence but to do so in a manner more audacious and spectacular than Incyte had the previous year; and preventing Incyte's spectacular publicity from having an easy outlet, through the organizational agency of TIGR, was clearly only half the battle won. Therefore Celera, who organized the 2000 TIGR party, did so at the Villa Vizcaya, an Italian Renaissance-style villa and gardens filled with art and antiques, which had been built as a winter estate of the industrialist James Deering in 1916. Included as part of the evening's festivities were a live band and plenty of food and alcohol.

If, on the one hand, reducing the "religious" aspects of capitalism to a dour austerity fails to take into account the actual and excessive forms through which capitalism operates, then on the other, it is too simple to reduce this excess to an "irrationality," which is all too easily done, especially today (2004), especially in places like Silicon Valley, where such exuberance is disdainfully marked off as an "aberration" of the dot.com boom, as somehow only spectacle, from which we have returned to the "reality" of rational accumulation. And yet such forms of excess are always undergirded by forms of rational calculation, just as rational accumulation in capitalism is always undergirded by excess — excess and rational accumulation are dialectically intertwined components of capitalism. Therefore the head of sales of a bioinformatics company, with me at the 2000 TIGR party, was completely unimpressed with its extravagance, to the extent that he saw it as a perfectly sound and fiscally conservative sales and marketing decision. After all, he told me, it is much cheaper to advertise one's presence in dramatic fashion to many potential investors and customers in one place, especially if it is a place they have happy memories of and at which they are not explicitly being sold something, than it is to make individual sales calls across the world to each one of them.

How such modes of explicit consumption can be situated in the context of the reemergence of scandal as central to the dynamics of contemporary corporate America (Enron, WorldCom, Tyco, and the like) is an important question to ask. Excess consumption is a central aspect of sites of speech such as industrial biotech conferences, and in addition to the major conference parties such as those sponsored by Incyte and Celera were other smaller parties that occurred every evening in what was, primarily, an industrial trade show. Perkin-Elmer, for instance, had organized a casino for conference participants at the 1999 TIGR conference, and these parties are not just sites of corporate excess, consumption, but also quite explicitly libidinal sites. I am reminded, for instance, of one inebriated Perkin-Elmer employee I met at the casino party, who, in the midst of a series of advances to the various women at the party, found the time to confide to me that his company's real aim was to take over the world. Instead of dismissing such statements as alcohol-induced gibberish, I would like to point, again, to the sense of invincibility that such modes of ritual performativity foster among their participants, an invincibility that translates into making sacred the source of such power, the corporation.

Of course, corporate scandals are always framed in terms of delinquent morality, and therefore as aberration. Such a framing thereby allows the everyday business of excess to continue, unscathed and unstopped. The dialectic relationship of the sacred is not to its binary opposite, the profane, but to its dialectic counterpart, the scandalous. Sacred power can only arise from the constantly deferred but always present risk of scandalous misappropriation — the very excess that lends sacred power to the corporation or enterprise at sites and moments of surplus consumption carries within it the risk of the recognition of that excess as somehow aberrant, abhorrent, immoral, scandalous. By deferring such recognition, of course, the corporation or enterprise in question gains not only an aura of power and invincibility but also an ethical legitimacy, as *not* therefore immoral or scandalous — simply powerful, the cult that demands to be bought into. Performativity provides material force, which gets consecrated in the body of the corporation, but especially in its name, *brand*. Hence the relevance of Derrida's questions regarding what is in the name, what it is we do when we act in the name of something (religion, for instance, but here also of science, of nation, of capitalism, of specific corporations) (see Derrida 1995, 2002a). And further, says Derrida, the very possibility of such faith that we can act in the name of (religion or, I add, science, nation, capitalism, corporation) has (today at least, and in the ways that faith gets mediated through performativity and ritual), as its condition of possibility, the *technical*. As he puts it:

> The technical is the possibility of faith, indeed its very chance. A chance that entails the greatest risk, even the menace of radical evil. Otherwise, that of which it is the chance would not be faith but rather program or proof, predictability or providence, pure knowledge and pure know-how, which is to say annulment of the future. Instead of opposing them, as is almost always done, they ought to be thought together, as *one and the same possibility*.[26]

I have already referred to the pervasive salvationary discourse that underlies the enterprise of drug development in the United States. There are two ways in which "the technical" can be read into such discourse. The first is one that Derrida himself is intimately concerned with, which is the way in which faith is mediated, that is, disseminated through technologies of the media. The corollary to biocapital here would be the symbolic capital of the drug development industry as being in the business of "food, health, and hope," and as articulated through the salvationary potential of particular therapeutic molecules (which are configured as objects that can simultaneously generate wellness among their consumers and instantiate them as consumers with free choice), which depends in large measure on the discursive and media apparatus that allows a fashioning of such a message.

There is a broader way in which "the technical" becomes the possibility of faith, as suggested by my description of the DNA chip in the previous chapter. I showed there that some technologies themselves work as "technologies of representation," by virtue of their being what Donna Haraway (1997) calls "material-semiotic" objects. Here the technical object both mediates and is itself the object of faith. It mediates faith by virtue of being the thing that represents, provides a portrait of, one's predisposition to future possible illness. But it also represents, stands in for, the "individual," who is represented by his or her genes, which in turn is represented by the DNA chip.[27] By functioning simultaneously as portrait and as proxy, the DNA chip becomes an object of faith, a fetish. Indeed, the fetish exists in the becoming-proxy (as in representative of individual "identity") of that which is just a portrait of an individual's nucleotide profile.

Derrida points to the "chance" of technically mediated faith, thereby also calling into account all the forms of risk that I argued for in the previous chapter. Specifically, the two forms of risk that I outlined were that of a patient-consumer's future probable illness as foretold by genomics, and of a company's high-risk capital investment in a drug that might never be realized, or that might not garner sufficient market revenue to make the investment worthwhile. But there is a third form of risk that entails a cultic faith in the salvationary potential of technoscience, or a market system, or, especially, specific corporate entities that claim to uphold value systems in all senses of the word, and that is the risk of "scandalous misappropriation."

One of the defining features of this current conjuncture of American capitalism has been the spate of corporate scandals that have rocked Wall Street over the last couple of years. While the drug development marketplace has so far been comparatively, though not entirely, unscathed by these scandals, I take them seriously as a tendential manifestation of particular currents in capitalist value systems, and as not irrelevant to understanding the underlying belief systems that animate biocapital.

Technoscience, especially when it concerns the ability to manipulate and intervene in "life itself," is risky even without situating it in the context of its free market emergence. The trope of science run wild is an old romantic trope that has constantly reinvented itself since the Industrial Revolution, and the specter of *Frankenstein* (Shelley 1992 [1831]) remains as strong today as it did at the time of its writing. The therapeutic promise of genomics is always already haunted by its eugenic promise. Even if scientists take pains to distinguish the "good" eugenics of new genome technologies from the "bad" eugenics of the Nazi era,[28] the trope of Aldous Huxley's *Brave New World* (Huxley 1998 [1946]) remains as potent as that of Shelley's *Frankenstein*. In other words, if the magic of innovation lies in its potential to pull rabbits out of hats, then that magic holds within it the fear that the rabbits might, in fact, turn out to be demons. While I refuse to subscribe to, or repudiate entirely, the fears attendant to new biotechnologies (just as I refuse to do either regarding the hype attendant to them), I do wish to take them seriously as dialectic components of the political economies I am trying to trace.

In addition to the potential "evils" inherent to the technologies themselves, though, are the "evils" of their misappropriation. "Misappropriation" here refers not just to their "misuse" in reference to an accepted norm, as Nazi science, for instance, could be argued to be,[29] but also to its misappropriation, where "appropriation" is specifically a term concerning ownership, exchange, and representation. In other words, not only do new technologies, and perhaps particularly new biotechnologies, contain the possibility of horrific emergences consequent to the possibilities of creation and manipulation inherent to the technologies themselves, but they also contain all the dangers attendant to the sacralization of purported representative bodies (in this case, often specific corporations, or the "free market" writ large) that allows acts of excess, or other forms of inappropriate behavior, on the parts of such "sacred" institutions.

Derrida once again points to the importance of temporality, which has been a constant theme in my arguments. The very possibility of a future, certainly for either a capitalism built on future promise, or a technoscience built on its potential for salvationary innovation, lies in the fact that they are indeterminate, even if tendential in many ways. It is this indeterminacy that leads to the fetishistic maneuvers of, for instance, reifying statements of probability into statements of prophecy; but this very indeterminacy also leads to the faith that is placed in institutions and belief systems such as the nation, the free market, religion, fact, or individual corporate entities — institutions and belief systems that promise, in their own ways, a coming to terms with the future that technologies like genomics predict in new ways.

Therefore I have argued here for the fetishism of the symbolic capital of the biotech and pharmaceutical industry as being in the business of saving lives, imploding into the fetishism of capitalism, fetishes that become reified into belief systems and power structures through the constant re-performance of ritual. In the process, the sacred is literally incorporated into the body of the corporation. And yet the suspicion that this is a particularly American mode of spectacular capitalism begs the question of the *missing nationalism* in these stories — especially since it is precisely the explicitness of nationalism that is so marked in the Indian stories of technoscience and globalization. It seems particularly ironic that what is silent or invisible in such situations of corporate excess is the particularly *American* nature of this excess, especially considering the overt and spectacular display of nationalism that is so constitutive of American public life. I suspect that this "missing" nationalism is not a case of American techno-capitalism *not* being animated by nationalist sentiments, but rather that the question of *what* constitutes nationalism is less questioned and less at stake in the United States than it currently is in India.

The other side of the comparative question also needs to be asked here, if briefly — is this a uniquely American mode of performative ritual excess? Certainly such forms of excess are not immediately evident in India. Is this simply a consequence of "cultural difference," or is it because biotech has not yet arrived in India the way it has in the United States? Answering such a question would begin at least partly addressing the question of the specificity of such excess to biocapital, since, as I have argued, such forms of (potentially) scandalous excess are hardly restricted to the drug development marketplace in

American corporate culture. Meanwhile, in the United States, to some extent, the biotech industry is already, in many ways, a very similar (if smaller-scale) version of the pharmaceutical industry: while the upstream-downstream terrain of drug development represents a real hierarchical differentiation between the power and resources these two types of companies have, the biotech industry is established enough now that it has itself begun the process of drug development. Indeed, there is a distinct market pressure for upstream companies to move further downstream. The difficulties they face in doing so point to the stark power differentials between the two types of companies, but the fact of the intimate rhetorical and market association of biotech with drug development means that the salvationary symbolic capital associated with, say, a Merck is very much associated with the upstream biotech industry as well.

The other difference between the United States and India that is worth marking here is that the visible locus of new biotech innovation in India is still the state rather than private industry, and hence the regime of symbolic capital that needs to be tapped into is quite different from one of investors and consumers. That nationalism is the explicit mode of biocapitalist articulation in India is a function not just of particular historical contexts but also of this distinct institutional context.

Therefore, on the one hand, we have messianic actors, such as Scott and Terry, as well as the corporate messiahs such as Incyte and Genentech, who are forging one set of visionary biocapitalist agendas. But let us recall that the commodity itself is theological: it is imbued with mystical and religious force. When that commodity is a therapeutic, it becomes salvationary. The drug's magic does not simply stem from its use value as an object that makes sick people better, but arises from the modes of abstraction that allow drugs to be commodities. Further, the *promise* of medicine, as mediated by the drug, does not need to be articulated: it is a promise that is *inherent* in the mundane objects, which are, as Marx put it, full of "metaphysical subtleties and theological niceties" (Marx 1976 [1867], 163). The social life of drugs, as commodities, is defined both by their cultural life (the different cultural contexts within which drugs travel and are consumed) and by their imaginary life (imaginaries that drugs both operate within and help create).

In addition to messianic actors and theological commodities is what Derrida calls a *structural messianism* — "a messianism without religion, even a messianic without messianism, an idea of justice" (Derrida 1994, 59), which is the promise that science holds for human emancipation.[30] This is a structural messianism that is as much a part of the foundational ideology for post-independence India, enshrined in Jawaharlal Nehru's famous description of science and technology as the "temples of modern India" (Nehru 1958), as it is a part of Randy Scott's rhetoric. The questions for comparison, then, are questions of how such structural technoscientific messianism articulates with other structures of promissory imagination, such as, in the case of Indian technoscience, the nation.

### The Council for Scientific and Industrial Research

I begin here with two quotes. The first is from India's first prime minister, Jawaharlal Nehru, speaking at the Indian Science Congress in 1938: "It is science alone that can solve these problems of hunger and poverty, of insanitation and illiteracy, of superstition and deadening custom and tradition, of vast resources running to waste of a rich country inhabited by starving people." The second is from the manifesto of the Congress Party for the first national government, declared in 1945: "Science in its instrumental fields of activity has played an ever-increasing part in influencing and molding human life. . . . Industrial, agricultural and cultural advance, as well as national defense depend on it. Scientific research is, therefore, a basic and essential activity of the State and should be organized and encouraged on the widest scale" (both quoted in Krishna 1997, 236–37).

As is quite clear from these quotes, Nehru and the Indian National Congress, the major nationalist party in the anti-imperialist struggle (and the party that has ruled postcolonial India for forty-four of the fifty-six years since India's independence), accorded a huge importance to science and technology in India's development. Indeed, one of the central features of the Congress-led struggle for independence was that it was very much tied into an intellectual struggle against colonial science policies that stifled the growth of local technoscientific institutions. V. V. Krishna explains colonial science in India as being a "planned activity from the metropolis," where "the colonies were assigned the subordinate tasks of 'data exploration' and application of existing technical knowledge, while the theoretical synthesis took place in the metropolis. Devoid of its intellectual essence, the goal of scientific practice in the colony was not the advancement of science . . . but the exploration of natural resources, flora and fauna to feed to intellectual and industrial 'revolution' in the metropolis" (Krishna 1997, 238).

Two things emerge here: the first, that the Indian state's anxiety over what it sees as expropriation of genetic resources from India for commercialization in the West is an ethical-political issue of some sensitivity that has its basis in firm historical, material colonial relationships. The second point is the emergence of India in the 1990s as a major contract research site for Western corporations, especially in software, data mining, and back-end corporate activities — a labor dimension to global ethical-political questions that exists beyond biocapital alone, of course. This development is a central part of contemporary global relations between the industrialized West and rapidly industrializing "Third World" countries like India and China.

These are issues that manifest themselves not only in structural relations of production but also in the everyday lives of scientists in Indian molecular biology labs, who still feel slighted that only "me-too" work that reproduces conceptual advances already made in the West gets accepted for publication in top Western journals, whereas novel conceptual work invariably tends to be met with suspicion. A scientist at the Centre for Biochemical Technology (CBT), where I did some of my fieldwork, for instance, had this to say:

> Getting things accepted in the international community is a problem. . . . Anything new, I think they feel we are not competent to propose a hypothesis or . . . they would be more demanding in terms of data, in terms of amount of work done. . . . It is very disheartening, actually.
>
> We had a person . . . who works abroad on schizophrenia, and he works with a professor who I think is from South Campus. . . . He came to our lab and he was trying to find out whether we could work together with them. He comes to our lab, he sits over here, and he says, "Whatever you are doing, you give us your samples, we will reproduce the same work abroad and then you will have an easier way of communicating your paper because nobody will accept any of the data that you send from here." And he is taking samples from India and doing the same analysis abroad. He has the cheek to come in our lab and say that we will not believe your data unless we produce the same thing abroad.[31]

The perceived bias does not just have to do with the acceptance of cutting-edge results in academic publications abroad. It also has to do with the poor quality of materials and reagents with which Western companies supply Indian researchers, setting up a vicious cycle in which Indian labs produce less-legitimate results partly because they (at least sometimes) have reagents and kits of spurious quality sold to them, and consequently become a dumping ground for such kits because the work produced is less legitimate and powerful than work emanating from Western labs. The same researcher at CBT, which is engaged in the sorts of high-throughput genome research that many Western labs perform, had the following disclosure to make:

> We went for a kit that Amersham had come up with . . . which was a resin-based kit, and what we were finding was that for four months we struggled and we were thinking . . . and at that time our sequencing facility was also getting set up and every time we would set up the reaction, we found that their results were very inconsistent. That at times the system worked, at times half of it worked and at times nothing worked. Then one day we did it with Qiagen and we found that whenever we were using Qiagen columns, it was much better than the Amersham column. Then we found that the Amersham kit actually kills the sequencing reactions and Amersham people knew about this and they were not selling this in the U.K. and they sold it to us here.[32]

In other words, getting work evaluated in objective, unbiased ways, and being sold reagents of the same quality as the ones sold to researchers in the West, are, quite explicitly, "ethical" questions for the work being done in molecular biology labs in a country like India.

At one level, then, there are ethical articulations as they emanate from, and manifest themselves in, everyday work practices; at another level there are the ethical-political articulations of the postcolonial Indian state, often manifested through policy statements and initiatives. Some context on the framing of science policy in postcolonial India, albeit brief and sketchy, would be informative in shedding light on the ways in which biotechnology policy today gets shaped by institutional actors such as CBT, and scientific-political actors such as CBT's director, S. K. Brahmachari.

An important historical frame in which to locate Indian genomics, the history of Indian molecular biology, and the larger political contexts that have coproduced Indian technoscience writ large is the history of the Council for Scientific and Industrial Research (CSIR). Much of the history of the CSIR has been a failed one, at least in terms of R & D productivity, and in terms of fulfilling its mandate, which is to facilitate technoscientific commercialization. Established in the 1940s, CSIR is a behemoth of forty research laboratories and institutes spread all over India. Although federally funded, these laboratories constitute an autonomous structure governed by the director general of the council, as well as the individual directors of each institute, and supervised by the Ministries of Science and Technology, Finance, and Human Resource Development.

The CSIR has been a major vehicle for transforming Indian science and technology since 1990 into a body that is in tune with India's new project of economic liberalization and globalization (see Turaga 2000 for an overview of these changes). The transformation of the CSIR began with the recommendations of a committee chaired by the CSIR's current director general, then director of the National Chemical Laboratories (NCL), Ramesh Mashelkar (see Mashelkar et al. 1993). The Mashelkar committee suggested changes in the incentive structure for CSIR scientists to provide them with explicit economic incentives that until the 1990s had been largely lacking.

Mashelkar's global vision for CSIR involves generating external, nonfederal revenue, increasing annual earnings from overseas R & D, developing licensable technologies (of which there were none in 1994), and obtaining foreign patents and using them to fund operational expenditures. Indeed, Mashelkar's mantra for the CSIR explicitly replaces "Publish or Perish" with "Patent, Publish, and Prosper" (see Council for Scientific and Industrial Research 1996).

Uday Turaga, in his enthusiastic overview of the globalizing changes sweeping the CSIR throughout the 1990s, refers to its earlier, pre-Mashelkar committee avatar as a "wastrel," because it did not link its research proactively to the marketplace. However, this hides the still live tension between the Mashelkar orientation (which Turaga subscribes to, and S. K. Brahmachari at CBT follows) and another orientation that links research to "national needs" that are explicitly framed in more local terms.

Mashelkar's vision is not criticized only by those who would oppose the global to the national or local. Manjari Mahajan, for instance, is a science policy expert whose criticism of Mashelkar is not a criticism of globalization per se but a criticism of a *mode* of globalization that she feels will in fact lead to less-effective global competitiveness.[33] Mahajan feels that Mashelkar is too focused on applied research without appreciating enough the value of basic research as it translates into applications (something that, in the case of drug development, is foundational). Indeed, Mashelkar wishes to change the very name of CSIR from "the Council for Scientific *and* Industrial Research" to "the Council for Scientific Industrial Research." And yet, says Mahajan, the latter has *always* at some level been a better reflection of CSIR's mandate (rather than a new visionary articulation), and also the cause of CSIR's failures, because Indian industry has traditionally never been willing to take up the technologies that CSIR institutes have provided them. What this accent on application at the cost of basic research has led to, according to Mahajan, is an ossified CSIR, with labs doing old work and not keeping up with advancements in the field. For example, many CSIR labs are still doing classical breeding experiments while the rest of the world has started doing molecular breeding. Mahajan thinks that CSIR will continue to fall into disrepair if its focus does not shift to basic research. Of course, institutes like CBT are not so ossified precisely because the CSIR is too diverse a body for any "vision" to apply uniformly across all its institutes. Therefore, even though Brahmachari believes quite strongly in Mashelkar's vision, CBT is one of the CSIR labs whose individual mandate is basic research, and is therefore trying — perhaps almost too hard for some of its scientists — to keep up with the latest global advancements in molecular genetics and genomics.

Mashelkar himself sees his use of the "and" in a slightly different light from Mahajan. (However, she is correct in her diagnosis that what he hopes to do is collapse the distinction between basic and applied research in ways that basic research always already translates into applied priorities — thereby putting under erasure the notion of basic research itself — and that those applied priorities are naturally assumed as being commercial priorities.) Mashelkar sees his erasure in the following terms:

> This name of Council for Scientific and Industrial Research. I do believe that it's
> got this message incorporated, that we're supposed to do scientific research, we're

supposed to do industrial research. The only problem is of that "and." So we did pure scientific research which has no industrial relevance, or we did industrial research which had pretty little scientific base, because we were doing in a reverse-engineering mode in a protected environment. So the other thing that I have tried to do is to remove that "and," by saying "scientific industrial research," where industrial research is done at cutting-edge science, and remove that confusion. Because I believe in what Louis Pasteur says, that there is science, and its application, there is nothing like "basic science" and "applied science."[34]

Mapping on to this collapsing of "basic" and "applied" science is the collapse between "science" and "technology," which are often taken to correspond to the basic/applied dichotomy. While Mashelkar's reasoning resonates with the STS usage of the word "technoscience," Mahajan argues for the strategic importance of keeping that distinction alive. Indeed, the distinction between science and technology is clearly articulated in India's 1958 Science Policy Resolution (Government of India 1958), independent India's first such formal and comprehensive document, which concedes the potentials for the application of science but also considers "technology" as something temporally distinct and following from basic "scientific" activity. What is at stake in this semantic game is not just a conceptual false dichotomy between science and technology that needs to be collapsed (which is the STS motive in troubling this binary), but also the fact that this dichotomy ties into a host of others that arise from the perception of this dichotomy and operate in certain ways as a consequence. Therefore the way Mashelkar collapses science and technology, basic and applied, is a way that collapses institutional demarcation as well and suggests (as was suggested implicitly in the 1980 Bayh-Dole Act passed by the U.S. Congress, thereby laying the grounds for venture science in the United States) that the purpose and rationale for academic research is to generate knowledge that can be commercialized.

The case model of the Mashelkar approach as criticized by Mahajan, indeed, is not CBT but Mashelkar's own former institute, NCL, and its alliance with General Electric (GE) to provide contract research services: an arrangement that GE has declared as a model for its external R & D alliances (Mashelkar 1999). And yet it is precisely this model of doing contract work for foreign companies without sharing in their intellectual property that mirrors Krishna's assessment of colonial science described earlier, whereby Indian labs exist primarily to perform work that has been designed in the metropolis, which again is where the maximum value gets realized. In other words, there is a fundamental contradiction between the Mashelkar committee's vision to generate external, nonfederal revenue (generated through contract work) and its vision to generate intellectual property (which can happen only through work for which ownership resides with the Indian institute).

Some of these tensions are articulated by the current director of NCL, S. Sivaram, whom I interviewed in 2001 when he was still deputy director of the institute. Sivaram himself sees contract work not as an end in itself but as a means, first, to get initiated into standards and work practices — such as, for instance, workplace safety conditions — that are established in other parts of the world; and second, as a means to enter into tacit networks that can subsequently be formalized into strategic alliances and collaborations. He is nonetheless acutely aware of the asymmetries embodied in relationships such as NCL's with GE, asymmetries that have everything to do with India's postcolonial condition, but also with the ways that states chart their strategic involvement in global commercial politics, with profound impacts on the abilities of public institutions such as NCL to negotiate contractual market terrains. Therefore, Sivaram says:

> See, today, GE comes here, walks in and works with me. I cannot come and work with just anyone. . . . It's a question of asymmetric axis. It's basically all about the competitiveness of nations. Today we are not bothering in this country, but U.S. surely bothers about it. Europe bothers about it, Japan bothers about it.[35]

The challenge therefore becomes for Sivaram explicitly one of moving beyond a dependence on contract work for revenue generation and toward a culture of indigenous innovation. It is precisely this move that is not given enough attention by many other Indian state and private actors, located both in India and in Silicon Valley, who believe that globalization is simply about increasing foreign direct investment in India, as an end in itself, rather than as a means to effect certain types of technoscientific advances and social developments. Sivaram distinguishes contract research from entrepreneurial science thus:

Contract research is to solve somebody else's problem. So you get paid for it. It's a service. It is like a consulting service. Contract research is nothing but a kind of consulting service, except that it is somewhat higher valued. . . . But when you do contract research the ownership rests with the contractor, the ownership does not rest with you, so you really have no stake in that development. You get current income, but you don't get future income. . . . I will be dealing in both. I can't be only surviving on future promises, I need to have current resources at the same time. But to depend only on current resources is also not fair. We need to have some eggs in the basket for the future. . . . And I think the rate of entrepreneurship generation in science today is insignificantly low.[36]

And, of course, contract research has its own set of challenges:

The difficult thing is to sustain the relationship. To get a contract is not difficult but to sustain the relationship is quite difficult. Even with the multinational contracts. Yes, yes, sustaining is difficult. The leadership changes are very frequent. And there are philosophical differences between people as to what can be done and what should be done. And therefore as the leadership changes, the philosophy changes.[37]

Sivaram therefore explicitly sees NCL as reaching a phase change, where the phase of contract research needs to give way to a phase of entrepreneurial research — not because of any ideological angst about doing work for Western multinational corporations but because of the structural reasons that pressure a shift away from contract work that have to do with the tensions inherent to a dependence on economic forces and strategic decisions made elsewhere for continued revenue generation. The move beyond contract research, for Sivaram, is dictated by the very exigencies of the contract research relationship, which translate into ways in which being a "global player" fails to be in the "national interest." This failure is due to the asymmetries of global equations and relationships that have to be negotiated as a means to fulfill global desires. The Gandhian-Nehruvian–Indian Marxist opposition of the national to the global breaks down completely, yet questions of nationalism, anti-imperialism, and global inequity refuse to go away. And the solution, ironically, is seen to lie in the ability to more aggressively leverage global market instruments, the very instruments that cause a deferral of India's global ambitions.[38]

According to Mashelkar, there are two aspects to the essence of CSIR: to "advance knowledge, and to use it for the good of the people." Further: "How do you relate to the good of the people? Through economic and social development. And how do you contribute to that economic development? By contributing to industrial research."[39]

In the following vignette, I indicate how "the good of the people" gets conceived in India in ways other than globally competitive market science. This account of a scientist at Hyderabad's Centre for Cellular and Molecular Biology still shows how huge faith is pinned on the potential of science for human emancipation, but by means other than market mechanisms.

Satish Kumar is the archetypal left-leaning scientist, a member of a dying breed that makes some very old points that are perhaps vital correctives in this very new moment. He holds on to the fact that India has been unique in applying science policy with specific public objectives in mind,[40] and those needs have not vanished yet—indeed, far from it. These are objectives that are very different from the market-driven Mashelkar objectives and are perhaps not even entirely resonant with Nehruvian objectives (though they have been pursued in what might be called the "Nehruvian era" of Indian science policy). Kumar is acutely aware of the confusion between the pressure to do science with social values and the pressures of the marketplace. But he feels there is no need to play the game of the West, because India still needs to focus on food security and health.

If the first myth is the myth of the technoscientific marketplace as in itself and unaided the panacea to the country's developmental ills, then the second myth, according to Kumar, is that technology will solve all of India's problems, since, as he says, "technology is not politically neutral."[41] Kumar feels that India's priorities should be to solve problems like providing drinking water and improving investment in, and quality of, food crops, animals, and health care. He sees in the current regime of biotechnology a continuation of colonization by remote control. This is because India still "buys their biochemicals, follows the agenda set by them, and our best scientists immediately publish in those journals that most Indian universities can't afford to buy."[42] He emphasizes the importance of publicly funded health care and agriculture systems. In the case of agriculture, for instance, he feels that Indian scientists could focus on generating drought-resistant crops rather than creating pesticide-resistant crops. Kumar feels there has been total confusion over what India should be doing with regard to genomics, which means that he is at odds in his thinking on the matter with Brahmachari, who believes that he knows exactly what India should be doing as far as genomics is concerned.

When I pointed out that the thrust of India's science policy has changed from self-reliance to innovation, Kumar wondered why innovation and self-reliance cannot both be attained simultaneously. He sees innovation as a tool to attain self-reliance and does not see why one has to choose between the two. What he is against, therefore, is not innovation or development of "global" science per se, but knee-jerk imitation. He strongly feels that government agencies should not change their focus from the fact that they exist for the people.

Kumar's own work in tune with this is to create a genetic map of the buffalo. Even though this is in his own words an "unglamorous" project, he thinks it is important as a scientist to start by asking, "What if I'm successful with what I'm doing?" Keeping that in mind, Kumar feels that research efforts in genomics should concentrate on mapping and sequencing pathogens rather than playing around with population genetics (which is the buzzword for people like Brahmachari). Indeed, Brahmachari himself started his own demand for India to enter the genomics fray in the late 1980s and early 1990s with the suggestion that the ideal project to initiate India's genome efforts would be to generate a map of *Mycobacterium tuberculosis*. This intention has now been sacrificed by Brahmachari himself at the altar of human population genomics.

The fundamentals, according to Kumar, are not going to change, and those fundamentals are that over the next fifty years, you cannot take people off the land. Even wealth creation, he argues, ultimately has to be addressed in terms of the people on the land. Scientists in the lure of the market, however, pretend that only one section of the population exists, the urban. Whatever your politics, says Kumar, you cannot divorce your work from the fact of the existence of your people.

His own research, as mentioned, involves first creating a genetic map of the buffalo, a project that took him three years to obtain funding for. This is unique work because conventional knowledge of animal population genetics has not found application in India. The second strand of Kumar's work involves documenting buffalo biodiversity at the DNA level, with the objective of actually knowing the existing genetic resources in order to prioritize conservation of diverse resources. His idea is to feed his results back through cooperatives to landless peasants who depend on livestock for their livelihood. Doing buffalo genomics is in some ways easier than human genomics because of the different priorities in animal genomics compared to human. With animals, knowing the whole genome is not essential: one needs only to target specific traits such as milk production, and Kumar's plan is to work with the peasants, through the medium of cooperatives, to pursue research that can target the traits essential to enhancing productivity of milk in order to most benefit those he sees as his primary "consumers."[43]

Kumar, then, is attentive to the mechanics of how to get scientific advances down to places where they can help marginal people. On the other hand, people such as the chief minister of Andhra Pradesh, Chandrababu Naidu, or the Silicon Valley Indian entrepreneurs who are trying to establish an entrepreneurial culture in India, or Mashelkar himself all believe that scientific advance will somehow "trickle down" on its own if the market is allowed free rein. Brahmachari, the director of the CBT, differs slightly from these positions in believing that science should be in the hands of the state (while himself claiming to be "for" globalization), as a resource for the public good. The key, however, is that the entire spectrum of scientist and policy positions is animated, quite explicitly, by nationalism — though the meanings of that word are implicitly, in each case, quite different.

### Silicon Valley NRI Entrepreneurs

I now examine nationalism's relationship to globalization and to capital, as informed by Indian entrepreneurial and venture capitalist communities (many of whom operate or network out of and into Silicon Valley). In the process, I highlight how the Indian nation, in the context of these actors, becomes one way of "linking fraternity, power and time meaningfully together" (Anderson 1991 [1983], 36). Even if a range of actors whose views are broadly in consonance might have similar underlying visions (that of India "going global," or developing an "entrepreneurial culture," both of which, I argue, are sometimes, and sometimes not, the same thing), their own strategic and tactical conceptions, combined with the institutional constraints and formative pedagogies that provide them with their situated perspectives, serve to differentiate their modes of action, leading to a range of ways in which India in fact "goes global" or "becomes entrepreneurial."

I begin by talking about two major nonresident Indian organizations with powerful presence in the United States, one of which has something to do with biotechnology, the other apparently nothing at all. The former is the indUS Entrepreneurs (TiE), and the latter the Vishwa Hindu Parishad (World Hindu Forum, or vHP).

TiE's mission is the "advancement and nurturing of entrepreneurship."[44] Established in 1994 in Silicon Valley, the organization now has a presence in North America, Europe, and India. The story of TiE, and of its related and younger offspring focusing on life science entrepreneurship, the Entrepreneurial Pharmaceutical Partners of the Indian Continent (EPPIC), is, at one level, the story of a venture capital approach to governance. A thicker analysis of organizations such as TiE or EPPIC, of course, would have to comprehend them as part of the assemblages that constitute the Indian diaspora, as part of Silicon Valley as a particular locale, and as part of a certain sort of social movement that, like any governmentality, cannot bring about formal political economic change without being driven itself by conceptions of broader social change. The vHP, on the other hand, is a much older organization, founded in 1964, its purpose being the global dissemination of Hindu values and the strengthening of Hindu networks around the world. Not surprisingly, the vHP has risen to public prominence and grown in stature during the 1990s, along with the rise of Hindu nationalism as a mainstream political force in India, but also with the rise of NRI communities becoming powerful and vocal political actors in Indian affairs in their own right.

TiE's conception of change is very much based in its vanguard elite, Indians who have made it big in American entrepreneurial worlds and therefore act both as role models and as networking nodes for other aspiring subcontinental entrepreneurs. TiE's objectives are threefold, to "foster entrepreneurship and nurture entrepreneurs; provide a networking platform for its members; [and] help members integrate with the mainstream community."[45]

At one level, these objectives, of nurturing what is simultaneously a community, a cause, and a way of life, eerily echo the focus and activities of organizations like the VHP. Further, both TiE and the VHP go beyond simply spreading ideology to actively participating in creating capital flows between the United States and India, in circuits closely tied to India's ruling corporate-political elites. The VHP in America, for instance, has been singularly involved in channeling funds back to the Hindu nationalist movement in India. TiE, meanwhile, aims not just to foster an Indian entrepreneurial community in the United States but to transpose to India the sorts of cultures and mechanisms of innovation that typify high-tech entrepreneurial capitalism in places like Silicon Valley. There are also structural and cultural similarities in the way the two groups function organizationally, through seminars, lecture tours, mentoring and counseling, and operating projects back in India.

There is, however, a crucial difference between the belief systems of the two organizations. At the risk of an apparent digression, it is necessary to explore this difference a little to lay the ground for further analysis of the way India is envisioned by entrepreneurial communities such as TiE. This difference has to do with the fundamentally *exclusionary* ideology of organizations like the VHP, which therefore have to be able to innovate for themselves accessible modes of grassroots functioning. TiE, on the other hand, is ideologically inclusive and, as part of its mission, explicitly claims respect for religious, ethnic, and political diversity. Indeed, while most TiE management and members are from India, there is a play on words in the name of the organization itself: InDUS represents not just the confluence of India and the United States but also the river that flows through Pakistan, has tributaries in India, is considered the cradle of subcontinental prehistoric civilization, and forms the basis for a water treaty between the two countries that is almost sacred in its symbolization of the links between them even in times of great diplomatic stress. TiE believes that its success stems from its "single-minded focus on the mission of advancing entrepreneurship and on its unrelenting value that successful entrepreneurship eschews all culture, religious, and political boundaries."[46]

Leaving aside for the moment both the impossibility of an entrepreneurship without culture and the contradiction of an organization that is explicitly formed on the basis of ethnic and geographical identification as "eschewing" such boundaries, I tell the story of Kanwal Rekhi, a founder and former president of TiE, and arguably the best-known Indian venture capitalist in the world. Rekhi's biography is the classic one of the poor outsider who made good in the American melting pot. Of Sikh parents, and born in Rawalpindi (current-day Pakistan), Rekhi moved to the United States in 1967 as an engineer, got laid off thrice in the early 1970s, and finally moved to San Jose, where he realized the Silicon Valley entrepreneurial dream. He cofounded an extremely successful computer company called Excelan, which merged with Novell in 1989, and then moved on to become a highly successful venture capitalist and angel investor. Rekhi was one of the generation of early (1980s) NRI entrepreneurs who learned from experience that while there were an increasing number of Indian software professionals (usually highly educated and highly qualified) coming to the Valley, there were very few who were actually in management positions or starting their own companies. A major reason for that, of course, was the Catch-22 that all entrepreneurs find themselves in when first trying to start a company with venture capital money without significant entrepreneurial or VC contacts: Rekhi himself, for instance, was constantly turned away by VCs while trying to start Excelan because he did not have the "right management team." Rekhi read that, probably accurately, as meaning that there was no white person on his team. This was the situation that he hoped to rectify not by fighting against the closed networks that ultimately served to perpetuate a form of racial-ethnic discrimination but by becoming "as white as the whites" by forming his own sets of networks and mentoring relationships that would foster a community for the next generation of aspiring Indian entrepreneurs.

Rekhi's ambitions, however, are far from merely local, and far from merely being about enabling Indian professionals to be successful in the United States. He dreams, indeed, of changing India, of turning it into an innovative and entrepreneurial society. These are visions that are based firmly in an idea of meritocracy and vanguard intellect. Himself a product of an Indian Institute of Technology (IIT), the prestigious set of institutions that are the training grounds for most of Silicon Valley's Indian software professionals, he subscribes completely to the IIT belief that this group is the best of the best. In other words, an organization like TiE, which is deeply inflected by the views of

Rekhi and those like him, is, in spite of its religious and cultural inclusiveness, precisely *not* the sort of grassroots organic movement that the VHP is: these are entrepreneurs who truly believe that change can come from the top, that they represent the top, and that they can change India on their own steam. In terms of strategies and tactics, therefore, TiE and VHP believe in completely inverted fields of hegemonic action.

In addition to this strategic-tactical binary of exclusive-grassroots versus inclusive-vanguard are related binaries in conceptions of community and family. The VHP, like any fundamentalist religious movement, is deeply family centered in its focus. The entrepreneurial ideal type, however, is that of the Lone Ranger, and indeed the risks of starting a company are so great that it is deemed exponentially harder to do so when the entrepreneur has other people to provide for. Most male Indian professionals who come to places like Silicon Valley from institutions like IIT, indeed, do come as bachelors and invariably "make good" before they return to India to get married. The mantra of entrepreneurialism that TiE espouses, and indeed seeks to establish as a way of life in India, is intensely centered around a vision of a community that is formed by a more American vision of *networked individuals*, not, as in the VHP's case, a community of strong patriarchal families.

TiE transposes back to India, then, ways of starting companies that are normal in the United States, and the financial and institutional backing to follow those ways. Rekhi, for instance, has set up a start-up incubator at IIT Bombay, a model of corporate incubation in university settings, where the university provides entrepreneurs with subsidized space and some funding to see them through the earliest stages of company formation, in a way that is quite typical of models followed at a number of U.S. universities. As he says:

> The people who are at IIT Bombay, the professors and the students, they wouldn't have thought of being start-ups, so we brought this notion in. . . . You know, just . . . bringing this tradition of entrepreneurship — like they have at Stanford, like they have at MIT — to Indian universities. The Indians . . . followed the British model, by and large [for universities]. There is the notion of being very pure [and] non-commercial in your studies. In the U.S. there's a big notion of how do you use your knowledge very quickly to create wealth, create jobs? So we're bringing this concept to India now.[47]

Such a conception as Rekhi's does not see ideology as something that is spread or diffused but sees it literally as a *thing*, plantlike, perhaps, that can be packaged, physically transported, and deposited on new soil, where it will take root, spread, and grow. Notions are "brought in," like a laptop, and one can almost imagine Rekhi declaring his notions at customs as he flies into Bombay.

Related to this faith in vanguard individualism as the engine for economic growth is, not surprisingly, a disdain and contempt for the state:

> India took a wrong, a left turn, about 50 years ago and became socialist. It was a tragic mistake India made, and it's paying for that one. . . . One of the messages that I deliver when I travel there is [that] entrepreneurs are the only hope. They are the wealth creators, job creators of the society. They are the locomotives which will pull the whole train along, which is a new concept for India because the . . . mindset under Nehru, Gandhi was central ownership of industry.[48]

Indeed, at a meeting of EPPIC that I attended, one member talked of a recent visit to Bangalore where a high-level state official asked him how the state government could assist in setting up entrepreneurial ventures, and he responded that the best way the government could help would be by staying as far away from them as possible. While this entrepreneurial community professes a neoliberal philosophy, it does not take into account a fundamental contradiction that dismantling the state requires a huge amount of state intervention.

For Rekhi, spreading the free market is no less a calling than it is for Randy Scott or Patrick Terry. However, this is a calling explicitly of nation rather than religion—but a national calling that reflects what in the previous section, quoting Derrida, I called a "structural messianism." Rekhi talks about himself and his comrades thus:

> We see ourselves as missionaries now. The Indian independence movement in the '20s was led by the Indians who came back from England. They came to India [where there was] no thought of lawful society, liberal society, and they applied those concepts, and that was the basis of our freedom movement, in the '20s and '30s.

> Essentially what we're doing [now] is the economic freedom movement for India.[49]

The question of the motivation for NRI groups to get involved in channeling capital back to India is not just one of ideology or philanthropy and further cannot be explained simply by the "guilt" of NRIs who feel they "owe" something to their home country, as many Indians in conversation often postulate. Rekhi himself is quite contemptuous of explicitly "philanthropic" entrepreneurs. For instance, a group of entrepreneurs that I know pitched their business idea to him, in which a part of their business plan promised to set aside 5 percent of their profits for the development of science and technology in India—something that, one would imagine, would be in consonance with Rekhi's own ambitions. Rekhi was openly disdainful of the idea and chided them that they were supposed to be starting a business, not a charity. Easy psychological attributions of feelings of guilt as being the motive force for channeling capital back to the country are likewise little more than conjecture and fail to take into account the larger structural forces that create such feelings of obligation to one's home country. The virtually free college education provided by the Indian state is one such factor, which in this case functions with the obligatory force of the gift.[50] Rekhi himself acknowledges the quality of the highly subsidized education that IIT graduates receive, which makes his contempt for the state even more ironic. These are obligations that I argue are part of a new set of legal and incentive structures constituting citizenship and structures of feeling.

Of course, what is repatriated by members of organizations such as TiE is not simply capital but also *expertise*, in an odd quasi inversion of that oft-repeated malady of Indian technoscience, "brain drain." There is thus a confluence of repatriated capital, labor, and imaginaries. Labor, because there is an increased incidence of Indians who have gone abroad for graduate or postdoctoral study or work returning to India to further their careers; imaginaries, because the "expertise" that is repatriated is not simply formal technical expertise (which, after all, is garnered in abundance and in quality by these professionals at institutions like the IIT *before* they leave India) but cultural ideals like entrepreneurship, ideals that get reflected in mimetic institutional structures, but also in larger urban landscapes. Hyderabad, which, along with Bangalore, has been the favored city for the repatriation of capital and expertise to set up high-tech industries in India (initially mainly information technology, but now increasingly biotechnology as well), has designated six hundred square kilometers of land called "Genome Valley," explicitly conjuring an image, and thereby, it is hoped, eventually a reality, of an entrepreneurial technoscientific haven on the model of Silicon Valley.

As my account of CSIR shows, though, it is not just NRIs who have techno-scientific imaginaries about India. Such imagining is very much at the heart of the public Indian scientific establishment as well, especially in cutting-edge high-tech fields such as genomics. The question, then, is how NRI (and re-ciprocal "local" Indian) technoscientific imaginaries are at odds, or not, with NRI (and reciprocal "local" Indian) cultural-religious imaginaries, such as those of the VHP and the BJP, and how "nationalism" differentially inflects these different sets of actors.

Nationalism exists in many different varieties — a self-evident observation, perhaps, but one that is all too easily overlooked when a particular brand of nationalism becomes the dominant discursive form through which one is expected and allowed to express allegiance for the nation. Secondly, these varieties do not simply polarize into two opposed varieties, an anti-imperialist, secular, "Congress" nationalism versus a culturally aggressive, Hindu, "BJP" nationalism. In places like Silicon Valley, and for expatriates in particular, nationalism is often necessarily defined as an inchoate affective "love" for one's country and people, but it is also defined in relation to the American Other. The modes of articulation of this relationship are starkly different in the case of, on the one hand, the cab driver whose story I narrated at the start of this chapter, and on the other hand, organizations like TiE. Both recognize them-selves as racially marked, even in the absence of an explicit self-admitted racial violence that is so much a feature of everyday life for South Asian expatri-ates in, for instance, Britain. While the cab driver distances himself from the "white-blooded" American (under which category he might include the In-dian who does not speak to him in Hindi), TiE, as part of its institutional mandate, seeks to identify with the Americans, play their game, be "whiter than the whites." This is clearly stated in the organization's objectives, one of which, as mentioned, is to "help members integrate into the mainstream com-munity." The way TiE seeks to deal with minority status is by becoming such a model minority that they stop being recognized as minorities anymore.

Not surprisingly, Rekhi has been an activist lobbying for the relaxation of

U.S. immigration restrictions on Indian high-tech professionals. He has become actively involved with the Immigrant Support Network (ISN) to help foreign high-tech workers lobby to change immigration laws. But again, the way Rekhi involves himself is by projecting American interests, and himself as an American, rather than by addressing issues such as racial disparity or discrimination. For instance, he said, "My generation came here and became strong Americans. We were productive citizens, creating wealth and jobs for society, everybody was a winner. This whole new thing worries me because it ties people down, disenfranchises them economically . . . and I am worried that this will not produce a strong American economy or help entrepreneurship. So my point is to raise awareness that this situation is not very healthy for society, and if the U.S. needs engineers, it must step up and offer them a fairer deal" (quoted in Din 2001a).

And of course, the cost of easing restrictions on high-tech model immigrants has to be a tightening of restrictions on those who are not professionals. In this interview, Rekhi continues:

> When immigrants were first allowed in the '60s, they were engineers and highly skilled people. Then there was family reunification, and parents and brothers and sisters were allowed in. All of a sudden, primary immigration of professionals became secondary immigration of taxi-drivers. . . . That secondary immigration was of very poor quality, and that caused a backlash. For one engineer, you'd get ten others. It's time to go back to the original setup, where you allow professionals and only their spouses and children, not one's brothers, sisters, parents. . . . The U.S. cannot take everyone in the world. I brought my brother and sisters here, don't get me wrong, but none of them turned out . . . if you let things continue, you get an endless loop of poor quality immigration.[51]

These remarks are well in keeping with the highly individualized visions of meritocracy that TiE repatriates to India as its "entrepreneurial culture."

Joseph Dumit (1998) talks about the formation of identities by scientific fact through his notion of "objective self-fashioning," a notion that I engaged with in the previous chapter as I discussed genomic fetishism. Identity in technoscientific capitalism, however, is shaped not just by the knowledge provided by technoscience, but by the hybrid de- and relocalizations that often accompany global knowledge production enterprises. TIE entrepreneurs therefore engage in a *subjective* self-fashioning, which is a mimetic American self-fashioning that does not just confine itself to "nonresident" locales but is repatriated in the form of imagined constructions such as Hyderabad's Genome Valley. Further, it is a form of self-fashioning in the image of the American Other that already exists, before the act of repatriation, in the Indian middle-class consumer population, fed as it is on America in every form through satellite television and the flooding of its markets with foreign consumer goods.

While objective self-fashioning is, at one level, a highly individualized and individualizing form of identity formation, it is also a form of identity formation that often occurs, or subsequently manifests itself, as collective social movements, such as patient advocacy groups. Therefore it is a mode of collective individualized identity formation that, on the one hand, often propagates beyond the individual through media such as the Internet. It is also, on the other hand, often the preserve of those who have recourse to the "culture of no culture" — scientific fact shapes identity not just because it is deemed supremely authoritative but also because it is deemed to be somehow *outside* culture. Sharon Traweek refers to the culture of high-energy physicists as being a "culture of no culture," which she describes as "an extreme culture of objectivity . . . which longs passionately for a world without loose ends, without temperament, gender, nationalism, or other sources of disorder — for a world outside human space and time" (Traweek 1988, 162). By allowing the authority of science to mold one as consumer (rather than scientist), objectively self-fashioned subjects take on an identity that is perceived to be supremely objective.

The notion of a "culture of no culture" has been used in a very different sense, however, by Ruth Frankenberg (1993) in her analysis of racial-cultural self-identifications of white women, based on interviews with women in northern California. The space of no culture here is the privilege of not being racially marked that accrues to a dominant culture that does not have to define its identity in relationship to another race but can assume itself as normative. If the "culture of no culture" represents *objectivity* when the identity-forming agent is science, then it is *normative* when the identity-forming agent is race.

The question for an analysis of biocapital then becomes the following: given that there is no shortage of American companies targeting the consumer capabilities of the middle class in India, one would imagine that the problematic of understanding emergent forms of biosociality in comparative context should *not* be the question of how biosocial communities such as PXE International and Genomic Health emerge as articulate (and articulated) entities in the United States. Rather, it should be the question why such biosocial arrangements that depend on a consumer market of precisely the sorts of networked individuals envisaged by organizations such as TiE *have not* emerged in India in spite of their mimetic efforts. In other words, why have the importation and repatriation of corporate technoscientific cultures of production to India not led (as yet, at least) to the same kinds of biosocial emergences as these productions do in the United States? Why has the subjective self-fashioning of both the productive entrepreneurial community (and its allied state actors) and the consumer middle class, as explicitly "Americanized," not led to a salvationary objective self-fashioning in the image of corresponding American identity formations through processes of production and circulation of facts, technologies, and commodities? It is in asking the question of a *failure* of homogeneous emergence in spite of the explicit attempts by many actors to reproduce such homogeneity that one comes up against the importance not just of nebulous attributions of cultural difference, but also of the different salience of precisely those cultural and ideological categories, such as nation and salvation, that completely imbricate, and thereby differentiate, "cultures of no culture" as capable of being understood and made sense of only through cultural analysis.

In other words, entrepreneurial "cultures" emerge from complex institutional, material, and semiotic assemblages, which in the United States, for instance, involved the coming together, at a certain historical moment, of legislative changes (such as the 1980 Bayh-Dole Act); legal precedents (such as *Diamond v. Chakrabarty*, which allowed patents on genetically engineered microorganisms in June 1980); technological advancements (recombinant DNA technology); changing business terrains (the emergence of venture capital as a serious force in enabling technoscientific research); and business events that either anticipate or respond aggressively to these changing events (for instance, the hugely successful Genentech IPO in October 1980). Thus the question of the failures of homogeneous imitation that I pose can be answered in terms of the fact that while one can replicate components of an assemblage, it is not so easy to replicate their stratified dynamics or their structural conjunctures. To assume that India in 2002 will replicate the United States in 1980 is ultimately to buy into a deeply ahistorical discourse, because the material relations of production, the institutional relations, and the larger socioeconomic contexts are simply not comparable.

## Conclusion

At one level, this chapter is about salvation and nation in two locales of radical asymmetry, the United States and India, when it is impossible to separate the two concepts in any oppositional fashion. But it is also a chapter about the radical asymmetry between the two locales. A fundamental point that I am trying to make is that what constitutes "the global" is an American free market imaginary, one that has retained certain value systems historically but is itself at stake, emergent, and inflected with salvationary and messianic overtones. It is the articulation of particular imaginaries as global that makes American-style free market innovation an object of desire in places like India, but also makes it an ambivalent object of desire. It is the hegemony of American imaginaries, whether of the free market, property regimes, or sovereign consumers, that makes countries like India articulate their national interests in terms of being able to buy into that imaginary, but also makes them selectively resist or attempt to remodel those imaginaries, attempts that are themselves born of a simultaneously modernist and nationalist desire.

So far in this book, I have explored, through different ethnographic and narrative strategies, multiple theoretical issues concerning biocapital — exchange and value, life and debt, vision and hype, promise and fetish, salvation and nation. These are issues and concepts that constantly merge into each other. It is difficult, nonetheless, to locate all these issues in one location or another, because while the sites and processes I have traced are globally interconnected, they are so in ways that manifest in particular, incongruent manners in different locales. In many ways, therefore, this book performs George Marcus and Michael Fischer's call for multisited ethnography as a means to follow and make sense of mobile, transnational, interconnected, emergent worlds (Marcus and Fischer 1986; see also Marcus 1998). It also heeds Akhil Gupta and James Ferguson's (1997) warning about the lack of necessary or direct correspondence between particular field sites and the "field" being written about in contemporary ethnographies, between the "where" and the "what" of anthropological analysis. In other words, it is impossible to write about global processes of exchange simply by localizing them to their manifestations at particular field sites; but it is equally impossible to appreciate the complexities of these global processes *without* making them specific, since for all the hegemonic potential of globalization today, it *does* manifest in particular, tendential ways in particular, tendential places. Multisited ethnography, in that sense, is not unlike quantum physics — localizing the velocities and the positions of globally mobile actors and processes is impossible to do simultaneously and constantly requires shifting perspective from one to the other, "global" to "local," "theory" to "ethnography," without privileging one over the other as definitive. In my final chapter, I make such a shift in perspective to write perhaps the most explicitly "ethnographic" chapter of the book through the story of a San Francisco–based start-up, GeneEd.

# 6. Entrepreneurs and Start-Ups
*The Story of an E-learning Company*

A project such as this, not surprisingly, brings with it a host of ethnographic challenges. A major challenge has to do with access, in an environment that is often defined from the ground up by its secrecy. This is especially a problem in the United States, where secrecy as part of corporate culture is culturally sanctioned and legally institutionalized. Corporations are understandably wary of researchers like me who will be traveling to a range of other sites, including possibly visiting their competitors. In addition, corporations are very careful about regulating what gets said about them, their public relations apparatus often being sophisticated and forming a central component of their corporate strategic apparatus.

I received a range of responses from various companies to which I tried to get access, including three of the best-known genome companies. Millennium Pharmaceuticals in Cambridge, Massachusetts, refused to even give me a tour of their facilities, citing reasons of lack of time. Celera Genomics, the controversial company that raced the public Human Genome Project to sequence the genome, was willing to give me a tour but wanted to know exactly what the purpose of my visit would be. When I explained my research project, their investor relations person said, "Oh, I get it! You want the media tour, not the investor tour!" thereby letting on that Celera's PR apparatus is so evolved as to be compartmentalized into "media" and "investor" components.

Incyte Genomics, based in Palo Alto (unlike Millennium and Celera, which are both East Coast companies), was in contrast by far the most open of the three major genome companies, and I received a wonderful and extremely informative tour of their premises. In addition, Incyte executives that I have met have always been willing to spend lots of time talking to me, suggesting that cultures of openness and secrecy are established at the top and permeate to become normative corporate behavior — "corporate culture," if you will. This difference might to a certain extent simply reflect a more laid-back, informal, and friendly West Coast attitude compared to the hard-nosed formality of the East Coast. Having said this, when I pressed Incyte with a request for doing longer-term ethnographic research there, I was asked to send a research proposal so that it could be vetted by Incyte's team of sixty lawyers (in a company whose strength at the time was seven hundred). Needless to say, I never saw my proposal again or heard back from Incyte.

It is, of course, much easier to negotiate with a company that has twenty people as opposed to one that has sixty lawyers, since in the former case the CEO often has a definitive say in deciding on issues such as access to a traveling ethnographer. This makes me no less grateful to the people at GeneEd, the company whose story I tell in this chapter, for the time and information they gave me. Before meeting with them, however, I had engaged in lengthy negotiations with another Bay Area start-up called Neomorphic. I met with a number of people in their management team, all of whom were intrigued, if cautious, regarding my proposal, but was finally denied access when Neomorphic got bought up by Affymetrix, making it overnight part of a company of 750 from being a whole one of 25.

Indian corporations, while keen to protect their confidential information, do not adopt their American counterparts' attitude of extreme defensiveness. Getting formal approval to conduct research at CBT nonetheless proved fraught, this time not because of the concerns of the defensive American corporation but because of the concerns of the defensive Indian state, as made operational by its bureaucracy.

S. K. Brahmachari, the director of CBT, was open to my doing ethnographic research there. My presence was also accepted by the director general of the CSIR, Ramesh Mashelkar, who was the ultimate authority to sanction my access. And yet doing the paperwork to actually get access at CBT was an intricate and frustrating maneuver that highlights the bureaucratic contexts in which Indian institutions work; the security concerns of the Indian state; and a whole local political economy of red tape that is of some importance to grasp if one is to adequately understand India's path to globalization in ethnographically informed ways.

The formal paperwork at CBT had to be negotiated with the person in charge of their Business Development and Marketing Group, a man called Pawan Gupta.[1] I had initiated correspondence with Brahmachari more than two months before I was due to start my fieldwork at CBT, because he had warned me that it would take time to get all the clearances, especially from the Ministry of External Affairs (MEA), since I qualified as a "foreigner" on account of my American institutional affiliation. I had been assured by Brahmachari the week before reaching India that all the clearances had been obtained. Here was Gupta, however, who was clearly ignorant of any of these happenings and decided to go about reinventing the wheel.

Gupta started off by saying that I needed to get both MEA clearance and security clearance. I told him that Brahmachari had already obtained these. Gupta said, How can Brahmachari obtain these on his own, he has to go through proper channels (which meant Gupta). So I was told that I could not start tape-recording conversations until Gupta himself had sorted out clearance issues, and he suggested that until then I just have "broad" conversations with various people so that I could decide whom I wanted to formally interview later. I told him that I had by then had "broad" conversations with people three times over (since I had made earlier shorter visits to CBT, when I talked to a number of people there off-tape. Also, Brahmachari had arranged that I give a talk to the entire institute explaining my work and what I wished to achieve). Further, I had already drawn up a list of people I wanted to interview, and Brahmachari had formally approved that list. None of this, of course, was good enough for Gupta, who kept talking about security considerations, and about how he would be in trouble if I turned out to be a Pakistani spy. Gupta then telephoned someone in Ramesh Mashelkar's office to consult with him. This other person made it clear that I would have to get all the clearances and that getting them would take a lot of time.

Gupta then started looking over a nondisclosure agreement I had drafted, and ruminated over the document for twenty minutes. As a part of any ethnographic agreement that I draw up with my informants, I tell them that they will get transcripts of on-tape interviews for review, in order to address proprietary concerns. Gupta said that getting transcripts for review was all very well, but there might be written notes that I took that would not include what was in the tapes, and that CBT would like to see those too. I made it clear that showing him written notes was impossible, and a clear violation of my professional ethics, but that I would be willing to provide CBT with a written synopsis of what I had observed at the end of my time there.

Gupta then had an assistant draw up a list of people I could talk to, even though Brahmachari had already formally approved the list that I had come up with. Needless to say, Gupta's list was much more selective than mine. Gupta then asked his assistant to e-mail the people on the list he had made, to sound them out about the questions I was likely to ask, and to ensure that they gave "proper" answers.

I spent the next morning in continued negotiations with Gupta, who was suddenly much friendlier, since he had spoken to Brahmachari and realized that, as I had been insisting, all the paperwork had indeed been done. However, friendly, it was evident from the outset, did not mean productive. Gupta had wanted me to e-mail him a copy of the agreement that I had drafted, since he did not want to retype it all. This I had done the previous day, but he still had not received it. I told him that I would e-mail it again from the Centre, but I could not follow through because the servers at the Centre were down all day. No more progress.

The following day, I did manage to get the agreement e-mailed to Gupta, but by the end of the week I found that he had still not signed it, because he was not the person vested with the authority to do so. The only person who can sign agreements of this sort in a public institution like CBT is their administrative officer, and CBT did not have one. A new one was supposed to join the following week, which ended up delaying the whole process by another week. Once the new AO did join, Gupta insisted that it would only be fair to give him a few days to review my proposal before being asked to sign it.

Finally, two weeks after starting at CBT, I got the agreement signed. This, however, was no simple feat, but rather a protracted ritual. Gupta outlined the projected modus operandi for me to follow, since as far as he was concerned the moment of signing the agreement was the time when I actually started my research at CBT. This modus operandi involved my having to report every move to Gupta's assistant, so that Gupta could constantly monitor who I talked to, and when. The agreement itself had to be signed on judicial stamp paper, because plain paper agreements in India are not legally valid.

Gupta and I then went up to see the new AO, a rather pleasant man called Ramanathan.[2] But that did not make him any less bureaucratic. While Ramanathan was not trying to obstruct the signing any further, it was clear that he was quite perplexed by this agreement, and it was clearly not the sort of thing he was used to encountering. More than anything else, it was evident that he wanted to cover his back in case anything went wrong, and kept saying that people should not later put him on the spot and ask him questions if anything went wrong. Therefore he wanted me to pass on to him not just the transcript but also the actual physical audiotape after recording, which seemed to me a bit excessive.

Ramanathan had meanwhile ordered tea for all of us from the canteen. The waiter from the canteen brought tea in plastic Nescafe cups, and Gupta threw a fit at him. He said that the canteen had no business sending tea in plastic cups to the room of an officer such as the AO, and insisted that the canteen manager be summoned. He then ticked off the canteen manager for his impropriety, in public, and threatened to fire him if proper deference was not shown to the officers in the future (deference here meant that tea should always be served in the ancient, chipped bone china cups that one gets in government offices, rather than in plastic cups).

Gupta then decided that he would continue to make things hard for me, so after all these conversations, and in spite of the fact that Ramanathan had had two days to read my proposal and all the paperwork, he insisted that I once again describe my project to them. Fortunately, Ramanathan was as keen to end the conversation as I was, and just wanted to go ahead with the signing. The actual signing itself was quite a ritual, since each person's signature had to be countersigned by a separate witness. This meant quite a congregation for tea in Ramanathan's room. But the job was finally done, and I was finally ready to officially roll.

I mention these stories to point to the situations that ethnographers have to face when access is not just a question of personal intrusion into lived individual or community lives but a question of access to *information*, which is always already overdetermined as something that can be commodified, that is valuable and sensitive, whether by corporations or by the state. While at some level Gupta was acting difficult, at another he was merely playing an institutional role that in all likelihood would have been played out in similar ways (though perhaps in less antagonistic fashion) by others in his position. Having said this, though, I will point out that the level of petty bureaucracy that prevails at CBT is a function both of its institutional culture and of its location in Delhi, notoriously the most bureaucratic city in India.[3] As also seen with the different cultures of openness and secrecy between West Coast and East Coast biotech companies in the United States, it is evident that place matters, leading to differences even within entrenched and institutionalized normative behavior.

## Grounds, Arguments, and Sites

Many of the defining differences between biotech and pharmaceutical companies are a consequence of the differences between companies that are operated, or have operated for a significant portion of their history, in "start-up" mode — often (though not always) venture capital financed, high risk, small, innovative, and managerially supple — and those that have the capital reserves and organizational depth of an established corporation. Meanwhile, as India moves to a "culture of innovation" that explicitly attempts to imitate the Silicon Valley model, start-up dynamics, especially as they exist and play out in Silicon Valley, become central.

In this chapter I trace some of these dynamics, and the political economic terrains faced by start-ups, by telling the story of a start-up that is in some ways emblematic, and in other ways atypical, of the "romantic" start-up narrative.[4] GeneEd is an e-learning start-up in San Francisco, cofounded by two Indians, that sells life science courses to biotech and pharmaceutical companies. Therefore GeneEd's story is also a story of nonresident Indian entrepreneurs in Silicon Valley and provides a situated perspective on the drug development marketplace as seen from the vantage point of a company that sells to both upstream biotech and downstream big pharmaceutical companies.

In the process I hope, once again, to show biocapital, relentlessly, as emergent *processes*. The perspectives that I provide in this chapter are very much situated perspectives. Situated perspectives serve a political function, as Donna Haraway has forcefully argued (Haraway 1991). In anthropology even more so, and the importance of reflexively situating the perspective that one is writing from and about (which may or may not be the same thing) is increasingly obvious. This is accentuated by the fact that in this book I choose to investigate the systems of techno-capitalism from the inside: trying to get into the belly of the corporate beast that I have politically often thought about in adversarial terms. The ethnographic challenge here is to be able to narrate my multiple (usually corporate) subjects' perspectives with respect and understanding without abandoning the right, or the ability, to be critical.

GeneEd is an e-learning company. E-learning is a mode of online course preparation and a substantial industry in its own right. The company was incorporated in 1997, though it really only started operating as a full-fledged company in early 2000. It sells online courses relating to the life sciences to biotech and pharmaceutical companies.

E-learning in the life sciences is a small but growing market niche, but many companies sell courses to physicians to educate them about emergent life sciences or therapies, while others educate lay consumers. GeneEd is relatively unique in (for now) exclusively targeting biotech and pharmaceutical companies as its customers. This means that GeneEd has a particularly invested, and well situated, perspective on the upstream-downstream terrain of drug development, a terrain that has had significant consequences for GeneEd's own development as a company.

GeneEd provides situated perspectives not only on the drug development marketplace but also on Silicon Valley, on entrepreneurship, and on trajectories of the Indian diaspora. A start-up is an emergent form of life in both senses of the term: it is both an emergent entity and an emergent sociality of action.[5] The question of corporate identity—what, or who, or who all, constitute(s) a corporation—troubles me throughout this book. A start-up allows some insights into a definition. Start-ups, literally, are emergent entities: every day that they survive is a triumph, often against great odds; their days are numbered, quite literally, by the amount of cash they have left in the bank.

GeneEd develops two types of courses. The first are catalog courses, which are textbook courses developed on specific topics such as bioinformatics, microarray technology, or cardiovascular diseases. The second are custom courses, which are specifically tailored for particular customer needs. Initially, many of the custom courses were tailored catalog courses that could be accessed on customers' Web sites. For example, an important early client for GeneEd was Celera Genomics, whose Web site had a genomics tutorial that was created by GeneEd. This was, in effect, GeneEd's own catalog course on genomics, tweaked to highlight Celera's achievements. Increasingly, however, customers requested custom courses for in-house use. As GeneEd's clients shifted from being small biotech to big pharmaceutical companies, a major example of such in-house use was sales force training regarding the company's products or technologies, which is an essential and otherwise relatively labor intensive activity for pharmaceutical companies. Not surprisingly, as GeneEd consolidated itself as a well-known name in the life sciences e-learning industry, it started to depend increasingly on custom rather than catalog courses for the bulk of its revenue. But it must be remembered that GeneEd was not entering a marketplace with a product that its potential customers already knew they needed. Rather, GeneEd had to convince their customers of the value of e-learning as much as they had to convince them of the qualities of their particular e-learning packages.

In this chapter, I wish to highlight some of the themes explored in this book, through stories of a particular corporate site, rather than "theorize" them. While GeneEd is not offered as a compendium of these themes, it nonetheless offers a fascinating, situated vantage point on a number of issues and terrains I am concerned with.

Most central to this chapter is the question of entrepreneurship and starting up companies. This is important at two levels. First, the biotech industry is itself a "start-up" industry, both because of its relatively recent history and because most biotech companies do follow the classic high-tech start-up trajectory of an academic professor developing a technology in a university, raising venture capital funds, and starting his or her own company. Biotech famously operates in a start-up culture, as recounted by Cynthia Robbins-Roth in her accounts of Genentech (Robbins-Roth 2000), Paul Rabinow in his account of Cetus (Rabinow 1997), and Barry Werth in his account of Vertex Pharmaceuticals (Werth 1994).[6] Second, a start-up culture, especially a Silicon Valley start-up culture, is precisely the culture that Indian companies and public labs are trying to incorporate in their own functioning. Entrepreneurship, then, is both a cultural form and a form of subjectivity, and it is this relationship between the two that I am trying to trace here.

The principle of entrepreneurship is that there is a tried and tested formula for starting companies, and it is this formula that is taught, for instance, in management courses relating to starting up new (especially high-tech) companies.[7] And yet, not surprisingly, actual stories of start-up companies are as varied as the companies themselves, a lesson that is equally strongly communicated in management pedagogy. This is the incongruence of "theoretically" learning how to start companies—on the one hand, there is the "correct" approach that is enshrined by authors such as Sahlman, while on the other there is the case study approach, emphasized by most MBA programs, which highlights the actual variations in start-up stories.

One sees a similar sort of incongruence as India attempts to incorporate a start-up culture into its technoscientific establishment—on the one hand, there is the American formula, Silicon Valley; on the other, the radical incongruence of actually starting up such a culture on the ground, a process full of particularities. In this sense, GeneEd is a typical start-up only by virtue of its being atypical. Through the stories I narrate, it is clear that however much the company may claim to subscribe to "tried and tested" formulas or buck them, there is always a pressure to do things according to the pedagogical norm, just as actual events invariably pan out otherwise. The best example of this is GeneEd's constant, and so far unsuccessful, attempts to raise venture capital money—something that the company's CEO, Sunil Maulik, is extremely ambivalent about, at least partly because it will lead to his having to relinquish considerable hold over the company, but something that he constantly attempts to do nonetheless. In the context of GeneEd's being a typically atypical start-up, I tell a number of stories that all emphasize the particularities of GeneEd's own historical emergence while nonetheless showing how these emergences occur in the shadow of, and are shaped by, capitalist logics that are themselves at stake through emergent corporate entities.

### Beginnings

GeneEd was conceived in the early 1990s, to the extent that even before the existence of the World Wide Web, one of the company's founders, Sunil Maulik, conceived of the possibilities of using the computer to teach science. Born in Bombay, Maulik grew up in England, where he studied biology before moving to Brandeis University for a Ph.D. After his degree, he moved in the late 1980s to Silicon Valley to join a company called Intelligenetics. Intelligenetics was a "bioinformatics" company before bioinformatics existed. Maulik's contemporaries at Brandeis thought he was crazy. It was still relatively unusual to leave academics to do research in a company at that time; but more than that, who would ever do biology in a company that only had computers? From Intelligenetics, Maulik moved through a series of other companies before ending up at Pangea Systems (which subsequently became Doubletwist before going out of business).

It was during this time that Maulik met Salil Patel. Of Indian descent, Patel spent his early childhood in Uganda before his family became one of the many Ugandan Indian refugee families who moved to England because of their persecution at the hands of Idi Amin. In England, Patel grew up with many other refugee families in Greenham Common, the site of a U.S. Air Force base made famous by antinuclear demonstrators during the 1980s. Patel did a Ph.D. at Stanford and a postdoc at Caltech before joining a biotech firm to do research on angiogenesis in order to develop gene therapy.

In his spare time, Maulik used to teach seminars on bioinformatics, often at evening colleges and university extension schools, and once they became friends, Patel would occasionally stand in for him. They both shared and developed together a love for teaching, which blossomed in Maulik's mind into a corporate opportunity. Bioinformatics was just becoming big; it would be the future. Why not start a company to teach bioinformatics? And why not teach it on the Web, in order to reach a really wide audience?

It was easy for Maulik to think of leaving a job to start his own company. He typified the Silicon Valley entrepreneur. Divorced, he did have a child to support, but not a traditional nuclear family structure to seriously distract him from the manic commitment and risk that any entrepreneurial activity entails. In any case, Maulik, again fitting the Silicon Valley stereotype made famous by Jim Clark (the founder of Netscape), was someone who dared to think differently. Maulik is extroverted and fun loving, and he enjoys talking about his ideas for a company — precisely the sort of person that financial communities in any other place and at any other time in history would immediately have run away from. In Silicon Valley, he was perfect CEO material.

It was a lot harder for Patel to leave his job and jump into the world of entrepreneurial unknowns. In addition to the commitments of marriage, he had grown up being a scientist: relatively shy, passionately committed to his research, and not, in his own mind, at all an entrepreneur. Only his friendship with Maulik and his love of teaching made Patel even seriously consider jumping ship. GeneEd, therefore, was founded and incorporated as far back as 1997, but the company really remained in a state of limbo for the next couple of years as Maulik and Patel balanced their new company with their existing jobs. During this time, in Maulik's terms, GeneEd lacked the "activation energy" to function as a real company doing real business on its own.

Starting a company often requires some form of crisis to make the risk worthwhile. For Patel, it was a progressive disenchantment with his current employer, a disenchantment that really stemmed from the type of scientist that he is. Patel has a firm belief in science — in the truths it provides, and in the ways it must be performed — that harkens back to an era of positivism and loyally reflects Merton's norms of science, an ethos that seems strangely out of place in today's postmodern venture science environment that thrives on the ability to be cynical. Patel's almost myopic principle that science is about the quest for truth encountered considerable friction from the everyday activities of an aggressive biotech company.

Patel, in any case, was not terribly happy with the way his former company was managed, an unhappiness that clearly proved to be a learning experience as he moved on to become a manager of a company himself. He was involved in gene therapy work that was constructed as the company's flagship project, and yet he was given meager resources and only four researchers under him. After a year of working on his project, his team reported generally negative results, which he took to the management, advising them to drop the project altogether. The next day, the company put out a press release announcing the stunning advances they had made toward gene therapy, using as examples the sorts of seriously troubled projects such as Patel's that the company was actually pursuing (or considering not pursuing). This public relations stunt got them the desired publicity and allowed their stock prices to shoot through the roof at a time when stock markets were highly responsive to the slightest hint of promise. In Patel's belief system, however, this piece of what in many circles might be admired as clever marketing was nothing other than scientific fraud. His disenchantment, increasingly, was not just with the way the company was being managed but with the form of life that the company stood for. Maulik's entreaties to join him were looking more and more attractive. What finally gave Patel the courage to make the jump was the support of his wife Tejal, who insisted that he should do what gave him satisfaction, rather than simply what brought home the proverbial bacon.

Maulik, meanwhile, was running the idea of GeneEd by John Couch, the CEO of Pangea, where Maulik was at that point in charge of business development, and was generally getting Couch's blessings. As far as Couch was concerned, anyone who could go out and educate other biotech and pharmaceutical executives about bioinformatics was in effect creating informed customers for companies like Pangea. By December 22, 1999, the company incorporated two years previously had slowly gathered enough momentum to appear ready to go on the road. Maulik had been promised money by venture capitalists and had made eight job offers. On that day, he threw a party for the new employees to celebrate the "beginning" of GeneEd.

The real beginning, according to both Maulik and Patel, happened neither when GeneEd was incorporated, nor when they made these initial hires, but on the day after the party, December 23, when Maulik, in the midst of a hangover, was informed by the venture capitalists who had promised him funding that they had decided not to give it to him after all. This was the crisis that provided Maulik with the activation energy to really get GeneEd started, as he was faced with no money and eight employees as a single parent who had maxed out four credit cards. The option remained to return to Pangea and resume his job there, but the withdrawal of the VCs' commitment made Maulik determined, more than ever, to convert what he was by now convinced was a very good idea into reality.

Over the next few weeks, Maulik went into money-raising frenzy. He called up a couple of his friends who had struck gold in the dot.com boom and were toying with the idea of doing some angel investing.[8] His friends asked him if he needed money in the next few months. No, said Maulik, he needed it in the next few days. Meanwhile, Maulik was on the road trying to sell what GeneEd had to offer in terms of products, and was receiving expressions of interest from biotech companies like Celera Genomics. Maulik also approached Celera's Silicon Valley rival Incyte, not just as a customer but as an investor. Like John Couch at Pangea, the management at Incyte was enamored with the idea of a company that would effectively be educating the industry about products it made and services it offered, and agreed to invest $500,000 in GeneEd.

One Saturday morning when Maulik was spending time with his mother, he received a call from a friend saying that he should make a pitch to Ernest Mario, CEO of Alza Corporation, a Silicon Valley biotech company (since bought by Johnson and Johnson) that made improved drug delivery systems. Getting an appointment with Mario for that very afternoon, Maulik drove unshaven to Alza's headquarters. He strolled through Alza's spacious, fountain-bedecked grounds into Mario's huge executive suite and talked him into investing another $500,000 in GeneEd. Within the next few weeks, Maulik, who had really been looking for about $500,000 in total to get his company going, had $2.25 million, and not a cent of it venture capital money. His failure to obtain venture capital funding has had serious long-term consequences for GeneEd's corporate culture, allowing it to be molded by the personalities of the management and employees, but also making it acutely dependent on constant sales in order to stay afloat: the sort of desperate fiscal discipline and pressure to produce, innovate, and sell that most dot.com companies, flush with millions of dollars of venture capital money, never had to deal with. I will have more to say about some of these pressures, and the culture they have given birth to. For the time being, however, GeneEd had emerged.

As mentioned earlier, GeneEd sells its courses to both small biotech and large pharmaceutical companies. It is therefore extremely invested in the drug development marketplace, which is the space that I am trying to elucidate. GeneEd is not a neutral site: no situated observation site can be. By selling to both small and large, biotech and pharmaceutical, upstream and downstream companies, however, GeneEd's worldview is more encompassing than those of these companies themselves, who tend to view marketplaces and market logics very much through a situated perspective that discursively constructs terrains and logics as *only* existing the way a given company sees things. One of my arguments throughout this book is that capitalism draws its sustenance, and encounters its resistance, from the multiple contradictions of the marketplace; for biocapital, many of those contradictions play out between biotech and pharmaceutical companies. GeneEd is able to "see" those contradictions in a more complete, though by no means less self-interested, manner than many companies that are actually in the business of making drugs, because GeneEd's business strategy depends on such a nuanced understanding of the upstream-downstream terrain of drug development.

A start-up's location is itself important to identify. Biotechnology is a form of venture science. Genomics in particular, taking place as it is in the midst and aftermath of the dot.com boom, has as central to its calculus entrepreneurs and venture capitalists. GeneEd itself is not a company funded by venture capital, though not for want of effort. It is nonetheless very much a company at the heart of venture science.

The particular location of this company in geographical terms adds to its interest. Being in San Francisco, GeneEd is a Silicon Valley company, and yet not a Silicon Valley company. Location does count for start-ups, and being in places like, especially, Silicon Valley enables the creation of networks and contacts that are of prime importance in hiring the best workers and managers, being in corridors of conversation with investors, and being able to easily access customers and collaborators. It is much harder to be a start-up in Kalamazoo, Michigan. GeneEd is very much a product both of its times and of its place. And yet that place is not alongside a freeway in Palo Alto, Fremont, Santa Clara, or San Jose but in a run-down part of San Francisco south of Mission Street. Within two blocks' walk, one can reach a rather trendy part of San Francisco's shopping district; an ornate Hispanic church; a community kitchen where homeless people get fed; a cafe-cum-laundromat where one can have lunch while washing one's clothes; a bakery that sells X-rated cakes; and a transvestite nightclub. GeneEd initially shared its office building with a company that manufactured jeans.[9] Many of GeneEd's employees, including Maulik, live or have lived in the Mission district and share in the general community concerns over the progressive corporatization of their locality. That GeneEd is a part of that corporatization is an irony that is acutely felt within the company. GeneEd's Silicon Valley is not the Silicon Valley of strip malls and suburban villas that most northern Californian biotech companies inhabit, or even that other sought-after biotech locality made famous by Genentech, South San Francisco (which calls itself "the Industrial City").

Maulik and Patel are both of Indian descent, both grew up in Britain, and have both lived in Silicon Valley for over a decade. There are stories of friendship and of hybrid backgrounds in their biographies. As is the case with many start-ups, the founders' biographies leave a significant mark on the culture, identity, and even (perhaps unwittingly) corporate strategy of the company they create. The Indian entrepreneurial community in Silicon Valley is one of the central links in this book between the drug development worlds of India and the United States. Maulik and Patel both belong to, and yet by virtue of their British upbringing are distinct from, that community.

In terms of being a site of knowledge production, GeneEd is an interdisciplinary space that reflects the centrality of interdisciplinary border crossings in the scientific-corporate worlds that I am studying. GeneEd's courses are physically designed by a team of graphic designers (who mostly have no advanced training in the life sciences and so pick up their biology on the job); their computers are maintained by programmers, and content is provided by Maulik and (mainly) Patel, who are both biologists. Indeed, my own function, in exchange for the access I was given, was to deliver a weekly seminar on the history of biology to the entire company in order to get the employees aware of, and talking about, issues in the life sciences. These seminars proved to be fascinating ethnographic moments for me.

### Access

I first met Sunil Maulik at one of the many receptions that define industrial genome conferences, in September 2000. After an engrossing initial conversation, I met him again on a trip to the Bay Area in November of that year, when he was in the midst of dealing with a company that wanted GeneEd to design a bioethics course for them. By this time, I had broached to Maulik the idea that I might do fieldwork at GeneEd. Maulik was open to the idea and arranged for me to give a talk at GeneEd as a way of introducing myself to the other people in the company to see how they felt.

In my talk, I provided a quick overview of science studies and cultural anthropology, how the two came together, how they met in my work, and how I expected GeneEd to fit into it. I actually thought I would have to do a lot of explaining about the last part, as GeneEd is not a genomics company, and I expected them to be preoccupied with the question of how they would fit into a contemporary (which generally gets understood as linear) history of genomics. On the contrary, they seemed to assume that GeneEd would quite obviously fit into a story such as mine, and in fact picked up on a lot of the history I was giving to ask me questions, something I had not really expected.

I received many questions and comments on my summaries of science studies literature. For instance, they really took on Bruno Latour and actor-network theory, and Salil Patel in particular really wanted me to explain how actants *work* (being quite readily convinced at the outset that science is basically a recruiting exercise!).[10] Maulik meanwhile wanted to know what *I* thought scientists' motivations were, since scientists constituted GeneEd's consumers, and thus the company really needed to understand what drove them. In other words, I was already being co-opted into GeneEd's interdisciplinary enterprise as a marketer.

After the talk, the employees went around the table introducing themselves, and then Maulik stood up and started what he called a "values and visions" session. Apparently the management (which at that point consisted of Maulik, Patel, Paul Eisele [the chief operating officer, a much more senior man who was steeped in years of sales and marketing experience in the entertainment industry], and Barry Giordano, the vice president of sales) had sat down together and tried to come up with a series of core values for the company. This was an acknowledgment and a reflection of the fact that the relationships between their primary markets (executives of other biotech and pharmaceutical companies) and their secondary and tertiary markets (which really could be anyone, including other biotech and pharmaceutical companies, but also lay consumers as the company made its courses more accessible to laypeople) were so complex. Maulik started by talking about an article in the *New York Times* (January 31, 2001) on direct-to-consumer advertising to parents of children with respiratory syncytial virus (RSV), put out by the biotechnology company MedImmune, in order to highlight GeneEd's complicit and complicated relationship with the marketplace that the company is so invested in.

Even though GeneEd itself is in no way involved in direct-to-consumer advertising,[11] issues like these point to situations that directly confront it as "value" questions, in both senses of the word. This is because GeneEd is caught in a peculiar dialectic between being an education company and an advertising company. In the former role, it creates its own, supposedly "neutral," education packages: neutral in the way a textbook would be neutral, drawing on generally known scientific literature to create the packages. But much of GeneEd's immediate revenue comes from doing contract work for other companies. In these cases, GeneEd does not provide the content, only the form. Therefore situations such as the MedImmune advertisements immediately highlight the need to question and critique what is meant by "public education." Further, these are not hypothetical situations: GeneEd had already developed an antibodies course and had already been approached by one of MedImmune's competitors to develop courses that they could use.

So Maulik talked about GeneEd's values. There is a tension in that word itself which reflects the tensions in GeneEd's complex relationships with its primary and secondary or tertiary markets. These values, as mentioned earlier, were initially outlined by the company's four executives, and Maulik was now opening them up for discussion by everyone else. Eisele summarized some of the "internal" values by saying that basically GeneEd wanted to be a company that allowed its employees to "have a life." One of the younger workers mentioned the need for the company to have an ethic, to have "unbiased opinions" on ethical issues. Patel immediately scorned the possibility of such a thing as "unbiased opinion" and said instead that they needed to have at their disposal "enough information to make up our own minds." Maulik now introduced the central tension for the company, that half of their courses are customized for companies. The question then becomes what to do when the company has ethical conflicts. The question, as Maulik posed it, was "Should it be the company's business to walk away from business?"

A graphic designer immediately translated the hypothetical company with which GeneEd might have ethical conflicts into an "evil company," and then immediately into the hypothetical case that Monsanto might approach

GeneEd for business.[12] She said that companies like Monsanto, whether re-garded as "evil" or not, should be allowed to say (through the medium of GeneEd) whatever they wanted to. She did not think it was unethical to work with a company whose business plans or projects were controversial. Her argument was for a company's free speech.

Eisele, however, said that GeneEd's walking away from a company did not deny that company its free speech. A visiting bioinformatic programmer said that it was important for a company like GeneEd to maintain its credibility. Patel said that in fact one of the first suggestions making the rounds among the executives was to prepare courses on genetically modified foods, but that he was personally disinclined because it was such a polarized issue, and GeneEd did not want to get caught in the middle. Maulik then asked the central question: Is it GeneEd's role to rule on the content? Do we want to be a cen-sor? Patel admitted that GeneEd had already developed a number of custom courses in which the content was not a hundred percent honest, or was some-how misleading. Eisele argued that in these cases GeneEd was the messenger and not the message. Again, therefore, the central question being contended with here was: Is GeneEd an education company or an advertising company?

Maulik arrived at the in many ways happy (albeit easy?) compromise that "if we get lots of money from pharmaceutical companies, we can redistribute it." He then suggested that 5 percent of GeneEd's time and resources would be used to contribute to nonprofit sources. He also, in that vein, mentioned the possibility of being involved in technology transfer to developing countries, and of course all sorts of possibilities exist for a company like GeneEd in a place like India.

So that was the conclusion of the values and visions session. Maulik then took me aback by asking everyone publicly and in front of me what they wanted to do with me, whether I should be invited back for a longer-term interaction. I suggested that this might be a conversation better had in my absence. One designer said she would be happy to have me back if it meant free lunch again. Generally, everyone seemed receptive, though it was sug-gested that they eventually decide through secret ballot. But Maulik was very upfront about the fact that he certainly wanted me back, and was equally upfront about the fact that it was his ego prompting him to be written about as much as anything else. On the other hand, both he and I realized that I might be valuable to him precisely because his consumer base is potentially anyone, and he knew that I might give him access to consumers such as patient groups, social scientists, and other scientist-businesspeople, and that I might also be invaluable in helping him think through ways of moving into India. This was always already a complicit ethnographic relationship.[13]

What remained at GeneEd, then, was negotiating the terms of access, especially as they related to confidentiality. After two weeks of negotiation, we finally agreed on a fourteen-point, legally binding nondisclosure agreement, modified from one of their standard templates to fit an academic ethnography. It required me to respect GeneEd's confidential information but allowed me to write or speak about their nonproprietary information for academic purposes. On the strength of this contract, I was given full access to the company, including their weekly management operations meetings and their company financial documents.

### Labor

There are two "labor" stories that I recount about GeneEd. The first has to do with the management structure of the company, which, when I first spent time there in 2001, had only one woman in the management team. The second has to do with the graphic designers who design GeneEd's e-learning courses, the "workers" of the company.

The management team of GeneEd in mid-2001 was pretty much its founding management team. Its cofounders, Sunil Maulik and Salil Patel, were the chief executive officer and chief scientific officer respectively. Paul Eisele, a more senior man with years of experience in the entertainment industry, was the chief operating officer; and Barry Giordano, an old friend and past boss of Maulik's, was both an investor in the company and its vice president of sales.

Directly reporting to Patel was Cynthia Kilroy, who had joined a few months after GeneEd started operations. She was in charge of product development. While Patel's job was to actually develop course content, Kilroy's job was to coordinate the development of that content into a visual, online e-learning course by the graphic designers, in consultation with the client if the course in question was a custom course. Kilroy had started her career as a software developer, went on to manage projects for health care organizations, and then spent five years doing consulting at Arthur Andersen.

Being a project manager at GeneEd in 2001, of course, was very different from consulting in one of the "big six" firms, because one of the defining features of working in a start-up is that it is impossible to rigidly enforce a strict division of labor: it is often essential for everyone in the company to multitask. In these early days of GeneEd, therefore, Kilroy saw herself as a "chameleon," doing whatever needed to be done on a particular day: a job description that fitted most of the GeneEd employees, from Maulik downward.[14]

The fact that Kilroy was the only woman on the management team, of course, was quite significant for her work situation at GeneEd. Most difficult for her at the time was her relationship with the two salespeople, Giordano and Mark Greenbaum, who were both experienced at sales and felt that Kilroy needed to prove herself. Of course, there was a certain amount of territoriality involved, in the very way GeneEd sold its product. GeneEd constantly made "sales and science" pitches. Their idea was that one of the salespeople would always be accompanied by either Maulik, Patel, or Kilroy, first of all to lend a certain gravitas to the impression they conveyed, as a "serious," "scientifically oriented" company, and also because their products were technically quite complicated, making it useful to have someone who was involved in a product's development there to explain it. Following up with the client also involved a delicate division of labor. The product developers interacted with the client to ensure that the courses (especially if they were customized) were developed to the client's satisfaction, while the salespeople had to stay attentive to closing the deal and to opening up other possible deals with the same client (as well as with others). The potential for one group of people stepping on the other's toes was significant, especially as issues of seniority, experience, and gender were superimposed.

Kilroy was extremely attentive to the gender dynamics in her interaction with the sales force, as she said:

> This is the first place I have ever worked where Salil and Sunil came to me and said, We don't like the way X is treating you and we're going to take care of it. I don't want it to sound the way it's going to, but it's probably because I'm the only woman on the management team and I think some of the sales guys probably get

away with things and treat me like crap, and I just have no respect for that. . . . And I think I played into some of that because I let those guys fight for me. I'm pretty outspoken and stuff but I can go nervous and sit at the back, and when I get more nervous, I get more spelling mistakes in my e-mail and I wasn't taking the time and then they didn't have the respect.[15]

Nonetheless there was no doubt in Kilroy's mind that a start-up still provided a more egalitarian system than what normally prevails in big companies in the American corporate world:

Like I said, I come from a huge consulting house that was very male-dominated. It was plain they strategically picked all women to interview me and had a partner that I was reporting to that was a woman. The problem is that for me when I look back now, while I had made the decision to go there because there were a lot of women, it's definitely still an old-school, old-boys' network.

Kilroy's opinions are hardly atypical, and they have recently become the sorts of opinions that have been the center of conversation in corporate America, consequent to the publication of the economist Sylvia Ann Hewlett's 2002 survey *Creating a Life*, which argues for the incompatibility, for women, of having a high-powered corporate career with having a family. Kilroy's own way of dealing with this situation is to

just prove myself and simply claim I've been smart enough that I've always wound up being able to do a good job. And then sometimes there is an opportunity, where you're kind of joking around the table and you can make a joke of what people know, that you know what they are about and then hopefully then they will look at their behavior and then realize.[16]

Of course, as a manager, Kilroy had herself to be sensitive to people-management issues, especially since she, more than anyone else, formed a direct bridge between the management and the designers who designed the courses. And here too the situation at GeneEd underwent a change as the company's clientele changed.

GeneEd started off primarily offering online e-learning courses on various life-science-related topics to people in the industry. The company designed a series of what were called catalog courses, which were basically generic textbook courses on a number of aspects of emergent life science, such as, for instance, bioinformatics or microarray technology. GeneEd also designed custom courses. Initially, these courses were often animated presentations that would go onto a company's Web site, such as Celera's genomics "tutorial," which was designed to highlight Celera's achievements. Predictably, custom courses were proving to be better revenue earners than catalog courses, when the target market was largely people who were in the industry already, and GeneEd spent most of its time designing these customized courses. It was Kilroy's job to allocate responsibility for the courses to the designers and to ensure their proper execution.

By mid-2001, it was clear that the designers were the indispensable labor force for the company. Indeed, there was not a group of what could be called "workers" independent of them. All the content was provided almost single-handedly by Patel, Kilroy's job was to ensure follow-through on projects, two salespeople handled the West Coast and East Coast respectively, one systems administrator made sure the computers were working properly, Eisele ran the nitty-gritty operational aspects of the company, an office manager assisted with whatever tasks needed help, and Maulik went out and sold the company's vision to prospective investors and customers. It was the group of (at the time) four designers who really executed the creation of the courses.

Kilroy felt that her job at the time was very much to be a mentor to the design team. Further, whole courses were allocated to specific designers, which meant that each designer was able to imprint his or her own artistic style on the course. Course allocation was a strategic exercise for Kilroy, as she tried to match each designer's artistic temperament to the requirements of the client. This meant that there was lots of room for artistic creativity. For instance, one of the graphic designers, Cyane Rollins, described her work, and the division of labor, to me in the following terms in mid-2001.

> CR: We have a project manager who keeps an eye on all of our schedules and an eye on projects down the line and then she'll allocate these projects to us and watch our schedules and keep tabs on our progress. We as developers work under her and work for Sunil, and because we're so small, it's not obviously very hierarchical. We have me down here and Salil and Sunil up there, which is great because I have plenty of room for feedback, and they listen to our feedback, which I think is great

on their part. It's great because I feel they listen to us and then make changes or whatever or help us out, but also it's good for them too because we have ideas. They are sort of looking at the more business and marketing side and we are looking at the more technological side—what's out there, how can we improve, what we're doing, that sort of thing. So that we have this little ecology. That's why I think this is a little ecological system. And that's pretty much the main thing— there's the management and then there's the project manager and then there's developers and then there's the HIPAA Department and then Robin, and I think that we're also working side by side. . . .

We [developers] critique each other and rely on each other for feedback, but when we get a project, we pretty much work on that from start to finish ourselves, and it's good because it's good to know. . . . You know you're beginning to know this stuff from the top, you're beginning to learn, and we know how to do animation and how to load it, what flaws and bugs might happen. The downside of that is that I know a lot about bioinformatics and drug design but I know nothing about microarrays or the other courses that other developers are doing and it takes a while to learn those courses. So that's one downside, and I don't know, I mean, it seems like . . . we're all seeing, I think in the future we'll see our goal because we all have different strengths, which is great. . . . You know like Jill has her 3-D modeling, and Jerry and Jill are very into the action scripting, and Tara has traditional animation which she brings to the table, and I have the educational background and then I have video stuff, so that's something that I could use. So we all have the different things that we're interested in and we can bring them together to the table. And between us . . . maybe it'll be in the future that, I don't know . . . I'm thinking that it could be really cool if one of us becomes a real expert in one area, and then we start dividing up in that way.

But right now it's working perfectly well the way we have it.

KS: So do you see a more defined sense of rules and responsibilities since you have joined?

CR: I think it's very defined now. I think it is very defined now.[17]

In other words, even in 2001, a year and a bit into the functioning of GeneEd as a fully operational company, the designers were beginning to see a certain amount of streamlining in the company's operations, but it was a streamlining that still left considerable agency to each designer to design his or her own courses. There was also a perceived sense of collegiality, what Rollins referred to as an "ecology," whereby both middle and upper management were accessible not just to mentor the designers but to receive feedback from them that could drive the company's decisions.

A number of things have changed for GeneEd structurally since then. The biggest change came in the summer of 2001, when GeneEd landed Astra Zeneca, a big pharmaceutical company, as a customer for a series of in-house courses such as sales force training. Astra Zeneca is a company of fifty-five thousand people, orders of magnitude larger than any of the biotech companies for which GeneEd had developed courses until that time. This meant three things for GeneEd.

First, there was the possibility of a sustained buy-in. A successful execution on their initial assignments, they knew, could lead to GeneEd being given other assignments by other divisions of the company. There was a chance to grow their market even within a single company, in a way that had never existed when GeneEd was developing courses for their biotech clients. Second, there was a possibility of gaining brand recognition within the pharmaceutical industry. Even though the GeneEd brand was visible on many biotech Web sites, for instance, that was hardly enough of a selling point to ensure that big pharmaceutical companies would be interested in giving them business. As Maulik always liked to point out, the difficulty — and the challenge — of selling a company like GeneEd's products is that one has to convince the customer not only that GeneEd offers the best product on the market but also that it's a product the customer needs in the first place. Getting the Astra Zeneca project gave GeneEd a toehold in the market of big pharmaceutical companies. Third, the amount of work that now had to be done to simultaneously implement the Astra Zeneca courses, continue their custom courses for other clients, and continually improve their existing catalog courses meant that it became essential to further streamline the process of course creation.

The way GeneEd did this was to develop what the company called "learning objects": modules or vignettes of courses that might already have appeared in their other courses, which could exist as independent objects in a searchable database, which could then be pulled out and inserted into a new course. In other words, GeneEd was shifting away from being a design company that would craft individual customized courses as if each was the creative product of a single graphic designer, to being a *knowledge management* company that would generate courses by an assembly line cutting and pasting of existing course modules (with, of course, the development of new course vignettes or modules as and when necessary).

Once a course becomes a collection of independently assembled objects, it becomes vitally important to standardize those objects. One just could not have a course that was put together by objects from previously designed courses that each had a distinct artistic signature. Very quickly, therefore, the role of the graphic designer stopped being one of artistic creation and became one of industrialized assembly. This did not even need a conscious strategic change of direction: it was simply the consequence of scaling up the enterprise and growing the company.

In the process, however, Maulik realized that the very assemblage of learning objects and the software infrastructure needed to support them and make them searchable was, independent of the *content* of the objects, itself a set of software applications that had value. In other words, while GeneEd, as an e-learning company, could sell courses to clients, it could also, as a *knowledge management* company, sell software applications to other e-learning companies. What this led to was an increased dependence on programmers.[18]

Therefore, largely as a consequence of selling courses to downstream big pharmaceutical companies instead of upstream biotech companies (who, as more big pharmaceutical companies became interested in GeneEd, became less and less a source of significant value), the entire work structure changed within a year. Suddenly it was the programmers who were doing the glamorous work, while the designers were merely assembling content.

Robin Lindheimer, who had been hired as a systems administrator in 2001, had by 2002 been promoted to manager of information technology. Just the challenge of automating processes as the company grew was for him a major programming challenge. While earlier Lindheimer had felt that his role was "just that of a plumber," he now felt that he was "dealing with the technology of GeneEd rather than with the technology of the world that helps you run an office."[19] He saw the company moving in a direction where selling courses would become incidental to developing salable software.

Indeed, GeneEd in 2002 had the sort of glamour—of doing something "cool" while doing something "good"—for programmers that it had held for graphic designers in 2001. Chris Palmer, a programmer who chose GeneEd over two other job offers, compared it to choosing to work at Apple rather than at Microsoft, where "Microsoft is just another job. Whereas Apple is a mission that people believe in, a community of far-thinking researchers that is a part of the business culture. That means a much better product—a product in which the labor of love has been put into it. It's a product that's better than good enough, it's actually great, and that has an economic effect and a personal effect."[20]

Conversely, and unsurprisingly, the graphic designers by 2002 felt increasingly stifled and unenthused, as evidenced by the following quotes (all kept anonymous):

> It's harder now for each designer to express herself. There are tensions between the individual creativity of graphic designers and the requirements of a corporate structure. Therefore, working here is not that creatively fulfilling. . . . I rarely see Cynthia on a day-to-day basis.

> The content is much more modular. We are more conscious of the process now. It takes a lot of energy to keep people interested and motivated. From the developers' side, our creative license as artists is missing. Earlier, we could create entire projects ourselves. . . . I don't know what Cynthia does.

> A change to bigger projects has meant a more streamlined process. We're not responsible for whole courses now. Streamlining and efficiency means less creativity for the artist. It's not good for the artists because the job isn't artistic anymore. I think most of the artists would have left if the economy was better. The company has become more hierarchical. Earlier, there was a pancake structure, anyone who had an idea got listened to. Now that's not the case anymore. . . . We'll probably get funding, get bigger, and have more growing pains.

> There is considerable freedom in terms of how I want things to look in terms of graphics themselves. But in terms of the interface, templates have been created which can't be redesigned. As an artist, I get bored really easily. I'm a *graphic* designer rather than an *instructional* designer. I try not to let the boredom show,

but it does. There's not a lot of interaction with the other developers. I miss that. . . . There's no communication with management, and rare interactions with Cynthia. The instructional designers are the bottom of the totem pole. We were really important when the company was a start-up. [The designers] pretty much made or broke the project. I enjoyed smaller-scale projects more, because I had more freedom, I could bring more design sense to bear. . . . The biggest frustration is being held down by management.[21]

In other words, the loss of artistic license, which was felt without exception among the graphic designers at GeneEd, was accompanied by the loss of the company's nonhierarchical management structure. It was also accompanied, not surprisingly, by an increased dispensability of individual designers. Indeed, this was almost logical. As one designer told me, almost the only way the company could have motivated designers was by constantly hiring new and inexperienced designers who would be motivated because they would be learning how to design on the job. Of course, that would compromise the quality of design, a quality that itself was becoming increasingly incidental and prepackaged. Sure enough, in May 2002, the company laid off two of its designers, one of whom had been with the company since its inception.

This dispensability was felt not just by the designers; it was echoed by the management. Therefore Kilroy, who in 2001 was explicit about the importance of mentoring the designers, and about her own central role in that mentoring process, was by 2002 admitting that there was now a line between management and "staff" (in 2001, she was still referring to them as "designers"). But then, she felt: "That's not a bad thing. I don't think I have to be friends with the staff. Getting rid of people is not a bad thing. . . . I don't miss anything about the start-up phase. Now it's not just about creativity but about software development. Possibly a lot of the present people won't work in the new model."[22]

There were necessary changes in the management structure as well, as GeneEd grew out of being a start-up and into being a "real corporation." What earlier used to be termed "sales" became the much more grandiose-sounding "business development." Heading that was a new middle manager, Glenn O'Classen, who comes from a family steeped in the pharmaceutical industry (his grandfather had built a pharmaceutical business), which meant that

O'Classen had many contacts in that world. In the process, GeneEd had to lay off their vice president of sales, Barry Giordano.

This was probably one of the most painful moments for GeneEd as a company, not least because Giordano was part of the founding management team and an early investor. Perhaps even more, he was Maulik's old friend, a close friendship that has probably terminally ruptured as a consequence of the layoff, which Giordano took very badly. Maulik, who is very good at wearing the CEO mask when he needs to, rationalized the decision as inevitable, since GeneEd was not getting the customers it needed to stay afloat. Indeed, even after the Astra Zeneca deal, GeneEd's revenue situation remained extremely precarious for much of fall 2001 and early 2002, since the company never had reserves of venture capital money to fall back on. Thus, a number of people in the company felt that the exit of Giordano, who had difficult relationships with both Kilroy and Eisele, was both necessary and good for the company.

This was not, however, a uniform sentiment in the least. While Giordano had certainly not shown much sensitivity in dealing with fellow women managers, as in Kilroy's case, there were many others in the company, men and women, who felt that he was precisely the sort of mentor that they just did not have anymore. They felt that O'Classen was too immersed in business development to bother about fostering mentoring relationships with those who reported to him, and in any case, those were relationships that could best be developed by someone senior who had been in the company from the beginning.

Meanwhile, Patel had moved from San Francisco to start a new GeneEd office in New Jersey. This was necessitated by the fact that GeneEd was shifting its clientele away from biotech companies toward the pharmaceutical industry, and the corporate headquarters of almost all the big pharmaceutical companies are on the East Coast. If the place of being in San Francisco mattered immensely to GeneEd's existence and identity as a start-up, then that too was completely at stake once big pharmaceutical companies became the major customers.

If Giordano's mentoring was missed by some, it was nothing compared to the way Patel was missed. Every single employee I spoke to, without even being asked the question, told me that he or she missed having Patel around.

Patel is in many ways a corporate anomaly, driven by a system of personal values that refuses to buy into the sort of hardheaded cynicism—what might politely be called "flexibility"—that is almost constitutive of American "corporate culture." This does not mean that Patel is romantic or naive—far from it. What it does mean is that, first, he has a commitment to truth (which makes him uncomfortable even with sales forecasts and investor pitches, which by definition cannot possibly be "truthful" events); second, he is deeply committed to teaching; and third, he is deeply committed to fostering an ethical relationship with his employees. While this does not stop him from supporting management decisions to, for instance, lay off certain employees, it also means that he would never be caught talking about their dispensability as part of the changing priorities for the company. It is his position of pragmatic principle that has earned him such respect in the company.

This means, on the one hand, that he spent a lot of time mentoring the graphic designers. This was not simply because he felt that mentoring was important for their well-being, or that of the company, but because, at the end of the day, the reason why he agreed to risk leaving a secure job to start this company with Maulik was because Patel loved teaching.

While Maulik was equally respected as a teacher, his job description as CEO ensured, even before GeneEd shifted its client focus, that he was more absent than present in the everyday running of the company. His job was always to sell the idea of the company outside, especially to potential investors; and Patel, for as long as he was in San Francisco, complemented Maulik perfectly by being the "resident" founder, translating the corporate vision into everyday work practices, providing precisely the inspiration and motivation that so many of the employees felt was lacking once Patel moved east.

But he also provided a certain managerial stability, often being the mediator in difficult relationships such as Giordano's with Kilroy or Eisele. He showed both sensitivity and evenhandedness and was a stickler for procedure. This made Patel easier for the middle management to relate to than Maulik, whose ability to sell the company outside the company came precisely from an absence of these qualities, came from his ability to think on his feet, act on the spur of the moment, make off-the-cuff remarks, take risks. As Eisele says: "Sunil jumps the chain of command all the time, which drives his managers crazy. It's a challenge not having Salil here. Sunil's mercurial; Salil's the Rock of Gibraltar."[23]

In other words, shifting the client base from small biotech to big pharmaceutical companies, a process that started with the Astra Zeneca contract and has expanded since, had profound consequences for GeneEd as a company. It changed the company from a content provider to a software company; from a "start-up" that was constantly bootstrapping to a "real company" that had more stable revenue flows; from a company with a bunch of gifted artists with room for self-expression to one with a group of dispensable designers and excited programmers. It changed the very critical mass of the company, which increasingly started depending on its New Jersey operation to leverage pharmaceutical sales. It changed the management structure of the company, and the way management interacted with employees. Indeed, in April 2002 I spent an afternoon at GeneEd, where I read out some of my accounts of GeneEd's emergence. After my talk, one of the employees told me, "I didn't recognize what you were talking about. I was saying to myself, This isn't GeneEd. And then I thought, maybe that was GeneEd a year ago. It seems so long ago, I've forgotten it now."[24]

What I want to emphasize constantly, however, is not just an attribution of credit or blame to individual people or circumstances that have made GeneEd evolve in certain ways, but rather to a deeper structural logic, of a start-up "growing up" into a corporation, that leads to certain tendential outcomes. This is not to say that this evolutionary path for GeneEd was in any way predetermined, or not the outcome of strategic, contingent, occasionally even lucky, events. It is to say that had those contingencies not occurred, the "alternative" GeneEd would not have remained a happy-go-lucky, selling-to-biotech, artistically expressive start-up but would have run out of funds and ceased to exist. There is a logic of capitalism that pushes toward growth *in certain ways*, that necessitates streamlining, dispensability, and standardization, and that pushes against all those qualities of exuberance, innovation, and risk taking that allow start-ups to start up in the first place, and also to create a certain type of community that everyone, management and employees alike, can buy into and feel part of. It is this logic, perhaps, that explains the managerial inertia of big pharmaceutical relative to small biotech companies, an inertia that is often hugely profitable; and it also perhaps explains why successful entrepreneurs, such as, most famously, Jim Clark (the founder of Silicon Graphics and Netscape), become "serial" entrepreneurs instead of staying on to manage and grow the company they have founded. It is, most starkly, a logic that in its acting out shows the alienation of the workers from the products of their labor, which Marx diagnosed as fundamentally symptomatic of capitalism a century and a half ago.

### Performance and Conjuration

I now recount stories from GeneEd that relate to my arguments in chapter 3 about vision and hype. Specifically, I am interested in the ways in which the everyday operations of (high-tech) start-ups, confronting as they do the necessity of selling stories of the future to create the present that enables them to go into that future, function in a discursive terrain of truth telling, a truth that is under erasure, undoubtedly operates on grounds for intentional deception, but can neither be dismissed as "simply hype" or cynicism nor be established as a lie. It is an ambiguous type of nontruth whose ambiguity resides in the temporal structures within which forms of start-up discursive performance operate. The question that arises when the start-up is involved in *scientific* knowledge production, and therefore is trading in an enterprise of supremely authoritative *fact* production, relates to the ways in which such acts of fact production articulate with the truths of corporate PR.

Salil Patel, as mentioned earlier, shows an almost idealistic adherence to, and belief in, the truth of science, a belief that exists in some tension with his role as manager of a start-up company that has to improvise and be flexible with its discourses, albeit without ever explicitly lying. Indeed, that he could not quite escape this mode of "lying" at GeneEd, in spite of his own best intentions to be "honest," was made quite clear on at least a couple of instances: once, in the values and visions session described earlier, when Patel admitted that he knew that at least one of the custom e-learning courses GeneEd was building (a course that as chief content editor Patel had a significant hand in designing) had "lies" in it; and again at a semiannual reception that GeneEd threw for its investors, where the company made a pitch about its current situation and promised an exciting future, and where again Patel felt squeamish about the fact that such pitches were not entirely "truthful." In fact, Patel felt uncomfortable about aspects of the pitch that could not possibly be statements of truth, such as sales forecasts, which are precisely that: forecasts, based on reasonable intuition, necessarily subjective and subject to all sorts of contingencies that could lead to outcomes radically different from those forecast. In other words, even calculating what is essentially incalculable had, for Patel, the manifestations of a "lie," with the same moral connotations that lying intentionally in a scientific paper would have.

This is precisely the conflict between Patel the scientist and Patel the businessman, subjectivities that are increasingly conflated as venture science becomes naturalized, but that are not at all unique to Patel. Indeed, in *The Billion Dollar Molecule*, Barry Werth (1994) recounts in great detail precisely such conflicts among many of the early management of Vertex Pharmaceuticals. Thus, on the one hand, it is important to tease out the different categories of the performative discourse of the truth, which is what Derrida does in "History of the Lie" (Derrida 2001 [1995]). On the other hand, it is important to simultaneously stay attentive to the institutional groundings from which such discourses emanate and within which they operate, especially when, as in the case of venture science, the germ of conflicts of interest is always already inherent. The notion of conflict of interest is a normative notion that draws attention to the possibility of nontruth emanating as a consequence of the institutional space from which statements might emanate. It is, indeed, one that has for many years functioned as a good watchdog that has allowed only a certain mode of truth accountability to operate in techno-corporate discourse.

Sunil Maulik has many things to say about vision, and one of the first is that being visionary is being interdisciplinary in a profound sense — not just allowing different disciplines and perspectives to cohabit in some bland acknowledgment of mutual tolerance, but actually putting what might be considered incompatible regimes of knowledge, and their practitioners, into the same enterprise, where the very success of that enterprise depends on these various forms of knowledge articulating in productive, and often unpredictable, new ways.[25] Second, for Maulik, being visionary involves *not* recharting paths that he has already been treading. He says: "As a person, the type of company I would want to start wouldn't have been a nuts-and-bolts company; it wouldn't have been a 'They are making clones, let's make clones. They're sequencing the genome, let's sequence the genome.' It was a company that was going to do what nobody had done before."[26]

However, having the vision to do something that has not been attempted before is not sufficient to ensure a successful enterprise. Maulik, in words that resonate with some of my arguments from the previous chapter, goes on to argue for *evangelism* as a third component of vision:

> Because a company is visionary . . . it does not make a business a success. In fact some people are going to argue that it almost ensures business failure because it is hoisting something new into a business climate. So not only do you have to convince people to buy your product, you have to convince people that the product is worth buying in the first place. So in a sense you're attempting to answer a question that nobody has thought of asking you. So first you have to convince them that there is a question worthy of answering, and then you have to convince them that you're worthy of answering it using your particular product or service. And in that sense, what GeneEd is doing, e-learning, is I think a bit of evangelism and missionary selling. First you have to convince them that they have the problem, and then you have to convince them that you are the only company who can solve their problem. That leads to the other side of vision, which is that visionary companies have a certain cultlike image attached to them, and there's a certain degree of brainwashing attached to the idea of vision, and it is that you create the market by basically . . . by not just the force of one person's personality but by the force of a group personality which you try to foster and create and build, and then you find the champions of the industry and people who can mouth the same words. So after a while it becomes a self-sustaining entity, and then you've got this culture, this sort of drum beating of people, "This is the next way," "This is the next way," "This is the next way."[27]

Vision, in this third conception of Maulik's, is ideology, in a manner very similar to that in which Marx conceives of religion as ideology in *The German Ideology*. But fourth, Maulik compares vision to a set of guiding principles, "a set of principles that are far-fetched, but not too far-fetched that people can't believe in them if they stretched their minds sufficiently."[28] Vision, then, serves simultaneously as imagination and as prescription, as an ambitious statement that says, "We're going to draw a line in the sand, we're going to do something nobody has ever done before, it's going to be a mission, it would be crossing the Sahara with one bag of water,"[29] but implicitly indicates to those who have a stake in realizing the vision *how* this improbable goal might be reached. It is in this sense that vision, in the ways that Maulik articulates it, is different from hype.

The question of the *distinction* of vision from hype is one that I have tried to trouble in chapter 3 by referring to hype as a type of promissory visionary articulation that allows the conjuration of certain types of futures to create the conditions of possibility for presents that allow those futures to materialize. And yet in Silicon Valley in 2001 and 2002, the distinction between hype and vision was acutely made manifest by entrepreneurs like Maulik, where hype refers to that dematerialized and somehow *false* conjuration that was epitomized by the dot.com era — an "era" that was already, by mid-2002, spoken of in firm historical terms as an "aberration" by the same people who had been extolling its invincible capacity for continued growth, revolution, and creating paradigm shifts just a couple of years previously.[30]

There is no question, however, that this is a distinction of some importance to GeneEd, which resisted calling itself GeneEd.com, a resistance that probably protected against the company's obsolescence with the receding dot.com wave. At least part of the reason why GeneEd was not caught up in the dot.com frenzy was that the company really was conceived in a pre-dot.com era, having been incorporated in 1997. Thus it effectively incubated through the dot.com years, somewhat befuddled by the dot.com goings-on around it. As Maulik says:

Part of the reason GeneEd had such a long incubation period was that none of us was really comfortable to really take that leap. The other part of it was [19]98–99 were two years when this extraordinary ferment was going on all around us, this Internet boom, dot.com hysteria, and it did have an effect on us in the sense that we were no longer sure if having this hard, well-thought-out, well-defined business plan that called for so much market penetration and so much revenues and so much time with so many products with so many people made sense anymore. A lot of supposedly very smart people were telling us it made no sense. They said, Why are you setting this up, create a large database instead . . . You know, things like that, like do not worry about revenues, use advertising and this . . . all kinds of things. And all that went against all that I had learnt in the prior fifteen years, so it was a very strange time to be considering starting a company. If you were a Harvard MBA who was twenty-four years old who didn't have those previous fifteen years of working experience, you might go, This is a great time to be starting a company. But having learnt the careful business models of how to build. . . . I'd worked for companies all my life, for a variety of small companies, and here there were plans on the back of a napkin and now you get a company the moment you see it, it was actually disconcerting.[31]

In this portrayal, then, GeneEd is almost like a caterpillar in a time-warped cocoon, insulated by its own pedagogical background against the "realities" that were now propounded as fundamental to start-up corporate dynamics. It was a period when Maulik felt that GeneEd's vision was being incubated, suggesting that vision is not just a onetime articulation but an entire discursive and material apparatus that needs nurturing and needs to be articulated with strategies and tactics in many ways. Indeed, Maulik's explicit assertion that vision is not vision until it is articulated "in the way that people see that, oh yes, I can see how this is going,"[32] is an understanding of entrepreneurship as explicitly hegemonic in the way that Stuart Hall understands hegemony (see, for instance, Grossberg 1996). Maulik's idea of a visionary is someone who is involved in cutting, pasting, and synthesis; he thinks that tropes of romantic genius inventors are somewhat bogus.

An important part of the entrepreneurial process is the relationship of the start-up to venture capital funding. GeneEd was able to get companies such as Incyte and Alza on board as early investors, instead of venture capitalists, though not for want of effort at attracting the latter. In fact, as mentioned earlier, Maulik actually had promises for VC funding that were withdrawn at the last minute. He had therefore been let down badly by venture capitalists, but it was a letdown that he felt ultimately made the company possible, made it come out of its incubation period and gave it the activation energy necessary to become a real company.

The first company to invest in GeneEd was the major Silicon Valley genome company Incyte, whose founder, Randy Scott, has himself figured prominently in this book. Typically, like almost any investment in high-tech capitalism, this was made possible not by the superiority of GeneEd's business plan as much as by Maulik's personal contacts at Incyte. It was, however, a fraught investment on both sides, given Incyte's own history of ups and downs with Pangea, which was always a company that might have been Incyte's competitor. Maulik feels that what eventually carried the day at Incyte was the personal credibility he had there, even though he had worked for a competitor. Trust and credibility are subjective judgment calls that are absolutely central to the dynamics of start-up worlds.

Getting Incyte as an investor, however, was always potentially a double-edged sword, because there was the danger of GeneEd being seen as a company seeded by Incyte, which Maulik knew could have huge consequences for the trust and credibility GeneEd might or might not have among potential customers, many of whom would have to be Incyte's competitors if GeneEd was to succeed as a company. Maulik expresses his ambivalence thus:

> A part of me didn't want to take the investment because I was concerned that if we were seen to be in Incyte's pocket, nobody will accept our products. And the other part of me wanted to take the investment from Incyte because I didn't get an investment from Pangea and I probably just wanted to thumb my nose at Pangea, say to them that your biggest competitors are investing in me, why aren't you, and there was definitely some of that. And I think, again, the rationalization for the investment — and it is a rationalization — is that we will take the investments from a large variety of companies, and not be beholden to any one of them. Now that's easy to say and much harder to do. I mean, the fact is that there is always a little bit of string that they can pull with us.[33]

In fact, however, GeneEd managed to sign up Celera Genomics, Incyte's biggest competitor, as one of their first customers, and it was Incyte, not their customer, who was put into a position of having to show trust. Maulik recalls the moment when Incyte learned of GeneEd's sale to Celera:

> The day we were going to close our investment with Incyte . . . this was the day the Celera Genomics Web site went live [with GeneEd courses on it], which we had conveniently forgotten to tell Incyte about. So it's five o'clock on a Friday afternoon, it was a classic afternoon. Marion [Marra, vice president of corporate development at Incyte], and Randy Scott and the two of us [Maulik and Barry

Giordano, GeneEd's vice president of sales at the time]. They said there were two things we needed to discuss, there were some issues with this contract we needed to get clearance on. And the second thing is — what the hell is going on with your being on Celera's Web site? What we said was, Take off your Incyte cap for a moment, put on your investor cap. You should be glad we're getting Celera Genomics as a customer, just as we intend every other genomics company to be our customer. And as an investor, that only enhances our value, and gives you return on your investment. We're doing business with companies of the stature of Celera Genomics, and just from a monetary standpoint, every dollar that Celera Genomics pays us is indirectly going back to you. So I think they do look at that rationally.[34]

GeneEd's failure to attract venture capital funding had certain positive consequences for the company. First, it forced a certain fiscal discipline on the company that many richly funded start-ups in the dot.com era simply did not have, to their eventual detriment. Second, it allowed Maulik to stay in control of the company's vision and execution in a way that would have been hard to maintain had the founders' ownership been significantly diluted by venture capitalists at the start.

These were, however, fraught positives, and there were a number of times when it seemed almost certain that GeneEd would run out of funds, and out of business. It is impossible to get out of bootstrapping mode through sales alone, and a certain significant amount of capital as cushion is probably essential for most companies. In addition, one of GeneEd's initial investors had invested in the company through a bridge loan, which meant that the investment was made on the condition that a further significant financing event (such as venture capital funding) would occur within a stipulated period of time, which was by September 2002.[35] If that financing event did not take place, then the investment would be treated as a loan, meaning that GeneEd would have to pay back a significant sum of money: significant enough to bankrupt the company. In other words, if GeneEd's drive for big pharmaceutical clients was constrained by the need for stable revenue, then the drive for venture capital funding was dictated by the terms and conditions of previous investment agreements.

Perversely, but not surprisingly, venture capitalists refused to invest in

GeneEd when the company really needed funds, before it landed its big pharmaceutical clients. By 2002, when GeneEd had pharmaceutical clients that ensured a certain stability in revenue flows, the VCs were much more enthusiastic about investing. This highlights venture capitalist logic, contrary to intuitive perception, that suggests an enterprise of risk *minimization* rather than risk taking. Indeed, Patrick O'Malley (2000), reading the work of the 1920s economist Frank Knight, makes the distinction between risk and uncertainty, the latter being the statistically noncalculable "risk" that is the source of entrepreneurial creativity. One could, indeed, see the interaction of entrepreneurs and VCs as being one in which entrepreneurs are involved with uncertainty, while VCs calculate risks. Although calculating risk is most certainly taking a gamble, it is done so that risk can be minimized.

Nonetheless, even though VC money was less of an urgent need for GeneEd in 2002 than it was in 2001, the terms of GeneEd's early bridge loan, combined with a risk minimization logic that operates in the entrepreneurial world as well (which states, emphatically, that you *never* turn down investment when you get it, because you never know when or if you will get some later), ensured that GeneEd returned to aggressively pursuing VC funding.[36]

The person whose job was to explore that funding was Maulik, both because it is part of his job description as CEO and because as founder, he, more than anyone else, provided the vision for GeneEd. Ironically, the person whose job was most on the line if he succeeded in getting funding was Maulik. This was for a number of reasons.

The first is an almost pedagogical insistence by venture capitalists that the founder of a company should not be its CEO, a line that is constantly reiterated in, for instance, business school classes on how to start new companies (in spite of many successful examples of founders who have in fact successfully run the companies they founded). The reason for this, largely, is that venture capitalists like to have, on the one hand, a "professional" CEO: founders are often the visionaries who get companies going, but one of the transitions a start-up has to make as it grows into a "real" company is precisely a shedding of the mercurial nature that made it a successful start-up in the first place. While Maulik's creative unpredictability could be an asset in a start-up with a small management team, it could make for an increasingly volatile situation in a larger management team, spread across two coasts, with a number of managers more senior and experienced at managing than Maulik himself. The transition that VCs like to see is one from an idea-driven company to a procedure-driven company, the latter often being precisely what successful entrepreneurs run away from to start their own companies in the first place. On the other hand, VCs also like to have a dispensable CEO, someone who can be blamed and made the scapegoat if things go wrong, and thereby replaced. From the point of view of the structure of capitalist versus worker, the CEO is very much also a "worker" once the company gets venture capital investment. At that point, the CEO is effectively an executor of a whole range of wills to increase return on investment. While the company is still private, VCs look ideally for a 60 to 70 percent return on their investment in the company, so that they can in turn generate a 20 to 30 percent return on investment for the investment funds that have invested money in the VC fund and still make a profit. Once the company (ideally) goes public (this constitutes for the VCs one of their ideal "exit strategies"), CEOs have a fiduciary responsibility to their stockholders, which makes them answerable to Wall Street.

I am not, here, trying to portray the CEO as a weak victim of a greedy capitalist system, especially since the incentive structures for CEOs are often grotesquely attractive. What I am trying to indicate is a certain constrained field of action that these executives have to operate within once they become answerable to other investors, private or public, in a way that they do not have to be accountable if they are a non-VC-funded start-up like GeneEd has been. It is often difficult to be both visionary and constrained tactician-manager, and VCs therefore often prefer those roles to be filled by two different people. Often getting rid of a flailing CEO, if he or she is also the founder, is, for the VC, throwing out the baby with the bathwater: they are reluctant to put the prime visionary of the company in such a constrained position.

Indeed, Maulik himself reflects on this position of venture capitalists, and their potential relationship to GeneEd, as follows:

> There is a clear "formula" to VC success, based around a "tried-and-true" manage-
> ment team, usually of the VCs' own choosing, and one that has succeeded before.
> There is also a clear formula for the profile of company that they will fund, typi-
> cally one based around a well-developed University project, preferably from a

researcher that is well known and with a proven track-record of success. In this way, all the "risk" and early groundbreaking hard work is done in an academic environment under (usually) government funding, and the VCs are simply funding the commercialization.

Neither of these models applies to GeneEd. In some way, we may be "unfundable" from a VC perspective, simply because we don't fit these pigeon-holes. I believe GeneEd could be a very profitable company generating nice returns for its investors, but I think this is irrelevant from a VC perspective (!). If the deal does not fit the profile, they simply pass on the deal (they have hundreds more to review, after all).

What does this mean for GeneEd's culture? Obviously it is very different from Pangea/Doubletwist, which was the most VC-influenced company I have experienced. But better? More successful? All I can say is that we are having lots of fun, a talented and motivated workforce, and compelling and exciting products. Doubletwist may go out of business too,[37] so there are no guarantees. Millennium is interesting, their CEO, Mark Levin, comes from Mayfield Fund, but they clearly are a deal-making machine. . . . My contact raves about Levin as a CEO she would follow to the ends of the earth.

So what is my point? A big part of the corporate culture (for better or worse) is dependent on the founders/CEO. If they are in sync, the culture is strong, if there is conflict, this will be reflected in the organizational values.[38]

In the case of GeneEd, Maulik's position was further made vulnerable because of the changing client base toward pharmaceutical companies and the consequent change in GeneEd's critical operational locale to the East Coast. Here, all the attributes that made Maulik so attractive to his initial angel investors and his initial management and employee team, and made him so much a part of the Silicon Valley entrepreneurial stereotype of *not* fitting a corporate American stereotype, become potential liabilities. East Coast business, goes the normative belief, is run by serious, gray-haired, tight-lipped white men in pinstriped suits, not by a young Indian immigrant who makes it a point to start up a conversation with anyone whom he sits next to on an airplane (he actually once managed to talk someone next to him on a flight into a small investment in GeneEd before the plane landed), and whose invariably bare-chested presence at parties was what gave one of his early angel investors in Silicon Valley the confidence that his money was being soundly wagered.

Everyone at GeneEd, to some extent even Maulik, does believe that in the long term, GeneEd will have to be run by that industry caricature, the "gray-haired pharmaceutical manager," someone who has worked for years in a big pharmaceutical company and is keen in his later years to do something more "risky" and "exciting," and so brings his staid management style to a younger company, thereby giving it legitimacy and an apparent seriousness of purpose when it presents itself to its big pharmaceutical customers. Indeed, Maulik himself has been claiming for the past four years that it is not his long-term ambition to run a nuts-and-bolts company, that what he really wants to do is to take GeneEd to a point where he feels that whoever runs it will have to run it on the terms set by Maulik's initial vision. What Maulik aspires to is not management power as much as a legacy, at which point he claims that he wants to retire on his stock options, sit on a beach, and write a novel.

Nonetheless, it is clear that no one knows, least of all Maulik, when he will willingly pass the reins to experienced management; but it is fair to say that whether or not Maulik's desired point of exit coincides with the desires of his investors will be a crucial determinant of how painful GeneEd's future growth will be. As of June 2002, Maulik's potential investors (and the managers of two companies that GeneEd, at that point, was potentially planning to merge with) did want Maulik to continue running the company, a point in which, in spite of his carefully stated indifference to being a long-term CEO, Maulik clearly found huge amounts of affirmation.

### Conclusion

I have ended this book with a series of stories about a start-up, GeneEd, that I think is an emblematic institutional node in biocapitalist terrains, albeit perhaps an atypical, maybe even somewhat marginal, one. Its particularities, however, do not make its stories a digression from the grand narratives of biocapital. Rather, it is completely constitutive of the multiple narratives, discourses, institutions, practices, and events — the circulations and articulations — of biocapital. In spite of the multiplicities of these circulations and articulations, as I have argued throughout the book, GeneEd's stories cannot be reduced simply to stories of contingency.

Indeed, there are structural and cultural logics at play throughout these stories. Many of these logics involve interactions between entrepreneurs and venture capitalists, which always tend to result in entrepreneurs spending lots of time, money, and energy seeking venture capital funds that they might in fact feel extremely ambivalent about. These interactions also usually involve venture capitalists adhering to a relatively conservative set of criteria and guidelines for evaluating the companies that approach them for funding. In spite of both entrepreneurs and venture capitalists sticking to rather formulaic modes of interaction (or perhaps because of it), GeneEd's history diverges markedly from that of many high-tech start-ups, in that it is not funded by venture capital but has grown "organically."

Similarly, there are certain discursive and performative operations, such as the conjuration of futures through investor pitches or sales forecasts that enable the present, that speak to the structural logics (that are always already strategic and tendential rather than inevitable) that I have argued for in chapter 3. These modes of discourse and performance are not just for external consumption; they also, as Chris Palmer implied in an earlier quote, form the grounds for GeneEd to foster a cultlike loyalty among its employees, another structural yet always already strategic logic I explored in chapter 5. Indeed, Sunil Maulik himself explicitly states that visionary articulations are meant to foster cultic formations.

And yet there are other labor dimensions than the cultic, and here too structural and tendential capitalist logics are at play. Specifically, there is the alienation of labor as the company grows from its intimate, improvisational start-up phase to become a more "mature" corporation, a form of growth that threatens redundancy all the way up to Maulik himself, but one that everyone, management and employees alike, nonetheless accepts as inevitable. This alienation, while structurally inherent to capitalism as Marx diagnosed, is equally the outcome of particular market terrains, in this case because of the upstream-downstream terrain of drug development. Since downstream big pharmaceutical companies represent a significantly greater market opportunity for GeneEd than upstream biotech companies, there is a strategic pressure to focus on big pharmaceutical customers. This leads to concomitant pressures to standardize the courses developed by GeneEd, so much so that the courses acquire a new name, "learning objects," suggesting their standardization and their becoming commodities. In the process, a business model whose value depended on the creativity of graphic designers shifted to become one where the designers became alienable, dispensable, replaceable units of an assembly-line manufacturing process, while software programmers became the integral creative center of the company, mere "plumbers" no longer.

This coexistence of the alienated with the cultic is an essential dimension to labor issues in capitalism writ large and allows an analysis of capitalism as a *hegemonic*, rather than a merely coercive, formation — and thereby a formation that has enduring social power in spite of its multiple contradictions. Indeed, I mentioned in my story of Genentech in chapter 5 my informant's surprise at the cultlike feeling of invincibility of Genentech employees despite the fact that most of them had "pretty crummy jobs." It is the multiple ways in which magic imbricates not just the objects and discourses, but also the *sites*, of capitalism that animate the fetishes of capitalism and provide it its performative force and social power.[39]

I have used GeneEd, in concluding this book, as an emblematic site through which to explore and illustrate some of my larger arguments relating to bio-capital. These arguments have related to the performative conjuration of techno-corporate futures, the continued alienation of labor in high-tech capitalism (as Marx diagnosed for industrial capitalism), and the cultlike fetishes that animate techno-corporate activity, especially in the United States.

# Coda

*Surplus and Symptom*

In conclusion, I return to this book's originating claim: that biotechnology represents a new face, and a new phase, of capitalism. This might seem to be a difficult statement to sustain, because the coproduction of life and capitalism is in itself not new. It is, historically, especially seen in the green revolutions of the 1960s, leading to new methods and institutional arrangements of agricultural production, new discourses and strategies around the management of risk, and new safety and lifestyle concerns as articulated by an emergent environmental movement. Both states and corporations were involved in such reorganizations.

Biocapital thus does not represent a new phase of capitalism in a temporal sense. Instead, as I argued in the introduction, my sense of the relationship of biocapital to systems of capitalism writ large is similar to Jean-François Lyotard's sense of the relationship of postmodernism to modernity—a constitutive component of a larger set of institutions, regimes, and practices that are themselves defined and exceeded by their incongruent components.

At the same time, there is an uncanny sense that something new is happening here. Part of this sensibility of novelty is due to the very discourse that sustains biocapital—for instance, the hype that is such an integral part of the biotech industry (and this hype itself, of course, is not necessarily such a new thing but can be located within the very discursive ethos of American nation building and nationalist consciousness). Another part of this sensibility is due to the fact that there are new institutional and technological assemblages that are being presented to us, new events that herald novelty. These include, to name some of them I have talked about in this book, DNA patents; the SNP Consortium; the ability to make sensible information out of biological material at speeds and resolutions that were earlier inconceivable; global benefit sharing agreements; biotech start-ups in India; knowledge parks; venture capitalism in high tech; new arrangements for technology transfer between academe and industry; the generation of the working draft sequence of the human genome; the dot.com boom and bust; automated sequencing machines; DNA chips; personalized medicine; genomic-based diagnostic tests; pharmacogenomics; globally standardized clinical trials regimes; World Trade Organization–mandated trade and intellectual property practices; nonresident Indian entrepreneurial communities in the United States; patient advocacy groups; consumer genomics, population genomics; and direct-to-consumer advertising. At the same time, some very old patterns of resource extraction and global inequities persist, even if they articulate or are resisted in new ways.

But a good part of the sensibility of novelty that we might experience is also conceptual, as the humanities and social sciences attempt to keep pace with events and emergences that are undoubtedly *rapid*, regardless of their novelty or familiarity. Michael Fischer poses the challenge to, and potential of, anthropological research in keeping pace with and making sense of what he calls "emergent forms of life," where, he says, "life is outrunning the pedagogies in which we were trained" (Fischer 2003, 37). The theoretical challenge, then, is not to abandon these pedagogies, the conceptual inheritances with which we formulate our explanations and descriptions, but to *recalibrate* them. In other words, the question is, What work does old vocabulary do in the face of new events and articulations, and when and with what sorts of new vocabularies do we need to come to terms with them?

Michel Foucault, as I have mentioned at a number of points in this book, argues for the constitution of the modern subject at the intersections of life, labor, and language (Foucault 1973). All three have been distinct themes throughout this book — life, especially, as the recalibration of life as a credible future that can be invested in, life as a business plan (chapter 4); labor, especially, as the labor of consumption, of consuming as a sovereign consumer or of being consumed as an experimental subject (chapters 1, 2, 5, and 6); and language, as in the discourse of hype and hope, salvation and messianism (especially chapters 3 and 5). But the question for Foucault remained one of how these intersections rearticulate at different moments in history to *constitute* modernity as some kind of temporally intelligible (if not temporally seamless) concept.

Paul Rabinow argues that Foucault, during the course of his writing, transformed his initial understanding of modernity as an epoch into an understanding that is based on "a new philosophic relationship to the present" (Rabinow 2003, 14). This relationship, according to Rabinow, is

> one in which modernity was taken up not through the analytic frame of the epoch but instead through a practice of inquiry grounded in an ethos of being oriented toward the present, of contingency, of form-giving. Perhaps today one, but only one, significant challenge of forging a modern ethos lies in thinking about how to relate to the issue of anthropos. . . . What if we took up recent changes in the logoi of life, labor, and language not as indicating an epochal shift with a totalizing coherence but rather as fragmented and sectorial changes that pose problems, both in and of themselves and for attempts to make sense of what form(s) anthropos is currently being given?[1]

The analytic problem of articulating biocapital as a novel form of capitalism is similar to the problem of depicting modernity as an epoch that Rabinow outlines here. A solution, as he indicates, is to resist an attempt at a totalizing formulation of a contemporary structure and instead to proliferate accounts of the fragments that constitute (and, indeed, exceed and surprise) such structures.

Rabinow, then, proposes a way to account for *epochs*, for those concepts of structure that structure our own understandings of the presents we live in, in terms of *contingency*. But there is a related analytic problem that is still at stake and unresolved. This is the parallel problem Fischer poses, of understanding *emergence* in terms of *structure*. In other words, if contingent, fragmented, multiple reality constantly exceeds our structural boundaries, then at the same time rapid, incongruent, emergent reality constantly calls for some kind of conceptual grounding, however provisional, in a kind of structural framework. Biocapital as a concept attempts, on the one hand, to point to the *insufficiency* of capitalism as an explanatory structure for rapid emergences in the life sciences and biotechnologies but, on the other hand, tries to provide, through the vehicle of received theoretical inheritances, familiar words and concepts through which to ground these emergences that otherwise threaten to overtake our pedagogical limits.

Biocapital, then, is always already all too new and all too familiar; all too specific to new emergences in the life sciences and all too general a symptom of a rapidly mutating political economic structure that we call "capitalism." I wish to point to two themes that I believe need emphasis in order to go beyond the argument that the emergence of a global commercial genomics has had structural effects driven by particular, sometimes new, forms of value creation and exchange networks. The first is that new epistemic and technological assemblages such as genomics can only be understood through an analysis of the market frameworks within which they are emergent. The second is the argument that an understanding of globalization needs an accounting of its biopolitical dimensions, but that equally, an understanding of biopolitics needs an accounting of its global dimensions.

### Subject to Surplus, or Symptomatic Speculations on Biocapital

Let me begin this section by referring to the story of Wellspring Hospital in Parel, Mumbai, which was the subject of analysis in chapter 2. This is the story of a hospital located in Mumbai's mill districts that houses a genome start-up, Genomed, which is seeded partly by a public institution, the Centre for Biochemical Technology (CBT), and partly by a local pharmaceutical company, Nicholas Piramal India Limited (NPIL). This is one of a number of attempts in India that I have mentioned in this book that seeks to imitate an American "start-up culture." A major research focus at Wellspring/Genomed is pharmacogenomic drug response in clinical trials, and major proposed clients for these clinical trials experiments are Western biotech and pharmaceutical companies. The subjects on whom these experiments will be performed are, according to scientists I spoke to at Wellspring, most often unemployed millworkers in Parel, an area that has, over the last twenty years, seen the dramatic disintegration of the textile industry that formed the basis of the local economy for much of the twentieth century.

I argue that the experimental subjects in Parel are *subject to speculation*, where speculation means, simultaneously, two different things. On the one hand, they are subject to the speculative enterprises of capitalism, both those of Western companies seeking to outsource clinical trials and those of the Indian state attempting to leverage global market terrains. In that sense, the story I have told of Wellspring reflects an old story, of colonial expropriation of Third World resources, where the resources in question are the genetic information and medical records of the experimental subjects of Parel. What makes this different from a mere resource-mining exercise, however, is that these are *experimental* subjects. As Hans-Jörg Rheinberger (1997) has beautifully illustrated, experiment is a speculative exercise of a very different register, a practice of inquiry that is constantly open-ended. The experimental subjects of Parel get incorporated, quite literally, into the implosion of these two forms of speculative enterprise, having to do with the *market*, on the one hand, and with the *life sciences*, on the other. It is a flavor of this implosion that I hope to provide with the term "biocapital."

The logics seen in Parel point to *one logic* of biocapital, leading to certain particular forms of subject constitution consequent to certain enterprises of speculation. Let me now shift frames to another story I have narrated in this book (in chapter 5), that of the Bay Area consumer genomics company Genomic Health. The vision of consumer genomics as articulated by Randy Scott, CEO of Genomic Health, sees the intertwining of diagnostic technologies that will enable the generation of personalized, high-throughput biological information at the genomic level with communications technologies such as the Internet, leading to the emergence of networked biosocial communities. Consumer genomics is a highly individualized practice, and the key here is that *every* individual, because of his or her genomic risk profile, is a potential target for therapeutic intervention. In this calculus, every individual is a patient-in-waiting and, simultaneously, a consumer-in-waiting.

Here again, the subjects of consumer genomics are subject to speculation. On the one hand, they (we) speculate about their (our) genetic "days of reckoning," the illnesses coming at them (us) in the future, and act in ways relevant to that. Such action could, for instance, involve lifestyle changes, or preventive or prophylactic therapeutic intervention. On the other hand, these subjects are again part of a speculative market enterprise, constituting a potential market for companies like Genomic Health. The difference, however, is that while the subjects of speculation in the Parel case are marked by their class position as a consequence of being *workers*, and therefore subject to the class logic of industrial capitalism, the subjects of speculation in Genomic Health's case are *all of us*, marked in this case as *consumers*, also consequent to class logic, this time of late or postindustrial or neoliberal capitalism.

We are faced with a complication while talking about biocapitalist subject configurations using the tools of Marxian political economy. This is that the relationship we are faced with in contemporary biocapital is not that of the *capitalist* to the patient-consumer but that of the *corporation* to the patient-consumer, and where market value implies value for the corporation, which depends on potential of the patient-consumer-in-waiting for therapeutic consumption over and above that which is necessary owing to illness.[2]

The corporation, conceptually, is a complicated beast. It is in itself a "capitalist" entity, but it is also answerable to "real" capitalists — who might be venture capitalists if the company is private, or might be Wall Street investors and stockholders if the company is public. If we are to extrapolate and use Marx for our contemporary purposes, we are faced squarely with the ontological question of what constitutes the corporation.

This is where reading volume 3 of *Capital* becomes interesting. It is at this late stage of his work that Marx first deals with the place of speculative capitalism, and with the emergence of the corporate form as a constitutive institutional *form* of capitalism. In fact, and most interestingly, Marx finds it very hard to do so, and his writing about the corporate form treats this form as somehow morally abhorrent. This is significant because throughout his writing Marx is arguing for a structural rather than moralistic analysis of capital (and hence, for instance, his famous tirade against the Young Hegelians in *The German Ideology*). I believe that this inability to deal with the corporate form can be explained by the likelihood that Marx, by the time he wrote volume 3 of *Capital*, was able to anticipate the (still emergent) corporate form in a manner similar to that in which, more than a century later, Slavoj Žižek would read capitalism. Žižek says:

> The "normal" state of capitalism is the permanent revolutionizing of its own conditions of existence: from the very beginning capitalism "putrefies," it is branded by a crippling contradiction, discord, by an immanent want of balance: this is exactly why it changes, develops incessantly — incessant development is the only

way for it to resolve again and again, come to terms with, its own fundamental, constitutive imbalance, "contradiction."[3]

Žižek regards the mutations of capitalism as the means of its adaptation and evolution to a higher form. Marx too realized toward the end of his writings that this "higher" form was not necessarily the higher form of communism; it could also be the higher form of the corporation. In other words, Marx was to realize by volume 3 that the corporate or speculative form of capitalism could in fact present an alternative, *capitalist* realization of the contradictions of mid-nineteenth-century capitalism — and about this he could only feel discomfort in moral rather than structural terms.

The specificity of biocapital as a *biopolitical* form of capitalism lies in the fact that the symptom shifts away from disease manifestation and toward disease potential. This happens through exactly the same logics whether we are considering emergent life science epistemologies such as genomics or emergent pharmaceutical company tactics such as direct-to-consumer advertising.[4] This indicates the implosion of the economic and epistemic that makes biocapital, in my opinion, something more than just the encroachment of capital on a new domain of the life sciences. Rather, the very grammars of the life sciences and of capital are co-constituted; life becomes a business plan. And the symptom is at the heart of this configuration.

My arguments here might appear to set up an incongruence, and it is one that is of some relevance to the narrative form that this book has taken. This is that the epistemology in question, which has indeed, I have argued, given "biocapital" its specific flavor, is that of the life sciences, especially as reflected in emergent techno-epistemic assemblages such as genomics. Obviously these are epistemologies that are inherently and in a direct way biopolitical. They draw their authority from the fact that they are scientific and therefore, by definition, universal. And yet, while the facts of genomics might indeed be universal, the biopolitical manifestations of genomics, as I have shown, are completely incongruent, manifesting in much "older" ways in India than they do in the United States.

Indeed, we are faced with a peculiar conundrum if we analyze epistemologies such as genomics, within the institutional and political economic frameworks that they both operate within and condition. While these epistemologies are placeless and universal by virtue of being scientific, the tactics of involved scientific-corporate actors are situated, conditioned by particular market regimes and legal, institutional, and policy frameworks. The task of tracing the former grammar, which happens to be a biopolitical grammar, is generally considered the domain of theory. The task of tracing the latter grammar, the grammar of cultural particularities, is similarly considered the domain of ethnography. The implosion of biocapital marks the implosion of a theoretical diagnosis regarding new configurations of subjectivity by the life sciences with an ethnographic diagnosis regarding new configurations of value generation by the American free market whose ideologies are increasingly globally hegemonic, but whose manifestations, as I have tried to show throughout this book, are hardly seamless in settings such as India.

Marx constantly argues for the importance of structural attentiveness in spite of the constant reality of tendential, incongruous, agential reality. In other words, incongruent manifestations of systems of exchange in India as compared to the United States are *not* merely contingent "exceptions" to a structural norm consolidated in the West. Rather, the exceptions are a *consequence* of these structural norms, their very evidence. The ways in which global systems of biocapitalist exchange — the explicitly Marxian concerns with value — manifest in India also *have to be analyzed in terms of structural logics*, even if (indeed, especially because) they are multiple, tendential, and contradictory.

A similar challenge faces theorizations of biopolitics: How does one account for incongruent manifestations of biopolitical emergences, such as modes of subject formation by emergent epistemological and institutional assemblages, without reducing these incongruent emergences, simply, to attributions of contingency? In other words, how can one theorize biopolitics "elsewhere," in places that are *not* advanced liberal societies, but that desire to be like them? The relationship of the sovereign American consumer described in chapter 4 to the Indian experimental subject described in chapter 2, for instance, is most reductively attributable to differences in economic standing. The difference that I wish to mark here from such a direct structural argument is that the Indian subject position is not just a consequence of *subjugation* to hegemonic logics and dominant relations of production but exists because of the *desire*, on the part of the Indian state, to buy into, and appropriate, these hegemonic imaginaries for itself, and for its selves.

In other words, there are two sets of relations to stay attentive to between, for instance, "India" and the "United States," as two sites structuring this analysis of "global" capital. The first, undeniably, are structural relations of production. It matters to the ways in which biocapital manifests in tendential fashion in the two locales that one of them is richer, stronger, and more powerful than the other. Indeed, similar structural logics operate within the United States, which is why the subjectivity of sovereign consumer does not automatically accrue from genomics to racially marked subjects, for instance.

But the second, again, has to do with *symptomatic* relations, with the fetish, this time of an American value system. This is a particular conception of the free market that is enforced not just through ideological mechanisms but through actual material structures, such as, for instance, World Trade Organization–mandated intellectual property regimes, which are considered across the board within India as regimes instituted to further American global economic interests (even by those who argue that India should be a willing and active participant in such regimes). And yet the ideal of the American free market becomes the value system that Indian actors, whether they are entrepreneurs based in Silicon Valley or state actors based in Delhi, desire to buy into. Indeed, power differentials between the United States and India can no longer be reductively attributed to differences in "facilities," the standard reason given by Indian scientists a decade ago for the relative impoverishment of scientific output compared to that in the United States. Indian public biology labs today have, or have access to, many of the state-of-the-art technologies that compare to those of top American labs (just as American biotech companies occasionally have leaky ceilings). The real power differential between the two locales lies in the ways that global imaginaries get structured, where doing science, and structuring the market *in the image of America* becomes the driving motivation for Indian techno-capitalist actors, the inverse never being the case. Indeed, it would be hard to suggest what a countervailing Indian vision or imaginary for the conduct of either technoscience or political economy would be.

I do not wish to attribute this desire to be "as if American" to a Marxian false consciousness. Indeed, as I argued in chapter 1, such Indian responses demand instead what Rosemary Coombe calls an ethics of contingency, a willingness to defer judgment on actions constrained by global inequities, but also enabled by global desires, to a future that is yet to come. But I do wish to diagnose a site of American global techno-capitalist hegemony, which resides in the realm of the construction and sustenance of imaginaries that the rest of the world, quite literally, buys into, even if in incongruent ways. It is because the *imaginaries of the American free market* become such global objects of desire — become *symptomatic*, indeed, of global power relations — that it is possible to talk of a culturally particular practice of free-market value generation with the same degree of theoretical fluidity as a universal practice of scientific knowledge production. The American free market is a peculiar beast, indeed a unique beast, probably never replicated in exact fashion anywhere else in the world. And yet, in spite of its absolute particularity, it exists everywhere; the world is built in its image. Ethnographic particularity becomes the object on which social theory gets built for our times, just as other parts of the world remain ethnographic locales.[5]

## Methodological Speculations

These concluding reflections, and this book, beg the question of theorizing emergent political economic structures using ethnography. Specifically, they ask questions of whose "postgenomic lives" are being constituted by biocapital, and who "we" are who are studying these emergences. George Marcus and Michael Fischer's call for anthropology as a form of cultural critique takes seriously the ways in which a discipline formed to study "the Other," "elsewhere," in fact holds much potential for having its insights repatriated in order to study "our" cultures (Marcus and Fischer 1986), especially as sites of ethnographic knowledge production proliferate globally in ways that cannot easily be reduced to the old colonial binary of an Occidental center and an Oriental periphery.

Fischer's problematic as posed in *Emergent Forms of Life and the Anthropological Voice* is that received theories and concepts often prove insufficient to contain and make sense of our rapidly emergent lifeworlds. Both technoscience and capital are particularly lively sites of such rapid emergence. At the same time, as Fischer would no doubt be the first to acknowledge, there is a value to reading theory, and to experimenting with reading theory in the context of new empirical emergence.

This is precisely what this book has attempted. I have tried to present a series of situations, some in India and others in the United States, that on their own lend themselves easily to particular reductive readings. Therefore it is easy to talk about, for instance, Genomic Health, and argue consequently for the *novelty* of our emergent techno-capitalist lifeworlds. It is equally easy to talk about Parel, for instance, and consequently of the *persistence* of very old forms and logics of subjection, alienation, and expropriation. One is a picture of the complete novelty of biocapital, coexisting with another that is a picture of its complete familiarity. Yet these two stories, and the others I have narrated, inhabit the same worlds of biocapital, and indeed the sites that I describe are linked by all manner of global techno-capital flows.

What I have attempted in conclusion, provisionally and in all too much of a hurry, is to question a certain relationship of ethnography to theory. We live in an intellectual milieu in which theory provides us with diagrams for under-standing worlds present, past, and future, with advanced liberal societies in-variably forming the templates on which these diagrams are formed; and in which ethnography is postulated as "the corrective" to these universalizing, homogenizing, and hegemonic theoretical tendencies, by claiming to force attention on those sites that constitute the margins or peripheries of theory. And yet this essential troubling of center and periphery is, necessarily, at least at this time, impossible, because if ethnography's function is to trouble taken-for-granted assumptions about center and periphery, it is also, at the same time, to *describe* those assumptions, to represent the reality of globally hege-monic alignments as faithfully as possible. If my own subjective desire as ethnographer and theorist is to be able to write an ethnographically attentive social theory of emergent globalizing structures where a site such as India was the crucible of theoretical formation, and the United States was the strange ethnographic particularity, then such a desire is, in its sensibility, not that distinct from the desire of the Indian state to be a global player. But like that of the Indian state, it is a desire that is deferred to the future in the manner in which Derrida speaks of it—*l'avenir*, the future that is to come, rather than that which will be, the promissory future without whose conjuration there will be "neither history, nor event, nor promise of justice" (Derrida 1994, 170). An unpredictable and tendential future, which in provisional, partial, fragmentary, and uncertain fashion, subjects such as the life sciences and social theory, value systems such as those of global capitalism and bioethics, and institutions such as corporations, nation-states, and patient advocacy groups, and indeed all of us who are interested in writing or reading books such as this, are working toward.

# NOTES

## Introduction

1. The book that Boguski was referring to was Paul Rabinow's *Making PCR*. See Rabinow 1997.
2. Base pairs are the chemical bases that join complementary strands of a DNA molecule via hydrogen bonds.
3. For an insider account of the many things that happened, see Shreeve 2004.
4. For the most famous articulation of this point of view at the time of the fall of communism, see Fukuyama 1992.
5. For an elaboration of the notion of coproduction, see Jasanoff 1995, 1996, 2004; Reardon 2001, 2004.
6. The four criteria for patentability in the United States are novelty, inventiveness, utility, and nonobviousness. In other words, for something to qualify as patentable, it must be new, actually invented (and not simply discovered), useful, and not obvious to others with prior experience in the field.
7. "Technoscience" is a terminology used by scholars in science and technology studies to argue for the impossibility of considering "science" and "technology" as easy binary counterparts to each other. I use "technoscience" through this book to refer interchangeably to the life sciences and to biotechnology, each of which influences and structures the development of the other.
8. According to Cynthia Robbins-Roth (2000), 11 percent of all federal research and development money was allocated to basic biomedical research, and the National Cancer Institute alone was spending nearly a billion dollars annually on basic research by 1981.
9. Indeed, Buck-Morss (2002) notes that Marx always referred to capital, rather than capitalism, as the phenomenon he was trying to make sense of.
10. For the notion of situated perspective, see Haraway 1991.
11. There are some significant differences between biotech and pharmaceutical companies, which I elaborate on later in the introduction.
12. Marx 1974 (1894), 298.
13. This also echoes Gayatri Spivak's 1999 argument with Fredric Jameson that postmodernism is repetition rather than rupture.

14. Political economy itself was structured by emergent social formations, since political economy was, in Marx's opinion, a fundamentally bourgeois science. Once again, one sees a coproduction between the "scientific" and the "social" as a diagnostic outcome of Marx's own critical method.

15. See Landecker 1999 for the way in which "biological" has increasingly come to function as a noun and not just as adjective.

16. For definitive explanations and critiques of Foucault's work, see Dreyfus and Rabinow 1983; Rabinow 1984.

17. For a key diagnostic analysis of late capitalism, see Jameson 2003 (1991).

18. It was only after completing this manuscript that I read Jason Read's excellent recent book, *The Micro-Politics of Capital*. While philosophical rather than ethnographic, and not concerned with technoscience, Read's method of reading Marx against Foucault has close resonances with what I am attempting here. Read 2003.

19. Marx and Engels 1963 (1845), 19.

20. See Doyle 1997, 2003; Jacob 1993 (1973); Kay 2000; Keller 1995, 2002.

21. See *Grundrisse* (Marx 1973 [1858]) and *Capital, Volume 1* (Marx 1976 [1867]) for Marx's labor theory of value.

22. Donna Haraway (2004) refers to this uncanny value of all exchange as "encounter value."

23. For the vexed relationship between notions of ideology and fetishism in Marx, which he diagnoses as a fundamental tension that grounds Marxian analysis of capital, see Etienne Balibar's essay "The Vacillation of Ideology in Marx" (Balibar 1994). For an argument that Marx's account of commodity fetishism inaugurates a *symptomatic* argument that prefigures a Freudian or psychoanalytic notion of symptom, see Žižek's essay "How Did Marx Invent the Symptom?" (Žižek 1994). My use of the word "uncanny" here is therefore not accidental but is a purposeful use of the Freudian concept. See also Maurer 2003 for an analysis of the ways in which systems of monetary and financial exchange are uncanny.

24. Many thanks to Nick King for making this evident through a workshop he organized on exchange networks in biomedicine called "The Moment of Conversion," which put this particular form of abstraction of this materialist process front and center in its analysis. The conversations in that workshop were particularly invaluable in developing my arguments in chapter 1.

25. See Deshpande 2003 for an articulation of the ways in which economics can be a nationalist discipline.

26. This, I believe, is the simplification that actor-network theory, an otherwise extremely provocative analysis of the mechanics of how technoscience functions, falls prey to. See, for instance, Callon 1999 (1986); Latour 1987, 1988.

27. See Haraway 1997 for her description of the "onion of technoscientific practice."

28. For a useful, if somewhat glorified, account of the biotech industry, see Robbins-Roth 2000. For accounts of the pharmaceutical industry, see Mahoney 1957; Mann 1999.

29. This becomes particularly pertinent in the wake of the recent bioterrorism scares in the United States, including the incidences of letters coated with anthrax spores in September and October 2001. At a venture capital conference that I attended in Boston at the end of October 2001, there was unmitigated excitement among the venture capitalists I

met, who saw anthrax as a pure and simple business opportunity because it would focus the attention of the Department of Defense on the biotech industry. See also Hoyt (2002), who analyzes the role of the military-industrial complex in post–World War II America in the innovation of vaccine development.

30. The most successful early biotech companies that have produced biopharmaceutical products are Amgen (which has developed granulocyte colony stimulating factor [G-CSF] and erythropoietin) and Genentech (which has produced recombinant insulin, tissue plasminogen activator [tPA], human growth hormone, and α-interferon products) (see Walsh 1998, 1–36, for a good summary, from which I have drawn for this account).

31. I discuss this IPO and analyze this fundamental driving temporal structure of the biotech industry in chapter 3.

32. There is a similar terrain in Europe, though the regulatory structure surrounding clinical trials and drug marketing is significantly different. These are consequential differences for understanding the terrain of drug development in the two contexts, but this is not an issue that I explore in this book.

33. This has predictably been labeled piracy by those with close ties to the U.S. pharmaceutical industry. However, it is hopefully evident from the formulation here that one could just as well see this as allowing free market competition in therapeutic molecules similar to that allowed, even in the United States, in many commodities central to daily consumption.

34. The difference of Reddy's and DRF from many U.S. biotech companies is that the former are organizations run by some of the most experienced members of the Indian pharmaceutical industry, many of whom have been in the business for the last twenty or thirty years, and therefore come much closer to the ideal type of the "gray-haired big pharmaceutical manager," the perceived managerial caricature of American big pharmaceutical companies. Indian pharmaceutical companies have not abandoned their generic manufacturing business models. WTO compliance just means that they need to restrict their generic business to molecules that have gone off product patent. However, Indian companies are slowly beginning to leverage their generic expertise to become competitive in the generic markets of the West. While generic markets are far less profitable than markets for drugs protected by patents, the ability to infiltrate Western generic markets is potentially very lucrative for Indian companies hoping to get a global toehold. Indeed, a few Indian companies, including Reddy's, have established R & D divisions in the United States. The emergent politics of generic drugs around the world is a particularly interesting terrain that requires close study, and Cori Hayden (2004) has embarked on such a study in Mexico.

35. For the notion of assemblage as it pertains to the analysis of technoscience, see Rabinow 1999.

36. The HGP used DNA from about fifty donors, created libraries from them, and chose eight libraries for subsequent sequencing. Celera used DNA from twenty-one donors and chose five libraries for subsequent sequencing. All eight libraries used in the HGP were from male donors, while three of the five Celera libraries were from female donors. See Gibson and Muse 2002, 20, for a diagrammatic representation of this.

37. The best account of the early days of the HGP is Cook-Deegan's (1994). For definitive

historical accounts of Cold War Soviet science, see, for instance, Graham 1990, 1993; Gerovitch 2002.

38. Some of the early model organisms to be sequenced were yeast (*Saccharomyces cerevisiae*), roundworm (*Caenorhabditis elegans*), and fruit fly (*Drosophila melanogaster*).

39. For a nice tabular summary of the stages of the HGP, see Gibson and Muse 2002, 14. See also Collins et al. 1998 for a summary of milestones and further challenges for the HGP as they existed at a time that could be considered the start of their race with Celera to sequence the genome.

40. For which see also Geertz 1983, 68.

41. See also Marcus 1998 for an elaboration of the methodological strategies of multisited ethnography.

42. The best way to proliferate analyses of various sites and forms of biocapital, I believe, is through collaborative inquiry. To that end, I organized a workshop called "Lively Capital: Biotechnologies, Ethics, and Governance in Global Markets," which brought together leading analysts of the life sciences and capitalism from a range of disciplines (primarily anthropologists, but also historians and literary theorists). The papers in this workshop trace forms and practices of biocapital in a range of national locales, including the United States, Mexico, Iceland, the United Kingdom, Germany, Nigeria, South Africa, India, China, Taiwan, and Singapore. Even this, evidently, is a fairly limited list of sites of analysis. The papers in this workshop are currently being gathered together for an edited volume.

43. The majority of the stories in this book trace events occurring between 1999 and early 2002, when the bulk of the field research was done. I performed follow-up research at various sites between 2002 and 2004 to trace the continuing changes occurring at a number of sites that I had studied. Given the rapid nature of some of these changes, it could be argued that this book is already something of a contemporary historical analysis, a succession of snapshots of dramatic and emblematic but by no means static moments in the history of technoscientific capitalism in two national locales.

44. This draws on Donna Haraway's notion of gene fetishism. See Haraway 1997.

## 1. Exchange and Value

1. This does not pretend to be an exhaustive account of the DeCode controversy, which has been well researched and debated not just among American bioethicists but also among American anthropologists. For contrasting positions on the controversy, see Palsson and Rabinow 1999 and M. Fortun 2000. Michael Fortun's book on the subject is forthcoming. An extensive archive of the literature surrounding the DeCode controversy is available on the Web site of the leading organization in opposition to DeCode, Mannvernd (www.mannvernd.org). Many thanks to Mike Fortun for conversations that have taught me much about the DeCode controversy, and also to Skuli Sigurdsson, whose indefatigable efforts have been instrumental in the creation of this archive.

2. As Stuart Hall points out (see Morley and Chen 1996), articulation too (like value) is a double-jointed word, implying simultaneously the ability to enunciate and make oneself heard, and the process of linking together.

3. The idea of "qualitatively compressed time" might seem anachronistic but in fact reflects the actual difference in modes of production — to the extent that new ways of doing

science emerge—from an increase in speed. This is reflected in the rapidly emerging high-throughput industries, which require battalions of advanced automated instrumentation that itself gives rise to new instrumentation industries. A particularly striking example of the qualitative effects of time compression can be seen in the business model and R & D activity of a San Diego–based company called Syrrx. Syrrx is a high-throughput proteomics company that seeks to automate all the steps of protein documentation and analysis. In the process, it claims it has robots that can actually crystallize proteins. Protein crystallization has always been one of the hardest things to do in biological research and is often considered more of an art than a precise science. That Syrrx believes it can automate such an intricate and unpredictable process is a testament to how drastically high-throughput technoscience (or its desire) can change the nature of scientific practice as much as it is to the rhetorical powers of a company capable of dynamically selling itself to investors.

4. For the essay that "fathered" information theory, see Shannon 1948.

5. This is still occasionally the case, though many genome companies have increasingly shifted their business models away from database generation toward functional genomics, drug discovery, and biopharmaceutical development. See the introduction for an explanation of these terms and business models.

6. One might think, however, that the state, were it so willing, might have the muscle to bring drugs to market. Historically, however, the state, and not just in the United States, has been good at initial capital outlay that enables the development of private industry, but has been bad at successful long-term execution on capital-intensive projects. Therefore, while the idea of a "public-sector" pharmaceutical company might be tempting to those who believe that the state should invest heavily in the development of accessible therapeutics, this is likely to remain out of even the spectrum of options that states generally explore. Further, in the United States, there exists an extremely strong pharmaceutical company lobby in Congress. Therefore the American state has close relationships with the pharmaceutical industry.

7. I am grateful to Alexander Brown for conversations that have helped me think through these parallels.

8. A "SNP" is a single nucleotide polymorphism. See the introduction for a definition of these DNA sequence markers.

9. A site at which this agitation, and dislike of Venter, was apparent was the 1999 Cold Spring Harbor genome meetings. The phrases quoted were mentioned in talks given by public researchers at these meetings. The reference to the worm genome was because the public researchers were just coming out with the sequence of the roundworm *Caenorhabditis elegans*, which was a major milestone at the time.

10. See also M. Fortun 1999 for an analysis of speed in genomics.

11. As Cook-Deegan (1994) points out, there was serious debate even within the NIH Office of Technology Transfer regarding the patentability of these sequences. A major reason why the NIH felt that it was necessary to patent the sequences was defensive: they felt that they would be in a vulnerable position if someone else patented the sequences instead and thereby prevented their release into the public domain.

12. Venter himself was not at the NHGRI but was working at the National Institute for Neurological Disorders and Strokes (NINDS).

13. As it happens, both the HGP and Celera generated a working draft of the sequence at roughly the same time.

14. Of course, the "official" summaries of this extremely contentious history are predictably formal and dyspeptic. For instance, Francis Collins, head of the National Human Genome Research Institute, in a review article coauthored with Victor McCusick, a leading public genome researcher at the Johns Hopkins University, written for the *Journal of the American Medical Association* summarizing the implications of the genome project for medical science phrases this history in the following terms: "By 1996, the complete sequencing of several bacterial species and yeast led to the conclusion that it was time to attempt sequencing human DNA on a pilot scale. The introduction of capillary sequencing instruments and the formation of a company in the private sector promising to sequence the human genome for profitable purposes added further momentum to the effort. By 1999, confidence had gathered that acquiring the majority of the sequence of the 3 billion base pairs of the human genome could be attempted. In June 2000, both the private company and the international public sequencing consortium announced the completion of 'working drafts' of the human genome sequence" (Collins and McCusick 2001, 541).

15. From *Signals* magazine, an online publication that analyzes biotechnology for executives, www.signalsmag.com, August 24, 1999. The genetic determinism in this quote is particularly striking: while not directly relevant to this chapter, it is interesting to see how it is precisely such deterministic language that is shed in, for instance, the promotion of cloning. It is also striking to note how SNPs simultaneously seem to represent information about individuals, populations, and the "globe."

16. The academic centers involved at the time the consortium commenced were the Whitehead Institute for Biomedical Research, Washington University School of Medicine, the Wellcome Trust's Sanger Center, the Stanford Human Genome Center, and Cold Spring Harbor Laboratory. The list of pharmaceutical members of the consortium was even more impressive and comprised AstraZeneca, Bayer, Bristol-Myers Squibb, Hoffmann–La Roche, Glaxo Wellcome, Hoechst Marion Roussel, Novartis, Pfizer, G. D. Searle, and SmithKline Beecham. Glaxo Wellcome and SmithKline Beecham have since merged to form GlaxoSmithKline (GSK).

17. Quoted in *Signals* magazine, www.signalsmag.com, August 24, 1999.

18. Why Merck, in spite of being a prime mover, was not among the consortium's ten pharmaceutical company members is something I have been unable to ascertain. Nonetheless, one might, in deference to Jacques Derrida, refer to the haunting of the SNP Consortium by Merck's influence and initiative as the "Specters of Merck." Thanks to Nick King for this bad pun.

19. As Pierre Bourdieu insightfully remarks, "We need to be able to recognize as such the strategies which, in universes in which people have an interest in being disinterested, tend to disguise strategies" (Bourdieu 1999 [1975], 35).

20. *Signals* magazine, www.signalsmag.com, May 19, 1998.

21. http://www.genxy.com/About/abt_history.html, accessed March 2000.

22. http://www.genxy.com/News/Releases/abbott.html, accessed March 2000.

23. *Signals* magazine, www.signalsmag.com, May 19, 1998.

24. *Signals* magazine, www.signalsmag.com, May 19, 1998.

25. For the notion of obligatory point of passage, see Latour 1987.

26. Equally important and often overlooked, however, is the obligation that Mauss emphasizes to gift in the first place. A realization of such obligations when exported to the corporate cause may not make new corporate activism seem less cynical, but certainly points to a much more constrained agency for these corporations. A difference between obligation and constraint is also important to tease out concomitant to their causal equation — by "constraint" I mean the limitation of strategic fields with the ultimate aim of maximizing profit, and therefore use the term specifically to define capitalist relations. By obligation I refer to a more intangible system of socio-moral pressures that operate as strongly in the societies Mauss describes as they coexist with the market in capitalism. A standard utilitarian move is to collapse all obligations into constraint. Godbout and Caille (1998) distinguish obligation and constraint as "a moral obligation, whose extreme manifestation is an obligation arising from love, and constraint, which comes from outside and at its extreme is embodied in physical force. Somewhere in the middle is the contract, which provides a space that separates the gift from constraint, a space that the market will enlarge, an intermediate type of social constraint that cannot, however, exist unless it is grounded in a prior gift relationship" (151).

27. Indeed, as Georges Bataille (1998 [1967]) would argue, the importance of gifting in capitalism is not just strategic but in fact a fundamental capitalist "impulse."

28. I am grateful to Bill Maurer for this reading of the gift that Godbout and Caille analyze as distinct from the "archaic" gift that is the subject of Mauss's analysis. Maurer reads Godbout and Caille's gift, which closely approximates the form of gifting I am talking about, as being akin to Dipesh Chakrabarty's "history 1" (the histories of precapitalism necessary to capitalism). He especially reads this in contrast to Marilyn Strathern's notion of the gift, which he sees as being akin to Chakrabarty's "history 2" (which exceeds and cannot be wholly co-opted by capitalism). See Chakrabarty 2000.

29. Academic research labs often aggressively pursue intellectual property protection. It is just that, in the context of DNA sequence debates, they have generally avoided doing so, thereby framing themselves as committed to the "public domain."

30. Three seminal studies show the importance of public research to private innovation in drug development. See Comroe and Dripps 1976; Maxwell and Eckhardt 1990; and Stallings et al. 2001.

31. For an analysis of the process of commodification that I have drawn inspiration from here, see Kopytoff 1986.

32. For an analysis of relationships between public domain and private property in the sphere of plant bioprospecting that inspired my argument here, see Hayden 2003. See also Smith 2004 for a description of the fluid and contested nature of the public/private boundary in the case of rice genomics.

33. For some useful literature on *Moore*, see Gold 1995 and Boyle 1997, 97–107. The best historical contextualization of *Moore* that I have read is Landecker 1999.

34. One could conceptualize this by the following relationship: Rx genomic information = genetic material + genotype information + medical information.

35. I have wrestled with the issue of whether to name this company, and I am still not sure that my decision to keep it anonymous is the correct one. However, there are a number of reasons why I have chosen to do so, and I think this extended footnote is of some

consequence in thinking through methodological questions surrounding the ethical choices that one makes while doing corporate ethnographies.

Joseph Dumit ponders these questions seriously in his recent work on venture science (unpublished), where he names two biotechnology companies and has therefore consciously decided to avoid interviewing people at these companies. In this case, however, I had already interviewed two people at Rep-X (one employee and one manager, one on tape and one off) before I learned of the company's controversial situation in India that I discuss in this chapter. At no point in the chapter do I draw on these conversations. As Dumit has shown, it is both legitimate and a challenge to do corporate ethnography by working from the public record in order to reserve the right to "tackle" certain actors. While that is precisely what I have done in this chapter (using not just the public record but public documents that Rep-X has had a significant hand in "spinning" to its own advantage), the problem of how to "forget" my conversations at Rep-X is a lingering one. I have decided to keep Rep-X anonymous until I have resolved that problem for myself.

This is, as much as anything, an acknowledgment that anthropology is different from journalism, and one of the lines of difference is the relationship with informants. Journalism is adversarial by nature: the work is to "get" a story out of a subject, even if there is a long-term relationship involved. The challenge for an anthropological account such as this is to be ethical and nonadversarial, which is not to say noncritical. At the end of the day, anthropologists write, in part, to their subjects, not just to their colleagues and beyond.

Corporate ethnography involves writing about what is fundamentally a culture of secrecy. It is possible to be fascinated by how and why things get made secret, without necessarily feeling the obligation to make public what the subjects want kept secret. This is precisely the opposite of the investigative journalist. On a basic level, the journalist wants the "truth" that is "out there," while the anthropologist wants, at least as one set of perspectives without which one cannot understand the motivational or intentional side of social action, something like the subject's truth. This is a "truth" in Foucault's sense of "the system of ordered procedures for the production, regulation, distribution, circulation and operation of statements . . . linked in a circular relation with systems of power that produce and sustain it" (Foucault 1980, 133).

One strategy I considered was going to Rep-X's investor relations department to ask for their comments on what I heard in India, but I decided against that journalistic tactic as well. My sense is that if this really is a public relations disaster waiting to happen for Rep-X, then there are strategies that can be employed in conversation with the involved representatives of the Indian state—who are, after all, extremely articulate and media savvy—in making that happen.

Finally, I believe that a number of people invested (in all senses of the word) in the world I am studying will read this chapter with an eye that will see through most attempts at keeping Rep-X anonymous. Also, any agreements I have with companies where I have done longer-term work (this does not apply to Rep-X, where I had only a couple of conversations) make it clear that I have the option of using the companies' names unless they would explicitly prefer me not to. Until shown otherwise, I adopt the methodological rule that the anthropologically interesting issues do not resolve into "dirty secrets" but are structurally interesting dilemmas.

I feel, in spite of that discomfort, that the story of Rep-X will be illustrative of situations I want to explain even if I do not directly locate it.

36. The name of the repository has been kept anonymous.

37. This quote was obtained from the Rep-X Web site. However, to preserve anonymity, the exact citation has not been provided.

38. That even the ethical questions are unclear seems to be lost on most bioethicists, who further believe they have most of the answers to these unarticulated questions. But that is well in keeping with the American institutional desire to have systems run by bodies of experts rather than through genuine public participation, and that is a topic for another day. Nonetheless, see *The Romance of American Psychology* (Herman 1996), a disciplinary study of the rise of "mind sciences," which becomes perceived as officially an expert discourse. This is a general post–World War II development in the United States. Thanks to David Kaiser for pointing me to this reference.

39. This is also a quote linked to Rep-X's Web site and therefore will not be cited to preserve anonymity.

40. The exact citation is not provided to preserve anonymity.

41. I am particularly intrigued by the way in which this article makes DNA sample delivery sound like groceries being delivered. This could, from the tone of the article, be a description of online grocery stores such as homeruns.com or namaste.com. This is not merely an interesting discourse; it is, I believe, a strategic one. After all, making controversial activities seem mundane is key to naturalizing them.

42. Yet again, I will not provide the exact citation, which is taken from Rep-X's Web site.

43. Marx and Engels 1963 (1845).

44. Donna Haraway, personal conversations with the author.

45. M. Fortun 2000, available at http://www.mannvernd.is/english/articles/mfortun.html.

46. Fortun's formulation draws deeply on notions of the ethical put forward by Jacques Derrida. See, for instance, Derrida 2002b.

47. For analyses that put questions of ethics and value squarely in the frame of encounters, whether they are global (and therefore transcultural) or across species, see, for instance, Haraway 2004; Zhan 2005.

48. For a conceptualization of ethics that takes as its starting point the striated rather than seamless terrain on which ethical-political emergence takes place, see Michael Fischer's notion of ethical plateaus (Fischer 2003). The disarticulation and incongruent nature of the ethical grounds on which new biotechnologies emerge is hardly restricted to the stories I outline here. Such disarticulation is, indeed, central to the ethical debates surrounding DeCode that Fortun writes about, and that I briefly introduced this chapter with. Another similar case is the failure of the public Human Genome Diversity Project (HGDP). This attempt by the NIH to document genetic variability among populations stalled as a consequence of different understandings of the ethical grounds for DNA sample collection held by the NIH and by Native American populations. For accounts of the HGDP, see Reardon 2001, 2004.

49. CBT has recently been renamed the Institute for Genomics and Integrative Biology (IGIB), reflecting its current mandate of genomic research. However, since it was called CBT throughout the period of my fieldwork there, I refer to it as CBT throughout this book.

50. Of course, neither of these is obvious or intuitive outside the constantly expanding rationality of population genetics as a discipline and enterprise that discursively constructs populations as units that "naturally" exist to be genetically studied.

51. This section is based on conversations with Indian scientists and policymakers. Instead of directly quoting specific conversations, I have summarized their general content and will keep specific informants anonymous.

52. India is often referred to as "India Inc." in the Indian business press.

53. The question of what constitutes "source" and what "invention" is, of course, a central one in IP debates writ large and is not just confined to biotech. The question of what, if anything, is distinct in the blurring of source and invention in biotech — other than the obviously different and dramatic political contexts that some of these biotech controversies operate within — is of central importance, and something I am very much grappling with.

54. I make these claims, again, based on conversations with Indian scientists and policymakers that I feel delicate about attributing directly to specific people. I do, however, wish to acknowledge one person by name, who has helped me greatly both as an informant and in helping me think through some of the conceptual issues at stake here. Manjari Mahajan is a student of science policy, who was briefly employed by S. K. Brahmachari at CBT to help him think through some of the science policy issues that emerged from genomics as a global practice, particularly as they pertained to IP issues. Mahajan has been particularly keen that the Indian state assert claims for intellectual property rights, rather than simply request benefit-sharing agreements with Western companies (which is the model adopted by most Latin American countries, and a model that Brahmachari, regardless of his personal feelings on the matter, feels might be the more strategic model to pursue because it might antagonize foreign investors less), because regardless of the possibly paradoxical framings of state-as-corporate-entity that this might lead to, intellectual property rights are precisely that: they confer proactive rights *to* exclude others from using "Indian" genetic material as they please, and they protect against Western companies obtaining precisely such rights. Benefit-sharing agreements, on the other hand, engage a terrain of (usually Western) corporate philanthropy rather than of rights. I thank Mahajan for these insights.

55. See, for instance, Victoria Bernal (2004), who traces the formation of an Eritrean nationalist consciousness as a consequence of global networks that are constituted simultaneously by members of the Eritrean diaspora and by communications technologies such as the Internet.

56. I narrate stories of Genomed in chapter 2.

57. For Derrida's notion of deconstruction that this draws on, see Derrida 1976.

58. I think Coombe's notion of a "cultural life" rather than a "social life" is of utmost importance, because understanding the lives of commodities cannot simply be an attempt to understand the circuits they travel as they are produced, circulated, and consumed. Commodities, by definition, are mystical things, and it is impossible to divorce their social life from an analysis of the imaginaries that they create, sustain, and traverse. Hence the salience of the notion of "cultural life." Coombe, indeed, is intimately concerned with the imaginaries associated with intellectual property.

59. For an example of which, see my story of PXE International in chapter 5.

60. Another American biotech company, AgriDyne, also received two U.S. patents for the bioprocessing of neem, and W. R. Grace was issued patents for neem-based biopesticides.

## 2. Life and Debt

1. See, for instance, "Suicides by Andhra Pradesh Farmers Continue," *The Hindu*, June 10, 2004.

2. See unpan1.un.org/intradoc/groups/public/documents/APCHIPAAY/UNPANO 13207.pdf.

3. This is a theme that encompasses Foucault's work. For his exposition specifically on governmental rationality, or what he calls "governmentality," see Burchell et al. 1990.

4. This is not only reflected in the governing ideologies of free market ideologues such as Margaret Thatcher, Ronald Reagan, and George W. Bush but also has very much been the mantra of "experts" of market globalization, as suggested by IMF/World Bank structural adjustment policies, or by publications such as the *Economist* or the *Wall Street Journal*.

5. For the notion of biosociality, see Rabinow 1992.

6. For background on the 1991 crisis, see National Council of Applied Economic Research 2001.

7. See Corbridge and Harriss 2003 (2000), 120. While part of the reason for India's move toward liberalization at the start of the 1990s was structural, part was very much ideological. A detailed account of the factors leading to a change in the economic rationality of the Indian state is beyond the scope of this narrative. Nonetheless it is useful to point out that some of the changes occurring in India at the start of the decade were a consequence of what Sudipta Kaviraj (1997) calls an "elite revolt," not just to four decades of state socialism inspired by the vision of Jawaharlal Nehru, but also to increased social mobilization among "backward" castes that was pronounced in the late 1980s. (The term "backward caste" is officially one of state classification. This includes Scheduled Castes [known politically as Dalits, these are groups of people deemed untouchable in the Hindu caste hierarchy] and Other Backward Castes, groups who are not Dalits but still deemed socially and economically backward by the state.)

8. For a discussion of Marx's distinction between commodity and commercial capitalism in *Capital, Volume 3*, and its relevance to this analysis, see my introduction.

9. I am inspired here by Saskia Sassen's consideration of how globalization "touches down" in different localities (see, for instance, Sassen 2000).

10. See, for instance, Bell 1998; Kassiola 2003.

11. Unlike in the United States, public institutions in India are not allowed to be monetary stakeholders in private enterprises. Instead, CBT holds equity in Genomed in the form of intellectual property, where CBT will get a fixed share of any intellectual property Genomed develops. This in itself is imaginatively different from the U.S. model for equity holding in start-ups. The advantage of this model, according to the director of CBT, S. K. Brahmachari, is that CBT's intellectual property stake cannot be diluted even if Genomed gets bought up by, or receives investment from, another entity, in the way monetary equity would have been.

12. For an analysis of the decoupling of the nation-state in global food politics, see Gupta 1998.

13. An important question is whether the relationship between regional parties and the transnational facilitation of capital flows is applicable to other regional parties beyond the Telugu Desam. A particularly instructive case is that of neighboring Tamil Nadu, which has been influenced since the mid-1960s by the Dravida Munnetra Kazhagam (DMK) and its offshoot and rival, the All India Anna Dravida Munnetra Kazhagam (AIADMK). These parties, as the Telugu Desam has for the Telugus, have based their ideology on Tamil regional identity while becoming important coalition players on the national political scene.

14. While Naidu's vision remains extremely attractive to investment communities based both in India and in the United States, it did not to the Andhra Pradesh electorate, who resoundingly voted him out of power in May 2004.

15. See, for instance, Hoare and Smith 1971.

16. The irony here is that Naidu himself could only be elected as chief minister for five-year terms and, as just mentioned, has been voted out of power before his vision could be successfully implemented.

17. This is not to say that there isn't a growing venture capital industry in India. The amount of venture capital investment in India increased from $3 million in 1995 to $342 million in 2000 (United Nations Development Program 2001, 38).

18. This has been the central mantra of World Bank/IMF structural adjustment policies all over the world.

19. This phrase is a play on Sharon Traweek's phrase "culture of no culture" to describe the culture of high-energy physicists. See Traweek 1988.

20. According to the 1991 census data, the rural population of Andhra Pradesh makes up 73 percent of the state's total population; there are 195.16 lakh (1 lakh = 100,000) agricultural workers as opposed to 104.48 lakh nonagricultural workers (a ratio of nearly 2:1, with the latter category including marginal workers).

21. I wish to be careful of making such predictions, especially since there has been innovative biotech research coming out of Hyderabad in recent years. Most well known has been the creation of a recombinant hepatitis B vaccine by the local biotech company Shanta Biotechniques. Shanta is currently located in the Biotech Park, adjacent to the ICICI Knowledge Park and conceived on similar principles. However, the research on the development of the hepatitis B vaccine occurred while Shanta was being incubated on the premises of an academic institution, the Centre for Cellular and Molecular Biology (CCMB). Rather than make pronouncements on the likely or unlikely futures of ventures like the Park, I wish here merely to emphasize Naidu's rationale for such ventures. Naidu's vision has not been the sole defining vision for the development of biotech in Hyderabad, but it has undoubtedly been a vital and enabling vision, one that has fashioned the priority and direction of biotech initiatives there to a significant extent.

22. The role of pedagogy, of course, is central here, which is why initiatives of Naidu's such as setting up the Indian Business School, modeled on the lines of American schools such as Wharton, become an integral component of such emergent stratified assemblages.

23. Indeed, as just mentioned, Shanta Biotech's development of its indigenous hepatitis B vaccine occurred while it incubated at CCMB.

24. See Srinivasulu 2004. Srinivasulu claims that the recent electoral failure of the Telugu Desam results from its failure to see the consequences of the changes it was bringing

about for the rural population of the state, coupled with a marginalization of the agrarian sector. I wish to thank Venkat Rao for conversations on the history and politics of Andhra Pradesh and its high-tech initiatives. Rao's insights have been invaluable in constructing this narrative.

25. All these figures are obtained from the 1991 Andhra Pradesh census, available at www.andhrapradesh.com, and also from Andhra Pradesh Government 1997. If these figures are adjusted for the relative population densities of Hyderabad city and the adjoining rural districts, the disparities are not quite as stark and amount to a hospital ratio, for instance, of roughly 4:1 between the city and the rural districts. Two things, however, trouble such an easy calculation. The first is that the utility of hospitals relates not simply to the number of people that they serve but also to their ease of access. It is not sufficient to say that hospitals serving a less dense population area can thereby be concomitantly fewer in number than one serving a denser population area, because in the former case the question of how sick patients in parts of the rural countryside far from hospital access then becomes a central question for development. Further, there is the question of the qualitative difference in hospitals and medical facilities in Hyderabad compared to its surrounding districts, vital comparative parameters that census figures cannot indicate. Indeed, hospitals in Hyderabad were seen by Naidu as an integral component of the state's *tourism* strategy, as he hoped to set up a number of "five-star" hospitals in the city that could cater to rich patients from various parts of the country (and perhaps also from other countries). He explicitly refers to the setting up of hospitals as a form of "health tourism" (Naidu 2000).

26. Genomed Mumbai has now (as of 2004) moved to a larger industrial facility in New Mumbai. However, Wellspring Hospital remains in Parel, a part of Mumbai whose political history I outline hereafter in the text. The story that I narrate, therefore, traces the particular situation of Genomed at the time I performed my fieldwork, 2001–2. Although my account is already dated because of the rapidly changing nature of the processes I am studying, I believe that it nonetheless allows me to highlight the structural logics and empirical specificities of biocapital "touching down" in India.

27. As briefly mentioned in the introduction, pharmacogenomics is the correlation of genetics to drug response.

28. It is estimated that of every five drugs that enter clinical trials in the United States, only one makes it to market.

29. Paradoxically, the more successful a drug is on the market, the greater the danger of recall due to adverse events, because a statistically small *percentage* of adverse responses would then get magnified to a numerically large *number* of people who experience negative side effects. The most dramatic example of a postmarketing recall because of the magnified effects of adverse responses in a statistically small percentage of people is the case of Pfizer's antibiotic Trovan, which was considered to be the best fluoroquinolone in its class until the small percentage, but increasingly large number, of patients showing liver failure as a side effect forced Pfizer to withdraw the drug from market.

30. Adriana Petryna is currently engaged in an ethnographic project that studies clinical trials; see Petryna 2005. The best historical work on clinical trials is H. Marks 1997.

31. S. K. Brahmachari, interview with the author, January 7, 2002. The difficulty of classifying populations for population genetics is constitutive to its epistemology; see chapter 4

for an elaboration of this fact. See also Reardon 2001 for an account of the difficulties encountered by the Human Genome Diversity Project as a consequence of this.

32. Sudha and Lalit Deshpande (2003) show that the decline of the textile industry in Mumbai actually started in the 1970s, before liberalization. They indicate that the last five years of the 1970s saw the loss of 34,000 textile jobs, while the first eight years of the 1980s saw the loss of 88,000 textile jobs.

33. Neha Madhiwalla (2003) shows how the distribution of private hospitals mirrors the distribution of elite residential areas. While Mumbai has among the best health coverage in India, the distribution of this health coverage is expectedly very uneven and skewed based on class.

34. My suspicion that what I describe is far from unique to Parel, even though Parel's political ecology might be unique, is suggested from conversations with Joao Biehl, who has for a number of years ethnographically studied an HIV testing center in the Brazilian province of Bahia. This is a center set up by the Brazilian state and is part of the widely hailed Brazilian state intervention in the diagnosis and treatment of AIDS, which has often been referred to as a model for other states to follow. On a recent visit to the center, Biehl found that adjoining the center was a huge five-star hospital, set up by a major multinational pharmaceutical company, that served primarily as an experimental site for clinical trials. In this case, it was the people getting tested for HIV who served as the population that could potentially be recruited into the trials in this hospital. Thanks to Biehl for conversations about this.

35. The relationship of bodies as sites of medical intervention to local forms of indebtedness is strikingly illustrated in Lawrence Cohen's 1999 account of organ transplantation in South India.

36. Datta Isswalkar, interview with the author, July 29, 2004.

37. In a similar vein, see also Susan Greenhalgh (2003) on China's "unimaginable populations."

38. One way they could conceivably be "included" in such circuits is if their genetic material and information was collected for population genetics experiments of the type being done by CBT/Genomed.

39. This is in contrast to the configuration of unmarked advanced liberal subjects of genomics, who are, as I argue in chapter 4, configured as *sovereign consumers*.

40. See Balibar 1995 for a theoretical exploration of the relationship between subjectivity and citizenship. See also Mamdani 1996.

41. Of course, the Indian (and Pakistani) nation-states were themselves formed along with the catastrophic events of the partition of the Indian subcontinent into two nations. It was, however, religion rather than biology that undergirded this citizenship order.

### 3. Vision and Hype

1. Balasubramanian 2002.

2. This account of Doubletwist's rather sorry but extremely entertaining history is reconstructed from conversations with former employees, who are both kept anonymous and not directly quoted.

3. Quote given by Williamson on Incyte TV, a closed-circuit TV channel that was covering the 1999 TIGR conference and airing it to the rooms of its participants.

4. I keep the firm anonymous, since I believe that the contours of this story, and the role venture capital has played in the lives of dot.com start-ups, can be conveyed without specifically naming the firm involved.

5. Bellenson and Smith, meanwhile, started another company in 1999 called DigiScents, which managed to get featured on the cover of the November issue of *Wired* magazine that year. This was a company that had nothing to do with biotech, and the products intended included the "iSmell" (a computer peripheral that would emit fragrances to enhance a user's multimedia experience), "ScentStream" software to drive iSmell, and the "Scent Registry," a licensable digital database of thousands of scents to sell to developers of Web sites, games, movies, advertisements, and music. In April 2001, DigiScents laid off all seventy of its employees and closed up shop after failing to attract enough venture capital funding to go beyond developing a prototype.

6. See the introduction for Marx's distinction between the two.

7. This is not to say that the stock market does not play a role in the lives of Indian companies. It is just that the metric by which Indian companies tend to be judged, even on the Indian stock market, is based less on speculation than on tangible material indicators.

8. See Comaroff and Comaroff 2001 for a collection of essays dealing with what they call millennial capitalism.

9. Dumit, unpublished essay.

10. For Merton's account of the normative structure of science, based on the four norms of universality, disinterestedness, communism, and organized skepticism, see Merton 1973 (1942).

11. This is consistent with Weber's famous argument that the role of the Protestant ethic in the small churches and denominations of North Carolina textile towns was business credit made by moral creditworthiness—the very function of sect organization was to enforce a moral creditworthiness. Also, the bidding among Jains in India for the honor of sponsoring ritual acts is a different but similar way of asserting business creditworthiness, often way beyond their actual means. The moral economy called into account in such situations of credibility/incredibility resembles that of the Balinese cockfight (Geertz 1973). Thanks to Michael Fischer for discussions about Weber's analysis of creditworthiness, and for pointing out the analogy to Jains.

12. Merton 1973 (1942). Of course, the corporatization of technoscience puts some of these norms more at stake than others. Clearly, the norm of communism is often violated when science gets increasingly commodified. Also, the norm of scientific disinterestedness is clearly at odds with that of corporate interest in maximizing market value from a technoscientific enterprise.

13. Among the most controversial of these arrangements is Novartis's funding of the College of Natural Resources at the University of California, Berkeley.

14. I have had one brief, perfunctory conversation with him that he himself is unlikely to remember.

15. Scott was also invited to present at a session on the ethical, legal, and social implications (ELSI) of DNA pátenting in the Cold Spring Harbor Genome meetings of 1999 that I attended. These meetings have constituted the "official" annual gathering of the public HGP, and 1999 was the year when the public researchers' animosity toward Craig Venter

and Celera Genomics was at its height (see chapter 1). Scott was then chief scientific officer of Incyte, which happened to be Celera's biggest and most direct competitor at the time.

16. Disclaimers such as the one put out by Incyte while announcing a collaboration with the Huntsman Cancer Institute to study the role of genes in the diagnosis, treatment, and prevention of cancer, which says: "Except for the historical information contained herein, the matters set forth in this press release, are forward-looking statements within the meaning of the 'safe harbor' provisions of the Private Securities Litigation Reform Act of 1995. These forward-looking statements are subject to risks and uncertainties that may cause actual results to differ materially. For a discussion of factors that may cause results to differ, see Incyte's SEC reports, including its Quarterly Report on Form 10-Q for the quarter ended June 30, 1999. Incyte disclaims any intent or obligation to update these forward-looking statements." See www.incyte.com/news/1999/huntsman.html. I expand on such statements later in the chapter.

17. See also M. Fortun 2004 for the role of promise in genomics.

18. See Robbins-Roth 2000.

19. What I have described so far is what Werner Hamacher (1999) refers to as "spectreality," which is a gesture toward the impossibility of separating the "real" from the "conjured," when at the same time the "real" *is* conjured, and the "conjuration" lays the grounds for the failure of the "real" to be realized.

20. It fascinates me that a number of biotech leaders in India are women. In addition to Mazumdar (now Mazumdar-Shaw), for instance, there is Viloo Patel, the founder and CEO of Avesthagen, another Bangalore-based biotech company. The CEO of the ICICI Knowledge Park, whose story I narrated in chapter 2, is also a woman, Deepanwita Chattopadhyaya, as was the head of India's Department of Biotechnology from 1995 to 2004, Manju Sharma. I cannot hazard the reasons for this, though it could be because of a gendering of occupational roles, with a large number and proportion of women in India going into the life sciences at the school and college level. Scarcely any of the U.S. biotech companies that I have mentioned in this book—a notable recent exception being Celera Diagnostics, the postgenomic reincarnation of Celera Genomics—are, to the best of my knowledge, headed by a woman. Of course, this rise of women to leadership roles coexists in India with some extremely low women's development indices, and the existence still of everyday atrocities against women in the home and workplace. This reflects the contradiction that Amartya Sen draws between women's well-being and women's agency (Sen 1999, 189–203). The conscious nurturing of female entrepreneurial talent in India is reflected in initiatives such as the recent setting up in Chennai of a women's biotech park by the M. S. Swaminathan Research Foundation, with the explicit goal of encouraging female entrepreneurs in the life sciences.

21. This quote is taken from *Business India*, December 8–21, 2003, 67. I draw my brief historical account of Biocon in this paragraph from this article.

22. Ibid., 64.

23. Indeed, Mazumdar-Shaw herself is into the vision game and heads the Karnataka state Vision group on biotechnology. This is, in a sense, Karnataka's, and Bangalore's, equivalent of Andhra Pradesh's Vision 2020.

24. This is based on a conversation that I had with a senior Biocon manager on June 16, 2004. I keep him anonymous.

25. Section 27A of the U.S. Securities Act of 1933, available online at http://www.sec.gov/divisions/corpfin/33act/sect27a.htm.

26. For the evolution of the Securities and Exchange Commission's regulation of the forward-looking statement from 1933 to the present, including a discussion of the landmark 1995 act, see M. Fortun 2004.

27. This is available online at www.incyte.com/news/1999/huntsman.html.

28. Derrida talks about the lie as distinct from error in "History of the Lie." See Derrida 2001 (1995).

29. Of course, this incalculability could be said to function even in noncorporate scientific contexts, such as academic grant applications. The difference between the two lies in the different relationships between promise (which tends toward the contract) and vision (which tends toward the imaginary). Even if the stated aims in, for instance, a scientific grant proposal are not examples of a legal contract, there are often elements in place that evaluate progress toward milestones and objectives as part of the condition of the grant. And, of course, the imaginary that is called into account in the corporate vision is embedded in a rhetoric and grammar that has everything to do with the institutional context of the market, and it is this relationship of institutional context to rhetorical structure that forms the basis of my argument in this chapter.

## 4. Promise and Fetish

1. For a description of SNPs, see chapter 1.

2. The Sanger Centre in the United Kingdom has also sequenced about a third of the genome, making it the other major contributor to the public sequence.

3. Getting access to the Whitehead is about as difficult as getting access to a biotech company. Unlike the biotech companies, the Whitehead's fears are not about an anthropologist having access to proprietary information but about the amount of time an anthropologist's presence might waste there. I was therefore formally refused permission to do extended participant observation at the Whitehead by one of the lab supervisors at the functional genomics center. This makes me particularly grateful to the postdoc who took the time to show me around the center on her own initiative.

4. Indeed, another company that makes chips for biomedical applications, Caliper Technologies (based in Mountain View, California), explicitly calls its products labs-on-a-chip (or LabChip).

5. Hybridizations onto Affymetrix chips are performed using a proprietary technology based on photolithography, which is a process of transferring shapes onto the surface of silicon wafers, and is used in the manufacture of integrated circuits.

6. Of course, such sites also immediately trouble Lander's extremely public image as a "public" scientist opposed to private genome companies patenting gene sequences. It must be mentioned here that Millennium, while broadly speaking a genome company, does not have the generation of sequence databases as its primary locus of value but rather concentrates on more downstream parts of the value chain and is ultimately trying to become a drug development company itself. Thus there is no business contradiction in Lander's opposition to gene patenting as a "public" scientist while being on the board

of a genome company. Rather, his opposition to aggressive gene patenting companies like Celera and Incyte could be seen as being not just in the interests of public researchers but also in the interests of Millennium.

7.  For the notion of obligatory passage point, see Latour 1987.

8.  "Subject" is one of those nice double-edged words that always already point in two complementary directions. It implies both a discipline and an individually or collectively constituted subjectivity. Thus there are subjects such as the life sciences and their various specialties and subspecialties; and there are human subjects of various sorts (subjects of the king, political subjects, and so on). As Etienne Balibar (1995) emphasizes, the latter meaning of "subject" (as individually or collectively constituted subjectivity) is itself an inherently contradictory term. On the one hand, it implies *subjection* — the subject as *disciplined*. On the other hand, it also implies *agency*, the subject that is not merely an object.

9.  The most well known of these situations is the controversy regarding the availability of anti-retroviral therapy to AIDS-ravaged Africa, which, according to activist groups, is in considerable measure due to price-gouging techniques of big pharmaceutical companies. Once again, in this situation, Indian pharmaceutical companies, which as of now operate on a distinct, albeit still capitalist, value terrain to U.S. companies, have emerged as strategic actors that denaturalize and destabilize hegemonic market terrains. Most notable is the offer by the Mumbai-based pharmaceutical company Cipla of generic anti-retroviral drugs to southern Africa at a fraction of the price charged by U.S. and European pharmaceutical companies. This offer is seen by those companies as an infringement of their intellectual property, as "piracy," but the extent to which they can successfully challenge such Indian companies is constrained by the PR disaster that could arise from being seen as aggressively protecting market interests in the midst of a devastating epidemic. Yet again, it is interesting to see how global biopolitical terrains and situations of health and illness, life and death, are overdetermined by market strategies and corporate fights. I do not describe the Cipla story in greater detail in this book, but there is no question that stories of such companies and actors are central to a striated understanding of global biocapitalist terrains.

10.  This latter understanding is given particular credence by the works of sociobiologists such as Richard Dawkins (see, for instance, Dawkins 1976).

11.  For example, look at the following titles of articles and correspondence in a single September 2000 issue of *Nature Genetics*: "Mutations in MKKS *cause* Bardet-Biedl syndrome" (Slavotinek et al. 2000); "Methylation of the CDH1 promoter as the second genetic hit *in* hereditary diffuse gastric cancer" (Grady et al. 2000); "Domain-specific mutations in TGFB1 *result in* Camurati-Engelmann disease" (Kinoshita et al. 2000); "A defect in harmonin, a PDZ domain-containing protein expressed in the inner ear sensory hair cells, *underlies* Usher syndrome type 1C" (Bitner-Glindcicz et al. 2000a); "A recessive contiguous gene deletion *causing* infantile hyperinsulinism, enteropathy and deafness identifies the Usher type 1C gene" (Bitner et al. 2000b); "Mutations in MKKS *cause* obesity, retinal dystrophy and renal malformations associated with Bardet-Biedl syndrome" (Katsanis et al. 2000); "The common PPAR Pro12Ala polymorphism is *associated with* decreased risk of type 2 diabetes" (Altshuler et al. 2000); "Heterozygous germline mutations in BMPR2, encoding a TGF-receptor, *cause* familial primary pulmonary hyper-

tension" (Lane et al. 2000); "Mutations of the gene encoding the protein kinase A type I-regulatory subunit *in* patients with the Carney complex" (Kirschner et al. 2000); "Autosomal recessive lissencephaly with cerebellar hypoplasia is *associated with* human RELN mutations" (Hong et al. 2000); "Mutations in MYH9 *result* in the May-Hegglin anomaly, and Fechtner and Sebastian syndromes" (Seri et al. 2000); "Mutation of MYH9, encoding non-muscle myosin heavy chain A, *in* May-Hegglin anomaly" (Kelly et al. 2000). "Nf1; Trp53 mutant mice *develop* glioblastoma with evidence of strain-specific effects" (Reilly et al. 2000); and "Identification of the gene *causing* mucolipidosis type IV" (Bargal et al. 2000). This is a total of fourteen articles linking single genes to disease, out of a total of thirty articles published in the entire issue. Some of the words are a little more innocuous: two groups merely *associate* genes with particular diseases; one group says that strains with a particular mutant *develop* x disease; one group says that a mutation *underlies* y disease; two mutations *result* in a disease, and another three mutations are merely [seen] *in* those diseases. But *five* mutations are claimed to *cause* diseases.

12. For an exhaustive analysis of the social consequences of classificatory maneuvers, see Bowker and Star 2000.

13. Dumit 1998, 88–89.

14. It should further be emphasized that this unmarked "Western (neo)liberal" subject is likely, though again not necessarily, white. The racial dimensions and implications of epistemologies and technologies such as genomics are immense, and I have not gone into their analysis in this book. For more on this essential topic, see, for instance, Duster 2003; Kahn 2000; Montoya 2003; Reardon 2001, 2004.

15. This argument owes much to conversations with Lawrence Cohen, for which many thanks. The phrase "biopolitics elsewhere," and the posing of the question in the terms I use at the end of this argument, are largely his formulations.

16. These steps are summarized from Collins and McCusick 2001.

17. I consistently noted during my fieldwork that it was the corporate actors who had a better conception of these ethnographic windows than public scientists, since it is the corporate actors who are often forced to take account, however problematically, of society.

18. As Jonathan Marks (2001) shows, the efforts to demonstrate continuity in the genes of Jewish priests have been equally troubled, yet registered as a "success."

19. Based on a conversation with one of the cofounders of Hibergen, Patrick Vaughan.

20. For Marx's section on commodity fetishism in *Capital, Volume 1*, see Marx 1976 (1867), 163–77.

21. Of course, the power of epistemic fetishism cannot be divorced from its functioning as truth-claim; rather than using the apparent "truthfulness" consequent to epistemic fetishism of the scientific fact as the explanation, however, it is precisely such a functioning as truth-claim that I wish ultimately to explain. See also Donna Haraway's notion of "epistemological fetishism" in Haraway 1997. My account is deeply informed by Haraway's argument.

22. Interpellation is the process of self-recognition that Louis Althusser (1994 [1970]) describes as forming the grounds of the operation of ideology. In Althusser's rendering, the classic example of interpellation is when a passerby, hearing a policeman shouting at someone indeterminate, recognizes herself as the subject being hailed. It is a process of

insertion into an apparatus of preexisting power, a call and a recognition of a call that can only operate within a framework of institutional structures that provide the agent who hails with authority, and make the agent hailed a *subject* to the voice of authority. At that moment, in Althusser's argument, the person who is hailed becomes a certain sort of subject, of the state, without even explicitly being called out to (indeed, it is quite possible that the subject of the policeman's hailing is someone else altogether). Interpellation, then, is the process by which an individual recognizes herself *as a subject* as a consequence of being inserted into a certain power structure (in this case, of the relationship of citizen to state) and a certain knowledge regime (in this case, the tacit knowledge of the power structure, which is expressed here through an abstraction).

23. And even if one were paid "enough," the nature of the work is still forced, because the worker is working for what the capitalist will pay.

24. I use male pronouns here, because Marx uses them when referring to workers.

25. Of course, this is again a particularly American manifestation and occurs simultaneously with the struggle for access to drugs in places such as AIDS-stricken Africa, where a very different pharmaceutical grammar is operational. While Dumit quotes a leading neurosurgeon as saying that being on five drugs, in his opinion, is an absolute minimum (Dumit 2003), the work of scholars such as Kristin Peterson shows how fraught the issues surrounding access to drugs are in places such as Nigeria, consequent equally to logics of global capitalism (Peterson 2004). India, by virtue of simultaneously being a "Third World" country and an emergent "global player," does not seem to manifest either of these extreme grammars, at least not at this time. Instead, as shown in chapter 2, the Indian subject of genomics tends to be configured as an experimental subject, again consequent to logics of global capitalism.

26. See Collins and McCusick 2001.

27. See Rapp 2000 for wonderful, embodied accounts of some of these dilemmas.

28. Similarly, it is this refusal to reify the provisional into a solid, preaffirmed ethics of intervention that Rosemary Coombe highlights the importance of when she refers to an "ethics of contingency" (Coombe 1998, 5). See chapter 1 for my use of Coombe's notion in this regard.

29. I am not saying here that born-again Christians are in any way fundamentally aggressive, but rather that evangelical Protestantism, which makes explicit a moment of transformation of consciousness into Christianity as a moment of definitive, unquestionable redemption, represents a certain form of Christianity, one that is certainly more millenarian than the ascetic Protestantism that Weber describes, and perhaps one that is more consonant with the millenarian celebration of risk, gambling, innovation, and excess that marks neoliberal capitalism.

### 5. Salvation and Nation

1. Organized by the Institute of Politics, Kennedy School of Government, September 16, 2002.

2. For ways in which religion can be understood as a cultural system through ritual practices, see Geertz 1973, 87–125; for an argument about capitalism as cultic, see Benjamin 1996 (1922).

3. During the freedom struggle, this party was called the Indian National Congress, sig-

nifying its pan-Indian hegemony and its subscription to the cause of the nation, both of the *Indian* nation whose freedom it was fighting for, and of the modernist *conception* of nation that it was very much fighting to uphold.

4. An example of such a political formation is Chandrababu Naidu's Telugu Desam party, which I described in chapter 2.

5. For an ethnographic exploration of the BJP's rise to prominence and power, and especially the ways in which this has been mediated by television, see Rajagopal 2001. The BJP-led coalition was voted out of power in May 2004.

6. For longer accounts of the pharmaceutical industry that equally subscribe to this idea of the history of drug development as being one of linear progress, see Mahoney 1959; Mann 1999.

7. Thinking about the salvationary tropes of drug development gets at the very question of the *historical* and *cultural* genesis of use value, which, as Marshall Sahlins (1976) points out, gets naturalized in Marx. Naturalizing use value makes *comparison* difficult, because ultimately the use value of an object outside a system of commodity exchange can be seen as irrelevant. It is, in fact, the very different use values of drugs in, for instance, the United States versus Africa (lifestyle drugs in the former versus drugs for survival in the latter), use values that are completely functions of the political economies in which they are situated, which become vital to stay attentive to.

8. By the end of 2004, Indian pharmaceutical companies have had to become WTO compliant, implying that they cannot reverse-engineer any new drugs developed after that date.

9. Including a secular-progressive activist context, as Rekhi has lent his voice in opposition to the exclusionary and often violent politics of Hindu nationalist organizations in India.

10. For a discussion of which, see chapter 3.

11. www.pxe.org.

12. This is stated on Genomic Health's Web site at http://www.genomichealth.com/message. htm. This was Genomic Health's focus in the months following their founding in 2000. By 2004, the company's focus has shifted specifically to cancer genomics. The messages on their Web site have changed to reflect this.

13. Observations based on two talks that I have attended given by Terry at very different forums — at a presentation at a conference on property issues in biotechnology, given primarily to academics and policymakers, and to a class at Harvard Medical School, given primarily to medical students. He followed the same structure in the two, highly similar talks and was equally open to talking about his religious faiths and beliefs in discussion and conversation after the talks.

14. Quote from personal conversations with Patrick Terry, May 2001.

15. www.genomichealth.com. While Terry was one of the founding members of Genomic Health, he is not currently (as of August 2004) on their board of directors. This account, therefore, is based on the relationships forged between Scott and Terry, and between Genomic Health and PXE, in 2001, and does not necessarily reflect either their personal or institutional relationships at present.

16. I draw my account of Scott's pitch for Genomic Health from a talk given at a session on postgenomic medicine at the 2001 Genome TriConference, an investor conference held in San Francisco, on March 7, 2001.

17. This, of course, is exactly what Incyte was.
18. Randy Scott, talk given at the Genome TriConference, San Francisco, March 7, 2001.
19. Ibid.
20. Marx points to the commodity as being "full of metaphysical subtleties and theological niceties" (Marx 1976 [1867]), 163.
21. For Merton's normative structure of science, see Merton 1973 (1942). For Joseph Dumit's notion of venture science, and how it puts Merton's norms at stake, see chapter 3.
22. Not his real name.
23. The company since then changed its name to Doubletwist and subsequently went out of business. For their story, see chapter 3.
24. Bataille would argue that this mode of excess is a fundamental playing out of what he calls "general economy," which he argues is marked by expenditure as a sign of the surplus consumption that is the fundamental logic and driving force of capitalism. See Bataille 1988 (1967). See also Coombe 1997 for the ways in which corporate brand names, trademarks, and similar images create certain types of popular imaginaries as a consequence of their lack of place.
25. Venter was heading TIGR at the time that Perkin-Elmer approached him to run Celera; TIGR was still being headed in 1998–99 by Venter's wife (then) and fellow genome scientist Claire Fraser.
26. Derrida 2002a, 83 (italics in original).
27. For a distinction between the two meanings of representation, as portrait and as proxy, see Spivak 1988.
28. See Silver 1998; Ridley 2000; see also Mendelssohn 2000 for a description of what he calls the "eugenic temptation."
29. Indeed, Merton's outline of the normative structure of science was explicitly in response to the dangers of Nazi science (Merton 1973 [1942]).
30. Derrida talks of this structural messianism in relation to Marxism, but then Marxism itself was explicitly regarded by its practitioners as scientific, and much of Marxism's potential for emancipation did stem for Marx from the fact that he believed his account of political economy to be properly "scientific."
31. Interview with a scientist (kept anonymous), Centre for Biochemical Technology, January 7, 2002.
32. Ibid.
33. Mahajan was hired by Brahmachari to help him with the policy initiatives that he was involved in — the sort of deregulated and imaginative hiring that would not have been possible in a pre-Mashelkar era. This account is based on conversations had with her in January 2002.
34. Ramesh Mashelkar, interview with the author, July 20, 2001.
35. S. Sivaram, interview with the author, June 13, 2001.
36. Ibid.
37. Ibid.
38. This is also seen in my example, in chapter 1, of India's attempt to regulate genetic expropriation through property mechanisms and market contracts.
39. Ramesh Mashelkar, interview with the author, July 20, 2001.
40. This is, of course, not entirely true, since countries like the Soviet Union, China, and Cuba have always done so.

41. Satish Kumar, interview with the author, August 6, 2001.
42. Ibid. Meanwhile, Brahmachari sees East-West inequity in the fact that Indian researchers are *unable* to immediately publish in those journals that Indian universities cannot afford. There are also now companies that are beginning to supply the reagent market locally, and CBT itself, indeed, was set up with this aim.
43. One would think that this is the sort of research that would have been done in a lab of the Indian Council for Agricultural Research (ICAR), and Kumar feels that the reason why it has not is because ICAR has basked for too long in the glory of the green revolution, which completely ignored the animal sector.
44. www.tie.org.
45. www.tie.org/library/about.asp.
46. www.tie.org.
47. In an interview to cnn.com, available at www.cnn.com/SPECIALS/2000/virtualvil lages/story/india/interviews/rekhi.html.
48. Ibid.
49. Ibid.
50. My total college fees for a three-year undergraduate degree, *inclusive* of tuition, accommodation, and utilities such as electricity, amounted to about Rs 720, which, at the exchange rate of the time, would be roughly $25. Meanwhile the United Nations Development Program (UNDP) 2001 *Human Development Report* estimates that an annual resource loss for India from software professionals who migrate to the United States is $2 billion, if one calculates the amount of state investment that is put into most of their higher education.
51. As might be expected, Rekhi's comments, made in April 2001, created quite a controversy, with heated debate ensuing in online Indian newsgroups and discussion groups. In May, Rekhi issued the following clarification on his remarks: "The raging debate about my views regarding secondary immigration were taken out of context. I hold no views about who should be or who shouldn't be allowed in. I am too much of a free marketer to worry about the quality of one profession over the other. I did make a distinction between primary and secondary immigrants, in that primary immigrants come on their own merit and compete like hell to survive on their own. Secondary immigrants often were sponsored brothers and sisters who were not qualified like primary immigrants and needed a lot of help to adjust here. Incidentally, I am somewhat of an expert here, having sponsored five brothers and their spouses over a 15 year period. I am not against family re-unification at all. Is an endless loop of sponsored brothers and sisters family re-unification?" (quoted in Din 2001b).

## 6. Entrepreneurs and Start-Ups

1. Not his real name.
2. Not his real name.
3. For instance, the Centre for Cellular and Molecular Biology (CCMB) in Hyderabad, a CSIR lab with an almost identical mandate to CBT's, is marked precisely by the absence of this type of bureaucratic hierarchy that is directed not just against outsiders like myself but also against CBT's own scientists. CCMB's more cooperative and egalitarian, and less bureaucratic, culture is a function both of its location in Hyderabad and of the managerial practices of its founding director, Pushpa Bhargava, who, according to scientists

at CCMB, ensured through personal example that bureaucratic one-upmanship would not be tolerated. An interesting hypothetical question to consider would be how similar, or different, CBT's culture might have been under Brahmachari had it in fact been in Hyderabad, not Delhi.

4. See, for instance, Lewis 1999, which recounts the story of Jim Clark, the founder of Netscape, in many ways the archetypal start-up of the recent dot.com boom.

5. For the use of "emergent forms of life" as a theoretical heuristic to open up questions of the study of rapidly emergent structures using ethnography, see Fischer 2003.

6. These three accounts, which all agree on the particularities of biotech start-up culture, in fact represent three quite distinct genres of writing about biotech. Rabinow's is the most academic and conceptual, Werth's is a popular-science account that reads like a thriller, and Robbins-Roth's is a feel-good investor manual written by a biotech industry consultant.

7. An exemplary "textbook" for starting companies is Sahlman et al. 1999.

8. This is a particular form of "benevolent" investing that is contrasted to venture capitalism in the generally smaller amounts invested, and in the investors' generally lower expectations for incredibly high returns on their investments. Venture capitalists ideally like a 60 to 70 percent return on their investment and usually take over a significant chunk of the company from the founders in return for their largesse.

9. GeneEd moved to fancier quarters in spring 2004, after four years in this office.

10. See Latour 1987.

11. Most custom courses developed by GeneEd are either for use on their clients' Web sites or, increasingly, for sales force training within the company.

12. The emblematic status of "Evil Company" that Monsanto has acquired in activist circles is interesting enough; even more interesting is that it has done so in corporate circles, as the benchmark either to avoid or to be distanced from.

13. Ethnographers are, after all, increasingly being used in the corporate world, especially in Silicon Valley high-tech companies such as Intel.

14. Indeed, on a typical day that I spent with Maulik, he followed up a meeting with a potential investor with a trip to Costco to buy plants for the office.

15. Cynthia Kilroy, interview with the author, May 24, 2001.

16. Ibid.

17. Cyane Rollins, interview with the author, May 14, 2001.

18. While the designers were, strictly speaking, also programmers, in that they needed to be comfortable with programming (mainly in Flash and XML), GeneEd's transition to becoming a knowledge management company saw a bigger role for more "traditional" software programmers, who were not responsible for the creative or artistic component of the output.

19. Robin Lindheimer, interview with the author, March 28, 2002.

20. Chris Palmer, interview with the author, March 28, 2002.

21. Each of these was told to me by a different graphic designer, in a series of interviews conducted between March 28 and April 2, 2002.

22. Cynthia Kilroy, interview with the author, April 1, 2002.

23. Paul Eisele, interview with the author, April 1, 2002.

24. I keep this employee anonymous. Quote from an interview with the author, April 2, 2002.

25. Needless to say, I feel there are profound lessons here for purported interdisciplines like STS, which often end up, in academic spaces such as STS departments, being carefully negotiated multidisciplines, with great care taken *not* to brainstorm across disciplinary preserves so that each component discipline's "sanctity" can be "respected," and a certain amount of peaceful coexistence maintained. The productivity of corporate spaces such as start-ups and new technoscientific endeavors such as bioinformatics comes precisely from the willingness to take the risk of encroaching on another's disciplinary turf and thereby creating the conditions of possibility for new forms of knowledge, strategy, and cohabitation to emerge. The parallels of multidisciplinary endeavors to the now highly critiqued notion and practice of multiculturalism, which allows, in the name of political correctness, an unquestioned coexistence of different cultural and religious beliefs and practices and their institutionalization, without adequately posing the "thick" questions of the historical genesis and political contexts of these "cultural forms," and further reifying the individual "cultural" components of a multicultural assemblage into homogeneous entities, need to be further examined. Perhaps corporate technoscience can provide some salutary lessons for progressive praxis after all.
26. Sunil Maulik, interview with the author, May 15, 2001.
27. Ibid. The parallels to Susan Harding's description of the forms of discursive and ritual performance involved in "brainwashing" people into born-again Christianity by evangelicals such as Jerry Falwell is striking (see Harding 2000).
28. Sunil Maulik, interview with the author, May 15, 2001.
29. Ibid.
30. The question of whether the dot.com era was indeed something that can so easily be dismissed as an "aberration" is, of course, an important one to ask. Indeed, such a dismissal stems from a deeply ahistorical supposition that the dot.com era marks, for the first time, a manifestation of capitalism in such an explicitly "excessive" mode. And yet one in fact sees the same forms of excess, albeit concentrated in different institutions (primarily Wall Street and investment banks rather than in Silicon Valley and high-tech venture-capital-funded industry), in the 1980s. Michael Lewis's accounts of both, in *Liar's Poker* and *The New, New Thing* respectively, in spite of a definite enthusiasm for Silicon Valley over Wall Street, provide a wonderful perspective from which to comparatively situate key institutional sites of excess in these two historical moments (Lewis 1989, 1999).
31. Sunil Maulik, interview with the author, May 15, 2001.
32. Ibid.
33. Ibid.
34. Ibid.
35. These words were written in June 2002. The conditions of the bridge loan were subsequently renegotiated.
36. Since the time of first writing, and over the next year (2002–3), GeneEd reached an advanced stage of negotiations with a number of VC funds before having the VCs pull out at the last minute once again. Maulik again justified the aggressive pursuit of VC investment while he was pursuing it, and rationalized that it was ultimately beneficial for GeneEd that the investments did not materialize once it became clear that they would not do so. As of August 2004, GeneEd remains a non-VC-funded entity.
37. Doubletwist has since gone out of business.

38. Sunil Maulik, correspondence with the author, November 20, 2001.

39. Of course, the fetishistic or cultlike dimensions of capitalism hardly manifest in uniform ways, or even in ways that necessarily lead to an enthusiastic buying in to the capitalist cause. At the end of the day, however "crummy" a job at Genentech might be, it is still a highly privileged site of labor in global capitalism. The fetish or cult of capitalism, especially in more marginal or subaltern sites, could often operate in ways that are still powerful but construct an aura of fear or hysteria rather than desire. For instance, see E. P. Thompson's account of the making of the English working class (Thompson 1966 [1963]), a process that he shows involved millenarian, religious, cultic, and fetishistic performance in ways that provoked a submission through the creation not of desire but of a "chiliasm of despair." Michael Taussig similarly shows how the making of South American working classes through forced proletarianization was accompanied by the fetishism of capitalism as the devil, as the cult to be submitted to rather than bought into (Taussig 1980).

## Coda

1. Rabinow 2003, 14.
2. This relates to Joseph Dumit's notion of "surplus health" (Dumit 2004).
3. Žižek 1994, 330.
4. For the latter, see Dumit 2004.
5. These arguments are hardly specific to the American free market but are relevant to a range of theoretical questions that inform our times. For instance, I am constantly amazed that democratic political "theory," in political science departments around the world, gets synthesized through an understanding of American interest-group politics (and occasionally, increasingly, by European grassroots politics), while the democratic political mobilizations (both representative and grassroots) of the world's largest democracy, India, get relegated to area studies.

# REFERENCES

Alinsky, Saul. 1989 (1971). *Rules for Radicals: A Practical Primer for Realistic Radicals*. New York: Vintage Books.

Althusser, Louis. 1969 (1965). *For Marx*. Trans. B. Brewster. New York: Pantheon Books.

———. 1994 (1970). Ideology and ideological state apparatuses (notes towards an investigation). In *Mapping Ideology*, ed. Slavoj Žižek, 100–140. New York: Verso.

Altshuler, D., J. N. Hirschhorn, M. Klannemark, C. M. Lindgren, M. C. Vohl, J. Nemesh, C. R. Lane, S. F. Schaffner, S. Bolk, C. Brewer, T. Tuomi, D. Gaudet, T. J. Hudson, M. Daly, L. Groop, and E. S. Lander. 2000. The common PPAR Pro12Ala polymorphism is associated with decreased risk of type 2 diabetes. *Nature Genetics* 26 (1): 76–80.

Anderson, Benedict. 1991 (1983). *Imagined Communities: Reflections on the Origin and Spread of Nationalism*. New York: Verso.

Andhra Pradesh Government. 1997. *Andhra Pradesh: Four Decades of Development*. Available at www.ap.gov.in/apbudget.

Balasubramanian, D. 2002. Molecular and cellular approaches to understand and treat some diseases of the eye. *Current Science* 82 (8): 948–57.

Balibar, Etienne. 1994. *Masses, Classes, Ideas: Studies of Politics and Philosophy before and after Marx*. New York: Routledge.

———. 1995. The infinite contradiction. Trans. J.-M. Poisson and J. Lezra. *Yale French Studies* 88.

Bargal, R., N. Avidan, E. Ben-Asher, Z. Olender, M. Zeigler, A Frumkin, A. Raas-Rothschild, G. Glusman, D. Lancet, and G. Bach. 2000. Identification of the gene causing mucolipidosis type IV. *Nature Genetics* 26 (1): 118–23.

Bataille, Georges. 1988 (1967). *The Accursed Share: An Essay on General Economy*. Trans. R. Hurley. New York: Zone Books.

Beck, Ulrich. 1986. *Risk Society: Towards a New Modernity*. London: Sage.

Bell, David, ed. 1998. *Political Ecology: Global and Local*. New York: Routledge.

Benjamin, Walter. 1996 (1922). Capitalism as religion. In *Walter Benjamin: Selected Writings, Volume 1, 1913–1926*, ed. M. and M. Jennings. Cambridge: Harvard University Press.

Bernal, Victoria. 2004. Eritrea goes global: Reflections on nationalism in a transnational era. *Cultural Anthropology* 19 (1): 3–25.

Biehl, João. 2001. Biotechnology and the new politics of life and death in Brazil: The AIDS model. Paper presented at the Society for the Social Studies of Science (4S) meetings, Boston, Mass.

Biehl, Joao, Denise Coutinho, and Ana Luzia Outeiro. 2001. Technology and affect: HIV/AIDS testing in Brazil. *Culture, Medicine and Psychiatry* 25 (1): 87–129.

Bitner-Glindzicz, M., K. J. Lindley, P. Rutland, D. Blaydon, V. V. Smith, P. J. Milla, K. Hussain, J. Furth-Lavi, K. E. Cosgrove, R. M. Shepherd, P. D. Barnes, R. E. O'Brien, P. A. Farndon, J. Sowden, X.-Z. Liu, M. J. Scanlan, S. Malcolm, M. J. Dunne, A. Aynsley-Green, and B. Glaser. 2000a. A defect in harmonin, a PDZ domain-containing protein expressed in the inner ear sensory hair cells, underlies Usher syndrome type 1C. *Nature Genetics* 26 (1): 51–55.

——. 2000b. A recessive contiguous gene deletion causing infantile hyperinsulinism, enteropathy and deafness identifies the Usher type 1C gene. *Nature Genetics* 26 (1): 56–60.

Bourdieu, Pierre. 1999 (1975). The specificity of the scientific field and the social conditions of the progress of reason. In *The Science Studies Reader*, trans. R. Nice, ed. Mario Biagioli. New York: Routledge.

Bowker, Geoffrey, and Susan Leigh Star. 2000. *Sorting Things Out: Classification and Its Consequences*. Cambridge: MIT Press.

Boyle, James. 1997. *Shamans, Software, and Spleens: Law and the Construction of the Information Society*. Cambridge: Harvard University Press.

Braga, Carlos. 1990. The economics of intellectual property rights and the GATT: A view from the south. In *Trade Related Aspects of Intellectual Property*, ed. L. Brown and E. Szweda. Nashville: William S. Hein.

Brahmachari, Samir K. 2001. Genome research and IPR: An Indian perspective. Presentation to the United Nations Educational, Scientific, and Cultural Organization (UNESCO).

Buck-Morss, Susan. 2002. *Dreamworld and Catastrophe: The Passing of Mass Utopia in East and West*. Cambridge: MIT Press.

Burchell, Graham, Colin Gordon, and Peter Miller, eds. 1991. *The Foucault Effect: Studies in Governmentality; With Two Lectures by and an Interview with Michel Foucault*. Chicago: University of Chicago Press.

Callon, Michel. 1999 (1986). Some elements of a sociology of translation: Domestication of the scallops and the fishermen of St. Brieuc Bay. In *The Science Studies Reader*, trans. R. Nice, ed. Mario Biagioli. New York: Routledge.

Canguilhem, Georges. 1989 (1966). *The Normal and the Pathological*. Cambridge: Zone Books.

Carnegie, Dale. 1998 (1936). *How to Win Friends and Influence People*. New York: Pocket Books.

Chakrabarty, Dipesh. 2000. *Provincializing Europe: Postcolonial Thought and Historical Difference*. Princeton, N.J.: Princeton University Press.

Chatterjee, Partha. 1997 (1989). *A Possible India: Essays in Political Criticism*. Delhi: Oxford University Press.

Cohen, Lawrence. 1999. Where it hurts: Indian material for an ethics of organ transplantation. *Daedalus: Bioethics and Beyond* 128 (4): 135–64.

——. 2000. *No Aging in India: Alzheimer's, the Bad Family and Other Modern Things*. Berkeley: University of California Press.

———. 2003. The sovereign's vasectomy. Invited lecture at Department of Anthropology, Harvard University.

Collins, Francis, Mark Guyer, and Aravinda Chakravarti. 1997. Variations on a theme: Cataloging human DNA sequence variation. *Science* 278:1580–81.

Collins, Francis, and Victor McCusick. 2001. Implications of the Human Genome Project for medical science. *Journal of the American Medical Association* 285 (5): 540–44.

Collins, F. S., A. Patrinos, E. Jordan, A. Chakravarti, R. Gesteland, L. Walters, and the members of the DOE and NIH planning groups. 1998. New goals for the U.S. Human Genome Project: 1998–2003. *Science* 282:682.

Comaroff, Jean, and John Comaroff, eds. 2001. *Millennial Capitalism and the Culture of Neoliberalism*. Durham: Duke University Press.

Comroe, Julius, and Robert Dripps. 1976. Scientific basis for the support of biomedical science. *Science* 192:105–11.

Cook-Deegan, Robert. 1994. *The Gene Wars: Science, Politics and the Human Genome*. New York: W. W. Norton.

Coombe, Rosemary. 1997. The demonic place of the "not there": Trademark rumors in the post-industrial imaginary. In *Culture, Power, Place: Explorations in Critical Anthropology*, ed. A. Gupta and J. Ferguson, 249–76. Durham: Duke University Press.

———. 1998. *The Cultural Life of Intellectual Properties: Authorship, Appropriation, and the Law*. Durham: Duke University Press.

Corbridge, Stuart, and John Harriss. 2003 (2000). *Reinventing India: Liberalization, Hindu Nationalism and Popular Democracy*. Delhi: Oxford University Press.

Council for Scientific and Industrial Research. 1996. *CSIR 2001: Vision and Strategy*. New Delhi: National Institute of Science Communication.

Davies, Kevin. 2001. *The Sequence: Inside the Race for the Human Genome*. New Delhi: Penguin Books.

Dawkins, Richard. 1976. *The Selfish Gene*. New York: Oxford University Press.

DBT. *See* Department of Biotechnology.

Department of Biotechnology. 2001. *Ethical Policies on the Human Genome, Genetic Research and Service*. New Delhi: Ministry of Science and Technology, Government of India.

Derrida, Jacques. 1976. *Of Grammatology*. Trans. Gayatri Spivak. Baltimore: Johns Hopkins University Press.

———. 1994. *Specters of Marx: The State of the Debt, the Work of Mourning and the New International*. New York: Routledge.

———. 1995. *On the Name*. Trans. D. Wood, J. Leavey Jr., and I. McLeod, ed. T. Dutoit. Stanford: Stanford University Press.

———. 2001 (1995). History of the lie: Prolegomena. In *Futures of Jacques Derrida*, ed. Richard Rand, 65–98. Stanford: Stanford University Press.

———. 2002a. *Acts of Religion*. Ed. Gil Anidjar. New York: Routledge.

———. 2002b. *Negotiations: Interventions and Interviews, 1971–2001*. Trans. and ed. E. Rottenberg. Stanford: Stanford University Press.

Deshpande, Satish. 2003. *Contemporary India: A Sociological View*. New Delhi: Penguin Books.

Deshpande, Sudha, and Lalit Deshpande. 2003. Work, wages, and well-being: 1950s and

1990s. In *Bombay and Mumbai: The City in Transition*, ed. Sujata Patel and Jim Masselos. Delhi: Oxford University Press.

*Diamond v. Chakrabarty*, 447 US 303 (1980).

DiMasi, J. A., R. W. Hansen, H. G. Grabowski, H. G. Lasagna, and L. Lasagna. 1991. Cost of innovation in the pharmaceutical industry. *Journal of Health Economics*, July, 107–42.

Din, Suleman. 2001a. Kanwal Rekhi takes up immigration issue. *Rediff.com*, April 28. Available at http://www.rediff.com/news.

———. 2001b. Rekhi clarifies on immigration issue. *Rediff.com*, May 24. Available at http://www.rediff.com/news.

D'Monte, Darryl. 2002. *Ripping the Fabric: The Decline of Mumbai and Its Mills*. Delhi: Oxford University Press.

Doyle, Richard. 1997. *On Beyond Living: Rhetorical Transformations of the Life Sciences*. Stanford: Stanford University Press.

———. 2003. *Wetwares: Experiments in Postvital Living*. Minneapolis: University of Minnesota Press.

Dreyfus, Hubert, and Paul Rabinow. 1983. *Michel Foucault: Beyond Structuralism and Hermeneutics*. Chicago: University of Chicago Press.

Dumit, Joseph. 1998. A digital image of the category of the person: PET scanning and objective self-fashioning. In *Cyborgs and Citadels: Anthropological Interventions in Emerging Sciences and Technologies*, ed. G. Downey and J. Dumit, 83–102. Santa Fe: School of American Research.

———. 2003. A pharmaceutical grammar: Drugs for life and direct-to-consumer advertising in an era of surplus health. Unpublished essay.

———. 2004. Drugs, algorithms, markets and surplus health. Workshop paper presented at Department of Anthropology, University of California, Irvine.

Duster, Troy. 2003. *Backdoor to Eugenics*. New York: Routledge.

Ewald, Francois. 1991. Insurance and risk. In *The Foucault Effect: Studies in Governmentality*, ed. G. Burchell, C. Gordon, and P. Miller, 197–210. Chicago: University of Chicago Press.

Fabian, Johannes. 1983. *Time and the Other: How Anthropology Makes Its Object*. New York: Columbia University Press.

Fischer, Michael M. J. 2001. Ethnographic critique and technoscientific narratives: The old mole, ethical plateaux and the governance of emergent biosocial polities. *Culture, Medicine and Psychiatry* 25 (4): 355–93.

———. 2003. *Emergent Forms of Life and the Anthropological Voice*. Durham: Duke University Press.

Fleck, Ludwig. 1979 (1935). *Genesis and Development of a Scientific Fact*. Trans. F. Bradley and T. Trenn. Chicago: University of Chicago Press.

Fortun, Michael. 1999. Projecting speed genomics. In *Practices of Human Genetics: International and Interdisciplinary Perspectives*, ed. M. Fortun and E. Mendelsohn. Dordrecht: Kluwer.

———. 2000. Experiments in ethnography and its performance. *Mannvernd*. Available at www.mannvernd.is.

———. 2004. For an ethics of promising. Workshop paper presented at Department of Anthropology, University of California, Irvine.

Foucault, Michel. 1973. *The Order of Things: An Archaeology of the Human Sciences*. New York: Vintage Books.

———. 1980. Truth and power. In *Power/Knowledge: Selected Interviews and Other Writings, 1972–1977*, ed. Colin Gordon, 109–33. New York: Pantheon Books.

———. 1990 (1978). *The History of Sexuality: An Introduction*. New York: Vintage Books.

Frankenburg, Ruth. 1993. *White Women, Race Matters: The Social Construction of Whiteness*. Minneapolis: University of Minnesota Press.

Frow, John. 1996. Information as gift and commodity. *New Left Review* 219:89–108.

Fukuyama, Francis. 1992. *The End of History and the Last Man*. New York: Free Press.

Geertz, Clifford. 1973. *The Interpretation of Cultures*. New York: Basic Books.

———. 1983. *Local Knowledge: Further Essays in Interpretive Anthropology*. New York: Basic Books.

Gerovitch, Slava. 2002. *From Newspeak to Cyberspeak: A History of Soviet Cybernetics*. Cambridge: MIT Press.

Ghosh, Jayati. 1998. Liberalization debates. In *The Indian Economy: Major Debates since Independence*, ed. T. Byres, 295–334. Delhi: Oxford University Press.

Gibson, Greg, and Spencer Muse. 2002. *A Primer of Genome Science*. Sunderland, Mass.: Sinauer.

Godbout, Jacques, and Alain Caille. 1998. *The World of the Gift*. Trans. Donald Winkler. Montreal: McGill–Queen's University Press.

Gold, Richard. 1995. Owning our bodies: An examination of property law and biotechnology. *San Diego Law Review* 32:1167–1247.

Golub, D. R., D. K. Slonim, P. Tamayo, C. Huard, M. Gaasenbeek, J. P. Mesirov, H. Coller, M. Loh, J. R. Downing, M. A. Caliguiri, C. D. Bloomfield, and E. S. Lander. 1999. Molecular classification of cancer: Class discovery and class prediction by gene expression monitoring. *Science* 286:531–37.

Goux, Jean-Joseph. 1990. General economics and post-modern capitalism. Trans. Kathryn Ascheim and Rhonda Garelick. *Yale French Studies* 78:206–24.

Government of India. 1958. *Scientific Policy Resolution*. New Delhi: Department of Science and Technology.

Grady, W. M., J. Willis, P. J. Guilford, A. K. Dunbier, T. T. Toro, H. Lynch, G. Wiesner, K. Ferguson, C. Eng, J.-G. Park, S.-J. Kim, and S. Markowitz. 2000. Methylation of the CDH1 promoter as the second genetic hit in hereditary diffuse gastric cancer. *Nature Genetics* 26 (1): 16–17.

Graham, Loren, ed. 1990. *Science and the Soviet Social Order*. Cambridge: Harvard University Press.

———. 1993. *Science in Russia and the Soviet Union: A Short History*. Cambridge, U.K.: Cambridge University Press.

Gramsci, Antonio. 1968. *The Modern Prince and Other Writings*. Trans. Louis Marks. New York: International Publishers.

Greenhalgh, Susan. 2003. Planned births, unplanned persons: "Population" in the making of Chinese modernity. *American Ethnologist* 30 (2): 196–215.

Grefe, Edward, and Martin Linsky. 1995. *The New Corporate Activism: Harnessing the Power of Grassroots Tactics for Your Organization*. New York: McGraw-Hill.

Grossberg, Lawrence. 1996. On postmodernism and articulation: An interview with Stuart

Hall. In *Stuart Hall: Critical Dialogues in Cultural Studies*, ed. David Morley and Kuan-Hsing Chen, 131–50. New York: Routledge.

Gupta, Akhil. 1998. *Postcolonial Developments: Agriculture in the Making of Modern India*. Durham: Duke University Press.

Gupta, Akhil, and James Ferguson, eds. 1997. *Anthropological Locations: Boundaries and Grounds of a Field Science*. Berkeley: University of California Press.

Halushka, M. K., J.-B. Fan, K. Bentley, L. Hsie, N. Shen, A. Weder, R. Cooper, R. Lipshutz, and A. Chakravarti. 1999. Patterns of single-nucleotide polymorphisms in candidate genes for blood-pressure homeostasis. *Nature Genetics* 22:239–47.

Hamacher, Werner. 1999. Lingua amissa: The messianism of commodity-language and Derrida's *Specters of Marx*. In *Ghostly Demarcations: A Symposium on Jacques Derrida's Specters of Marx*, ed. Michael Sprinker. New York: Verso.

Haraway, Donna. 1991. *Simians, Cyborgs and Women: The Reinvention of Nature*. New York: Routledge.

———. 1997. *Modest_Witness@second_Millennium.FemaleMan_Meets_OncoMouse™: Feminism and Technoscience*. New York: Routledge.

———. 2004. Value-added dogs and lively capital. Workshop paper presented at Department of Anthropology, University of California, Irvine.

Harding, Susan. 2000. *The Book of Jerry Falwell: Fundamentalist Language and Politics*. Princeton, N.J.: Princeton University Press.

Hayden, Cori. 2003. *When Nature Goes Public: The Making and Unmaking of Bioprospecting in Mexico*. Princeton, N.J.: Princeton University Press.

———. 2004. Pharma nation? The generic-ization of Mexico's pharmaceutical economy. Workshop paper presented at Department of Anthropology, University of California, Irvine.

Healy, David. 1997. *The Anti-depressant Era*. Cambridge: Harvard University Press.

———. 2002. *Psychiatric Drugs Explained*. Edinburgh: Churchill Livingstone.

Herman, Ellen. 1996. *The Romance of American Psychology: Political Culture in the Age of Experts*. Berkeley: University of California Press.

Hewlett, Sylvia Ann. 2002. *Creating a Life: Professional Women and the Quest for Children*. New York: Talk Miramax Books.

Hoare, Quintin, and Geoffrey Nowell Smith, eds. and trans. 1971. *Selections from the Prison Notebooks of Antonio Gramsci*. New York: International Publishers.

Hong, S. E., Y. Y. Shugart, D. T. Huang, S. A. Shahwan, P. E. Grant, J. O. Hourihane, N. D. T. Martin, and C. A. Walsh. 2000. Autosomal recessive lissencephaly with cerebellar hypoplasia is associated with human RELN mutations. *Nature Genetics* 26 (1): 93–96.

Housman, David, and Fred Ledley. 1998. Why pharmacogenomics? Why now? *Nature Biotechnology* 16:492–93.

Hoyt, Kendall. 2002. *The Role of Military-Industrial Relations in the History of Vaccine Development*. Ph.D. diss., Program in Science, Technology, and Society, Massachusetts Institute of Technology.

Huxley, Aldous. 1998 (1946). *Brave New World*. New York: Harper Perennial.

Jacob, Francois. 1993 (1973). *The Logic of Life: A History of Heredity*. Princeton, N.J.: Princeton University Press.

Jameson, Fredric. 2003 (1991). *Postmodernism; or, The Cultural Logic of Late Capitalism*. Durham: Duke University Press.

Jasanoff, Sheila. 1995. *Science at the Bar: Law, Science and Technology in America*. Cambridge: Harvard University Press.

———. 1996. Beyond epistemology: Relativism and engagement in the politics of science. *Social Studies of Science* 26 (2): 393–418.

———. 2004. Ordering knowledge, ordering society. In *States of Knowledge: The Co-production of Science and Social Order*, ed. Sheila Jasanoff. London: Routledge.

Jazwinska, Elizabeth. 2001. Exploiting human genetic variation in drug discovery and development. *Drug Discovery Today* 6 (4): 198–205.

Kahn, Jonathan. 2000. Biotechnology and the legal constitution of the self: Managing identity in science, the market and society. *Hastings Law Journal* 51:909–52.

Kalow, Werner. 1962. *Pharmacogenetics: Heredity and the Response to Drugs*. London: W. B. Saunders.

Kassiola, Joel, ed. 2003. *Explorations in Environmental Political Theory: Thinking about What We Value*. Armonk, N.Y.: M. E. Sharpe.

Katsanis, N., P. L. Beales, M. O. Woods, R. A. Lewis, J. S. Green, P. S. Parfrey, S. J. Ansley, W. S. Davidson, and J. R. Lupski. 2000. Mutations in MKKS cause obesity, retinal dystrophy and renal malformations associated with Bardet-Biedl syndrome. *Nature Genetics* 26 (1): 67–70.

Kaviraj, Sudipta. 1997. The general elections in India. *Government and Opposition* 32:3–24.

Kay, Lily. 2000. *Who Wrote the Book of Life? A History of the Genetic Code*. Stanford: Stanford University Press.

Keller, Evelyn Fox. 1995. *Refiguring Life: Metaphors of Twentieth Century Biology*. New York: Columbia University Press.

———. 2002. *Making Sense of Life: Explaining Biological Development with Models, Metaphors, and Machines*. Cambridge: Harvard University Press.

Kelley, M. J., W. Janien, T. L. Ortel, J. F. Korczak. 2000. Mutation of MYH9, encoding non-muscle myosin heavy chain A, in May-Heglin anomaly. *Nature Genetics* 26 (1): 106–8.

Kinoshita, A., T. Saito, H.-A. Tomita, Y. Makita, K. Yoshida, M. Ghadami, K. Yamada, S. Kondo, S. Ikegawa, G. Nishimura, Y. Fukushima, T. Nakagomi, H. Saito, T. Sugimoto, M. Kamegaya, K. Hisa, J. C. Murray, N. Taniguchi, N. Niikawa, and K.-I. Yoshiura. 2000. Domain-specific mutations in TGFB1 result in Camurati-Engelmann disease. *Nature Genetics* 26 (1): 19–20.

Kirschner, L. S., J. A. Carney, S. D. Pack, S. E. Taymans, C. Giatzakis, Y. Cho, Y. S. Cho-Chung, and C. A. Stratakis. 2000. Mutations of the gene encoding the protein kinase A type I-regulatory subunit in patients with the Carney complex. *Nature Genetics* 26 (1): 89–92.

Kopytoff, Igor. 1986. The cultural biography of things: Commoditisation as process. In *The Social Life of Things: Commodities in Cultural Perspective*, ed. Arjun Appadurai, 64–94. Cambridge, U.K.: Cambridge University Press.

Kramer, Peter. 1997. *Listening to Prozac: The Landmark Book about Anti-depressants and the Remaking of the Self*. New York: Viking Penguin.

Krishna, V. V. 1997. A portrait of the scientific community in India: Historical growth and contemporary problems. In *Scientific Communities in the Developing World*, ed. Jacques Gaillard, V. V. Krishna, and Roland Waast, 236–80. New Delhi: Sage.

Landecker, Hannah. 1999. Between beneficence and chattel: The human biological in law and science. *Science in Context* 12 (1): 203–25.

Lane, K. B., R. D. Machado, M. W. Pauciulo, J. R. Thomson, J. A. Phillips III, J. E. Loyd, W. C. Nichols, R. C. Trembath, M. Aldred, C. A. Brannon, P. M. Conneally, T. Foroud, N. Fretwell, R. Gaddipati, D. Koller, E. J. Loyd, N. Morgan, J. H. Newman, M. A. Prince, C. Vilariño Güell, and L. Wheeler. 2000. Heterozygous germline mutations in BMPR2, encoding a TGF-receptor, cause familial primary pulmonary hypertension. *Nature Genetics* 26 (1): 81–84.

Latour, Bruno. 1987. *Science in Action: How to Follow Scientists and Engineers through Society*. Cambridge: Harvard University Press.

———. 1988. *The Pasteurization of France*. Trans. Alan Sheridan and John Law. Cambridge: Harvard University Press.

———. 1993. *We Have Never Been Modern*. Trans. Catherine Porter. Cambridge: Harvard University Press.

Lewis, Michael. 1989. *Liar's Poker: Rising through the Wreckage on Wall Street*. New York: W. W. Norton.

———. 1999. *The New New Thing: A Silicon Valley Story*. New York: W. W. Norton.

Lewontin, Richard. 1993. *Biology as Ideology: The Doctrine of DNA*. New York: Harper Collins.

Lotfalian, Mazyar. 1999. Technoscientific identities: Muslims and the culture of curiosity. Ph.D. diss., Department of Anthropology, Rice University.

Love, James. 1997. Calls for more reliable costs data on clinical trials. *Marketletter*, January 13, 24–25.

Luhmann, Niklas. 1998. *Observations on Modernity*. Trans. William Whobrey. Stanford: Stanford University Press.

Lyotard, Jean-François. 1984. *The Postmodern Condition: A Report on Knowledge*. Trans. Geoff Bennington and Brian Massumi. Minneapolis: University of Minnesota Press.

Madhiwalla, Neha. 2003. Hospitals and city health. In *Bombay and Mumbai: The City in Transition*, ed. Sujata Patel and Jim Masselos, 111–33. New Delhi: Oxford University Press.

Mahoney, Tom. 1959. *The Merchants of Life: An Account of the American Pharmaceutical Industry*. New York: Harper and Brothers.

Mamdani, Mahmood. 1996. *Citizen and Subject: Contemporary Africa and the Legacy of Late Colonialism*. Princeton, N.J.: Princeton University Press.

Mann, John. 1999. *The Elusive Magic Bullet: The Search for the Perfect Drug*. Oxford: Oxford University Press.

Marcus, George, ed. 1995. *Technoscientific Imaginaries: Conversations, Profiles, and Memoirs*. Chicago: University of Chicago Press.

———. 1998. *Ethnography through Thick and Thin*. Princeton, N.J.: Princeton University Press.

Marcus, George, and Michael M. J. Fischer. 1986. *Anthropology as Cultural Critique: An Experimental Moment in the Human Sciences*. Chicago: University of Chicago Press.

Marks, Harry M. 1997. *The Progress of Experiment: Science and Therapeutic Reform in the United States, 1900–1990*. Cambridge, U.K.: Cambridge University Press.

Marks, Jonathan. 2001. Scientific and folk ideas about heredity. In *The Human Genome Project and Minority Communities: Ethical, Social, and Political Dilemmas*, ed. R. Zininskas and P. Balint, 53–66. Westport, Conn.: Greenwood.

Marshall, Eliot. 1997a. "Playing chicken" over gene markers. *Science* 278:2046–48.

———. 1997b. Snipping away at genome patenting. *Science* 277:1752–53.

Martin, Emily. 1998. Anthropology and the cultural study of science. *Science, Technology and Human Values* 23 (1): 24–44.

Marx, Karl. 1970 (1859). *A Contribution to the Critique of Political Economy*. Moscow: Progress Publishers.

———. 1973 (1858). *Grundrisse: Foundations of the Critique of Political Economy*. Trans. Martin Nicolaus. London: Penguin Books.

———. 1974 (1894). *Capital: A Critique of Political Economy, Volume 3*. Ed. Friedrich Engels. Moscow: Progress Publishers.

———. 1976 (1867). *Capital: A Critique of Political Economy, Volume 1*. Trans. Ben Fowkes. London: Penguin Books.

———. 1977 (1852). *The Eighteenth Brumaire of Louis Bonaparte*. Moscow: Progress Publishers.

Marx, Karl, and Friedrich Engels. 1963 (1845). *The German Ideology*. New York: International Publishers.

———. 1986 (1848). *Manifesto of the Communist Party*. Moscow: Progress Publishers.

Mashelkar, Ramesh A. 1999. *On Launching Indian Innovation Movement*. New Delhi: National Institute of Science Communication.

Mashelkar, R. A., T. S. R. Prasada Rao, K. R. Sharma, H. S. Ray, S. R. Bhowmik, N. C. Aggarwal, D. Kumar, H. R. Bhojwani. 1993. *Creating an Enabling Environment for Commercialisation of CSIR Knowledge Base: A New Perspective*. New Delhi: Council for Scientific and Industrial Research.

Maurer, Bill. 2003. Uncanny exchanges: The possibilities and failures of "making change" with alternative monetary forms. *Environment and Planning D: Society and Space* 21:317–40.

Mauss, Marcel. 1990 (1954). *Gift: The Form and Reason for Exchange in Archaic Societies*. Trans. W. D. Halls. New York: W. W. Norton.

Maxwell, Robert, and Shohreh Eckhardt. 1990. *Drug Discovery: A Casebook and Analysis*. Clifton: Humana Press.

Mendelssohn, Everett. 2000. Eugenic temptation: When ethics lag behind technology. *Harvard Magazine*, March–April.

Merton, Robert. 1973 (1942). The normative structure of science. In *The Sociology of Science*, by Robert Merton, 267–78. Chicago: University of Chicago Press.

Montoya, Michael. 2003. Biotechnology, genetics, and diabetes: Racial prescriptions of pharmaceutical science. Ph.D. diss., Department of Anthropology, Stanford University.

*Moore v. The Regents of the University of California*, 793 P.2d (Cal. 1990), *cert. Denied*, 111 S. Ct. 1388 (1991).

Morley, David, and Kuan-Hsing Chen, eds. 1996. *Stuart Hall: Critical Dialogues in Cultural Studies*. New York: Routledge.

Motulsky, Arno. 1957. Drug reactions, enzymes and biochemical genetics. *Journal of the American Medical Association* 165:835–37.

Naidu, N. Chandrababu. 2000. *Plain Speaking*. With Sevanti Ninan. New Delhi: Viking.

National Council of Applied Economic Research. 2001. *Economic and Policy Reforms in India*. New Delhi: NCAER Publications Division.

Nehru, Jawaharlal. 1958. *Jawaharlal Nehru's Speeches, March 1953–August 1957*. Calcutta: Publications Division, Ministry of Information and Broadcasting.

Nietzsche, Friedrich. 1973 (1886). *Beyond Good and Evil: Prelude to a Philosophy of the Future*. Trans. R. J. Hollingdale. London: Penguin.

O'Malley, Patrick. 2000. Uncertain subjects: Risks, liberalism and contract. *Economy and Society* 29 (4): 460–84.

Palsson, Gisli, and Paul Rabinow. 1999. Iceland: The case of a national genome project. *Anthropology Today* 15 (5): 14–18.

Peterson, Kristin. 2004. Biosociality in an emptied-out material space. Workshop paper presented at Department of Anthropology, University of California, Irvine.

Petryna, Adriana. 2002. *Life Exposed: Biological Citizens after Chernobyl*. Princeton, N.J.: Princeton University Press.

———. 2005. Ethical variability: Drug development and globalizing clinical trials. *American Ethnologist* 32 (2): 183–97.

Pietz, William. 1993. Fetishism and materialism: The limits of theory in Marx. In *Fetishism as Cultural Discourse*, ed. Emily Apter and William Pietz, 119–51. Ithaca: Cornell University Press.

Pinker, Steven. 2002. *The Blank Slate: The Modern Denial of Human Nature*. New York: Viking Books.

Rabinow, Paul, ed. 1984. *The Foucault Reader*. New York: Pantheon Books.

———. 1992. Artificiality and enlightenment: From sociobiology to biosociality. In *Incorporations*. New York: Zone Books.

———. 1997. *Making PCR: A Story of Biotechnology*. Chicago: University of Chicago Press.

———. 1999. *French DNA: Trouble in Purgatory*. Chicago: University of Chicago Press.

———. 2003. *Anthropos Today: Reflections on Modern Equipment*. Princeton, N.J.: Princeton University Press.

Rajagopal, Arvind. 2001. *Politics after Television: Hindu Nationalism and the Reshaping of the Public in India*. Cambridge, U.K.: Cambridge University Press.

Ramachandran, T. V. 1992. *Non-resident Indian Investment Policy Guidelines and Procedures: A Compendium*. Bangalore: Puliani and Puliani.

Rapp, Rayna. 2000. *Testing Women, Testing the Fetus: The Social Impact of Amniocentesis in America*. New York: Routledge.

Read, Jason. *The Micro-Politics of Capital: Marx and the Prehistory of the Present*. Albany: State University of New York Press, 2003.

Reardon, Jenny. 2001. The Human Genome Diversity Project: A case study in coproduction. *Social Studies of Science* 31:357–88.

———. 2004. *Race to the Finish: Identity and Governance in an Age of Genomics*. Princeton, N.J.: Princeton University Press.

Reilly, K. M., D. A. Loisel, R. T. Bronson, M. E. McLaughlin, and T. Jacks. 2000. Nf1; trp53 mutant mice develop glioblastoma with evidence of strain-specific effects. *Nature Genetics* 26 (1): 109–13.

Rheinberger, Hans-Jörg. 1997. *Toward a History of Epistemic Things: Synthesizing Proteins in the Test Tube*. Stanford: Stanford University Press.

Ridley, Matt. 2000. *Genome: The Autobiography of a Species in 23 Chapters*. New York: Perennial.

Robbins-Roth, Cynthia. 2000. *From Alchemy to IPO: The Business of Biotechnology*. Cambridge: Perseus.

Rose, Nikolas, and Carlos Novas. 2005. Biological citizenship. In *Global Assemblages: Technology, Politics, and Ethics as Anthropological Problems*, ed. Aihwa Ong and Stephen Collier, 439–63. Malden: Blackwell.

Roth, Daniel. 2002. Pat Robertson's quest for eternal life. *Fortune*, June 10, 132–46.

Sahlins, Marshall. 1976. *Culture and Practical Reason*. Chicago: University of Chicago Press.

Sahlman, William A., Howard H. Stevenson, Michael J. Roberts, and Amar Bhide, eds. 1999. *The Entrepreneurial Venture*. Boston: Harvard Business School Press.

Sassen, Saskia. 2000. *Cities in a World Economy*. Thousand Oaks: Pine Forge Press.

Scott, James. 1999. *Seeing like a State: How Various Schemes to Improve the Human Condition Have Failed*. New Haven: Yale University Press.

Sen, Amartya. 1999. *Development as Freedom*. New York: Alfred A. Knopf.

Seri, M., R. Cusano, S. Gangarossa, G. Caridi, D. Bordo, C. Lo Nigro, G. Marco Ghiggeri, R. Ravazzolo, M. Savino, M. Del Vecchio, M. d'Apolito, A. Iolascon, L. L. Zelante, A. Savoia, C. L. Balduini, P. Noris, U. Magrini, S. Belletti, K. E. Heath, M. Babcock, M. J. Glucksman, E. Aliprandis, N. Bizzaro, R. J. Desnick, and J. A. Martignetti. 2000. Mutations in MYH9 result in the May-Hegglin anomaly, and Fechtner and Sebastian syndromes. *Nature Genetics* 26 (1): 103–5.

Shannon, Claude. 1948. A mathematical theory of communication. *Bell System Technical Journal* 27:379, 623.

Shelley, Mary. 1992 (1831). *Frankenstein*. Ed. Johanna M. Smith. New York: Bedford/St. Martin's.

Shreeve, James. 2004. *The Genome War: How Craig Venter Tried to Capture the Code of Life and Save the World*. New York: Alfred A. Knopf.

Silver, Lee. 1999. *Remaking Eden*. New York: Phoenix Press.

Singh, K. S., ed. 1992. *People of India*. Calcutta: Anthropological Survey of India.

Slavotinek, A. M., E. M. Stone, K. Mykytyn, J. R. Heckenlively, J. S. Green, E. Heon, M. A. Musarella, P. S. Parfrey, V. C. Sheffield, and L. G. Biesecker. 2000. Mutations in MKKS cause Bardet-Biedl syndrome. *Nature Genetics* 26 (1): 15–16.

Smith, Elta. 2004. Making genomes and public property: Four efforts to constitute rice. Ph.D. qualifying paper, John F. Kennedy School of Government, Harvard University.

Spivak, Gayatri. 1976. Translator's preface to *Of Grammatology*, by Jacques Derrida, ix–lxxxvii. Baltimore: Johns Hopkins University Press.

——. 1985. Subaltern studies: Deconstructing historiography. In *Subaltern Studies IV: Writings on South Asian History and Society*, ed. Ranajit Guha, 330–63. New York: Oxford University Press.

——. 1988. Can the subaltern speak? In *Marxism and the Interpretation of Culture*, ed. Cary Nelson and Lawrence Grossberg, 271–313. Urbana: University of Illinois Press.

——. 1999. *A Critique of Postcolonial Reason: Toward a History of the Vanishing Present*. Cambridge: Harvard University Press.

Sprinker, Michael, ed. 1999. *Ghostly Demarcations: A Symposium of Jacques Derrida's Specters of Marx*. New York: Verso.

Srinivasulu, K. Political articulation and policy discourse in the 2004 election in Andhra Pradesh. Personal communication of draft manuscript.

Stallings, Sarah C., Robert H. Rubin, Thomas J. Allen, Charles L. Cooney, Anthony J. Sinskey, and Stan N. Finkelstein. 2001. Technological innovation in pharmaceuticals. MIT's Program on the Pharmaceutical Industry, Working Paper 59-01. May.

Strange, Susan. 1986. *Casino Capitalism*. Oxford: Blackwell.

Taussig, Michael. 1980. *The Devil and Commodity Fetishism in South America*. Chapel Hill: University of North Carolina Press.

Thompson, Edward P. 1966 (1963). *The Making of the English Working Class*. New York: Vintage Books.

Traweek, Sharon. 1988. *Beamtimes and Lifetimes: The World of High Energy Physicists*. Cambridge: Harvard University Press.

Turaga, Uday. 2000. CSIR: India's techno-economic revolution. *Chemical Innovation*, August, 43–49.

Unger, Brooke. 2001. A survey of India's economy. *The Economist*, June 2–8.

United Nations Development Program. 2001. *Human Development Report 2001: Making New Technologies Work for Human Development*. New York: Oxford University Press.

Vogel, Friedrich. 1959. Modern problems of human genetics. *Ergib Inn Kinderheild* 12:52–125.

Walsh, Gary. 1998. *Biopharmaceuticals: Biochemistry and Biotechnology*. New York: John Wiley and Sons.

Weber, Max. 1978 (1968). *Economy and Society: An Outline of Interpretive Sociology, Volume One*. Ed. Guenther Roth and Claus Wittich. Berkeley: University of California Press.

———. 2001 (1930). *The Protestant Ethic and the Spirit of Capitalism*. Trans. Talcott Parsons. New York: Routledge.

Werth, Barry. 1994. *The Billion Dollar Molecule: One Company's Quest for the Perfect Drug*. New York: Simon and Schuster.

Woodmansee, Martha. 1984. The genius and the copyright: Economic and legal conditions of the emergence of the "author." *Eighteenth Century Studies* 17:425–44.

———. 1992. On the author effect: Recovering collectivity. *Cardozo Arts and Entertainment Law Journal* 10:279.

Zhan, Mei. 2005. Cevic cats, fried grasshoppers, and David Beckham's pyjamas: Unruly bodies after SARS. *American Anthropologist* 107(1): 31–42.

Žižek, Slavoj. 1994. How did Marx invent the symptom? In *Mapping Ideology*, ed. Slavoj Žižek. London: Verso.

———. 2004. The ongoing "soft revolution." *Critical Inquiry* 30 (2).

belief systems (*continued*)
    evangelism, 188, 266, 313 n.27; messianism, 123–24, 181, 210–11, 310 n.30; millenarianism, 199, 308 n.29. See also fetishism; religion
Bellenson, Joel, 109, 303 n.5
Benjamin, Walter, 180
Bharatiya Janata Party (BJP), 70, 228
Bhargava, Pushpa, 311–12 n.3
Biehl, João, 99, 302 n.34
*Billion Dollar Molecule, The* (Werth), 123, 186, 265
biocapital: defined, 78–79, 111, 112, 136; history of, 72; rationale for term, 6–7; summary of institutional and technological assemblages, 277–78
Biocon company, 127–28
bioethical issues: biopiracy and, 73–74, 291 n.33; biotech industry and, 67, 297 n.48; clinical trials and, 93, 96–97; corporate values and, 250–51; DeCode Genetics and, 60–61, 297 n.48; ethical, legal, and social implications (ELSI) of DNA patenting, 303–4 n.15; ethical-political terrain and, 93, 96–97; GeneEd company and, 250–51; genetic variability information and, 50; genomics information and, 57; global market terrains and, 66; HGP and, 297 n.48; information ownership and, 64–66; moral vs. ethical distinction, 65–66; naturalizing acts and, 63, 297 n.41; NIH and, 297 n.48; nonmarket values and, 41; population genomics experiments in Iceland and, 40; Rep-X and, 62–64, 295–97 n.35, 297 n.38; truth and, 115
biopolitics: ethical-political terrain and, 93, 96–97; governance, 80, 97; local vs. global political ecologies, 83, 285–86, 314 n.5; modern life, and impact of, 12–14, 79, 99, 278–79; Naidu, and ideology of governance, 86–89, 93, 100, 300 nn.14, 16, 19, 21, and 22; structural relations of production and, 284–85; U.S. free market value generation and, 285–86. See also political issues

biosociality, concept of, 145–46, 159, 194–95
biotechnology industry: alliances between pharmaceutical industry and, 53; bioethical issues and, 67, 297 n.48; biosociality concept and, 194–95; capitalism and, 42; corporate PR and, 115; cult-like loyalty and images, 200–201, 275; defining features of, 42; disjuncture of production and circulation, 9; expenditure and excess in, 199, 200–206, 209–10, 310 n.24; expressed sequence tag (EST), 51; facilities for research in India and, 89, 300 n.21; female CEOs in, 304 n.20; fetishism of symbolic capital and, 123, 209; First World–Third World asymmetry and, 67, 297 n.48; gender issues and, 254, 304 n.20; haplotypes and, 157; history of, 5–6, 21–23, 112–13, 291 n.30; hype, and value of excess in, 113; India and, 27, 89, 300 n.21; "life itself" and, 142, 178, 208, 278; material culture, and impact on, 138–42; messianism in, 123–24, 181, 210–11; misappropriation, and evils inherent in, 208; neem-derived products, 74, 299 n.60; protein crystallization and, 292–93 n.3; public as enabler of private research and, 56; start-up model and, 239, 241; study of, 4; temporality issues and, 152, 209, 307 n.17; theology and, 123–24; truth and, 115; venture capital and, 6; Weber on element of calling in, 200. See also corporations; *specific corporations and companies*
Biotech Park, 300 n.21
bioterrorism, 290–91 n.29
Boger, Joshua, 123
Boguski, Mark, 1
Bourdieu, Pierre, 294 n.19
Bowker, Geoffrey, 165
Boyer, Herbert, 5
Braga, Carlos, 75
Brahmachari, S. K., 95, 117–18, 220, 221, 299 n.11
*Brave New World* (Huxley), 208
Brazil, 302 n.34
Breeden, Richard, 182–83

Bristol-Myers Squibb, 140–41, 142
Buck-Morss, Susan, 7, 192–93
buffalo, genetic map of, 220–21
*Business India*, 127

Caille, Alain, 55, 295 n.26, 295 n.28
California Supreme Court, 60
Caliper Technologies, 305 n.4
Canguilhem, Georges, 160, 162
capital: cities, and role in capital flows in
    global market terrains, 84–85; economic
    issues and, 9–10, 239, 246; flows between
    United States and India, 193, 227; Indian
    regional parties, and relationship to capital
    flows, 300 n.13; organization of corpora-
    tions and, 239, 246
*Capital* (Marx), 8, 97, 282
capitalism: biocapital as new phase of, 7–12,
    277–80; biotech industry and, 42; capital-
    isms, 7, 289 n.9; Christianity, and relation-
    ship to, 180, 195, 199; commodity fetish-
    ism and, 143, 198, 199, 210, 276, 310 n.20;
    coproduction of life sciences and, 4, 6, 11–
    12, 20, 290 nn.14 and 26; corporate PR
    and, 136; cult-like loyalty and images, 200–
    201, 275, 276, 314 n.39; fetishism of, 276,
    314 n.39; free market, 183, 285–86, 291
    n.33; gifting and, 295 nn.27–28; high-
    tech, 84, 86, 113; hype and, 136; implosion
    of life sciences and, 116, 136, 303 n.12;
    industrial, 86; labor issues and, 252–54,
    255–57, 275, 276; modern thought about,
    3; multiple and mutable forms of, 7, 10–
    11, 31–32, 59, 78, 200, 247, 276; nation-
    state, and relationship to, 85, 180; novelty
    vs. persistent forms of, 287; performative
    space and, 119, 121–25, 276, 303–4 n.15,
    314 n.39; religion, and relationship with,
    180, 184, 195, 199; social power and, 276
Carnegie, Dale, 53
Celera Genomics: ethnographic research,
    and access to, 234; GeneEd, and invest-
    ment by, 269–70; genetic variability and,
    29, 291 n.26; Human Genome Project vs.,
    2, 29, 48, 49, 294 n.13; patentability of

sequences and, 2; Perkin-Elmer and, 30,
    310 n.25; salvationary promise of biocapi-
    tal and, 204–5; speed issues, and Human
    Genome Project vs., 48
Center for Functional Genomics, 138–39
Centre for Biochemical Technology (CBT):
    bureaucratic hierarchy and, 239; clinical
    trials and, 93; ethnographic research, and
    access to, 235–39; Genomed company,
    and involvement of, 93; genomics and, 68,
    297 n.49; intellectual property and, 84,
    299 n.11
Centre for Cellular and Molecular Biology
    (CCMB): applied science policies and,
    219–21; bureaucratic hierarchy and, 311–
    12 n.3; description of, 91, 107; genetic
    map of buffalo research, 220–21; global
    market terrains and, 192; hepatitis B vac-
    cine and, 300 n.21; Indian nationalism
    and, 192
Cetus Corporation, 22
Chakrabarty, Dipesh, 295 n.28
Chakravarti, Aravinda, 51
Chatterjee, Partha, 82
Chattopadhyaya, Deepanwita, 304 n.20
Chernobyl survivors, 102
Christianity: capitalism, and relationship to,
    180, 195, 199; evangelism in Africa and,
    188; messianism in biotech industry and,
    123–24, 181, 210–11; Protestant, 113,
    199, 303 n.11
circulatory processes, 77, 80, 97, 103. *See also*
    exchange; value
citizenship issues, 102, 302 n.41
Clark, Jim, 243, 264, 312 n.4
clinical trials: Centre for Biochemical Tech-
    nology and, 93; ethical-political terrains
    and, 93, 96–97; Genomed company and,
    93, 191; inclusion-exclusion issues and,
    100–101, 302 n.39; volunteer subjects and,
    97, 102, 280–81, 302 n.34
Cohen, Lawrence, 190
Cohen, Stanley, 5
Cold Spring Harbor genome meetings, 1, 2,
    303–4 n.15

College of Natural Resources, 303 n.13

Collins, Francis, 294 n.14; history of genomics and, 294 n.14; National Human Genome Research Institute and, 50; on SNPs data, 51; therapeutic lag and, 152

commercial enterprises: commercialization of research in life sciences, 6; hype and commercial value, 116, 303 n.12; promissory biocapitalist futures and, 113; SNP Consortium and, 51, 52–53; vision, and commercial value, 116, 303 n.12

commodification: capitalism, and commodity fetishism, 143, 198, 199, 210, 276, 310 n.20; of e-learning courses at GeneEd, 257–58, 275–76; exchange and, 75–76; of information, 239; speed issues and, 56

communication issues. *See* language and communication issues

*Communist Manifesto, The* (Marx and Engels), 7

conferences as speech and ritual sites, 191–92, 200–206, 313 n.30

consumption issues: risk and, 174–76; sacrifice and consumption of workers, 98–99; subjects as sovereign consumers, 191, 278, 281–82; surplus production and, 113–14, 172–74, 308 n.23; surplus value and, 174. *See also* patient-in-waiting for drug development

Cook-Deegan, Robert, 48, 293 n.11

Coombe, Rosemary, 72–73, 83, 298 n.58, 308 n.28

Cooney, Charles, 127

corporate activism, 52–55, 294 n.19, 295 n.26

corporate public relations (PR): biotech industry and, 115; capitalism and, 136; as hype, 116–17; promissory biocapitalist futures and, 115, 118; scientific facts and, 135, 142

corporations: bioethics and corporate values, 250–51; capital, and organization of, 239, 246; corporate form and, 282; ethnographic relationship to, 252, 312 n.13; and ethnographic research, 234–39, 295–

97 n.35; fraud in United States, 182–83; gender issues and, 254, 304 n.20; gifting in United States and, 34; and implosion of economic and epistemic regimes, 142, 177, 180–81; model for, 239, 246; research sites for Western corporations in India, 212; scandal in United States, 205, 206, 208. *See also* biotechnology industry; *specific corporations and companies*

cortisone, as miracle drug, 186

Corzine, Jon, 182

Couch, John, 245

Council for Responsible Genetics, 40

Council for Scientific and Industrial Research (CSIR), 192–93; applied research and, 215; contract research and, 214–17; *CSIR 2001: Vision and Strategy*, 214; entrepreneurial research and, 217–18; global market terrains and, 84, 211–16; innovation and, 220; nation-state and, 74, 84; science and technology issues, 216; vision of, 214, 219

*Creating a Life* (Hewlett), 254

*CSIR 2001: Vision and Strategy*, 214

currency, analysis of multiple forms of, 43

Cytochrome P450 genetic profile, 94

Davies, Kevin, 51

DeCode Genetics, 39–40, 60–61, 165, 297 n.48

Deering, James, 204–5

Deleuze, Gilles, 93

Delhi, bureaucratic hierarchy and, 239

Department of Biotechnology (DBT), Ministry of Science and Technology, 69, 304 n.20

depression, psychotropic drugs for, 158

Derrida, Jacques: acts in name of something, 206; faith and technologies of media, 207; on norm, 160; on popular conception of the lie, 133; provisional worlds and, 179; on speculations and the future, 123, 288; structural messianism and, 210–11, 226, 310 n.30; temporality and, 209; truth and, 133, 265

Deshpanade, Lalit, 302 n.32

Deshpanade, Sudha, 302 n.32

diagnostic tests: DNA chips and, 140, 168; pharmacogenomics industry and, 143, 151; probability and, 178–80; risk issues and, 143, 144, 175

*Diamond v. Chakrabarty*, 6

DigiScents company, 303 n.5

*Dilbert*, 139

Din, Suleman, 229

diseases and illnesses: ADHD, 158; ALL, 140; AML, 140; anthrax spores, 290–91 n.29; anti-retroviral therapy, 306 n.9; cancer, 6, 140, 177, 187, 289 n.8; depression, and psychotropic drugs, 158; genetic effects on, 153; HIV/AIDS testing and treatments, 144, 302 n.34, 306 n.9, 308 n.25; medical information, genotyping and, 61, 68, 295 n.34; Myriad's tests for *brca* genes, 177; non-Hodgkins' lymphoma (HL) and Rituxan as miracle drug, 186–87; pharmaceutical industry, and early stages of disease, 158; preventive medicine, 168; Prozac, 158; pseudoxanthoma elasticum (PXE), 191, 194; public health issues, 188; rheumatoid arthritis, and cortisone as miracle drug, 186; single-gene correlation for, 146–47, 153–54, 306–7 n.11; SNPs and, 162; streptococcal fever, and penicillin as miracle drug, 186; syphilis research, 166; Trovan (antibiotic), 95, 301 n.29

DNA chips, 139–40, 141, 207, 305 nn.4–5

DNA patenting, 303–4 n.15

dot.com era, 267, 312 n.30

Doubletwist company (Pangea), 108–10, 245, 273, 313 n.37

downstream companies. *See* upstream-downstream terrain

Dr. Reddy's Foundation (DRF), 26–27, 291 n.34

Dravida Munnetra Kazhagam (DMK), 300 n.13

drug development marketplace: Africa, and use value of drugs, 187, 188, 309 n.7; anti-retroviral therapy, 306 n.9; capital-intensive process and, 45–46, 94, 293 n.6; capital risk and, 94, 301 n. 28; cortisone and, 186; Cytochrome P450 genetic profile and, 94; in Europe, 291 n.32; GeneEd company and, 246–47, 249–50; genetic effects on drug action, 153, 154; implosion of economic and epistemic regimes, 177; India, and overview of, 25–27, 291 n.33; information ownership and, 55; as miraculous enterprise, 186–87; penicillin as miracle drug and, 186; psychotropic drugs for depression and, 158; public health and, 188; recall issues and, 95, 301 n. 29; reverse engineering of generic drugs in India and, 188, 309 n.8; risk issues and, 143, 144; Rituxan as miracle drug and, 186–87; software industry compared with, 45–46; United States, and overview of, 21–27; U.S. FDA approval and, 93; use value of drugs, 187–88, 309 n.7. *See also* patient-in-waiting; pharmaceutical industry; therapeutic development; upstream-downstream terrain

Dumit, Joseph: corporate ethnography and, 295–97 n.35; on objective self-fashioning, 147, 159, 229; overdetermination of scientific research and, 114; surplus health and, 314 n.2

East-West issues. *See* First World–Third World asymmetry

economic issues: analysis of multiple forms of currency, 43; capital and, 9–10, 239, 246; indebtedness, 77, 80–83, 97; life sciences, and effects of capitalist political economic structures, 6; market logic, 33, 41–42, 53, 57–59, 63, 72; Marx on political economy, 7–12, 282; revenues and profits, India answerable to, 112, 303 n.7. *See also* expenditure and excess; market value

*Economist*, 100

*Economy and Society* (Weber), 199

*Eighteenth Brumaire of Louis Napoleon, The* (Marx), 7–8

Eisele, Paul, 249, 251

*Emergent Forms of Life and the Anthropological Voice* (Fischer), 286

Engels, Friedrich, 7, 16, 65, 266, 282

Entrepreneurial Pharmaceutical Partners of the Indian Continent (EPPIC), 222, 226

entrepreneurship: conjuration of futures and, 275; defined, 241–42; investment companies and, 268–71; Maulik and, 243–44; NRI and, 224–26, 239, 241; Patel and, 244; principle of, 242; TiE and, 222–23, 225; venture capital and, 242, 245–46, 271–72

ethics. *See* bioethical issues

ethnographic research: access to companies for, 234–39, 248–52; anonymity of sites and, 295–97 n.35; anthropology of science and, 4; biocapital studies and, 30–33, 292 nn.42–43; corporate ethnography and, 234–39, 295–97 n.35; corporations, and ethnographers, 252, 312 n.13; emergent forms of life and, 240, 278, 279, 286–87, 312 n.5; Fischer and, 1, 30, 278; Indian ethnographic sites, 33, 235–39; locality vs. universality, 150, 232–33; local vs. global political ecologies, 83, 285–86, 314 n.5; situated perspectives and, 239–40; social theory, and relationship to ethnography, 287–88; "the Other" and, 82–83, 286–87; U.S. ethnographic sites, 33, 234–35

eugenic technology, 179, 208

Europe: drug development marketplace in, 291 n.32; SNPs from DNA donations and Europeans, 50

evangelism, 188, 266, 313 n.27

Ewald, François, 167

Excelan company, 224

exchange: commodification and, 75–76; deconstruction and, 72; dialectic of materiality to abstraction and, 17–18, 290 n.22; Foreign Exchange Regulations Act, 190; gifting and, 75–76, 80; global market terrains and, 103; information ownership and, 34, 75; market contradictions and, 39; market value, and processes of, 41; public domain and, 34, 75; sites for study

of, 44; U.S. Securities and Exchange Commission (SEC), 120, 132, 304 n.16; volunteer subjects and, 102

expenditure and excess: in biotech industry, 199, 200–206, 209–10, 310 n.24; at conferences as speech and ritual sites, 200–206, 313 n.30; hype, and value of excess in biotech industry, 113

expressed sequence tag (EST), 51

Falwell, Jerry, 313 n.27

Ferguson, James, 233

fetishism: of capitalism, 276, 314 n.39; commodity fetishism and, 143, 198, 199, 210, 310 n.20; of genomic facts, 167–71, 307 n.21; genomic fetishism, 143–45, 147, 168–71, 207, 307–8 n.22; of symbolic capital of biotech and pharmaceutical industry, 123, 209; U.S. free market value generation and, 285–86

First World–Third World asymmetry: biocapital and, 75; biopiracy issues and, 73–74, 291 n.33; biotech industry and, 67, 297 n.48; East-West inequities and India, 219, 311 n.42; research sites for Western corporations in India and, 212; "the Other" and, 82–83, 286–87

Fischer, Michael: on multisited ethnography, 232–33; emergent forms of life and, 278; *Emergent Forms of Life and the Anthropological Voice,* 286; ethical-political issues and, 93; ethnographic research and, 1, 30, 278; on ethnographic study of "the Other," 286–87

Fleck, Ludwig, 166

Foreign Exchange Regulations Act, 190

Fortun, Michael, 65–66

forward-looking statement: defined, 131–32; fabrication of truth and, 120, 121, 129–35, 304 n.16; temporality and, 134; venture science and, 133–34, 305 n.29

Foucault, Michel: on biopolitics and impact on modern life, 12–14, 79, 99, 278–79; on governmentality, 177; *Order of Things, The,* 13; truth and, 295–97 n.35

Frankenberg, Ruth, 230
*Frankenstein* (Shelley), 208
Fraser, Claire, 310 n.25
*From Alchemy to IPO* (Robbins-Roth), 186
Frow, John, 73

Gandhi, Indira, 74–75
Gandhi, Rajiv, 74, 82
Geertz, Clifford, 113
Gelsinger, Jesse, 152
GenBank, 1
GeneChip arrays, 139–40
GeneEd company: as advertising company,
   250–51; angel investments in, 245–46,
   273–74, 312 n.8; bioethics and, 250–51;
   corporate capital investment and, 246,
   257, 263, 268–74, 313 n.35; description of,
   239; drug development marketplace and,
   246–47, 249–50; as education company,
   250–51, 254–57; ethnographic research,
   and access to, 248–52; gender issues and,
   253–54; graphic designers and, 248, 252,
   276; history of, 242–48, 267–68; as
   knowledge management company, 258,
   312 n.18; life science issues and, 248; location issues and, 247–48, 312 n.9; management structure of, 246, 249, 252–54, 260–
   64, 270, 273–74, 312 n.14; product of,
   240–41, 250, 312 n.11; programmers, and
   role at, 248, 259, 276; situated perspective
   and, 246–47; as software designer, 257,
   258, 263, 276; start-up model and, 242,
   263, 267–68; upstream-downstream terrain and, 240, 248; venture capital and,
   242, 268, 270–71, 272–73, 313 n.36
Genentech company: biotech research and,
   291 n.30; history of, 22; IPO and, 22, 119–
   20, 125–28; salvationary promise of biocapital and, 203–4
General Agreements on Tariffs and Trade
   (GATT), 73
General Electric (GE), 216
genetic studies: drug response, 94–95;
   genetic determinism, 144–45, 146;
   genetics of disease, 95; genetic variability

information, 49, 50, 60, 294 n.15; population of India and, 68; populations as units
   and, 298 n.50
"Genetic Technology and Society" conference, 39
Genomed company: Centre for Biochemical
   Technology, and involvement in, 93; clinical trials and, 93, 191; Council for Scientific and Industrial Research, and involvement in, 84; Genomed Mumbai, 93, 301
   n.26; history of, 71, 84, 299 n.11; Nicholas
   Piramal India Limited and, 93
Genome Valley, 77, 90, 228
Genomic Health company, 191, 194, 281–
   82, 309 n.12
genomics: bioethics and, 57; defined, 2, 289
   n.2; description of, 28, 47; eugenic technology and, 179, 208; genetic information
   vs. human biological material, 60; genetic
   map of buffalo research, 220–21; genetic
   variability, 28–29, 291 n.36; genomic
   facts, 114, 156–59, 167–71, 307 n.21; genomics information, 57; history of, 2–3,
   29–30, 32, 292 n.38, 294 n.14; Icelandic
   population genomics experiments, 39–40,
   60–61, 165, 297 n.48; market frameworks
   and, 33; moral value and, 56–57; overview of, 27–30; pharmaceutical industry,
   and genomics in public domain, 45; SNPs
   and, 28–29; speed issues and credit for sequencing, 19, 48; technological advances
   vs. conceptual advances, 33; upstream
   drug development marketplace and, 23–
   24
genomics industry: implosion of economic
   and epistemic regimes, 177; patentability
   of sequences and, 45; pharmaceutical
   industry, and relationship to, 45; public
   domain, and interactions with, 49–51,
   54–57, 59, 117–18, 142, 303 n.13, 305–6
   n.6; therapeutic lag and, 152; upstream-
   downstream terrain of drug development
   marketplace and, 44, 45, 293 n.5
*German Ideology, The* (Marx and Engels), 16,
   65, 266, 282

Ghosh, Jayati, 82
Gibbs, Richard, 145–46, 179
gifting, concept of: capitalism and, 295
nn.27–28; corporate activism and, 53, 295
n.26; description of, 55–56, 295 n.28;
exchange and, 75–76, 80; SNP Consortium
and, 53; U.S. corporations and, 34
Gilder, George, 199–200
Giordano, Barry, 249, 252, 253, 261
global market terrains: anti-retroviral
therapy and, 306 n.9; bioethical issues
and, 66; capital flows between United
States and India and, 193, 227; Centre for
Cellular and Molecular Biology and, 192;
cities, and role in capital flows of, 84–
85; Council for Scientific and Industrial
Research and, 192–93, 211–16; exchange
and, 103; indebtedness and, 83, 97; In-
dian state and, 34, 46–47, 67–71, 74–75;
nationalism and, 70–71, 188–90, 192–93;
National Chemical Laboratories and, 192;
territorial unit of nation-state and, 79
Godbout, Jacques, 55, 295 n.26, 295 n.28
Golub, D. R., 140
Goux, Jean-Joseph, 198, 199–200
governance issues, 80, 86–89, 93, 97, 100,
300 nn.14, 16, 19, 21, and 22
Gramsci, Antonio, 88
Great Britain, 305 n.2
Greenbaum, Mark, 253
Greenhalgh, Susan, 99
Grefe, Edward, 52
Grossberg, Lawrence, 268
*Grundrisse* (Marx), 173
Gupta, Akhil, 233
Guyer, Mark, 51

Hall, Stuart, 292 n.2
Halushka, M. K., 155
Hamacher, Werner, 304 n.19
haplotypes, 157
Haraway, Donna, 65, 168, 170–71, 240
Harvard-MIT Hippocratic Society, 39
Hayden, Cori, 291 n.34
health issues. *See* diseases and illnesses

Health Sector Database, 40
Healy, Bernadine, 48
Healy, David, 144
Hegel, G. W. F., 15
hepatitis B vaccine, 300 n.21
Hewlett, Sylvia Ann, 254
Hibergen company, 165
high-throughput gene expression studies,
140, 141, 154
"History of the Lie" (Derrida), 265
HIV/AIDS testing and treatments, 144, 302
n.34, 306 n.9, 308 n.25
Hoffmann-LaRoche, 61
Holden, Arthur, 51
Housman, David, 157
*How to Win Friends and Influence People*
(Carnegie), 53
Human Genome Project (HGP): bioethics
and, 297 n.48; Celera Genomics vs., 2, 29,
48, 49, 294 n.13; Cold Spring Harbor genome meetings, 1; description of, 47;
genetic variability, 28–29, 291 n.36; history of, 29
Human Genome Sciences, 51
Huntsman Cancer Institute, 132, 304 n.16
Huxley, Aldous, 208
Hyderabad: bureaucratic hierarchy and,
311–12 n.3; Genome Valley, 77, 90, 228;
high-tech capitalism and, 84; networks
between nonresident Indians and, 92; statistics, 92, 301 n.25
hype: capitalism and, 136; commercial value
and, 116, 303 n.12; corporate PR as, 116–
17; credibility-incredibility and, 114–15,
118, 303 n.11; dot.com era and, 267; Doubletwist company (Pangea), 108–10, 244–
45; innovation and, 111; as productive
mechanism, 110, 135; speculation and,
111; truth and, 251, 264–65; value of
excess in biotech industry, 113; vision vs.,
266–67

Iceland, population genomics experiments
in, 39–40, 60–61, 165, 297 n.48
ICICI Knowledge Park (the Park): female

information sciences, 3, 41
innovation: biocapital, and technological, 111, 113–14; Council for Scientific and Industrial Research and, 220; culture of, 188–89, 193, 227–28; hype and, 111
Institute for Genomics and Integrative Biology (IGIB), 297 n.49
Institute of Genomic Research (TIGR), 121, 201–5, 310 n.25
intellectual property (IP): Centre for Biochemical Technology and, 84, 299 n.11; cultural life of, 72–73, 298 n.58; Department of Biotechnology and, 69; DNA chips and, 141; DNA samples for research and, 194; GATT and, 73; India and, 68–70, 189, 298 n.54; information flow and, 76; materiality and, 72; *Moore v. the Regents of University of California,* 60, 63, 64; source vs. invention and, 60, 72, 298 n.298; start-up model and, 299 n.11; United States and, 55, 295 n.29; volunteer subjects and, 102; WTO and, 73, 74
interdisciplinary issues, 265, 313 n.254
International Monetary Fund (IMF), 82, 300 n.18
Isswalkar, Datta, 98

Jains, 303 n.11
Jameson, Fredric, 11, 289 n.13
Jazwinska, Elizabeth, 155
Johns Hopkins University, 294 n.14
*Journal of the American Medical Association,* 294 n.14

Kalow, Werner, 154
Karnataka state, 304 n.21
Kaviraj, Sudipta, 299 n.7
Kennedy School of Government, 182
Kilroy, Cynthia, 252–54, 260
Kinney, Catherine, 183
Kramer, Peter, 144
Krishna, V. V., 211, 212, 216–17

L. V. Prasad Eye Institute (LVPEI), 107
labor issues, 252–54, 255–57, 275, 276

Lander, Eric, 117, 139, 305–6 n.6
Lander lab, 139, 140
language and communication issues: conferences as speech and ritual sites, 191–92, 200–206, 313 n.30; information flow and, 43, 57–58, 76
Latour, Bruno, 147, 249
Ledley, Fred, 157
legal issues: *Diamond v. Chakrabarty,* 6; *Moore v. the Regents of University of California,* 60, 63, 64; patentability and, 4–5, 289 n.6, 303–4 n.15; patent rights, 6; Private Securities Litigation Reform Act of 1995, 120, 132, 304 n.16
Levin, Mark, 273
Lewis, Michael, 114, 313 n.30
Lewontin, Richard, 164
*Liar's Poker* (Lewis), 313 n.30
"life itself": biocapital, and transformations of, 47; biotech industry and, 142, 178, 208, 278; as business plan for biocapital, 144, 278; scientific fact about, 135
life sciences: applied science policies, 219–21, 310 n.40; biocapital, and relationship to, 11–12; biological material vs. biological information, 42; capitalist political economic structures and effects on, 6; commercialization of research in, 6; coproduction of capitalism and, 4, 6, 11–12, 20, 290 n.14, 290 nn.14 and 26; corporatization of bioscience, 4; GeneEd company and, 248; implosion of capitalism and, 116, 136, 303 n.12; implosion of market and subjects and, 281, 306 n.8; information ownership and, 41; information sciences, and evolution from, 3, 41; materialism, and effects on research in, 19; overdetermination and, 6; salvationary force and, 198; science and technology studies (STS), 313 n.254; social power and, 198
Linsky, Martin, 52
Livingstone, David, 188
Luhmann, Niklas, 178
Lyotard, Jean-François, 10, 11, 277

M. S. Swaminathan Research Foundation, 304 n.20

Madhiwalla, Neha, 302 n.33

Mahajan, Manjari, 215, 298 n.54, 310 n.33

Marcus, George, 30, 232, 286

Mario, Ernest, 246

market logic, 33, 41–42, 53, 57–59, 63, 72. *See also* Indian state; Rep-X; SNP Consortium

market value: bioethics, and nonmarket values, 41; creation of value and, 43; exchange processes and, 41; genomics and, 46; pharmaceutical industry and, 24–25; speed of generation of DNA sequences, and drug, 43, 292–93 n.3

Marks, Jonathan, 307 n.18

Marshall, Eliot, 50, 51

Martin, Emily, 4

Marx, Karl: *Capital,* 8, 97, 282; on capitalism, and alienation of labor, 275; commodity fetishism and, 143, 198, 199, 210, 310 n.20; *Communist Manifesto,* 7; corporate form and, 282; deproletarianization and, 97, 98; *Eighteenth Brumaire of Louis Napoleon, The,* 7–8; *German Ideology, The,* 16, 65, 266, 282; *Grundrisse,* 173; historical and dialectic materialism and, 15–18; on political economy, 7–12, 282; on religion as ideology, 266; on structural attentiveness, 284; surplus production and, 113–14, 172–74, 282

Mashelkar, Ramesh, 75, 192, 214–17

material culture, and impact on biotech industry, 138–42

Maulik, Sunil: biography of, 242–43, 248; entrepreneurship and, 243–44; management structure and, 249, 252, 253, 262–63, 273–74, 312 n.14; on starting a company, 267–68; values and, 249–51; venture capital and, 242, 245–46, 272–73; vision and, 249–51, 265–67, 275

Maurer, Bill, 295 n.28

Mauss, Marcel, 55, 199, 295 nn.26 and 28

Mazumdar, Kiran, 127–28, 304 n.20,23

Mazumdar-Shaw, Kiran, 127–28, 304 n.20,23

McCusick, Victor, 152, 294 n.14

Medak district statistics, 92

medical information, genotyping and, 61, 68, 295 n.34

MedImmune company, 249

Merck, 51, 294 n.18

Merton, Robert, 11, 114–18, 133, 199, 310 n.29

messianism, 123–24, 181, 210–11, 310 n.30

millenarianism, 199, 308 n.29

Millennium Pharmaceuticals company: ethnographic research and access to, 234; history of, 139, 141, 142; public domain, and interactions with genomics industry, 305–6 n.6; venture capital influence and, 273

Ministry of External Affairs (MEA), 236

Monsanto, 250–51, 312 n.12

Moore, John, 60

*Moore v. the Regents of University of California,* 60, 63, 64

moral issues, 56–57, 65–66

Motulsky, Arne, 154

Mumbai: Genomed Mumbai, 93, 301 n.26; hospitals in, 96, 302 n.33; industrialization and, 84; sacrifice and consumption of workers and, 98–99; textile industry, 96, 97–98, 302 n.32. *See also* Parel; Wellspring Hospital

mutagenesis, 159–60

mutants, 159–62

Myriad's breast cancer tests, 177

Naidu, N. Chandrababu: governance and ideology of, 86–89, 93, 100, 300 nn.14, 16, 19, 21, and 22; health tourism and, 301 n.25; state compensation for suicides and, 77; venture capital and, 88–89; Vision 2020, 77, 78. *See also* Andhra Pradesh state government

National Center for Biotechnology Information, 1, 6, 289 n.8

National Chemical Laboratories (NCL), 192

National Human Genome Research Institute (NHGRI), 48–49, 50, 294 n.14

National Institutes of Health (NIH), 47, 48, 50, 55, 297 n.48
nationalism: biocapital as embedded in, 181; global market terrains and, 70–71, 188–90, 192; India and, 182–86, 192–93, 201, 308–9 n.3; National Chemical Laboratories and, 192; nonresident Indians and, 227, 228; United States and, 182–83, 209; Vishwa Hindu Parishad and, 228
nation-state: capitalism and relationship to, 85, 180; Council for Scientific and Industrial Research and, 74, 84; natural resources, and claims of, 71; territorial unit of, 79. *See also* India
Native American people, DNA sample collections from, 50, 297 n.48
*Nature Genetics*, 146, 306–7 n.11
Nazi science, 208, 310 n.29
neem-derived products, 74, 299 n.60
Nehru, Jawaharlal, 211
Neomorphic company, 110, 235
*New Corporate Activism, The* (Grefe and Linsky), 52
*New, New Thing, The* (Lewis), 313 n.30
Nicholas Piramal India Limited (NPIL), 1, 84, 93
Nietzsche, Friedrich, 118, 144
nonresident Indian (NRI) entrepreneurs of Silicon Valley: capital flow from United States to India and, 193, 227; entrepreneurship and, 224–26, 239, 241; history of, 190; nationalism and, 227, 228; networks between India and, 92, 190, 193; objective self-fashioning and, 230; racial-ethnic discrimination and, 224, 228–29, 230; repatriation of culture of innovation from United States to India, 193, 227–28; structural messianism and, 226; the Park and, 83; venture capital and, 88–89
Novartis, 303 n.13
Novas, Carlos, 14
Novell company, 224

*Order of Things, The* (Foucault), 13

Palmer, Chris, 275
Pangea company (Doubletwist), 108–10, 245, 273, 313 n.37
Parel, 84, 101, 301 n.26; union activity and, 98. *See also* Mumbai
Patel, Salil: biography of, 243, 244–45, 248, 261–62; entrepreneurship and, 244; management structure and, 262–63; truth and hype issues, 251, 264–65
Patel, Viloo, 304 n.20
patentability of sequences: bioethics and, 303–4 n.15; Celera Genomics and, 2; *Diamond v. Chakrabarty,* 6; DNA patenting, 303–4 n.15; genomics industry and, 45; Indian patent issues and, 189; information ownership and, 2, 4; laws and, 4–5, 289 n.6, 303–4 n.15; NIH and, 48, 293 n.11; patent rights, 6; pharmaceutical industry and, 45; public domain and, 2, 4; SNP Consortium and, 51–53; WTO and, 25, 189. *See also* information ownership
patient-in-waiting (consumer-in-waiting): consumer genomics and, 196–97, 281–82; for drug development, 144, 148, 175–77, 195, 308 n.25; India and, 149, 308 n.25; personalized medicine and, 144, 148, 175–77, 195, 308 n.25; therapeutic development and, 144, 148, 175–77, 195, 308 n.25; United States and, 148, 195, 308 n.25. *See also* drug development marketplace
penicillin, as miracle drug, 186
*People of India* (Singh), 164
Perkin-Elmer company, 30, 310 n.25
personalized medicine: contingency and, 178–79, 308 n.28; defined, 114, 151–54; implosion of economic and epistemic regimes and, 177; patient-in-waiting and, 144, 148, 175–77, 195, 308 n.25; probability and, 178–80; risk minimization and calculation and, 176, 178; SNPs and, 167; therapeutic development and, 60
Petryna, Adriana, 102
Pfizer, 95, 301 n.29
pharmaceutical industry: corporation model

and, 239; disjuncture of production and circulation and, 9; early stages of disease manifestation and, 158; fetishism of symbolic capital and, 123, 209; genomics in public domain and, 45; history of Indian state and, 25–27; market valuation and, 24–25; market value of genomics and, 46; patentability of sequences and, 45; SNP Consortium and, 51, 52–53; SNPs and, 50; speculation and, 24; speed issues and, 41, 43–44; upstream-downstream terrain of drug development marketplace and, 44–45. *See also* drug development marketplace; therapeutic development

pharmacogenetics, 154

pharmacogenomics industry: defined, 153, 301 n.27; diagnostic tests and, 143, 151; high-throughput methods for genetic analysis and, 140, 141, 154; history of, 5; India and, 93–95, 149; pharmacogenomic process, 154–58; subject position of Indian population and, 149

Pietz, William, 169, 170, 171

Pinker, Steven, 145

political issues: ethical-political terrains, 93, 96–97; life sciences, and effects of capitalist political economic structures, 6; local vs. global political ecologies, 83, 285–86, 314 n.5; Marx on political economy, 7–12, 282; Telugu Desam political party, 86–88, 300 n.13. *See also* biopolitics

polymerase chain reaction (PCB), 5

populations: classification of, 163–66, 307 n.18; as consumers-in-waiting for drug development, 144, 148; genomic fetishism and, 143; implosion of market and subjects, 281, 306 n.8; as patients-in-waiting for drug development, 144, 148, 175–77, 195, 308 n.25; subject position of, 68, 143, 148–51, 306 n.8, 307 n.14; subjects as sovereign consumers in United States, 191, 278; and volunteer subjects for clinical trials, 97, 102, 280–81, 302 n.34

*Postmodern Condition, The* (Lyotard), 10

postmodernism, 11, 289 n.13

preventive medicine, 168

*Principles of General Economics* (Bataille), 113

private ownership of information. *See* information ownership

Private Securities Litigation Reform Act of 1995, 120, 132, 304 n.16

production issues: biocapital, and structural relations of production, 284; biopolitics, and structural relations of production, 284–85; consumption and surplus production, 113–14, 172–74, 308 n.23; coproduction of capitalism and life sciences, 4, 6, 11–12, 290 n.14; coproduction of Christianity and capitalism, 180; coproduction of life sciences and capitalism, 4, 6, 11–12, 20, 290 nn.14 and 26; disjuncture of production and circulation in pharmaceutical industry, 9; production of scientific facts, 111, 114, 134, 147; surplus production, 113–14, 172–74, 282, 308 n.23

promissory biocapitalist futures: commercial realization and, 113; corporate PR and, 115, 118; entrepreneurship, and conjuration of futures, 275; IPOs and, 119–20, 125–28; persona and performative space and, 119, 121–25, 303–4 n.15; reality issues and, 125–26, 304 n.19; scientific facts and, 115, 133–34, 142; speculation, 24, 111, 123, 288; therapeutic realization and, 113; unpredictability of, 288; venture science and, 133, 305 n.29

protein crystallization, 292–93 n.3

Protestant Christianity, 113, 199, 303 n.11

*Protestant Ethic, The* (Weber), 199

Prozac, 158

pseudoxanthoma elasticum (PXE), 191, 194

public domain issues: downstream companies and, 55; exchange and, 34, 75; genome sequence information and, 45; genomics and, 45; genomics industry, and interactions with, 49–51, 54–57, 59, 117–18, 142, 303 n.13, 305–6 n.6; Indian state, and information ownership vs., 73–74; NIH and, 55; patentability of sequences

public domain issues (*continued*)
and, 2, 4; pharmaceutical industry and,
45; SNP Consortium, and genomics in, 46;
speed issues and, 41, 43–44; temporality
of therapeutic development and, 152, 307
n.17
public health issues, 188. *See also* diseases and
illnesses
public relations (PR), corporate. *See* corporate public relations (PR)
PXE International, 191, 194–96

Rabinow, Paul, 145, 241, 279, 312 n.6
Rajagopal, Arvind, 180, 190
Ramachandran, T. V., 190
Rama Rao, N. T., 87–88
Rangareddy district, 92
Reardon, Jenny, 163
recombinant DNA technology (RDT), 5–6,
22
Rekhi, Kanwal, 193, 224–26, 227, 228–29,
309 n.9
religion: asceticism, 199, 308 n.29; biotech
industry and theology, 123–24; capitalism,
and relationship to, 180, 184, 195, 199;
as cultural system, 184; millenarianism,
199, 308 n.29. *See also* belief systems;
Christianity
Rep-X (Repository X): bioethics and, 62–
64, 295–97 n.35, 297 n.38; ethnographic
research, and anonymity of, 295–97 n.35;
information ownership and, 46
research issues: bias against scientists and
research in India, 212–13; commercialization of research in life sciences, 6; Council
for Scientific and Industrial Research and,
214–18; Dumit, and overdetermination of
scientific research by the market (venture
science), 114; facilities for research in
India, 89, 300 n.21; genetic map of buffalo
research, 220–21; intellectual property,
and DNA samples for research, 194; public
as enabler of private research, 56; research
hospitals, 68, 83–84, 93–94, 96, 301 n.26;
research sites for Western corporations in

India and, 212; vision, and original
research, 265–66
Rheinberger, Hans-Jörg, 138, 281
risk issues: calculation of risks, 178; consumption issues and, 174–76; diagnostic
tests and, 143, 144, 175; drug development marketplace, 143, 144; risk distribution, 166; SNPs, and probability or risk of
disease, 166; start-up model and, 143
*Risk Society* (Beck), 166
Ritalin, 158
Rituxan, as miracle drug, 187
Robbins-Roth, Cynthia, 186, 241, 289 n.8,
312 n.61
Robertson, Pat, 188
Rollins, Cyane, 255–56
Rose, Nikolas, 14

Sahlins, Marshall, 309 n.7
salvation: acts in name of something and,
206; biocapital in United States and, 181,
184, 185, 186, 194–200, 210–11; Genentech, and salvationary promise of biocapital, 203–4; messianism and, 123–24, 181,
210–11, 310 n.30; sacred power and, 206;
salvationary force of life sciences, 198; salvationary promise of biocapital, 194–96,
201–5, 309 n.15; typology of, 184
Sanger Centre, 305 n.2
Shanta Biotechniques company, 300 n.21
Sassen, Saskia, 84–85
science and technology studies (STS), 313
n.254
Science Policy Resolution of 1958, 216
scientific facts: about "life itself," 135; biosociality and, 145–46, 159; corporate PR
and, 135; correlation of SNPs with diseases
and, 146, 306–7 n.11; genomic facts and,
114, 156–59, 167–71, 307 n.21; objective
self-fashioning and, 147–48; production
of, 111, 114, 134, 147; promissory biocapitalist futures and, 115, 133, 142
Scott, James, 99
Scott, Randy: consumer genomics and, 196–
97; moral value and, 56–57; persona and

temporality issues (*continued*)
314 n.5; therapeutic development and,
152, 209, 307 n.17; truth and, 134
Terry, Patrick, 191, 194–96, 198, 309 nn.13
and 15
theology: biotechnology industry and, 123–
24. *See also* belief systems; religion
theology, biotechnology industry and, 123–
24
therapeutic development: consumers-in-
waiting for, 144; databases and, 61;
description of relationships between material and information, 295 n.34; DNA chips
and, 140; gene therapy and, 151, 152; genomics, and endpoint in, 143; patients-in-
waiting for drug development and, 144,
148, 175–77, 195, 308 n.25; personalized
medicine and, 60; promissory biocapitalist
futures and, 113; targeted therapeutics
and, 151–52; temporality and, 152, 209,
307 n.17
Third World. *See* First World–Third World
asymmetry
time issues. *See* speed issues
Traweek, Sharon, 230, 300 n.19
Trovan (antibiotic), 95, 301 n.29
truth: academic grant applications and, 305
n.29; bioethical issues and, 115; biotech
industry and, 115; Derrida and, 133, 265;
forward-looking statement, and fabrication of, 120, 121, 129–35, 304 n.16; Foucault and, 295–97 n.35; hype and, 251,
264–65; popular conception of the lie vs.,
133; promise and, 134–35; temporality
and, 134; venture science and, 133, 305
n.29
Turaga, Uday, 214

Unger, Brooke, 100
United Kingdom, 305 n.2
United Nations Development Program
(UNDP), 300 n.17
United States: biopiracy vs. free market
competition, 291 n.33; capital-intensive
process, and drug development market-

place, 45–46, 293 n.6; comparison of biocapital in India and, 20, 149–50; corporations, and gifting in, 34; Department of
Agriculture, 74; Department of Defense,
290–91 n.29; Department of Energy, 29;
ethnographic sites, 33, 234–35; free market capitalism and, 183, 285–86, 291 n.33;
free market value generation in India and,
285–86; gender issues at corporations in,
254; intellectual property and, 55, 295
n.29; nationalism and, 182–83, 209;
Native American people, and DNA sample
collections, 50, 297 n.48; nonresident
Indian repatriation of culture of innovation to India from, 193, 227–28; overview
of drug development marketplace in, 21–
27; patient-in-waiting and, 148, 195, 308
n.25; remodeling entrepreneurial cultures
in India and, 231–32; research hospitals
and, 68; scandal in corporations and, 205,
206, 208; Securities and Exchange Commission (SEC), 120, 132, 304 n.16; subject
position of populations of, 68, 149, 150,
307 n.14; Supreme Court rulings, 6; use
value of drugs and, 309 n.7; venture capital and, 112
upstream-downstream terrain (drug
development marketplace): description
of, 48; downstream companies and, 47,
55; of drug development marketplace, 21;
GeneEd and, 240, 248; genomics and, 23–
24; genomics industry and, 44, 54, 293
n.5; pharmaceutical industry and, 44–45;
upstream companies and, 23–24, 47. *See
also* drug development marketplace

value: access to information and, 239; biocapital and, 57, 76; dialectic of materiality to abstraction, and act of valuation,
18–19; as double-jointed word, 43, 292
n.2; hype, and commercial, 116, 303
n.12; market contradictions and, 39;
Scott, and moral value, 56–57; sites for
study of, 44; vision, and commercial, 116,
303 n.12

Venter, Craig, 2, 29, 48, 49, 293 nn.9 and 12, 310 n.25

venture capital (VC): angel investments vs., 245–46, 312 n.8; biotech industry and, 6; CEOs and, 271–72; entrepreneurship and, 242, 245–46, 271–72; GeneEd company and, 242, 268, 270–71, 272–73, 313 n.36; India and, 88–89, 300 n.17; Maulik and, 242, 245–46, 272–73; Naidu and, 88–89; nonresident Indians and, 88–89; Rekhi and, 224–26; returns on investment and, 312 n.8; United States and, 112; Vishwa Hindu Parishad and, 193, 225

venture science, 133–34, 142, 195, 199, 305 n.29

Vertex Pharmaceuticals company, 123, 265

Vishwa Hindu Parishad (World Hindu Forum, or VHP), 193, 222, 223, 225, 228

vision: commercial value and, 116, 303 n.12; of Council for Scientific and Industrial Research, 214, 219; Doubletwist company (Pangea), 108–10, 244–45; evangelism and, 266, 313 n.27; of Genomic Health, 194, 309 n.12; hype vs., 266–67; ideology and, 266; Indian context of, 111–12, 303 n.7; interdisciplinary issues, 265, 313 n.254; Maulik and, 249–51, 275; original research and, 265–66; persona and performative space and, 119, 121–25, 303–4 n.15; as productive mechanism,

110; as set of guiding principles, 266; venture science and, 133, 305 n.29

Vision 2020: The Right to Sight, 107, 128

Vogel, Friedrich, 154

W. R. Grace company, 74, 299 n.60

Watson, James, 48

Weber, Max: coproduction of Christianity and capitalism, 180, 199; dichotomy between asceticism and mysticism, 199; *Economy and Society,* 199; element of calling in biotech industry and, 200; multiple causalities and, 181; *Protestant Ethic, The,* 199; Protestant ethic and, 113, 199, 303 n.11

Wellcome Trust, 51

Wellspring Hospital, 83–84, 93–94, 96, 301 n.26

Werth, Barry, 123–24, 186, 241, 265, 312 n.6

Western and non-Western issues. *See* First World–Third World asymmetry

Whitehead Institute, 138–39, 142, 305 n.3

Williamson, Alan, 54

Williamson, Rob, 109

*Wired,* 303 n.5

World Bank, 82, 300 n.18

World Health Assembly, 75

World Health Organization, 107

World Trade Organization (WTO), 25, 73, 189

Žižek, Slavoj, 6, 59, 282–83

Sections of this book have previously appeared in article form. Parts of chapter 1 appeared in *Science as Culture* 12, no. 1 (2003): 87–121, and in the *Sarai Reader* 2 (2002): 277–89. Many thanks to Les Levidow, Jeebesh Bagchi, and Shuddhabrata Sengupta for helping me move my thoughts along through and in the process of writing these articles. Parts of chapters 2 and 5 appeared in *American Anthropologist* 107, no. 1 (2005): 19–30. Many thanks to Bill Maurer for helping to put this special issue together.

Kaushik Sunder Rajan is an assistant professor of anthropology
at the University of California, Irvine.

Library of Congress Cataloging-in-Publication Data

Sunder Rajan, Kaushik, 1974–

Biocapital : the constitution of postgenomic life /
Kaushik Sunder Rajan.

p. cm.

Includes bibliographical references and index.

ISBN 0-8223-3708-8 (cloth : alk. paper)

ISBN 0-8223-3720-7 (pbk. : alk. paper)

1. Biotechnology industries. I. Title.

HD9999.B442S86    2006

338.4′76151 — dc22      2005030718